The CHRONICLE
of the Catholic Church
in LITHUANIA

The CHRONICLE
of the Catholic Church
in LITHUANIA | Vol. 1

UNDERGROUND JOURNAL | nos. 1-9
OF HUMAN RIGHTS VIOLATIONS | 1972-74

Translated and edited by
NIJOLĖ GRAŽULIS

With an introduction by V. STANLEY VARDYS

Loyola University Press
and
Society for the Publication
of the Chronicle of the Catholic Church
in Lithuania, Inc.

Originally published in Lithuania
as **Lietuvos Katalikų Bažnyčios Kronika**, 1972-74

Translation © 1981 by the Society for the Publication
of the **Chronicle of the Catholic Church in Lithuania**, Inc

Library of Congress Catalog Card Number: 78-62412

Loyola University Press
3441 North Ashland, Chicago, Illinois 60657

Society for the Publication
of the **Chronicle of the Catholic Church in Lithuania**, Inc.
(member of the Lithuanian Roman Catholic Federation
of America)
6825 South Talman, Chicago, Illinois 60629

Typesetting and page composition by
The Sisters of the Immaculate Conception
Putnam, Connecticut 06260

Printed by Kingsport Press
Kingsport, Tennessee

Jacket design: Our Lady of Vilnius
by Sister M. Mercedes, S.S.C.

Printed in the United States of America

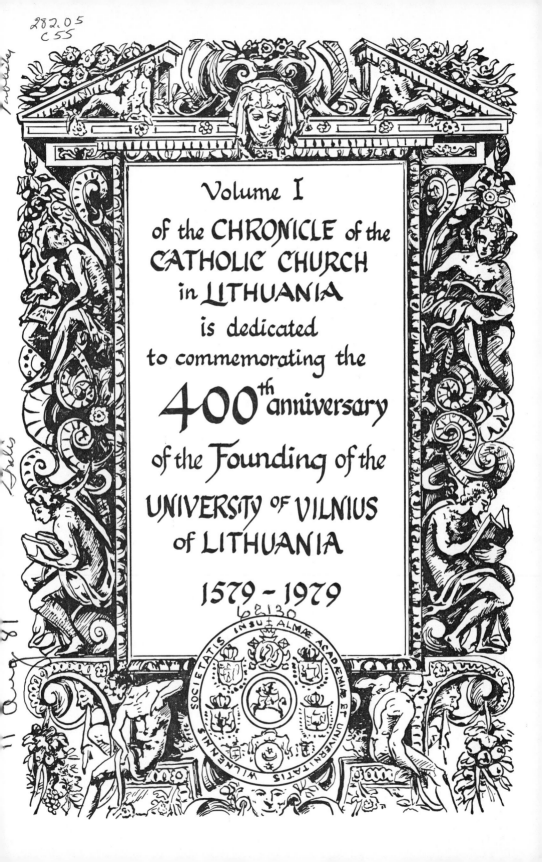

Volume I
of the CHRONICLE of the
CATHOLIC CHURCH
in LITHUANIA
is dedicated
to commemorating the
400th anniversary
of the Founding of the
UNIVERSITY OF VILNIUS
of LITHUANIA
1579 - 1979

CONTENTS

THE CHRONICLE
OF THE CATHOLIC CHURCH IN LITHUANIA

Issue Number 1

Issue Number 2

Issue Number 3

Issue Number 5

Issue Number 6

Issue Number 7

Issue Number 8

Issue Number 9

His Holiness Pope Pius XII on one occasion stated that Lithuania is the northernmost frontier of Catholicism in Europe. Lithuania is the youngest daughter of the Catholic Church on that continent; she was baptized in the thirteenth and fourteenth centuries.

Lithuania is at present a small nation of more than three million people. But, she is ancient and has a long and impressive history. She was an independent state since the thirteenth century. Her first king, Mindaugas, was baptized in 1251 and crowned in 1253. In the fourteenth and fifteenth centuries, the boundaries of Lithuania extended from the Baltic Sea to the Black Sea. As such, she was one of the largest and most powerful states of Europe with broad political, cultural, and commercial relations. The Lithuanian language is one of the most ancient living languages in the world and is of the greatest interest to linguists.

Lithuania, having to withstand German expansion to the East and Slavic expansion to the West, melted throughout the centuries. However, culturally she remained strong. Since 1579, Lithuania has had a university founded by the Jesuit Order in Vilnius, and it is the oldest university after the university in Cracow in Eastern Europe. The first university in Russia, for example, was established 200 years later, in 1775. Lithuanians throughout the world have been celebrating the 400th anniversary of the establishment of the Vilnius University. With the publication of this volume, the Jesuits of Loyola University of Chicago are pleased to join in this celebration of the opening of a sister Jesuit-founded institution of higher learning.

After 123 years of czarist occupation, Lithuania in 1918 regained her independence and was able to make great cultural and economic progress, being one of the free European countries. Unfortunately, disregarding the peace treaty of 1920 in which Moscow had guaranteed Lithuanian independence forever, and disregarding the non-agression pact of 1926, the Soviet Union occupied Lithuania in 1940.

It is already the fourth decade that Lithuanians under Soviet occupation have had to suffer mass deportations, liquidation of leading personalities, persecution of the Church. For the love of their country, for faithfulness to their religion, they are being exiled, jailed, kept in concentration camps and psychiatric wards. In that Catholic country, all religious communities are now suppressed, all Catholic societies disbanded, all Catholic press forbidden. With great risk of their freedom and their lives, some dedicated Lithuanians are publishing an underground paper, the *Chronicle of the Catholic Church in Lithuania*. This secret documentary reveals the cruel sufferings of this subjugated nation. We are happy to have in the United States of America, the Society for the Publication of the *Chronicle of the Catholic Church in Lithuania*. This Society now is presenting the translation of the first nine issues of the *Chronicle of the Catholic Church in Lithuania*. Loyola University Press is happy to recommend this impressive documentary publication to English-reading people.

DONALD J. HAYES, S.J.
Vice President—University Ministry
Loyola University of Chicago

Having no access to a free religious press, on March 19, 1972, believers in Soviet-occupied Lithuania began to secretly publish *Lietuvos Katalikų Bažnyčios Kronika* [The Chronicle of the Catholic Church in Lithuania], which cites concrete instances of brutal persecution of the faith and of the believers. By secret pathways, the *Chronicle* reaches Lithuanians living in the free world. Forty-five typescript issues have been obtained so far.

A total of five volumes containing thirty-nine issues of the *Chronicle* have been published in the United States in their original, the Lithuanian, language by the Society for the Publication of the *Chronicle of the Catholic Church in Lithuania.* Preparations are under way for publishing Volume 6.

The Society has also undertaken, jointly with Loyola University of Chicago, the publication of collections of English, Spanish, and French translations of the *Chronicle.* The Society, however, is solely responsible for the financing, printing, and distribution of these volumes throughout the respective countries. The first Spanish-language volume of the *Chronicle* appeared in 1979, and the first French-language tome is in the process of being printed. This initial English-language volume contains the first nine issues of the *Chronicle.* Later issues will be collected in future volumes in English and the other, previously mentioned languages and published in the near future.

The *Chronicle* is also being translated elsewhere into other languages. German-language volumes of the *Chronicle* are being published by Lithuanian priests living in Germany, Monsig. V. Mincevičius is publishing collections of Italian translations in Rome, and translations of the *Chronicle* into the Portugese are being published by Lithuanian priests in Brazil.

The Chronicle of the Catholic Church in Lithuania reveals how courageously Lithuanian Catholics are waging the fight for freedom of their religion and their nation. Many of them have ended up in prison or have been shipped to concentration camps in Siberia for their part in this publication.

The publishers hereby grant permission for the use of this documentary material in the press, on radio and television programs, and elsewhere, so as to publicize the ongoing struggle for religious freedom behind the Iron Curtain. Anyone who is interested in reprinting this book in its entirety would first have to contact the publishers, who retain copyright privileges.

The publishers would like to express their sincere gratitude to the Rev. Donald J. Hayes, S.J., the Rev. Dr. Paulius Rabikauskas, S.J., Dr. V. Stanley Vardys, Sister M. Mercedes, S.S.C. for the artwork; Antanas Beleška for the map, consultants Petras Aleksa and Bronius Kviklys, to all others who have taken a part in this venture, and to all those whose offerings have enabled its financing.

EDITOR'S NOTE

All references to an editor within the text apply to the original editor of the *Chronicle* in Lithuania (abbreviated *ed.*). In general, all matter enclosed by parentheses is found in the original, whereas anything between brackets has been added by the translator-editor (abbreviated *tr.*), whose main task, aside from rendering a faithful translation, was providing aids to the reader to enable the retrieval of data of interest from the wealth of information available in this underground publication as to the true situation of the Catholic Church in Lithuania.

Abbreviations were avoided, except the following, which are easily understood and remembered:

CPSU—Communist Party of the Soviet Union
KGB—State Security Committee (Soviet secret police)
LSSR—Lithuanian Soviet Socialist Republic
USSR—Union of the Soviet Socialist Republics

Except for well-known, public figures, the Lithuanian spelling of the names has been retained, including the inflected endings of the surnames, which indicate whether the person under discussion is male or female, and if the latter, whether married, (-ienė, -uvienė) or single (-aitė, -utė, -ūtė, -ytė).

The choice of the Russian word *rayon* (Lithuanian: *rajonas*), which ordinarily could be translated as district, subregion, or similarly, was prompted by the desire to avoid confusion, for the word *district* might also be used as a translation for *okrug*, which too is one of the administrative divisions of the Soviet Union. For administrative purposes, Soviet-occupied Lithuania (a takeover never recognized by the United States) is divided into forty-four *rayons* that are in turn subdivided into a number of localities (*apylinkė*). Eight towns are under the direct jurisdiction of the Republic (Birštonas, Druskininkai, Klaipėda, Neringa, Palanga, Panevėžys, Šiauliai, Vilnius).

Within the text the reader will encounter a great number of petitions addressed to both local and USSR government agencies. These may be summarized as follows. The highest organ of state power is the Supreme Soviet. Between its sessions, state duties are carried out by the Presidium of the Supreme Soviet. The highest executive body is the Council of Ministers. The Communist party plays a leading role in government. Its supreme organ is the Congress, and between congresses the Central Committee directs Party work. The Supreme Court of the USSR is the highest judicial organ in the USSR, and the Supreme Court of a Republic (Lithuania among them) is the highest judicial organ of the Republic. There is also a local network of People's Courts. Observance of the law is monitored by the Procurator's (or Prosecutor's) Offices, which are subordinate only to the Procurator General of the USSR, who appoints the Procurators of the Republics. The official overseer of religious matters is the Council for Religious Affairs attached to the Council of Ministers of the USSR, thus the many references to the Commissioner (for the LSSR) of the Council for Religious Affairs in the *Chronicle*. At the local level, each administrative division—*rayon*, town, locality, and village—has its own Soviet of Working People's Deputies, whose executive and administrative body is the executive committee.

400 YEARS FOR THE UNIVERSITY
OF VILNIUS

The very first school of higher learning not only in Lithuania but also in all of northeastern Europe was established on April 1, 1579, when Steponas Batoras (Stephen Bathory), the grand duke of Lithuania and king of Poland, issued a diploma in Vilnius granting the title and rights of a university to the Jesuit College, which had been in operation in Vilnius since 1570. On October 30 of that same year, by his bull *Dum attenta*, Pope Gregory XIII also elevated the college to a university and granted to it all the rights and privileges enjoyed or to be enjoyed in the future by any other universities established by popes, emperors, or kings. With the exception of the university in Uppsala, founded in 1477, all other universities in this part of Europe were established later: Tartu State University (Estonia)—in 1632; University of Helsinki (Turku, Finland)—1640; the university in Moscow—as late as 1775.

The new university was entrusted to the Jesuits. According to the customs of those times, the courses of study were divided into the fundamental and the advanced. The fundamental courses consisted of classes in grammar, poetry, and rhetoric; whereas the advanced curriculum comprised the departments of philosophy and theology. The royal founding diploma forbade the opening of departments of law or medicine, apparently due to the influence of the university in Cracow, which was apprehensive of possible rivalry (the papal bull contains no such prohibition). Only in 1641 did the King of Poland and Grand Duke of Lithuania Vladislovas IV (Wladyslaw IV) permit the establishment of these departments. The department of civil and canon law was inaugurated in 1644, whereas medicine was first taught only in the second half of the eighteenth century. The university, which was often called an "academy," a term preferred by humanists, was endowed with buildings, land, and funds by Lithuanian noblemen.

When the university was established (1579), the students numbered 500, and their numbers grew rapidly in succeeding decades: in 1597 there were about 800 students, and between 1616 and 1620, more than 1200. Later, when several Jesuit colleges were founded in Lithuania, the number of students in Vilnius declined (especially in the basic courses); nevertheless, in normal times there were about 700-800 students. A goodly number were from the nobility, but many townspeople also attended the university. There were also simple peasants among the students, for whom needy-student dormitories were provided. In addition, seminarians from the papal seminary (founded in 1583), from the Vilnius diocesan seminary (established in 1582), and for a time (1582-1620), seminarians from the Žemaitija diocesan seminary together with postulants from various monasteries attended the university. The national background of the students was quite varied: besides Lithuanians, Byelorussians, Latvians, Poles, and Ukrainians, the university served, among others, Prussians, Germans, Danes, and Swedes. Alongside Catholics studied schismatics and Protestants.

The *Ratio studiorum*, which was the same for all Jesuit educational establishments, took the place of university regulations. Scholastic theology dominated. In addition, controversial theology, the Bible, moral theology, and from the middle of the seventeenth century, canon law were taught. At first there was only one professor in the department of philosophy; in the seventeenth century there were already five: three taught parallel courses in philosophy, one taught mathematics, and one—ethics.

Under the university's care was a high-grade pharmacy, the most important printing press in Lithuania, and a large library, to which King Žygimantas Augustas (Sigismund II) himself left a number of rare and valuable books in his will when he died in 1572. At about mid eighteenth century, when there was a growing tendency toward the physical and the natural sciences, the following subjects were introduced into the curriculum: geometry, experimental physics, mechanics, astronomy (an astronomical observatory was in operation from 1753), and also geography, history, and French and German. After 1760 some lectures were given in the field of medicine.

The abolition of the Jesuit order in 1773 was a serious blow to the University of Vilnius. A governmental educational commission was formed to administer the university and other Jesuit colleges. The commission rearranged the country's school system and in doing so renamed the university in 1781 as the Principal School of Lithuania. The School was entrusted with the supervision of all the schools in the Lithuanian educational system (about thirty secondary schools and about 200 elementary schools). In that same year, the fundamental courses of study at the university were grouped together, forming a separate school for the district of Vilnius. After all of Lithuania and its capital, Vilnius, came under the rule of czarist Russia in 1795, the university was renamed the Principal School of Vilnius in 1797. Later, in 1803, by an edict of Czar Alexander I, it became the Imperial University of Vilnius.

During this period the program of studies in the fields of medicine, the natural sciences, mathematics, astronomy, geography, architecture, and art was further expanded. In 1797 the official language of the lectures was changed from Latin to Polish, but professors from abroad continued to teach certain courses in Latin.

Various student organizations came into being at the Imperial University. At first the members of these groups sought mutual help in matters of learning, but eventually they began to take an interest in the political situation. One such renowned society was the Filomatai, established in 1817. Beginning in 1823, the czarist government started to suppress these organizations and to attempt to russify the entire university. Because a large number of students had participated in the uprising of 1831, the Russian authorities closed the university in 1832. Only the Institute of Medicine, with 100 students, and the Principal Theological Seminary, with eighty students, were allowed to continue functioning. In 1842 the government closed both of these institutions as well.

Only after the hostilities of World War I had passed and Lithuania had regained its independence in 1918 was it possible to reestablish the Lithuanian University of Vilnius. But already by the year 1920 the Poles had occupied Vilnius and founded their own Polish University of Stephen Bathory, which was in operation until the start of World War II.

In October, 1939, Lithuania regained its capital city, Vilnius, and soon afterward the Lithuanian university was reestablished. Its normal functioning was soon hindered, however, first by the Soviet occupation (from June, 1940), then by the German occupation (from June, 1941), and once again by the Soviet occupation (from July, 1944). In March of 1943, the German occupational government had even closed down the university.

After the war, the University of Vilnius slowly began to return to normality. In 1955 it was given the name of V. Kapsukas, a Communist activist. Significant research has been carried out there in the areas of mathematics, physics, cibernetics, and the Lithuanian language; however, the forcibly propagated Leninist-materialist ideology significantly hinders the university's further development. The fields of philosophy, history, and literature especially have been adversely affected by this ideology, whereas theology has been banished from the university altogether. The human rights of university students of Catholic Lithuania are being flagrantly abused by this forcible indoctrination with a foreign atheistic world view.

Nevertheless, even as it awaits brighter days, Soviet-occupied Lithuania can be rightfully proud of the illustrious 400th anniversary of its university. The university was the first and, for a long time, the most important center of learning and culture in Lithuania. It has contributed significantly to keeping Lithuania faithful to Catholicism and open to the culture of the West.

PAULIUS RABIKAUSKAS, S.J.
*Professeur à la Faculté de
l'Histoire ecclésiastique de la
Université Pontificale Grégorienne
à Rome*

FREEDOM OF RELIGION, LITHUANIA AND THE CHRONICLE: AN INTRODUCTION

V. Stanley Vardys

In the Western tradition, freedom of religion constitutes an integral part of the basic rights of man. The historical struggle to gain this freedom has to a large degree shaped the development of the philosophical and institutional foundations of Western civilization in general and of constitutional, limited government in particular.

The *Chronicle* seeks to achieve for Lithuania what scores of philosophers, theologians, and political leaders had in earlier centuries secured for Western Europe and North America: the right, equal to that of the other citizens, freely and without any peril to personal security or welfare to profess and to communicate a religious belief. Especially in this respect, the *Chronicle* is not a narrowly denominational paper but a successor to the historical liberal tradition of Europe, and very much in tune with the philosophical and theological thinking of the Second Vatican Council.

Yet, in an age in which modern popes confer with Communist leaders, a journal which seeks religious freedom has to be published in the underground. Indeed, the *Chronicle's* sponsors and correspondents have been tried by

Soviet courts and sentenced to long prison terms for such daring.

To understand why despite such danger to personal security the publishers of the *Chronicle* continue issuing the journal—during 1972-79 forty issues appeared containing approximately 3,000 pages of typewritten text—it is imperative to examine at least three aspects of the current social and political context in which the *Chronicle* is being published. It is necessary to know, first, the traditions of the Catholic Church in Lithuania; second, the legal and social position of religion as defined by Soviet rulers today; and third, the recent historical situation that gave rise to the struggle by Lithuanian Catholics for their rights.

Lithuania is the only Soviet republic in which Latin-rite Catholics make up an absolute majority of the population. About one-half of all Soviet Catholics live in this southernmost Baltic republic. Perched on the shores of the Baltic Sea across from Sweden, Lithuania is the size of West Virginia and currently has a population of 3.4 million, of which solidly 80 percent are Lithuanian. Of the remaining people, 8.9 percent are Russian, 7.1 percent Polish, with the remaining 4 percent divided, in the main, between Jews, Ukrainians, and Byelorussians. An independent country in the interval between the two world wars, in June of 1940 Lithuania was occupied by the Red Army and shortly afterward forcibly annexed by the Soviet Union. With the exception of a harsh three-year occupation by Nazi Germany during World War II (1941-44), the country has been ruled by the Kremlin for almost two generations. During this period, Moscow has reorganized Lithuania not only politically but also economically and socially, to conform to the Soviet system of a Party-oriented society.

These revolutionary transformations have radically affected religion and crucially changed the social position of the Catholic Church. The Church is the oldest Lithuanian institution, dating back to the Christianization in 1387-1413. Lithuania, it may be noted, was the last nation in Europe to accept Christianity. The Lithuanian state, first established in 1231-51 and quickly expanded to rule Russian lands almost as far as Moscow and the Black Sea, at the end of the fourteenth century entered into, at first, a personal union with Poland and together with it fell victim to the rising Germanic and Russian empires. As a result, in 1795, Lithuania was annexed by Catherine II of Russia. The Catholic Church, however, survived the rule of Russian Orthodox emperors. In the nineteenth century, furthermore, it developed especially strong ties with the peasant population and under the leadership of certain bishops, primarily Motiejus Valančius (Wolonczewski), substantially aided in the articulation of modern Lithuanian nationality, helping to confirm the ensuing convergence between nationality and Catholicism.

In the twentieth century, important Church leaders supported the restoration of Lithuania's independence—based on ethnographic boundaries and not the historical union with Poland. The Church, that is, the clergy and the laymen intellectuals and political leaders, played a crucial part in the young nation's development. The Church, needless to say, enjoyed a constitutionally protected position of freedom. Similarly to other religious denominations, it had the rights of a legal person and was free to teach, to organize, and to publish. In 1940, after the incorporation of a portion of the Vilnius region into Lithuanian boundaries, the Church organization consisted of two archdioceses, four dioceses, and one prelature. The other vital statistics included the following: 708 churches, 314 chapels, over 150 monasteries and convents, three archbishops, nine bishops, 1,451 diocesan and monastic priests, over 1,000 nuns and monks, and almost 500 seminarians in four theological seminaries. In addition, church institutions ran scores of kindergartens and schools, orphanages, homes for the aged, and other charitable or health-related institutions. Finally, there existed a strong Catholic press and Catholic Action movement. Just before the country's occupation by the Soviets, Lithuania had approximately a 3.2-million population, of which an estimated 86 percent were

Catholic and 7-8 percent Jewish, with the several remaining percentage points divided up amongst the Protestants, the Orthodox, and other denominations.

Thus, while there was no established religion, its impact on everyday life was very strong. It also must be added that the secularization of social relations in Lithuania was not complete. As in some other Catholic countries, there was no civil marriage, and the various churches kept vital statistics for the state. Religion was taught in public schools, and the state paid for it for all religious groups. Cooperation between the Catholic Church and the state, however, frequently was not very smooth. Historically, the Lithuanian Church developed a sense of independence from the state, and especially during most of the nineteenth century, relations between the Church and the Russian rulers were generally hostile. Pursuing their own political and religious aims, and in an effort to wrestle the Lithuanians away from Polish influence, the czars had not only forbidden Lithuanian publishing in the Latin alphabet (1865-1904) but also imposed many limitations on the Church, making its canonical self-government very difficult. Thus, for example, episcopal appointments of parish pastors needed governmental approval; admission to the theological seminary was monitored and at times limited; and sometimes there was even government interference in the ordination of priests. Clergymen could not travel to perform religious functions outside their parochial boundaries without the authorities' approval; religious processions were confined to churchyards; sermons at one time had to be given from approved manuals, etc. The Church organization itself was controlled by a government council for religious affairs in St. Petersburg. The bishops, especially Bishop Motiejus Valančius, attempted to either neutralize or outrightly to disregard these limitations. For example, books printed in the Latin alphabet were published in the German-ruled East Prussia and smuggled into Lithuania; illegal Lithuanian-language schools functioned on farms; churches marked for closure were defended by parishioners.

The czars thus could not completely subdue the Church, and actually all of these restrictions were gradually lifted, especially after the 1905 revolution.

This relative freedom gained both by resistance to St. Petersburg and as a result of domestic political upheaval blossomed into a list of constitutionally guaranteed rights in independent Lithuania, institutionally insuring the Church's freedom from the state. The creation of a separate Lithuanian church province by Pope Pius XI in 1926 further strengthened the feeling of independence. A Lithuanian concordat with the Vatican signed in 1927 gave additional legal grounds for the Church to jealously protect itself from interference by the state in matters agreed as belonging under church jurisdiction. As a result, in the period between the two world wars the Church did not hesitate to resist what it regarded as encroachment on its legal rights by the government of President Smetona. The conflict between this government and the Church continued for a decade, 1929-39. Thus the Church asserted its independence not only against great odds under the Russian rule but also in the free Lithuanian state, which was, generally speaking, generous to religious groups.

The Church Loses Its Legal Rights

The flourishing church life in Lithuania between the wars indicated how closely the welfare of the Church was related to political independence of the country. Once the free national government was snuffed out by the Soviet occupation of June 15-17, 1940, the Church immediately lost its legal rights. Within four months after the official incorporation of Lithuania into the Soviet Union, which occurred on August 3, the Communist government introduced Soviet Russian laws concerning religious denominations. These laws were not enforced at once, but gradually, and while inoperative during the German occupation, they were aggressively implemented after the war. In legal terms, the conditions for the field of action of the Catholic Church in Soviet Lithuania today differ only in minor details from the general religious regulations anywhere in the Soviet Union.

In the Kremlin's empire, the legal status of churhes is regulated by a number of documents, beginning with the revolutionary decree of January 23, 1918, on the separation of Church and State. This decree established the basic principles for future legislation. Interestingly enough, it was more favorable to religious groups than the subsequent laws because it allowed the private teaching of religion, which now is forbidden. This decree of Lenin was implemented by constitutional definitions, laws, provisions of the criminal code, by administrative instructions passed by the Council for Religious Affairs in Moscow, and by various other government agencies, mainly local authorities.

Constitutionally, both the Stalin (1936) and the Brezhnev (1977) constitutions allow the freedom of performance of religious ceremonies but deny the right of disseminating religious information. Article 124 of the old and Article 52 of the new constitution equate freedom of performing religious rites to freedom of communication (antireligious propaganda) granted to the atheists. Thus, the constitution provides for an asymmetric allocation of freedom between the believers and the atheists. Two consequences have followed from this constitutional asymmetry: first, that freedom of religion is very limited; second, that this very limited freedom has to be exercised in a social environment in which antireligious propaganda is officially sponsored as the only allowed ideological view related to religious beliefs.

Limitations imposed on the exercise of freedom of religion were first codified in the law of 1929, which was in time amended and rewritten. The Russian republic initiated the rewriting, better to say rephrasing, in 1975. The Lithuanian republic followed suit in July of 1976. According to Soviet practice, there is no national statute on this (and many another public) matter, but republics have to follow uniform legislative principles. As a result, despite different authorities involved, the laws they pass are almost literally identical. The Lithuanian statute concerning religious associations thus does not really in any way differ from the Russian.

According to this legislation, the government has to license each religious association, that is, congregation or parish. A group of twenty adults may apply for registration, which is not automatic but may be denied. These twenty people, the *dvatsatka*, are responsible for the administration of the affairs of the parish and for the maintenance and upkeep of church buildings and religious church articles, all of which are state property leased to the association by the local government according to the terms of a written contract. The authorities may terminate this contract at will without judicial recourse for the religious association since the latter has no legal standing. The clergy are excluded from the parochial (*dvatsatka*) committee that is to run the parish; they are regarded as employees of this committee and cannot perform any liturgical functions without the group's consent. Religious centers —diocesan administrations—are recognized by the new law but they do not have a clear legal status of governance over parishes, which may refuse to accept diocesan decisions. Neither the parishes nor the dioceses have the status of a legal person in the Soviet state and thus enjoy neither legal protection (unless specifically agreed) nor can they go to court for the redress of grievances. Religious centers, however, are now allowed to acquire property and the means of transportation needed for the performance of their functions, and they may also reproduce any religious articles needed for services. Individual parishes are forbidden to own property. In addition, they are completely isolated from society. Article 17 of the Lithuanian statute forbids the parishes to organize "special children's or youth meetings and likewise work, literature, or other circles or groups which have no relation to the performance of religious rites." Article 45 further prohibits the creation of "mutual-aid funds, cooperatives, production associations," the giving of aid to parish members, and the "use of property at their disposal for any other purpose but the satisfaction of religious needs." Clergymen are "restricted to the place of residence of members of the religious associations which they serve and to the location of the corresponding premises of prayer" (Article 19). They are, finally, forbidden "to engage in visitations of believers" (Article 45).

The Teaching of Religion—A Crime

Of special concern to the law is the teaching of religion. To prevent it, as already mentioned, the law bars special religious services for the youth and also confines religious instruction to "clerical scholastic institutions," in actuality, to the sole theological seminary in Kaunas, which in 1965-66 was permitted an enrollment of only twenty-five students. (In response to the growing protest by the Catholics, this number was increased to about 100 by 1979). The Criminal Code (Article 143) of the Lithuanian republic declares the organization and "systematic" teaching of religion to minors to be a criminal act punishable by the "deprivation of freedom for a term of up to three years." Punishment is also provided for violating other provisions of the law. It is also important to note that the criminal code forbids the writing of petitions or leaflets requesting any changes in such laws ("which encourage noncompliance with the laws concerning religious cults," Article 143), if there is large-scale soliciting of signatures for such petitions.

In Lithuania these restrictions were enforced only gradually because, especially in 1945-47, they met with great resistance from the churchmen and the faithful alike. The struggle for religious education, but especially opposition to the principle of registration and "association"— considered uncanonical by several bishops—led to the liquidation of the Lithuanian hierarchy, as well as of many other churchmen. In February of 1946 the Communists arrested and in October of the same year executed Bishop

Vincentas Borisevičius of Telšiai. His Auxiliary Bishop, Pranas Ramanauskas, was arrested and exiled to Siberia, but released though not reinstated after Stalin's death in 1956. As 1946 was ending, the authorities further arrested Bishop Teofilis Matulionis of Kaišiadorys. He was sentenced to a seven-year term in prison. Although being a very old man, he survived the camps to reclaim his miter, but was again deposed. In 1947, the Communists, finally, arrested Archbishop of Vilnius Mečislovas Reinys, who perished in the notorious Vladimir Prison on November 3, 1953. For a decade, the only bishop left in Lithuania was Msgr. Kazimieras Paltarokas, the Bishop of Panevėžys, who now moved to Vilnius. During the same period, approximately 1947-51, the authorities exiled 350 Lithuanian clergymen, or about one-third of all the priests who were left in Lithuania at the time. This antichurch action coincided with the government's forcible collectivization of agriculture and with military action against the armed Lithuanian partisans who resisted the reimposition of Soviet rule (1944-52). As a result, the sentenced bishops and the deported clergy constituted only a tiny fraction of the approximately 350,000 Lithuanians deported to camps or exile for being people of the wrong social origins or political convictions or potentially dangerous to the Soviet system. These deportations, it became clear in perspective, represented a part of the Kremlin's deliberate plan for decimating the leadership strata of undesirable Lithuanian population groups. Execution of this plan had begun in June of 1941 with mass deportations of almost 40,000 people.

The death of Stalin brought relief. Amnesties in the final days of 1955 allowed the return of many surviving clergymen, though some stayed to minister to their countrymen and other Catholics in the remaining Siberian and Central Asian diasporas. The post-Stalin thaw promised relief from pressures on religious life; however, the churches were not eligible to benefit from the liberal winds that Khrushchev freed with the de-Stalinization he initiated in 1956. The new leader, it appeared, wanted the relaxation of social relations exclusive of religion. Already in 1957 new steps were taken against the Church. In Lithuania, a newly consecrated bishop, Vincentas Sladkevičius of Kaišiadorys, was deposed and banished from his diocese. In 1960, the government removed and sent into provincial exile another new bishop, Julijonas Steponavičius, who in 1955 had been appointed administrator of the Vilnius Diocese. In that same year, Moscow reorganized the national administration of church life in the Soviet Union and tightened up its restrictive legislation, pressing for stricter enforcement by local authorities. In 1966, the criminal code was clarified by openly spelling out as crimes activities heretofore not always publicly regarded as such.

At the same time, Moscow intensified its atheistic drive. As explained earlier, the churches in the Soviet Union not only have very limited freedom of action but also have to work in an officially atheistic environment. In the Soviet view, the state may tolerate religion, as it does, but the Communist party is committed to atheism and to its promotion. Since the party controls the government and all public organizations, it uses state machinery and resources for the indoctrination of people with atheism. Official atheism often embarrasses nonbelievers and intellectual atheists, but this surrogate for religion is promoted not only in the armed forces or in the factories but especially in schools and in society. In 1961, the Kremlin ordered a renewed attack on religion to completely eliminate it as a competitor in the freshly begun efforts to finally produce the "new Soviet man"—so stated the program of the Communist party in 1961—and in 1963 it coupled this antireligious struggle with a revised design of atheistic indoctrination. This latter campaign was begun in Lithuania even before a decision on the question was adopted by the all-Union Communist party—an unusual step in itself— and privately Communist leaders in Lithuania boasted that, as a result of this new action, Catholicism in the republic would be dead within one or two decades.

This did not come to pass. Atheist successes, too, were

very limited, and in the 1970s Catholic believers in Lithuania were estimated to constitute at least sixty to seventy-five percent of the population. By 1974, all chapels, however, and ninety churches had been closed by the government; monasteries and convents were outlawed; the number of priests had been reduced to 772. The country's religiosity suffered, raising the specter of future generations completely ignorant of religion, who, although they were uncommitted to atheism, would nevertheless be alienated from organized religion. Dedicated clergymen and laymen became deeply upset by this development.

All of these pressures, the new restrictions, the atheistic campaign, the chocking off of the supply of new priests, and new moves against the unofficially conducted religious instruction of the children were too much for Lithuania's Catholics to take. Local Catholic anxieties grew to alarming heights when it was realized that, at the same time when domestically the post-Stalinist liberalization did not produce much relief for religion, internationally the relaxation of tensions seemed to have won for the Kremlin the ear of the Vatican. The Papal *Ostpolitik*, in the view of Lithuanian Catholics, helped to bring about the appointment of subservient hierarchs and administrators who seemed to accept Soviet limitations on the teaching of religion, the education of priests, and on Catholic publishing. This would result in the destruction of the Church by the very hands within it.

Before this faith in the wisdom of the Vatican's *Ostpolitik* had been shaken, however, the clergymen had addressed their own Soviet authorities, asking for the redress of grievances: free religious instruction, theological education, publications; the reinstatement of deposed bishops; the end of discrimination against churchgoing Catholics. Collective petitions signed by up to eighty-five percent of diocesan priests and thousands of believers descended upon the authorities in Moscow and Vilnius. In this way, beginning with the summer of 1968, the Lithuanians adopted the practice of Baptist *Initsiativniki*, and of the Crimean Tartar,

Jewish, and Russian dissidents. These petitions, however, bore no fruit, most of the time not even a written response. When the government answered, it was in the form of arresting priests and laymen charged with the teaching of religion to minors. Four such trials were held in the sixteen months between September of 1970 and January of 1972. Three priests, the Rev. Antanas Šeškevičius, a Jesuit father; the Rev. Juozas Zdebskis; the Rev. Prosperas Bubnys; and Ms. Kleopa Bičiučaitė were sentenced to prison for giving such religious instruction. In Lithuania, these trials were perceived as indicating the failure of the Vatican's *Ostpolitik* that merely allowed the staffing of the hierarchy with the regime's collaborators. "The Vatican is misinformed," was the conclusion. Every effort had to be made, it was decided, to pass on to Rome undistorted information on the naked reality of religious life. Lithuanian Catholics should not let themselves be deluded into inactivity by vague expectations of help. In the winter-spring of 1972, therefore, an appeal was organized to the world: more than 17,000 people (a fantastic number under Soviet circumstances) signed a petition to Brezhnev asking for the correction of the situation. Since in the past Moscow's authorities had refused to answer similar petitions, this one was sent through Kurt Waldheim, Secretary-General of the United Nations in New York. In this way the petition became front-page news all over the world, and the voice of Lithuania's Catholics could not fail to be heard somewhere at long last.

The First Issue of the CHRONICLE Appears

At about the same time, largely to provide data for the Vatican, the Catholics began publishing (in Lithuanian) the *Chronicle*. Its first issue appeared on March 19, 1972, the feast day of St. Joseph. Its avowed purpose was to gather and publicize information on Soviet discrimination against the Catholics and on the violations of human rights as guaranteed in the Declaration of Human Rights by the United Nations and by other international agreements.

The journal also sought to induce the Soviet government to reinterpret the meaning of the constitutionally guaranteed freedom of religious ceremonies, hoping for an inclusion of freedom of communication.

In the Soviet Union, this philosophy of dissident publication was not new. The *Chronicle* shared it with the dissidents of Moscow. The very choice of the title for the journal showed that the publishers of the Lithuanian *Chronicle* felt close to the Russian sponsors of the *Chronicle of Current Events*, which had been published in the underground since 1968 and which had temporarily ceased publication because of the arrests of its chief editors. A number of *samizdat* documents, and especially the trial in Vilnius of Academician Sakharov's friend Sergei Kovalev, a Russian scientist and member of Sakharov's Human Rights Committee, revealed rather close ties between the Lithuanian Catholic and the Russian liberal dissidents. Both groups believed that the exposure of violations of human rights would restrain the government and that freedom of information constituted the basis of a just political society. In other words, both groups subscribed to democratic principles of civil rights.

The Lithuanian *Chronicle* was published for the purpose of informing world public opinion, but especially the Vatican, on the true situation in Lithuania. As the reader will see, its language is factual and moderate, and it is concerned not with editorializing but with hard data. For a publication issued under such forbidding circumstances, it has made extremely few factual errors, which were corrected when noticed. It disapproved of intemperate language that certain other, later-sprouting Lithuanian underground publications (at least six now appear periodically) occasionally used to describe government officials and practices. At first concerned solely with the religious situation, the *Chronicle* expanded coverage to the social and cultural scene and to other dissident activities and became, as an English publication has phrased it, the true "uncensored voice" of Lithuania and a sort of shield for the still-free or emigration-bound dissidents. Its tactics are moderate. It does not foment revolution or violence but urges a peaceful struggle for the guarantees of canonical rights to teaching, preaching, and administering the sacraments. Politically, it prefers an independent Lithuanian state, in the conviction that the latter would guarantee the rights of all citizens, including those of religious believers and the Church. However, it takes the current condition as it is, without nevertheless becoming resigned to the legal restrictions or the administrative browbeating. The *Chronicle* has vowed that it will cease publication only when these restrictions are abolished and religious rights are restored.

Indeed, the arrests of the *Chronicle's* workers did not even interrupt its publication, and on the average, the journal has appeared five-six times a year. In 1974-75, the Communists held four trials of the uncovered supporters of the journal, who received sentences of up to seven years in prison and additional years in exile. Petras Plumpa-Pliuira, who helped to duplicate the journal on an electric machine, was given eight years of hard labor. Ms. Nijolė Sadūnaitė, who typed it, was sentenced to three years in prison and to an additional three years in exile. Povilas Petronis, because of his advanced age, received four years, Juozas Gražys three, and Virgilijus Jaugelis, V. Lapienis, and Ms. O. Pranckūnaitė each received two years. The harshest sentence was meted out to Sergei Kovalev, a Russian from Moscow who had edited Moscow's *Chronicle of Current Events*, and who had incorporated within it the Lithuanian *Chronicle's* information. He helped Lithuanian dissidents in other ways as well. Kovalev was sent away for seven years to a strict-regime prison camp and, in addition, three years of exile. In 1978, the Soviets tried two other Catholic activists, Viktoras Petkus and Balys Gajauskas. Each received a fifteen-year sentence. Other arrests came in 1979.

The *Chronicle* represents a register of Lithuanian events and actually is a gold mine of rarely accessible information. It lists, for example, cases of discrimination against students for their religious beliefs; the fines and punishments inflicted upon clergymen and laymen for the teaching of religion; secret police activities aimed at intimidating the clergy and controlling theology students; persons arrested for Lithuanian cultural activities. It prints texts of submitted petitions and otherwise unavailable government documents; transcripts of political trials and investigations; lists of imprisoned or deported priests, etc. No historian will be able to bypass the journal when researching social and political life in post-World War II Lithuania. The journal, finally, deals in frank terms with the problem of collaboration within the clerical and the Catholic ranks in general and exposes detected collaborators, as well as the overeager or vulgar atheists. Generally, however, it considers that a person is not necessarily corrupted by membership in the Communist party, warning the readers not to judge a book by its cover. It must be noted, however, that unlike in Poland, Lithuania's Communists automatically lose membership for any personal involvement in a religious ceremony, e.g., allowing the baptism of one's child.

The Soviet regime has been propagating the view, fully reported in the *Chronicle*—and some Catholics possibly share it—that the *Chronicle's* tactic of seeking improvement by exposing government misdeeds is divisive, that it will split up the clergy and the Catholics in general, thus hurting instead of helping the Church. The *Chronicle* disagrees, though it has frankly admitted that both governmental restrictions and hierarchical practices have driven a part of the church into the underground (the convents, the monks, the preparation of theology students, even some ordinations, not to speak of religious teaching). While there apparently exists some disagreement on the tactics to be used for the advancement of freedom of religion in Soviet-ruled Lithuania, both the *Chronicle's* publishers and the officially appointed church administrators—of that there now is no question—agree to the goals of the struggle, namely, freedom of communication of teaching and instruction, the elimination of actual inequality between believers and nonbelievers, the abolition of restrictive qualifications on freedom of speech and assembly, the lifting of the barriers isolating the Church from society, etc., that are now imposed by the Constitution. If doubts existed as to Lithuanian Catholic unity on such aims, they were dispelled by a letter to General-Secretary Leonid Brezhnev which Lithuanian administrators of Catholic dioceses wrote in the summer of 1977. In this letter (published in the *Chronicle* as well), the Lithuanian hierarchs suggested concrete language for the incorporation of such goals into the current Soviet Constitution.

Leonid Brezhnev did not answer.

University of Oklahoma

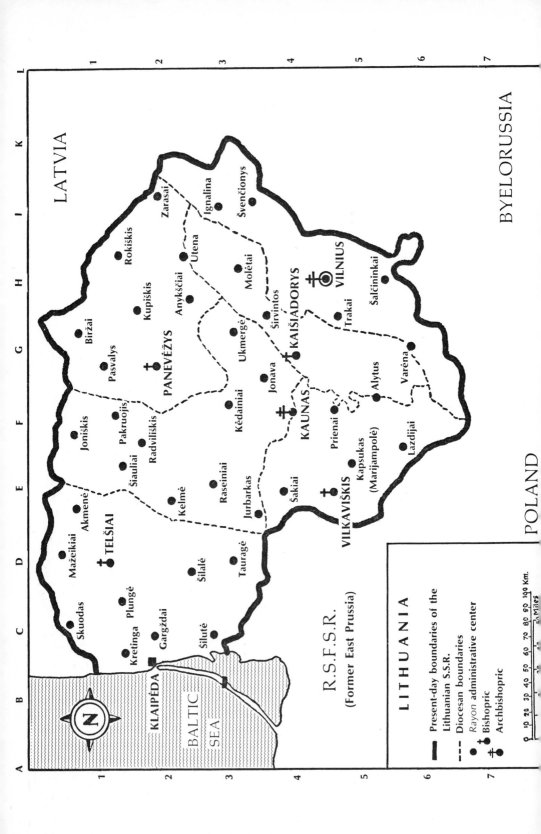

LATVIA

BYELORUSSIA

1

2

3

4

5

6

7

Zarasai

Ignalina

Švenčionys

Rokiškis

Utena

VILNIUS

Anykščiai

Molėtai

KAIŠIADORYS

Kupiškis

Širvintos

Šalčininkai

Biržai

Ukmergė

Trakai

PANEVĖŽYS

Pasvalys

Jonava

Alytus

Varėna

Joniškis

Pakruojis

Kėdainiai

KAUNAS

Radviliškis

Šiauliai

Prienai

Lazdijai

Akmenė

Kelmė

Raseiniai

Šakiai

Kapsukas
(Marijampolė)

Mažeikiai

Jurbarkas

VILKAVIŠKIS

TELŠIAI

Šilalė

Skuodas

Tauragė

Plungė

Kretinga

Gargždai

KLAIPĖDA

Šilutė

BALTIC
SEA

N

R.S.F.S.R.
(Former East Prussia)

POLAND

LITHUANIA

Present-day boundaries of the
Lithuanian S.S.R.

Diocesan boundaries

Rayon administrative center

Bishopric

Archbishopric

0 10 20 30 40 50 60 70 80 90 100 Km.

50 Miles

APPROXIMATE LOCATIONS OF PLACES MENTIONED IN THE CHRONICLE*

Adakavas D 3
Adutiškis K 3
Aleksotas F 4
Alksninė E 5
Alunta H 3
Antakalnis H 5
Anykščiai H 2
Apytalaukis F 3
Ariogala F 3
Aštrioji Kirsna F 5
Aviliai I 2
Ąžuolų Būda F 4
Babtai F 4
Bagaslaviškis G 3
Baisogala F 2
Balsėnai C 2
Baltašiškė F 6
Batakiai D 3
Bernotai I 3
Būbniai G 3
Buckūnai I 3
Čedasai H 1
Ceikiniai I 3
Dabužiai G 2
Darbėnai C 1
Daugai G 5
Daunoriai I 2
Davaisiai K 3
Deltuva G 3
Didžiasalis K 3
Druskininkai F 6
Dubingiai H 4

Ežerėlis F 4
Gardinas F 7
Garliava F 4
Gaurė D 3
Gerdašiai F 6
Girdžiai E 3
Girkalnis E 3
Gižai E 5
Griškabūdis E 4
Ignalina I 3
Ilguva E 4
Išlaužas F 4
Jakeliai K 3
Jakutiškiai G 3
Jieznas F 5
Jonava G 4
Joniškėlis G 1
Joniškis F 1
Juodaičiai E 3
Jurbarkas E 3
Jurgaičiai E 1
Kabeliai G 6
Kačergiškė I 3
Kaišiadorys G 4
Kaltinėnai D 2
Kalvarija E 5
Kapčiamiestis F 6
Kapsukas E 5
Karklėnai D 2
Karoliniškė I 2
Kašučiai C 1
Kaunas F 4

Kėdainiai F 3
Kelmė E 2
Kernavė G 4
Klaipėda B 2
Kretinga C 1
Krikliniai G 1
Krikštonys F 6
Krinčinas G 1
Krosna F 5
Kruopiai E 1
Kučiūnai F 6
Kuktiškės H 3
Kuršėnai E 1
Kybartai E 5
Lankeliškiai E 5
Lauksargis D 3
Lauksodis F 1
Lazdijai F 6
Leipalingis F 6
Leskava F 4
Liubavas E 5
Lukšiai E 4
Lygumai F 1
Marginninkai F 4
Marijampolė E 5
Mažeikiai D 1
Meškuičiai E 1
Meteliai F 6
Mielagėnai I 3
Miežiškiai G 2
Mindūnai H 3
Mištūnai H 3

Moliniškiai E 5
Naujoji Akmenė E 1
Naujoji Vilnia H 4
Nemaniūnai G 3
Nemenčinė H 4
Nemunėlio Radviliškis G 1
Pabaiskas G 3
Paežerėliai E 4
Pajūris D 3
Pakruojis F 1
Palanga B 1
Panevėžys G 2
Paringys I 3
Pašilė D 2
Pasvalys G 1
Pavidaujys E 3
Perloja G 6
Plokščiai E 3
Plungė C 1
Pravieniškės F 4
Prienai F 5
Punia F 5
Rageliai H 1
Ramygala G 2
Raseiniai E 3
Ratnyčia F 6
Rokiškis H 1
Rubinavas D 2
Rūdiškės G 5
Rumšiškės G 4
Salininkai G 5
Saločiai G 1

Salomenka I 3
Salos H 2
Sangrūda E 5
Santaika F 5
Šeduva F 2
Semeliškės G 5
Senosios Naniškės G 6
Šeštokai E 5
Šešuolėliai H 4
Šiauliai E 1
Šilalė D 2
Šilutė C 3
Šiluva E 2
Simnas F 5
Šimoniai G 1
Širvintos G 4
Skaudvilė D 3
Skriaudžiai F 4
Šlienava F 4
Smalininkai D 3
Smilgiai G 1
Šnaukštai C 2
Steponiškis G 2
Stirniai H 3
Šunskai E 5
Surviliškis F 2
Švenčionėliai I 3
Švenčionys I 3
Šventybrastis F 3
Svirkos I 3
Tauragė D 3
Telšiai D 1

Trakai G 5
Traupis G 2
Ukmergė G 3
Upyna D 2
Urkionys G 5
Urliai H 2
Utena H 2
Vabalninkas G 1
Vadžgirys E 3
Vaitiménai D 2
Valakampiai H 4
Valakbūdis E 4
Valėnai I 3
Valkininkai G 5
Vandžiogala F 3
Varduva D 1
Varėna G 6
Veisiejai F 6
Veiviržėnai C 2
Vepriai G 3
Viduklė E 3
Vievis G 4
Vilkaviškis E 5
Vilkija F 3
Vilnius H 5
Vinginninkai D 2
Viršužiglis F 4
Vištytis E 5
Žagarė E 1
Žemaičių Kalvarija D 1
Žemoji Panemunė F 4
Žiežmariai G 4

*Some could not be pinpointed

no. 1

- *Father Zdebskis: texts of petitions on his behalf; his trial on charges of catechization; the text of his statement to the court*

- *Father Bubnys is tried for catechization; the text of his statement of defense; the text of a petition on his behalf*

- *Father Keina is fined twice and his appeals are rejected*

- *Even after serving his sentence, Father Šeškevičius is still kept from performing his priestly duties*

- *Father Orlickas is fined and transferred for associating with children*

- *Residents of Panevėžys appeal to the LSSR and the USSR authorities to reinstate Bishop Steponavičius*

- *The text of a petition from the clergy to USSR authorities concerning the seminary, religious publications, the right of priests to perform their priestly functions, etc.*

- *Seventy-year-old woman is sentenced to one year in prison for preparing children for First Communion*

- *Father Lygnugaris is fined for visiting a seriously ill hospital patient*

THE CHRONICLE
OF THE CATHOLIC CHURCH
IN LITHUANIA

No. 1   [March 19, 1972]

THE TRIAL OF FATHER ZDEBSKIS

Every summer thousands of Lithuanian mothers prepare their children for their first confession and Holy Communion. This is a difficult task and a great responsibility that demands much dedication on the part of both the parents and the clergy. Soviet laws forbid priests to teach children in order that the atheists may all the more easily disseminate their ideas. A number of priests who lived through the Stalinist reign of terror do not want any conflicts with the authorities and content themselves simply with testing the children. Other priests are courageous and have resolved to obey God rather than men—risking their freedom, they teach children the fundamentals of the faith.

At the sizeable parish in Prienai, about 300 children are prepared every year for First Communion. It was the same in 1971. On July 16 the children, together with their mothers, gathered at the church in Prienai for catechization. As Father Zdebskis was teaching and testing the children, a group of officials forced their way into the church. They photographed the children, asked their names, and drew up a report. A commotion arose in the church. Scandalized by the self-will of the Soviet officials, the parents of Prienai appealed to the Control Commission of the Central Committee of the USSR:

"On July 16 of this year, we, the undersigned, brought our children to church so that a priest could test their knowledge—whether they were ready to receive First Communion.

"Suddenly a group of men and women forced their way into the church. It was the chairman of the executive committee, the secretary of the Young Communist League, several teachers and police officers, and others. The uninvited guests began to take over in the church: they photographed the children and asked their names. One frightened girl even fainted.

"The mothers could not help defending their children. A sad scene was taking place in the church. When asked not to interfere, the uninvited guests answered: 'We're not causing the commotion—the women are.'

"Such behavior by representatives of the government brings dishonor upon the Soviet laws. We ask that the persecution of believers be stopped."

This petition was signed by eighty-nine parents and sent to Moscow. Unfortunately, Moscow did not reply to the Catholics of Prienai.

* * *

Interrogations of the children, their parents, and of Father Zdebskis were begun by the Prienai Procurator's Office. Interrogator A. Pakštys searched Father Zdebskis' apartment.

On August 26 the interrogator telephoned Father Zdebskis and asked him to stop by his office "for a while." It was here that the priest was arrested.

When the people found out that the priest had been arrested, they came to the Procurator's Office and demanded the release of the priest. They said: "If you are arresting the priest, then arrest us first, for we brought our children to the priest. It is his duty to teach the children and to test them." From the Procurator's Office the believers marched off to see the Party secretary, who, however, refused to see them. A wave of indignation swept through the entire parish of Prienai and far beyond its borders. On Sunday a crowd of people could be seen waiting in line to sign a complaint addressed to several Soviet agencies:

"To: The Procurator General of the USSR

The Party Control Commission of the Central Committee of the CPSU

The Procurator of the LSSR

A Declaration by the Believers of the Parish in Prienai

"On August 26 of this year, our parish priest, the Rev. J. Zdebskis, was arrested.

"He had conscientiously carried out his priestly duties. He did no harm to anyone. We are convinced that the arrest of our priest is due to some kind of misunderstanding, and we therefore ask that the reasons for his arrest be examined and that the order be given for his release.

"The Rev. J. Zdebskis is accused of preparing children for their first confession. If he has committed an offense by carrying out the duties pertinent to his priestly calling, why does the USSR Constitution guarantee freedom of conscience and of worship? We believe that this arrest is a brazen violation of the laws of this Soviet state.

"We parents are unable to prepare our children for their first confession. We do not have the time since we work either in factories or on collective farms. Secondly, we have neither catechisms nor religious books. During the postwar years, our public officials did not permit the publication of even one catechism.

"Bearing in mind this lamentable situation of Lithuania's believers, what can we parents do? We take our children to the priests and insist that they help us prepare our children so that they would know at least the minimum about the faith. A priest cannot allow an unprepared child to make his first confession.

"It is a requirement of the Soviet government that priests do not teach children but only test them, and then only one at a time. But can a priest test in two months' time about 300-400 children, who come knowing almost nothing of the faith and confession? Besides, our priests have many other churchly duties, for the parish in Prienai is large, with about 8,000 Catholics.

"Our priest was arrested because of our requests and demands, and therefore we are very surprised, upset and indignant. Why disturb the regularity of work, why provoke the believers, why artificially create confusion among the people of the *rayon*?

"We think that our indignation and this protest are well-founded and will be acted upon, and that in the future similar events will not recur.

August 29, 1971"

The declaration was signed by about 350 persons. The people of Prienai themselves delivered the declaration to the Procurator's Office of the USSR. A promise was given that the matter would be investigated.

The believers also appealed to the Procurator of the LSSR and to Rugienis, the commissioner of the Council for Religious Affairs. He spoke angrily: "I know Father Zdebskis!" The parishioners answered: "We know him at least as well."

On August 30 Father Zdebskis was taken to Vilnius. Already early in the morning there was a crowd of people near police headquarters waiting for the time when the priest would be driven away. Security agents photographed the people and wanted to disperse them. "Why are you standing here? Do you want to see a miracle?" "More than a miracle!" answered the people. At 4 p.m., as the crowd of people wept, Father Zdebskis was seated inside a car and driven away.

On September 3 Father Zdebskis' apartment was searched thoroughly a second time. Someone was spreading rumors that Father Zdebskis had been arrested not for teaching children but that a radio transmitter had been found in his apartment, etc. Since even government officials were saying such things, apparently the intent was to deliberately compromise the arrested priest even more so that the believers would not dare to come to his defense.

* * *

In the latter half of September, the believers from Prienai took another petition to Moscow, one which resounded widely throughout the entire world:

"To: The Central Committee of the CPSU

The Supreme Soviet of the USSR

The Council of Ministers of the USSR

A Petition from the Believers of the Parish in Prienai

"The newspapers and the radio try to convince us that there is religious freedom in the LSSR, but in reality this is not so.

"We are not permitted to publish religious books— we have never seen any. We do not even have any small catechisms. The last printing was in 1940.

"Often we cannot hear mass because we are forced to work on Sundays, even though Church laws forbid it.

"We lack priests. Every year about twenty priests die, but barely ten are allowed to enter the seminary. In addition, we know the difficulties those who enroll in the seminary experience from government officials.

"Our priests are being arrested for preparing children for their first confession. On August 26 our priest, the Rev. J. Zdebskis, was arrested for catechizing, and we are now awaiting his trial.

"All this compromises in our eyes the Soviet Constitution and the laws.

"We therefore ask the government of the Soviet Union: give us true freedom of religion; give our priests the freedom to perform their duties without interference and without fear; arrange to have our priest, Father J. Zdebskis, released from custody.

Prienai

September 12, 1971"

The petition was signed by 2,010 believers. This was a courageous protest by the people against religious persecution.

The government had not foreseen that the believing people were like a temporarily inactive volcano. We cannot foresee the future consequences. One thing is clear—*Lithuanian believers shall fight for their rights!*

How intensely the people reacted to Father Zdebskis' arrest can be seen from certain facts. During the religious festival of the Nativity of Mary in Šiluva, about 200 people made offerings for masses to be said for Father Zdebskis' intention. Having lost their pastor, parishioners from Santaika appealed to the General-Secretary of the CPSU asking that Father Zdebskis be released because the bishop had no one he could appoint as pastor of the parish in Santaika:

"We, the undersigned Catholics, appeal to the Central Committee requesting that attention be directed to the difficult situation of believers in Lithuania.

"Our government officials do not permit all those who wish to enter the seminary to do so, and therefore the number of priests is rapidly decreasing. The bishop already lacks enough priests to take care of all the parishes. We have heard that during this past year, the parish in Lankeliškiai has been deprived of its pastor, and just this month we too were left without a permanent pastor. A priest who has to commute from elsewhere will not be able to take proper care of our spiritual affairs. This hurts us deeply and is arousing mistrust of the government's policy.

"Hardly had Father Šeškevičius, who was convicted for the performance of his priestly duties, returned from the prison camp in Alytus, when Father Zdebskis was once again arrested in Prienai for having, as we heard, prepared children who were brought by their parents for their first confession. If this is a crime, then how can we even think about freedom of conscience and of religion?

"We Catholics lack prayer books and pray from tattered ones. Several years ago, we received several prayer books published by the government, in jest, as it were. . . It is essential that every Catholic be able to obtain a good prayer book. Wo do not even have the Bible to read from.

"It is most regretful that the rights of Catholics, as though they were Negroes, are being flagrantly violated, and we ask the Central Committee to see to it that government officials would not interfere in seminary matters; that permission would be granted to our spiritual leadership for publishing annually a sufficient number of prayer books, the Gospels, and other religious books; and that Father Zdebskis would be released from custody. The bishop will then be able to appoint him or another priest as our pastor.

Santaika
September 26, 1971"

The petition was signed by 1,190 Catholics of Santaika.

* * *

Weeks and months raced by, but the day of Father Juozas Zdebskis' trial was constantly postponed and diligently kept secret. Late in the evening on November 11, like lightning the news flashed through the parish in Prienai: "Father Juozas will be tried tomorrow in Kaunas!"

The morrow would reveal the true nature of the Soviet government's attitude in regard to the believers.

Already early in the morning the staircase of the courthouse up to the third floor and the yard were teeming with people. Flowers could be seen in the hands of many persons. Everyone was waiting for the arrival of Father Zdebskis. Police officers were scurrying about in the vicinity. As the hour of the trial approached, they started to "put things in order"—to forcibly push the people outside. They even bloodied a woman they were pushing. The Catholics were ejected, and their places in the courtroom were taken by an enormous group of security agents. Besides them, there were witnesses in the courtroom—children, their par-parents, together with the employees of various agencies brought over from Prienai. A theatrical performance had to be played out—a public trial was taking place... to which the security agents were admitting only atheists. Without a doubt, the authorities did not want to popularize this trial.

The arrests of the faithful were begun on the staircase. One youth was arrested because he made a remark to the policemen questioning why they were allowing only atheists inside and not the believers. The youth was punished with fifteen days in jail. One priest who had accompanied Father Zdebskis' mother was arrested in the corridor and taken away to security headquarters for interrogation.

Outside, near the courthouse, the crowd continued to grow. The police began to arrest those people who could be seen with flowers in their hands and forcibly crowd them into paddy wagons. There was a great deal of confusion and shouting. The police were given the order to disperse the crowd, which consisted of about 500-600 persons. After the crowd had been rudely dispersed, they began to arrest certain individuals. A priest who happened to be passing by was arrested and charged with organizing the demonstration. Throughout the day the policemen stood guard on Ožeškienė Street and did not allow people to assemble. "Why are you standing here like pigs!" was one of the ways the police officials knew of "greeting" the people. People were even being chased out of the nearby stores. "Chase the sanctimonious grannies out of here," shouted a policeman who had run into one shop. Most of those arrested were released in the evening. One person was taken to a psychiatric hospital and later was punished with fifteen days in jail.

On that day the people admirably demonstrated their solidarity with the priest who was on trial, whereas the mob of security agents and policemen showed how the Soviet government takes into consideration the rights of believers.

In order to keep the Jewish nation living in fear, each month King Antioch of the Syrians would kill those he felt were still faithful to the laws of God; however, many chose to die rather than betray their faith (1 Mach. 1).

Father Zdebskis' trial had the same purpose—to keep the nation under an atmosphere of fear so that no one would dare to demand more freedom.

Persecution arouses fear; however, someone's self-sacrifice, made in God's name while suffering for one's faith, rouses the people into thinking about and fighting for the greatest human values.

* * *

The People's Court of Kaunas *Rayon* consisted of presiding People's Judge V. Gumuliauskas and People's Assessors [Mrs.] Palaišienė and Vasiliauskas. [Miss] Černiauskaitė served as secretary. Procurator A. Miliukas, "Public" Prosecutor S. Ratinskas, and Defense Counselor A. Riauba participated in the trial.

The judge read the minutes of a faculty meeting of the secondary school in Prienai, which had been called to elect the "public" prosecutor. Then after announcing Father Zdebskis' biographical data (born in 1929 in Naujiena Village, Kapsukas *Rayon*) and the charges, the judge began questioning the accused. (Some excerpts are presented):

"Have you ever been convicted by a court?"

"I have been."

"On what charges?"

"For the same thing. Later the Supreme Court reversed my conviction."

"Has your right to perform priestly functions ever been revoked?"

"Yes."

"Why?"

"That is something I am unable to tell the honored members of the court because in my mind it is unclear to this day why my rights were revoked."

"What have you to say about the charges against you?"

"I must state that I do not agree with the charge that I organized the teaching of the children. I did not organize it—that would have been just about impossible due to a lack of the time needed for going around to the homes or travelling to the villages. The testing of children who are preparing for their first confession goes on all year long, and whoever wants to may come. But in the summertime, during vacation, when the children have no classes, then it is most convenient for them; that's why a larger group of children formed spontaneously."

"How many children would be in the groups?"

"Sometimes one or more. . ."

"Could there have been as many as one hundred?"

"Yes," he answered joyfully, "at times there may have been as many as one hundred. To my delight there are quite a few conscientious parents who prepare their children very well. These children can be allowed to receive the sacraments as soon as they are questioned. There are also untalented children who cannot be allowed to receive the sacraments for as long as they have not learned the tenets of the faith."

"The interrogator has written down that some children came for instructions for as long as two weeks."

"That could have happened."

"Were the children registered?"

"No. I spoke with whoever came. To avoid confusion, after the examination of their knowledge, they were given a certificate, that is, a permit to receive First Communion. There were some children who could not answer the questions at first. Then I would explain things to them."

"Where did they find out that such instruction of children was taking place in the church?"

"Usually an announcement is made in the church

during the sermon that parents should taken an interest in their children and should teach them religious truths, and that during vacation is the most convenient time to bring the children, after preparing them, to have their knowledge tested."

"Were you the only one to announce this, or did other priests announce it as well?"

"Whoever preached the sermon, he would also remind them."

"Were you the only one who taught the children, or did other priests teach them also?"

"Since I was the youngest at the church in Prienai, I had to carry the greater work load, for the pastor has many other duties."

Father Zdebskis was charged with being the first among the priests to catechize children.

"I was not the initiator of the practice of preparing children to receive the sacraments. That would be conferring too great an honor upon me. Other priests are also fulfilling their obligation to teach, which has been imposed upon us by Christ and the Church. I would be a slanderer if I said that they do not teach. Each one must answer to his own conscience how he fulfills this obligation."

Afterward, the underage witnesses were questioned. After asking their name and surname, the judge would urge:

"Tell the whole truth to the court. Do you recognize him? Turn around and look!"

Some of them answered, "I recognize him"; others said, "No." One boy who had looked for a long time at the priest standing there and smiling at him replied: "He's changed a lot." When the judge questioned them about what the priest had taught, some said, "Prayers," and others said, "He didn't teach. He only asked questions." Still others answered, "He taught us not to break windows, pick pockets, fight, or steal, but to obey our teachers and parents." The judge asked at what times the lessons had started and ended, and when intermissions had occurred.

Some children gave the times, others answered that they could not remember. When asked by the judge what they had studied from and where they had received the cate- chisms, almost everyone answered that his mother or grand- mother had one. The more timid children cried or remained silent. Father Zdebskis stood up for each child, but the judge kept reminding him: "Remain seated!"

After this, they began questioning the parents.

Witness R.: "I instructed my child myself and took him to the priest to be tested."

"Did the child want to go, or did you just take him?"

"Our parents took us, and I also took my children."

The defense counselor: "Were you coerced into taking him whether you wanted to or not?"

"No. I took him in good faith."

The parents who were witnesses were questioned a great deal as to how often they had taken their children to see the priest, what the priest had talked about, how many children were in the groups, etc.

Later, representatives of the local authorities of Prie- nai were questioned.

The witness Kučinskas: "In early July, the executive committee received reports from the inhabitants that a priest of Prienai was teaching religion to children in the church. We went to the church and found about fifty chil- dren and several women. Father Zdebskis was expounding to them. When we arrived, he called for an intermission, and we went to the sacristy for a talk. We warned him that he was breaking the law with such actions, but he replied, "I have taught before and will continue to teach. When the laws of God and the Church conflict with those of the state, one must preferably obey God," and he paid no at- tention to our warnings. One week later I went there once more with the commission, and Father Zdebskis was teach- ing again. A report was drawn up.

"Was Father Zdebskis tactful?"

"Yes, he was tactful. He even joked at first: 'Perhaps

you've come about your children? If you wish, I am ready to help. . .' "

"And both times you drew up a report?"

"Both times."

The witness M. Naginevičius: "On July 9, 1971, I was included in the commission concerned with the teaching of children in the church. There was a group of children and mothers in the church. Father Zdebskis was expounding to them. We explained to him that the organized teaching of religion to children is a violation of the laws, and he answered that he was aware of this, but that he had been teaching the commandments of God and would continue to teach them. . ."

After a recess, the judge read aloud the documents of the case proving the "guilt" of Father Zdebskis.

From page 3 of the proceedings: "A report by the chairman of the Prienai *Rayon* Executive Committee written to Rugienis, the commissioner of the Council for Religious Affairs, states that on July 8 of this year, the retired priest Zakaryza was found in the parish church of Prienai with a group of fifty children. After being warned, Zakaryza had declared: 'I've been teaching, and I will continue to do so. I am only doing what God has commanded.' On July 9 Father Zdebskis, after being warned, stated the same thing. Father Zdebskis was warned that he was disregarding the laws."

From page 20 of the proceedings (from Father Zdebskis' previous place of employment): "The chairman of the Lazdijai *Rayon* Executive Committee writes that in Kapčiamiestis there has been an increase in religious activities under the influence of Father Zdebskis: they go around carrying crosses and crowns, even though they have no right to do so. They are attracting the Young Pioneers and the Little Octobrists, and are enrolling them into rosary societies. Father Zdebskis has a Java motorcycle and rides around from house to house. He visited one Communist family and said that he could even baptize their child at their own home if they so desired."

All these documents—the complaints, photographs, warnings—made up the fifty-three pages of the proceedings. After they were made public, Father Zdebskis asked to be permitted to present his motives as a concluding statement.

The legal arguments began.

"Public" Prosecutor S. Ratinskas, who heads the dormitory of the secondary school in Prienai, said in his presentation that Father Zdebskis knows the laws forbidding the teaching of religion to underage children, but he ignores these laws, basing his action on the premise that he must obey a higher law. The laws are not to be abused. Zdebskis was undoing what was being taught in the schools.

The students are finding it difficult to assimilate the school's program; they were having doubts... The Church was frightening the people. It has no experience in practical life... The religion primer is not pedagogical because it discusses disoluteness... The teaching of religion in the church was carried out in an organized manner because there had been an announcement about it during a sermon... There is a seminary for studying religion. Up to ten candidates are allowed to enroll there annually, but when that many are not to be found, three to four are accepted, and this entirely satisfies the needs of the believers, for their numbers are continually decreasing. The state is not hampering the believers...

The prosecutor concluded his presentation by relating some slanderous gossip about Father Zdebskis.

A summary of the procurator's presentation follows: Parents and guardians are completely free to teach children about religious matters. Those who interfere with the performance of religious rites are punished. The Declaration on Christian Education of the Second Vatican Council states that, in addition to the parents, the state also has rights regarding children. Father Zdebskis violated the law governing the separation of Church and State. During July and August in 1971, he organized and systematically carried out the instruction of minors—a total of about 200-

300 children—and therefore, punishment must be imposed on him in accordance with the appropriate article of the law.

Afterward, the procurator tried to prove that Father Zdebskis did in fact organize and teach the children. According to the testimony of the witnesses and the words of the accused, Zdebskis, an offense had really been committed and had been fully proven. The instruction of children was also carried out by Father Zakaryza, but because of certain circumstances the Procurator's Office had halted the criminal proceedings against him. In conclusion the procurator asked the court to sentence Zdebskis to the loss of his freedom for one year in a regular-regime prison camp.

Defense Counselor Riauba argued that Father Zdebskis had not organized the instruction of the children. He had only announced publicly that parents should show some concern about their children's knowledge of religion. There had been no coercion. In the addendum to the Criminal Code, the Presidium of the Supreme Soviet of the LSSR has indicated how the article regarding the separation of Church and State is to be applied, stressing the factors of organization and systematic execution. Execution alone is not enough. Besides, some of the children came only once. Is that systematic instruction?

The defense counselor recalled to the court Lenin's injunction against offending the believers, but the procurator had done just that, basing his action on the unfounded rumors about Father Zdebskis. As he concluded his presentation, the counselor asked the court not to apply Article 143 of the Criminal Code to Father Zdebskis but to reserve the right for the executive committee to penalize him with a fine of fifty rubles.

After this, Father Zdebskis made his final statement. His presentation was interrupted several times by the judge, who would not let the priest state his intended ideas; therefore, we are presenting here the written text of the Rev. Juozas Zdebskis' statement:

"Between two laws
"The right to live when one may not be born

I

"On August 25, 1971, I was arrested and criminal proceedings were started against me because this past summer I taught children the tenets of the faith at the church in Prienai. In one of the documents of my case it is recorded 'About seventy children and about fifty parents were found in the church. He is being charged with the violation of Article 143, section 1, of the LSSR Criminal Code, which refers to the separation of Church and State. The charge was announced during his arrest.'

"How do I justify my actions? I must repeat the same motive I stated in the church when a group of atheists who had come into the church asked me whether I knew that the teaching of children was forbidden. The answer must be given in the same words with which the first messengers from Jesus explained to the Supreme Court: "We must obey God rather than men' (Acts 5:29).

1. Thus, the answer to the question of why I taught children the tenets of the faith is essentially provided by Christ's command: 'Go therefore... teaching them to observe all that I have commanded you' (Matt 28:19). This command encompasses all people, both adults and children without exception. To teach—not one's own wisdom, not the way of life suggested by some philosopher, but the kind of life Christ demands of us, emphasizing especially His greatest requirement: to consider no man your enemy. Not one of those who have set themselves up as teachers of the art of living, has dared to make such a demand. Not even the Communist party.

2. The Roman Catholic Church has repeated this demand of Christ as a juridical person in three paragraphs of its code of laws (*Codex Juris Canonici*, pars. 129, 130, 131).

3. The command to teach children the tenets of the faith

and the way of life indicated by Christ is being put into practice by the children's parents, who have a natural right to do so. If the parents want their children to study music, they seek a music teacher; if mathematics, then a teacher of mathematics, and similarly.

"Thus we priests find ourselves between two laws.

"It seems that a state could have no other purpose in enacting laws other than the welfare of its citizens, which is impossible without freedom of conscience, without the right of parents to nurture their own children. The constitution of the USSR recognizes the freedom of conscience and the rights of parents regarding their children. The Universal Declaration of Human Rights has been signed. All this was quite comprehensively presented a year ago in equivalent proceedings against the Rev. A. Šeškevičius. Because the present case also does not concern only one individual—the accused—but concerns the Catholic Churh as a juridical person in a certain geographic area, it is therefore perhaps unnecessary to repeat all this again.

"It is worth remembering the latest official explanations regarding this matter. L. Brezhnev, the General-Secretary of the Central Committee of the CPSU, stressed the following in a report at the Twenty-Fourth Congress: 'Violations of an individual's rights or insults to the dignity of citizens cannot be allowed. For us Communists, adherents of the most humane ideals, this is a matter of principle.' (*Pravda*, editorial, August 29, 1971).

"Rugienis, the commissioner of the Council for Religious Affairs, in an official interview with the editor of an overseas Lithuanian newspaper, Jokūbka, emphasized that in Lithuania there is complete freedom of religion and of conscience. No one has the right to even inquire about anyone's religious convictions. That is how Jokūbka depicts the religious situation in Lithuania in his book *Tėvų žemė* [Land of our Fathers], which was published earlier this year in Chicago. The same thing is also stated in the booklet *Bažnyčia Lietuvoje* [The Church in Lithuania], which recently appeared in Lithuania in the Italian and the English languages. It would seem that not only the previous year's, but also this year's official explanation of this matter sounds identical—that there is total freedom of religion in Lithuania.

"Freedom, to the Catholic Church as a legal entity, should mean the ability to function. For example, if one is permitted to live, then one is also permitted to breathe, eat, etc. If there is official permission for priests to exist, then, by the same token, they are allowed *to perform their basic functions*, that is, to offer sacrifice, to forgive sins in God's name (to judge), and to teach.

"It follows that I am being tried for the performance of the duties pertinent to my calling.

"A glance at the pages of documents of this case reveals that my characterizations written by atheists from my various former places of employment also accuse me *of having carried out my duties*. It is unfortunate that I did not find there any characterization from the chancery of the Curia. Would it also have accused me of performing my duties?

II

"It is also necessary to indicate to the court the psychological circumstances which doubtless influenced the actions for which I am being tried.

"These circumstances were created by the facts of life brought about when either *the atheists themselves or certain institutions failed to observe the very same law* which refers to freedom of conscience according to which I am being tried today.

"The word 'atheists' is being used here as the most suitable in this matter, because an atheist—whether he is an operative of the security forces or whether he works in administration or in the field of education—acts the same in this regard—as one who wages a fight against God.

"The laws of the USSR solve the problem of freedom of conscience by separating the Church from the state. Unfortunately, due to some atheists, the Church perceives itself as being not separated from the *state but on the contrary, as subjugated to the interests of the atheists* and even that, quite often *by means of guile and deceit.*

"For the same reasons, the believers feel they are "outsiders"; *they feel themselves unequal before the law.*

"The facts which are widely known by the public cannot be unknown to the Procurator's Offices. Why do they remain silent?

"Let us bring to mind one or two facts which are relevant to the case at hand.

"First of all, the inequality of believers before the law is illustrated by the fact that the atheists have their own press and schools, but the believers are not permitted this.

"If priests are being punished for preparing children for their first confession, then one is inclined to ask whether even one atheist has been brought to trial for violating the rights of believers on the basis of the supplement to Article 143 of the Criminal Code which was promulgated in 1966? After all, there have been such violations. For example, one year ago a teacher from the secondary school in Vilkaviškis was dismissed from work because she was a believer and therefore had no right to function as an educator or to even work elsewhere. Is this not a violation of the freedom of conscience? And this is not a solitary occurance in our environment.

"Another aim of the atheists is to have the public, especially the youth, students, and office workers, stop attending mass. They probably sense intuitively that it is easiest to know God face to face; they can feel that everything we call the working of grace, and at the same time the steadfastness of one's faith are inseparably linked with the Mass. In other words, there is freedom of conscience; however, the inner culture of the people, and especially of the youth, is not to be nurtured. There have been a number of instances when teachers either did not allow students who were participating in funeral services to enter a church or made them leave it. Is this not a transgression against the freedom of conscience? These and similar facts which are widely known by the public cannot be unknown to the Procurator's Offices. Why do they remain silent? Is it a wonder then, that believers do not feel equal before the law?

"It is particularly incomprehensible to believers why the authorities have failed to respond to any of the believers' petitions in which the existing irregularities as far as the believers are concerned were pointed out to the government. It had been announced in the newspapers, after all, that the appropriate agency must respond to petitions within one month's time. The action taken by the believers in connection with this case might serve as a fitting example. This past summer when the children were being taught the tenets of their faith and a group of atheists came into the church and began to furtively photograph the children and to ask their names, then the mothers came to the aid of their children. There was an uproar in the church—it takes so little to affect the psychology of the masses, in order that something similar to the events in Kražiai during the days of czarist oppression might recur. (One would ask whether all this increases the people's respect for the constitution?) After this occurrence, eighty-nine parents wrote a joint complaint to the Control Commission of the Central Committee of the CPSU demanding that 'the tormenting of the believers be stopped.' There was no official reply to the petition, even though a return address had been given.

"In the face of such and similar facts, the question naturally arises whether the community of believers is outside the bounds of the law? Should one be surprised if it occurs to the public that the freedom of conscience granted by the constitution and the signing of the Universal Declaration of Human Rights, etc., are only propaganda? Likewise with the 1966 addendum to Article 143 of the Criminal Code concerning the penalties for violating the religious freedom of believers; and also Rugienis' interview by Jokūbka; and the publications *Tėvų žemė* [Land of our Fathers], *Bažnyčia Lietuvoje* [The Church in Lithuania], and others which concern the freedom of conscience.

"Why do the Procurator's Offices remain silent seeing all this? Do certain *secret laws* exist which contradict the official laws and are unknown to the public?

"Let us look further.

"In a number of instances *the actions of the atheists reek of unmistakeable guile and deceit* in regard to the requirements of conscience. Why is none of this being punished? More than once, the atheists' actions in regard to believers were similar to the behavior of the fifteenth-century Duke of Gloucester depicted in the writings of Shakespeare. In attempting to attain the throne of the King of England, he secretly murdered all his competitors, but was capable of appearing in public with a prayer book in his hands.

1. Do not the atheists' guileful efforts to undermine the Church from within violate the freedom of conscience? —this in a country whose constitution guarantees the freedom of conscience—by creating the impression that the bishops are at their posts, that instructions are being issued from the bishop's chancery, even though actually the assignment of priests to their places of ministry and many other instructions are dictated by the atheists in the hope that the situation of the Catholic Church in Lithuania would begin to resemble that of the Russian Orthodox Church.

2. Do not the efforts to compromise certain priests and even bishops in the eyes of the believers and even in the Vatican reek of guile? For instance, is it the wish of believers that the energetic and healthy Bishop V. Sladkevičius be listed as *'sedi datus'* in the Vatican's register of the world's bishops?

3. Is not guile indicated by the fact that although a theological seminary exists only four or five candidates are allowed to be admitted annually, and hence, graduated, when twenty to thirty priests die every year in Lithuania? Equally indicative are the efforts being ex-

pended to keep especially talented and refined students
and professors out of the seminary.

4. The same can be said about the teaching of children.
Although they are permitted to receive First Communion, what is the significance of the requirement that
children be questioned one at a time? (for no such
juridically formulated law exists) How can children
be prepared one at a time in those parishes where one
is faced with several hundred little children in the
summertime? The parents rightfully expect help from
us priests in this matter. And what is one to do? Should
the children be allowed to receive First Communion
unprepared? A person cannot love what he does not
know. Is it possible that a guileful attempt *to quietly
wrest the children from their parents* lurks here? Then
the atheists would be able to say that we have freedom
of conscience—the people themselves are renouncing
the faith.

"But then such freedom of religion is like *being allowed to live when one is not permitted to be born.*

"Honorable Judges, I am inclined to think that you,
too, like many people of the younger generation today have
come to know God from *Biblijos linksmybės* [Pleasantries
from the Bible] and from similar books, rather than the
God who died for us on the Cross; thus, even though you
have advanced degrees in your field of specialization, it is
doubtful if at this moment you could pass the kind of examination on religious matters that the children take before their First Communion.

"Upon recalling this fact alone (since, in the words
of Rachmanova, you too are among the people produced
by 'the new people factory'), we must forgive you for
holding this trial and pray for God's forgiveness. On that
day, as I have already mentioned, when the disturbance
was created in the church, I later asked the children: 'Children, should we hate these people?' They answered: 'No!'
'And what is the most important command Jesus gave us?'
'To consider no man your enemy,' they again replied.

"Again recalling those facts, a few of which I have mentioned as examples, which are widely known by the public and which the Procurator's Offices cannot be unaware of, I would like to ask: why is all this tolerated, while I am being tried, having been charged with violating the freedom of conscience? How can a citizen be punished on the basis of laws which, as we see, are not observed in many instances even by certain state institutions? That such charges are being brought against a priest is already a violation against the freedom of conscience, exactly like the efforts to take children away from their parents. Perhaps I could have been accused of violating the freedom of conscience had I taught them without their parents' knowledge.

"Can it be that the state itself is forgetting the requirements of its own constitution by tolerating all this?

"Finally, the very article on whose basis I am being tried appears to *lack distinct contours*. As an example, we can recall an identical case in 1964 in which, also for teaching children, I was sentenced to one year in prison. Then, several months later, the order was given by the authorities to release me and to overturn the conviction. In the statement of acquittal was the following explanation: 'It has been determined that there had been no coercion of the children.' Yet the court had known this when I was being sentenced to imprisonment. Coercion of the children had not even been mentioned in court. During the trial, Article 143 had been explained in the following way: it is forbidden to organize and to teach religious truths in school (not in church). Even though I had not been charged with the above, the court nevertheless proceeded to try me. How is one to understand this? And if I was later acquitted, why am I once again being tried under the same article? This time too, the court is aware that the children were not coerced. This is also attested to by the petition sent by the parents to the USSR government regarding this matter, pointing out that the children were not being instructed in school, that they were being taught in accordance with the wishes of their parents.

"For when the circumstances are the same, a law cannot be interpreted in one way at one time and differently on another occasion.

"I have also been unable to determine where 'the regulations designated by law' have been promulgated. Neither the interrogator, nor the juridical consultation office of Vilnius have replied to this question.

III

"What can be concluded from all this?

"Looking from a human, shortsighted viewpoint, in similar situations one is always inclined to repeat the words of Jesus: 'Father. . . remove this cup from me'; yet in truth, we priests should *thank you* for this and similar trials. These facts force our consciences to speak out. They don't let us fall asleep, they force us to make up our minds, they place us between two possibilities.

"One possibility is to choose the so-called path of *'peaceful cooperation with the atheists'*: to attempt to serve two masters, to toady to the designs of the atheists—that a priest perform his duties but be innocuous to atheism; that he himself would drive away the youth from the church and not allow them to participate in the rites or in processions; that he would not let them serve mass; that when preparing children for First Communion he would be satisfied if they only know their prayers, although they lack understanding of the mystery of the Mass, the center of all Christian life; that the clergy would not stop to consider what the country's situation will be in ten or twenty years! This means that priests should not carry out the duties pertinent to their calling, that they must resolve to struggle with their conscience as they concern themselves merely with the dinner menu. The priest must try to forget that the children will nevertheless be told of God, but of *a God who really does not exist.* (I too do not believe in the God which is portrayed by our local press and radio.)

"You have shown me thousands of youths behind bars. Not one of them knows the God who should be loved and who loves us. No one has spoken to them of such a God; no one has taught them to find happiness in doing good to every human being, even to an enemy. I know very well that if we priests shall not speak about this, the very stones will begin to exclaim, and God will hold us responsible for their fate.

"This is what peaceful cooperation with atheism means in our surroundings, which is something that believers living abroad cannot comprehend.

"The second possibility is to be the kind of priest that Christ had in mind by resolving to carry out the duties Christ and Church Law demand, and at the same time accepting whatever Providence wills one to experience, choosing—as is evident in this case— windows with bars, exactly like the interrogators said: 'You didn't want roast duck, so now you'll eat prison bread.'

"And yet, if we priests are not tried in court here and now, in time our nation will judge us! Eventually the Supreme Being's hour of judgement will come. May God help us priests to fear it more than these trials of yours.

"I again recall those thousands of youths behind bars. In their childhood they did not know how to obey their parents... This land along the banks of the Nemunas is dear to me. I know very well that it will no longer exist if its children will be incapable of obeying their parents. I spoke to them about this. I told them that this is something God demands of us.

"If this is a crime according to your conscience, then pronounce me a fanatic and judge me, but in doing so you will also be judging yourselves!

"I ask the court to consider the aforementioned psychological circumstances and not to forget that the decision of this court may force the community of believers into thinking that some paragraphs of the constitution are there simply for propaganda purposes. Can one respect the requirements forcing one to go against one's conscience?

Can there be respect for a law that punishes one for performing one's duty?

"There still remains for me to repeat the words of the first Apostles, which were already spoken to the court: 'We must obey God rather than men.'"

A two-hour recess followed the Rev. J. Zdebskis' statement. Returning after lengthy deliberations, the court handed down the following verdict in the name of the LSSR:

"Zdebskis, Juozas, the son of Vincas, born in 1929, is adjudged to have committed an offense under the provisions of Article 143, section 1 of the Criminal Code of the LSSR, and is sentenced to be deprived of his freedom for one year, which sentence is to be served in a regular-regime corrective labor colony. August 26, 1971, will be considered the onset of the sentence."

On December 9, 1971, the Collegium for Criminal Cases of the Supreme Court of the LSSR ruled that the Rev. J. Zdebskis had been justly found guilty and that his sentence was appropriate for the crime committed and suited his character.

At present (1972) the Rev. J. Zdebskis is serving his sentence in Pravieniškės.

May the self-sacrifice of those suffering for the faith rejuvenate the land of our fathers!

THE TRIAL OF THE REV. PROSPERAS BUBNYS

During the summer of 1971, the bishop was to have come to Raseiniai to administer the Sacrament of Confirmation. The clergy of the *rayon* had been directed by the bishop to test the knowledge of the faith of those about to be confirmed and to issue certificates.

The pastor of the parish in Girkalnis, Father P. Bubnys, informed the believers that the parents should bring their children to the church for the testing. The parents were doing this until one day a group of representatives of the Raseiniai *Rayon* Executive Committee forced its way into the church. Upon finding the children waiting in church for the priest, the representatives proceeded to round them up and drag them through the town to the fire station; there, by means of intimidation and threats, they forced them to write statements claiming that Father Bubnys had taught them the tenets of their faith. The children were so terrified that they even cried, and some even became ill afterward.

On November 12, 1971, the People's Court met in session in Raseiniai. Only officials and witnesses were permitted to participate in the trial. The believers had to stand outside the doors. No one expected Father Bubnys to be convicted, for the government officials had come upon him as he was questioning but one child while the other children awaited their turn in the church. Only when the court left for deliberation and a police car drove up to the courthouse, did it become clear to everyone—Father Bubnys would indeed be convicted. The court's decision, in the name of the LSSR, was to find Father Bubnys guilty, and it handed down a one-year sentence to be served in a strict-regime prison camp. After the decision was read, Father Bubnys was seized, and as the people wept, he was driven to Lukiškis Prison.

* * *

Before the trial had begun, Father Bubnys wrote his statement of defense, which is presented below:

"Honorable members of the Court,

"I have the important duty as a citizen to state my views concerning an important existential question: am I guilty for teaching religion? The question arises whether the profession of religion (profession not to trees or stones but in the presence of other people) and its propagation thereby is an intrinsically evil and forbidden act? If it is permissible, then do I have the right and the duty to do this?

"The community of the United Nations and our country's constitution have transcended the medieval principle that whoever rules determines the people's religion by recognizing freedom of conscience and freedom of religion.

By acknowledging that religious instruction is an offense, I would be sinning against the concept of man and the spiritual progress which mankind has achieved through agelong efforts. I respect the right of parents to decide for themselves whether their children must be religious or not. They themselves brought their children to have their religious knowledge examined. No one was assigned a certain day for bringing his children. In order to save the working people's time, we accomodated ourselves to the timetable of the sole bus which services Girkalnis. I did not try to deliberately disregard the officials and their demands.

"Besides my obligations to the state, I, as a priest and pastor, have obligations to my religion and to the Church which are binding upon my conscience.

"A priest's essential duty, which Christ himself has conferred, is to preach the Gospel, to teach the nations, and to dispense God's grace by administering the sacraments. Since the Soviet government still has not ordered the seminary in which religious matters are studied and learned to be closed, then it agrees that the knowledge obtained there should be used in the teaching of religion. When he is ordained, every priest becomes obligated to God, and by means of the appointment he is given by the bishop, he receives the command, which is governed by Church regulations, to teach and bless the Nation of God. Therefore, if he is to act conscientiously, he cannot avoid propagating and teaching religion, for as the Apostle St. Paul has said: 'Woe to me, if I do not preach the Gospel!' (1 Cor. 9:16). The parents also have the right to teach religion to their children. If they are supporting a priest at their expense, then does that priest have the right to refuse to serve the parents in these matters? How absurd it would seem to have the right and the means, and yet to forbid use to be made of them? This would be like allowing a man to hold a hammer in his hand but forcing him to drive nails with his fist. Such a requirement is not in accord with the workings of a sound mind, and thus it is not surprising that, to a majority of the people, it is entirely incomprehensible.

"If every decent person should not be indifferent to
matters of truth and morals, then all the more so must a
priest not remain silent, for through Christ he has been
allowed to know divine truth. For no other name has been
given to us under heaven through which we can be saved
except the name of Jesus (cf., Acts 4:12). Christ's teaching
is the foundation of mankind's culture and goodness. As
a rational being is on a higher level than an irrational one,
so culture of the spirit is of a higher value than material
culture. The laws of men are altered by time and place,
and they become contradictory to the previous ones. The
laws of Christ are based on the very nature of man and
will not cease to exist as long as man exists. The story of
Christ did not end with His death upon the cross. He is
eternal. This very day testifies to that. He comes as He has
promised, without delay, with great power and majesty,
as the One to whom all power in heaven and on earth has
been given. To Him belong both all the believers and all
the atheists, no mater how many of them there are. His
winnow is in His hand, and He will separate the chaff
from the grain.

"In view of this, my conscience causes me to feel
somewhat apprehensive, not about my 'crime' for having
taught the tenets of the faith to the children, but about
my negligence in carrying out such important duties because, as calculated by my accusers, the total amount of
time devoted to examining each child's knowledge of the
most essential matters (for First Communion) did not
even amount to ten minutes. Thus, can one speak of it as
teaching?

"My sole justification is that there was not enough
time available before the coming of the bishop to Raseiniai. I can attribute to myself neither merit before God
nor guilt before the laws.

"If I must publicly state today whether I did teach
religion, then I cannot deny this, nor do I regret it, because that would indicate a distorted conscience and the

disregard of what is due the Creator in favor of the laws of men. If the laws of men are not in harmony with the Creator's Natural Law, then it is not nature which errs, but man's understanding; and because of this, human beings are suffering and will continue to suffer until they perceive where they erred in deviating from the Creator's plan.

"At this solemn hour which has been allotted to me, a speck of dust, I cannot renounce Jesus, who loves us and who urges that the little ones would not be kept from coming to Him. I want to say: *'Praised be Jesus Christ!'* "

* * *

A month after his conviction, on December 9, 1971, the Supreme Court upheld the decision of the People's Court of Raseiniai.

The believers of Girkalnis and of the neighboring parishes, who were greatly distressed because of the injustice inflicted upon their priest and disillusioned with the local authorities, sent a petition to the President of the Presidium of the Supreme Soviet of the USSR and to the Procurator General of the USSR:

A Petition

"On November 12, 1971, in Raseiniai (the LSSR), the Rev. Prosperas Bubnys, who resides in the parish of Girkalnis, Raseiniai *Rayon*, was sentenced to one year in prison. On December 9, the Supreme Court of the LSSR upheld that decision.

"The priest's 'guilt' consisted in the conscientious carrying out of his duties by helping parents prepare their children for First Communion and confirmation.

"We do not want to believe that this was not a mistake. After all, our constitution guarantees freedom of religion and of conscience, and Lenin has decreed the following concerning the separation of the Church from the state: 'Citizens have the right to study religion on their own initiative.' Our pastor taught on his own initiative; he did not go into a school to teach the children. Just the opposite occurred: representatives of the Raseiniai *Rayon*

Executive Committee, together with several teachers that they had invited, practically broke into the church, and, finding the children waiting for the pastor (to test their knowledge of the faith), created a disturbance. The representatives rounded up the frightened children and dragged them through the village to the fire station; there they were closeted and forced through intimidation to write statements accusing the pastor. (Some of the children even became ill from the terrorization.) The intimidated, frightened, and crying children wrote the statements without making any distinction between the words 'to teach' and 'to examine.' This was taken advantage of by the enemies of the freedom of conscience in order that they could accuse the priest of the systematic instruction of children. Then again, if the priest did teach the children not to steal and not to be naughty but to respect their parents and to love their neighbor—is that a crime? From our experience of life we can clearly see that children nurtured in the Faith grow up to be better people, people without bad habits. We naturally want to raise our children to be like that, but we have no textbooks from which we could teach the tenets of the faith to our children. (For during the years of socialism in Lithuania, neither catechisms nor other religious textbooks have ever been published.) We are left with only one solution: to ask the pastor to help us. Unfortunately, for this religious ministration, our pastor has been sentenced to prison.

"The self-will of the atheists and of the authorities greatly insults and demeans us believers, because the existing inequality between believers and nonbelievers is being forcibly manifested. Only atheists have been granted the possibility of raising their children without constraint, that is, atheistically; but the believers have had all their rights and all the possibilities of raising their children according to their convictions taken away. Furthermore the atheists have been given the right to concern themselves with our children's upbringing more than the parents themselves. They attempt to force somebody else's children to become atheists, they chase them out of churches, they try to frighten them, they do not let them receive First Communion. As for the priest, who 'on his own initiative' taught the children, when asked by the parents, on matters of faith and morals—they are punishing him with imprisonment.

"We ask you not to permit such arbitrariness by which the rights of us parents over our children are being violated. We ask for freedom of conscience and for equal rights, as Lenin has promised and as the Soviet Constitution proclaims.

"We ask that catechisms be published, so that we would have the means for instructing our children.

"We ask that priests be permitted to teach children the tenets of the faith in church—in keeping with Lenin's decree.

"We also ask your help so that the Rev. P. Bubnys would be released from prison.

"P.S. A total of 1,344 believers from Raseiniai *Rayon* have signed this petition, 570 of whom are from the parish in Girkalnis. Forty-three pages of signatures are being attached to this petition.

"We await a reply at this address:

> The LSSR, Raseiniai *Rayon*
> Girkalnis,
> [Miss] Lukinskaitė, Blasė,
> [Miss] Kazimierskytė, Anelė
>
> December 11, 1971"

Although the people of Girkalnis requested that their rights be upheld and that Father Bubnys be released from prison, the voice of the people remained unheard by the Soviet government.

Meanwhile, Father Bubnys is serving his sentence at the Kapsukas strict-regime prison camp, and he does not complain about his lot. On the occasion of Christmas he wrote: "When I was faced with the prospect of imprisonment, I found myself partly longing for it and rejoicing at this opportunity to detach myself from the world, to sink into oblivion, and to consciously take upon myself the spirit of penance and self-sacrifice. . ."

THE PERSECUTION OF THE PASTOR
OF THE PARISH IN VALKININKAI

On September 28, 1970, the Administrative Penalties Commission of Varėna *Rayon* fined the pastor of the parish in Valkininkai, Father Algimantas Keina, fifty rubles for violating "the laws concerning religious cults." Father Keina brought an accusation against the Penalties Commission before the People's Court of Varėna, requesting that the unjust fine be nullified.

On November 3, 1970, the People's Court of Varėna *Rayon* deliberated on the case of the Rev. A. Keina. The chairman of the court was People's Judge J. Burokas, the defendant—the vice-chairman of the Soviet of Working People's Deputies Executive Committee, J. Visockis.

The court rejected the claim for the following reasons:

1. "On July 4, 1970, three children were being prepared for their First Communion at the sacristy of the church in Valkininkai; they were being taught collectively by Citizen [Miss] E. Kuraitytė."

2. "On August 30, 1970, the Rev. A. Keina publicly announced that mass would be said for the students' intention."

3. "On September 6, 1970, the Rev. A. Keina allowed two underage boys to serve mass."

The other reasons were less important.

Father Keina then appealed to the chairman of the Supreme Court of the LSSR explaining why he considered the decision of the People's Court of Varėna *Rayon* to be unjust:

1. "Citizen E. Kuraitytė was not teaching the children because she is only employed as the church's cleaning lady. When the parents failed to find the priest within the church, they enquired of her what questions the priest

usually asks the children, and she had indicated the appropriate questions in the catechism. Is the pastor to blame for this?"

2. "In August, during high mass (on Sunday), at the request of the parents, a mass was said for their children's intention, so that they would be good, diligent, and exemplary. Since when have fines been imposed for praying in church for a worthy cause? To pray for parents and children is a priest's obligation."

3. "There is no law which would forbid minors to serve mass. The boys came voluntarily with their parents' permission. The pastor does not have the right to drive away either the parents or the children when they come to church to pray. Everyone prays wherever he wants to: near the door or at the altar."

The deputy chairman of the Supreme Court of the LSSR, Čapskis, responded: "From the additional information presented, one must conclude that the commission had the right to penalize you for violating the law concerning religious cults."

On November 5, 1971, Father Keina appealed to the Procurator's Office of the USSR, which replied that the pastor had been justly punished. The Procurator's Office ignored the fact that, in its desire to punish the pastor, the Varėna *Rayon* Administrative Penalties Commission had even *falsified the date*: actually, the bill regarding the "instruction" of the three children had been drafted in 1968, but the commission had dated it as 1970 because they knew that a fine cannot be imposed later than one month after the offense is committed.

* * *

On October 4, 1971, the very same commission of the Varėna *Rayon* Executive Committee once again fined the pastor of the parish in Valkininkai fifty rubles because he allowed minors to serve mass. During the meeting of the commission, Father Keina *was not even permitted to explain himself.*

The pastor again appealed to the People's Court, seeking the nullification of the fine. The first court session was held on November 15, 1971, in Varėna. Father Keina explained that he had not organized the children, nor had he taught them how to serve mass. The children would come voluntarily and with their parents' permission. The pastor pointed out that the decree issued on May 12, 1966, by the Presidium of the Supreme Soviet of the LSSR does not forbid minors to serve mass, and that his penalization had been based on this very decree. According to Article 85 of the LSSR Constitution and Article 8 of the Code of Criminal Procedure, the court must heed only the laws and not some sort of instructions.

Because there was no proof in writing that the pastor had organized the children to serve mass, the court session was postponed.

The second session occured on December 7, 1971. The court was presented with two affidavits testifying that Father Keina had organized children to assist at the altar.

The pastor showed that the *affidavit of the boy Vytas Kazlauskas was not genuine because it had been written in the handwriting of J. Visockis, and the signature had been obtained by threatening* the child that his conduct grade would otherwise be lowered. The boy himself, in tears, testified to the court that they had intimidated him, and that therefore he had signed the statement written by J. Visockis.

The other affidavit was a complaint against the pastor by the principal and two teachers from the secondary school in Valkininkai, stating that he spends time with the children and thus interferes with their atheistic nurturing. Father Keina explained that *the complaint was falsified, for one of the teachers referred to* had not signed the complaint, and *his signature had been forged.* The pastor also noted that the instructions on whose basis he had been penalized were not legally binding because they have not been made public anywhere, and their cover actually bears the inscription *"Not for distribution to the press."*

The statement of the procurator who spoke at the trial was more like an atheistic lecture with a nuance of menace. "What will happen if the parents themselves begin to teach their children?" he asked angrily, thereby stressing the parents' lack of rights in the nurturing of their children.

The court confirmed that the pastor had been justly fined. *The sole "proof" was the testimony of a coerced child which he had tearfully retracted in court.*

The courtroom was full of believers. During the trial people were crying, being unable to remain indifferent witnesses to such guile and deceit. When they heard the verdict of the court, they were all so indignant that the officials even called the police as a precautionary measure.

Because even after the second decision of the court the pastor failed to banish the children from the altar, a note was sent from the *rayon* office to the chairman of the executive committee of the parish in Valkininkai threatening with the possible closure of the church in Valkininkai if Father Keina continued to violate the laws concerning religious cults.

Neither threats, nor trials, nor any other kind of persecution can break the spirit of those who are determined to obey God rather than men.

THE PERSECUTION OF FATHER ŠEŠKEVIČIUS

For teaching religion to children, Father A. Šeškevičius was sentenced on September 9, 1970, by the People's Court of Molėtai *Rayon* to one year in a strict-regime prison camp. Having completed his sentence on September 9, 1971, he appealed to the ecclesiastical administrator of the Diocese of Kaišiadorys requesting that he be appointed to a parish. The commissioner of the Council for Religious Affairs refused to issue him a registration certificate and ordered him to find work in some other occupation, supposedly because he had failed to obey the Soviet laws. Then

Father Šeškevičius appealed to the chairman of the Council of Ministers of the LSSR:

"If I have supposedly violated Soviet laws, then I have served my sentence and have even received a good charactrization. In addition, when I was released my rights were not curtailed, thus why am I being punished once again and even lifelong without any trial? Even the worst tyrants, when punishing people, specify the article of the violated law, the duration of the sentence, and the agency for appeals. I alone am denied this knowledge. Is there any state in this world which would permit such treatment of its subjects? How can this be reconciled with the Universal Declaration of Human Rights, which has been signed by the Soviet Union?

"By preventing me from carrying out my priestly duties, you are forcing me into transgression, for I have not ceased being a priest and I shall have to perform at least some of my priestly functions; but the state will consider this to be illegal work, and prison will again await me."

Father Šeškevičius did not receive a reply to his appeal. He then appealed to the Procurator's Office of the LSSR, but from this agency too no answer was forthcoming. Having almost lost hope, Father Šeškevičius appealed to the Procurator General of the USSR and to Academician Sakharov's Human Rights Committee. Twice he personally met with the Council for Religious Affairs and spoke with its dignitaries. Eventually he was promised a position in the Diocese of Telšiai.

In this way, even after having completed his undeserved sentence, Father Šeškevičius was a victim of discrimination for another half year. The Soviet authorities were trying to crush the spirit of the priest and thus to intimidate the others so that in their fear they would obey the authorities rather than God.

To the joy of Lithuania's believers, there are still many spiritual leaders who are faithful to their calling, who are determined to make any necessary sacrifice for the good of men's souls and the propagation of the Kingdom of Christ.

EVENTS IN MARGININKAI

On December 3, 1971, the pastor of the parish in Margininkai, the Rev. Petras Orlickas, was penalized for violating Article 143 of the LSSR Criminal Code—*he played volleyball with a group of children!*

The decision of the administrative commission of Kaunas *Rayon* stated that Father Orlickas had worked with children (he had participated in sports, played volleyball), showed cartoons, and so forth.

For a long time it was as if the atheists and Party workers never saw the children playing rowdily and cursing near the collective farm office. The pastor noticed this and set up a volleyball court. Even the most mischievous youngsters did not swear here.

What caused the administration of the Kaunas *Rayon*, the Party workers, and certain teachers to become uneasy? At the funeral services of a student it was noticed that many students were in the church. The teachers even attempted to take them by the hand and lead them out of the church. In addition, it was known that several boys used to serve mass. The principal did not succeed, though she tried her utmost, in dissuading these children. Then, as usually happens, the officials of the *rayon* authorities came to the aid of the Soviet school. Either official security policemen or covert security operatives—we are not certain which—photographed the children at the altar so that they would not think of denying their "misdeed." Government officials came to the school and started an interrogation. The students were grilled for a long time. Some mothers who had waited in vain for their children to return home from school came looking for them. Disgusted by such terrorization of their children they took them home.

The pastor was warned by the government representatives not to associate with the children, but he knew very well Christ's command: "Suffer the little children to come unto me," and for them he was determined to sacrifice whatever was necessary.

On December 3, 1971, Father P. Orlickas was summoned to a session of the Administrative Penalties Commission of Kaunas *Rayon*. Here he was accused of causing harm to Soviet youth, and a fine of fifty rubles was imposed. To the pastor's explanation that even his doctors had advised him to participate in sports, S. Jančiauskas, chairman of the commission, retorted: "You can play with the housekeeper." Throughout the entire session the chairman was tactless and coarse.

As was to be expected, Father Orlickas was immediately transferred from the parish in Margininkai. This was done on the initiative of the commissioner of the Council for Religious Affairs—an active priest is removed from his parish so that the atheists could all the more readily undermine the faith of the students.

* * *

Through fines, interrogations, even prison, the atheistic government seeks to win over the youth of Lithuania. No doubt these are extreme measures, but they are not rare. Their purpose is to intimidate the clergy, so that they would abandon their duties, and to frighten the children away from the church. Sometimes they succeed.

Lately, the opposite phenomenon is being noted—the persecutions are steeling not only the priests but also the parents and the students. More and more priests are appearing who willingly risk even their freedom rather than make compromises with their conscience; more and more parents are beginning to understand that their children must be defended from coercers of every sort who attempt to forcibly wrest the faith from the believers and who put their careers before humaneness and the rights of parents. More and more students are daring to proclaim their convictions publicly in the classroom or to criticize the atheists' contentions.

Religious persecution is undermining the government's authority more and more, for it is becoming clear to everyone that it is being conducted not on the initiative of individual atheists but through pressure from the Party and the Soviet authorities.

Hasn't the time come to put an end to the discrimination of the believers in order to narrow at least partly the abyss between the Communist party and the believing public?

A PETITION FROM 134 RESIDENTS OF PANEVĖŽYS

As 1971 was ending, the clergy of the Diocese of Panevėžys appealed to A. Kosygin, the chairman of the USSR Council of Ministers, and to the LSSR Council of Ministers. Their petition stated that, since 1961, the Diocese of Panevėžys has been deprived of its bishop, who, by order of the LSSR government, was exiled to Žagarė, which is in Joniškis *Rayon*. The priests asked that Bishop Julijonas Steponavičius be permitted to perform his duties in the Diocese of Panevėžys, for the LSSR Constitution and the laws do not provide for such curtailment of the rights of those citizens who have not been convicted in court. Also noted in the petition was that the absence of a bishop from his diocese is a great irregularity because in the absence of a bishop Church law permits an ecclesiastical administrator to oversee a diocese for only a short period of time.

The Soviet government did not reply to the petition. The commissioner of the Council for Religious Affairs upbraided some of the priests reminding them that it is senseless to write such petitions because they will be ignored.

The Soviet government considers H.E. Bishop Steponavičius disloyal to the government because he had carried out his duties as the shepherd of the diocese without making any compromises.

A PETITION FROM THE CLERGY OF THE
VILNIUS ARCHDIOCESE

"To: The General-Secretary of the Central Committee
     of the CPSU
   The Chairman of the USSR Council
     of Ministers
"Copies to:
   The Chairman of the LSSR Council of Ministers
   The LSSR Commissioner of the Council
     for Religious Affairs

A Petition from the Clergy of the Vilnius Archdiocese

"Believers constitute the greater part of the inhabitants of our Republic. They would participate much more actively in the social and political life of our country if conditions were more favorable to them. The Constitution, the Criminal Code, and various international agreements theoretically guarantee that the rights of the believers are equal to those of other citizens. Radio broadcasts to foreign countries, the press, and Lenin's postrevolutionary decrees also speak of this; but in reality very often it is otherwise.

"The number of priests in Lithuania is constantly decreasing. This is occurring not through some fault of the believers but because of the administrative obstacles created by the government. The field of action of the sole seminary in Lithuania, the theological seminary in Kaunas, is extremely restricted. The authorities strictly limit the number of those who study there; thus many who wish to enter are not accepted. Those who wish to study there are interrogated by various officials and terrorized at their place of employment. Conditions being thus, some candidates are studying theology and becoming priests outside the bounds of the seminary; however, the commissioner of the Council for Religious Affairs, which is attached to the USSR Council of Ministers, does not permit such priests to carry out their duties (this happened to the Rev. Vytautas Merkys and the Rev. Petras Našlėnas).

"Is this normal? Yet J. Rimaitis asserts in *Religion in Lithuania* (Vilnius: Gintaras, 1971), an informational booklet intended for foreign readers, that 'the government does not hamper the training of new priests' (p. 21).

"The Soviet government proclaims to the whole world that 'the Church is free to make use of all the means of religious propaganda' (ibid., p. 30). But in reality this is not so. The believers in Lithuania do not have their own press. They cannot make use of the services of radio and television. They do not even have the simplest textbooks on religious truths. 'Every citizen can purchase prayer books, the Bible, and other religious literature,' writes J. Rimaitis further (p. 24). But in fact, the Bible has never been published, just as the religious books needed by the average believer have not been published; the prayer books which were published in very small editions long ago have been unavailable for a long time now, yet we need more than half a million of them.

"The Soviet press claims that the canonical activity of the Church here is unrestricted, and yet Bishop Julijonas Steponavičius and Bishop Vincentas Sladkevičius have not been allowed to perform the duties pertinent to their position for more than ten years now. Priests who have served their sentences (even those whose convictions have been overturned) must sometimes wait a number of years before the commissioner of the Council for Religious Affairs deigns to permit them to carry out their priestly functions.

"Lenin's decree issued on January 23, 1918, allows children to be instructed privately in religious matters. In the press, the priests and the parents are given to understand that Lenin's decree is in force even now, yet more than one priest and layman (Father A. Šeškevičius, Father Juozas Zdebskis, Father Prosperas Bubnys, [Miss] Ona Paškevičiūtė) have been sentenced to forced labor solely for the performance of canonical duties—the preparation of children for their First Communion inside a church.

"According to the international agreement signed by the USSR on November 15, 1961, parents must be guaranteed the feasibility of raising their children religiously and morally in accordance with their convictions; nevertheless, government organs in our country sometimes forbid children (boys as well as girls) to take even passive part in the services, even though their parents demand or desire this. In our country's schools, the children are sometimes forced to fill out various questionnaires which are contradictory to the freedom of conscience or to publicly declare their religious convictions; the activities of the Catholic Church are being explained to them in a distorted way; antichurch literature is being foisted upon them; they are being mocked and even punished for attending church; through moral compulsion they are enrolled in antireligious groups.

"Adult believers often suffer for their religious convictions, too; they are not permitted to hold responsible positions. Those who are suspected of being believers are threatened with dismissal and are even dismissed from work under cover of various other reasons. For example, [Mrs.] O. Brilienė, a teacher at the secondary school in Vilkaviškis, was not allowed to work even as a cleaning lady in that city even after the Supreme Court of the LSSR handed down the verdict that she must be reinstated (because she had been dismissed from work solely for church attendance). In general, the practices of the People's Courts in deciding the cases of believers are often shocking: the courts (and similar agencies) often base their decision on some sort of secret instructions (which are unknown even to Soviet jurists), for whose nonobservance they hand down sentences (for example, the cases of Father Šeškevičius in Molėtai, of Father Zdebskis in Kaunas, of Father Keina in Varėna). In Soviet courts children are being questioned, are being forced to act as witnesses even against their will and that of their parents; and sometimes they are even being forced to commit perjury (viz., at the People's Court of Varėna on December 7, 1971, in the case of Father Keina).

"We therefore ask you:

1. To permit the theological seminary in Kaunas to function freely and to accept all candidates which are suitable to the Church.

2. To put into practice the freedom of a religious press guaranteed by the USSR Constitution, i.e., to permit the publishing of prayer books, catechisms, hymnals, the Bible, and other religious books, which the people lack and which they demand.

3. To permit bishops Julijonas Steponavičius and Vincentas Sladkevičius to perform their duties as bishops and to permit all priests living in our country (among them also the Ukrainians) to freely and openly perform their priestly functions.

4. To repeal the explanatory text of Article 143 of the LSSR Criminal Code—'The organization of religious instruction activities for minors in violation of regulations established by law'—which is not in accord with the international agreement of November 15, 1961, or with the constitution of the Soviet Union, and which is being abused by our country's People's Courts.

5. To abolish all of the secret instructions which are unknown to us and which concern our religious life.

6. To review the cases of individuals convicted because of their faith and to acquit them.

"We request that the matters set forth in this petition be decided in Moscow because previous petitions from the believers, which were forwarded from Moscow to Vilnius, were not examined objectively but only brought new unpleasantness for the believers.

"These complaints of ours are based on numerous grievances, more of which could be presented if necessary.

December 24, 1971

[Signatures]: Rev. R. Blažys, Rev. B. Budreckis, Rev. A. Merkys, Rev. D. Valiukonis, Rev. Č. Taraškevičius, Rev. A. Ulickas, Rev. J. Kardelis, Rev. J. Jakutis, Rev. J. Grigaitis, Rev. K. Žemėnas, Rev. A. Čiūras, Rev. K. Garuckas, Rev. V. Miškinis, Rev. A. Petronis, Rev. A. Simonaitis,

Rev. B. Laurinavičius, Rev. M. Žemaitis, Rev. J. Kukta, Rev. K. Vaičionis, Rev. J. Baltušis, Rev. B. Jaura, Rev. K. Pukėnas, Rev. J. Vaitonis, Rev. A. Dzekan, Rev. D. Akstinas, Rev. L. Ivančyk, Rev. I. Karukievič, Rev. P. Jankus, Rev. A. Lakovič, Rev. K. Molis, Rev. P. Valičko, Rev. S. Valiukėnas, Rev. V. Merkys, Rev. P. Daunoras, Rev. V. Černiauskas, Rev. A. Tamulaitis, Rev. V. Zavadzkis, Rev. A. Keina, Rev. A. Jašmantas, Rev. N. Jaura, Rev. J. Budrevičius, Rev. S. Tunaitis, Rev. M. Petravičius, Rev. N. Pakalka, Rev. K. Vasiliauskas, Rev. J. Lauriūnas, Rev. A. Andriuškevičius.

"Please send your reply to the following addresses:

1. The Rev. B. Laurinavičius, Adutiškis Post Office, Švenčionys *Rayon,* the LSSR
2. The Rev. K. Pukėnas, Nemenčinė Post Office, Vilnius *Rayon,* the LSSR
3. The Rev. R. Blažys, Tilžė Post Office, Zarasai *Rayon,* the LSSR"

* * *

The commissioner of the Council for Religious Affairs regards the priests' efforts to attain greater freedom of conscience and religion as impudence.

THE TRIAL OF KLEOPA BIČIUŠAITĖ

On January 13, 1972, in Naujoji Akmenė, the People's Court heard the case of a seventy-year-old resident of Žagarė, [Miss] Kleopa Bičiušaitė. She had violated the Soviet laws by preparing children for First Communion. To confirm her guilt, twenty-seven witnesses were summoned, mostly children between the ages of seven and fourteen. When Bičiušaitė herself admitted that, over a period of six days in July, 1971, she had taught prayers to children, these witnesses were no longer necessary—they only interfered with the smooth functioning of the trial because of their contradictory testimony. Seeing that some of the children were denying what others had affirmed, the judge began examining the children's political awareness— how many of them were members of the Young Pioneers. Only four stated that they belonged to the Pioneers.

In his statement the procurator recalled that the constitution permits all citizens to freely profess whatever religion they choose, or to be atheists. No one restricts this freedom or uses any coercion. But the Soviet form of government strives against religion and hoodwinkery because it cannot tolerate the use of religion to hoodwink its citizens. According to the constitution, the Church is separate from the state and the school from the Church. The accused, Bičiušaitė, however, had taught children in an organized manner such prayers as the Our Father, the Hail Mary, the Apostles' Creed, the Angelus, and the Ten Commandments. This the Soviet system cannot allow. It cannot allow anyone to teach children differently from the way they are taught in school.

The procurator accused the school's teachers of negligence, claiming that because of it, many children have not been enrolled into the Pioneers. He criticized and censured the Party element for their lack of political awareness, because their children also had gone to learn the tenets of the faith.

In concluding his presentation, the procurator recommended that Bičiušaitė be sentenced to one year in prison.

In her concluding statement Kleopa Bičiučaitė explained that she had taught the children at their parents' request, and that it is permissible for those parents who cannot teach their children themselves to request help from another person. She had provided such assistance to the parents. And besides, she had taught the children only what was good: that they should not steal or lie but should obey their parents, etc.

The verdict of the court was that Bičiušaitė be deprived of her freedom for one year.

After the announcement of the verdict, the police immediately arrested the elderly lady and drove her to their headquarters so that she would no longer be able to teach the children of the people what the people wanted them to be taught.

THE REV. P. LYGNUGARIS IS PENALIZED

On December 9, 1971, the Rev. Petras Lygnugaris from the parish in Akmenė visited a seriously ill patient at the hospital in Akmenė. Noticing this, the chief physician halted the administering of the last sacraments, and after berating the priest, made him leave the hospital. On December 28 Father Lygnugaris was summoned by the Akmenė *Rayon* Executive Committee and fined fifty rubles for visiting the patient in the hospital.

no. 2

- *Text of the memorandum signed by 17,054 Catholics of Lithuania sent to Brezhnev through the Secretary of the United Nations in 1972; texts of related petitions*

- *Text of petition to Brezhnev signed by 3,023 believers concerning the church in Klaipėda which was turned into a philharmonic hall*

- *Texts of petitions from parents concerning the discrimination against religious schoolchildren*

- *Text of petition concerning the church in Ignalina which was turned into a cultural center*

- *Text of a petition concerning the clergy*

- *Students are interrogated concerning First Communion*

- *Priests are fined, warned, searched, and upbraided*

- *Text of a poem in honor of Father Zdebskis*

THE CHRONICLE
OF THE CATHOLIC CHURCH
IN LITHUANIA

No. 2   [1972]

A MEMORANDUM FROM THE CATHOLICS OF LITHUANIA

Restrictions placed on the rights of Catholics, and especially the trials of Fathers J. Zdebskis and P. Bubnys, prompted the appearance of the memorandum.

The signatures were collected over a period of about two months. Because the memorandum was intended for the USSR government, no particular precautions were taken in collecting the signatures. Some of the signatures were obtained on Sundays near the churches as the faithful came to or went from the services, and the rest by visiting homes. On each page was a copy of the complete text of the memorandum so that the signers could acquaint themselves with its contens. For those unable to read, the signature gatherers would either read the memorandum or explain what matters this petition to the USSR government pertained to.

Catholics signed the memorandum with great enthusiasm. Only a small number refused to sign because they feared reprisals. The gathering of signatures was a spontaneous process—people would copy the text of the memorandum from one another and volunteer their help.

Fairly soon the news spread that the KGB was apprehending the persons who were gathering signatures, interrogating them as to where they had obtained the text of the memorandum, and confiscating the signatures already collected.

The collection of signatures was halted. Before the signatures were sent to the USSR government, a difficult question was posed: by what route should the signatures be sent to the General-Secretary of the CPSU? Complaints sent through the mail from the territory of Lithuania are usually intercepted by the KGB. The situation is no better when the complaints are presented directly to the addressees in Moscow. Undoubtedly not even one petition which the Catholics and priests sent to Moscow to Brezhnev, the General-Secretary of the Central Committee, or to Kosygin, the chairman of the Council of Ministers, or to Podgorny, the President of the Supreme Soviet, reached its addressee. They were all redirected to Vilnius and eventually reached J. Rugienis, the commissioner of the Council for Religious Affairs, which is attached to the Council of Ministers of the USSR, who, with the aid of the KGB, would attempt to ascertain just who had organized these petitions so that he could intimidate them and "explain" to them that the principles of freedom of religion and of conscience are not being violated in Lithuania.

In order to avoid a similar fate for the Catholics' memorandum, the decision was made to ask for help from the Secretary-General of the United Nations, Kurt Waldheim.

The memorandum reached the United Nations by a fortuitous route before Easter of 1972. The texts of the memorandum from the Catholics and the postscripts are presented below.

***

"To: L. Brezhnev, General-Secretary of the Central
     Committee of the CPSU, Moscow—the Kremlin

A Memorandum from the Roman Catholics of Lithuania

"After World War II had ended, the nations rose from the ruins and now desire lasting peace. The foundation of true peace is justice and the respect of human rights. We, the Catholics of Lithuania, grieve that to this day the freedoms of the believers are being restricted and the Church is being persecuted in our nation.

"Bishops J. Steponavičius and V. Sladkevičius have had to bear the burden of exile for over ten years now with no end in sight although they have not been sentenced in court and are innocent of any offenses.

"In November of this year two priests, J. Zdebskis and P. Bubnys, were sentenced to a year in prison because at the request of the parents and in the performance of their priestly duties they explained to children the fundamentals of the Catholic faith. These priests helped the children to prepare for First Communion not in school but in church, and they did not coerce anyone—whoever wanted to, studied.

"At the same time, the children of believing parents are being taught atheism against their will in school; they are even being forced to speak, write, and behave at variance with their conscience, yet no one reprimands such violators of the freedom of conscience or tries to bring them to justice.

"The priests are unable to properly minister to our needs as believers because there are not enough of them. Already in many places one priest has to take care of the needs of two and sometimes even three parishes. Even aged invalid priests have had to continue working. Matters are such because the theological seminary's affairs are being managed not so much by the bishop as by an agent of the government. The authorities permit but ten seminarians to be enrolled in the seminary each year.

"Government officials also control priestly appointments to parishes.

"Although the Criminal Code of the LSSR prescribes penalties for the persecution of believers, in practice they are not being implemented. In 1970 the education department of Vilkaviškis dismissed from work teacher [Mrs.] Ona Brilienė because of her faith, and the authorities of

Vilkaviškis *Rayon* will not even give her a job as a cleaning lady in her own town. No one punishes such officials even though persons of intelligence are afraid to practice their faith publicly because of the arbitrariness of such officials.

"Government officials do not permit the believers to rebuild, at their own expense, the churches destroyed by fire, for instance, in Sangrūda, Batakiai, Gaurė. After strenuous efforts permission is granted for a chapel to be furnished in the presbytery, but under no circumstances can it be transferred to the churchyard.

"We could point out many more distressing instances of persecution which have embittered our lives and have engendered disillusionment with the Soviet Constitution and the laws. Therefore we ask the Soviet government to grant us the freedom of conscience guaranteed by the Constitution of the USSR, which has not been enforced to this day. It is not pretty words in the press or over the radio that we desire but serious efforts by the government which would enable us Catholics to feel like equal citizens before the laws of the Soviet Union.

December, 1971"

* * *

"To: the General-Secretary of the Central Committee of the CPSU

(A supplement to the memorandum)

"Included with this memorandum are 17,054 signatures. It is essential to point out that only an insignificant number of Lithuania's believers signed this memorandum because the police and the KGB resorted to a number of means in order to disrupt the large-scale collection of signatures. In Kapsukas, Šakiai, Išlaužas, and Kapčiamiestis the persons collecting signatures were apprehended, and the petitions found in their possession were confiscated in spite of the fact that the memorandum was addressed to the Soviet government.

"If in the future the state agencies will also react to the believers' complaints as they have until now, we will be forced to appeal to international organizations: the Pope in Rome, who is the Head of our Church, or to the United Nations, as the authoritative institution which defends human rights.

"In addition, we want to remind you that this memorandum is an outgrowth of a national misfortune: during the years of Soviet rule in Lithuania, certain social ills have increased tenfold, such as juvenile delinquency, drunkenness, suicide; there has also been an ominous increase in the number of divorces and abortions. And the further we recede from our Christian past, the more apparent become the dreadful consequences of a forced atheistic upbringing, and the more widespread is the inhuman way of life without God and without religion.

"We appeal to you, the supreme authority of the Communist party, asking you to examine with a sense of seriousness and responsibility the facts we have presented and to make the appropriate decisions.

February, 1972
Representatives of
the Catholics of Lithuania"

* * *

"To: Kurt Waldheim, the Secretary-General
of the United Nations

An Appeal from the Catholics of Lithuania

"Bearing in mind that Lithuania does not have its own delegation at the United Nations, we Catholics of Lithuania have been compelled to appeal to you, Secretary-General, by means of fortuitous routes.

"We were prompted to turn to you by the circumstance that the believers of our Republic cannot make use of those rights which are set forth in Article 18 of the Universal Declaration of Human Rights. Our clergy, our organized believers, and individual Catholics have appealed more than once to the highest state organs of the Soviet Union regarding this matter, demanding that the violations of the believers' rights be stopped. The Soviet leaders were sent several petitions from the faithful, among them: the petition from 2,000 Catholics of Prienai mailed in September, 1971; the petition from the believers of the parish in Santaika, in Alytus *Rayon*, signed by 1,190 persons and mailed in October, 1971; the petition from 1,344 believers from the parish in Girkalnis, Raseiniai *Rayon*, mailed in December, 1971. All these petitions were sent to several of the highest institutions of the USSR; however, not one of them has provided an official reply although state agencies are obliged to respond to citizens' petitions within one month's time. The unofficial response was increased repression of the believers.

"The Catholics of Lithuania decided to remind the Soviet government of their disenfranchised position through a memorandum to the General-Secretary of the CPSU, Mr. Brezhnev; however, the Soviet police and KGB organs disrupted the large-scale collection of signatures by means of intimidation, arrests, and handcuffs.

"Such actions by the authorities have convinced us that this memorandum signed by 17,000 believers would not attain its goal if it were sent by the same route as the previous collective petitions.

"Therefore, we Catholics of Lithuania are appealing to you, Honorable Secretary-General, and we are asking you to forward this memorandum with all its signatures, which we are sending you through the channels of the United Nations, to the General-Secretary of the CPSU, Mr. L. Brezhnev.

> Respectfully,
> Representatives of
> the Catholics of Lithuania
> February, 1972"

* * *

The foreign press, radio, and television widely publicized this memorandum. The world's public opinion supported the 17,000 Catholics who had dared to publicly demand their rights. Pope Paul VI also remembered "the silent Church" in his Easter address.

How did the Soviet government organs react?

In their opinion this memorandum was slandering Soviet reality, and that was why the KGB was conducting a search for the initiators of the memorandum, but in vain, for so far they have exposed only a few of the signature collectors. Government agencies suspect that "anti-Soviet" priests had been the organizers of the memorandum.

* * *

On April 11, 1972, J. Rugienis, the commissioner of the Council for Religious Affairs, summoned to the office of the Kaunas Archdiocesan Curia all the bishops from the Lithuanian dioceses (who are actively fulfilling their functions) and all the ecclesiastical administrators. Together with Orlov, a representative of the authorities in Moscow, he forced them into signing a so-called "pastoral letter to the faithful," in which both those who had gathered the signatures and those who had signed the memorandum were slandered:

"3. Finally, recently in certain parishes, supposedly in the name of the clergy and the faithful, some irresponsible individuals have been collecting signatures on sheets of paper containing a text or even without one, near churches or even inside them and sometimes by visiting homes, ostensibly so that some pastor would be transferred, that some church would not be closed, that a priest would be appointed, that the pastor or the vicar would not be transferred, etc. These signature collectors later alter or add a text and attach to it the collected signatures. But this—is a falsification. We are astonished that there are believers who sign things without knowing why or for whom, and without considering what the consequences will be. We must not forget that the signing of irresponsible documents affects the relations between the Church and the State and gives rise to misunderstandings. Such matters bode no good for the Church..."

This letter was ordered to be read on Sunday, April 30, 1972, in place of all the sermons to be delivered that day.

It was immediately evident to all the clergy that this letter had been written by order of the government because the bishops had not received the information about the collection of signatures from authentic sources, and most importantly, the "pastoral" letter's allegations about the collection of signatures were clearly untrue. The clergymen discussed among themselves what should be done—whether to read the letter or not?

Many priests received a request with the following contents:

"Reverend Father,

"Days that will test the mettle of the Catholic Church in Lithuania and of its clergy are before us. On April 30 all the priests are obligated to read a letter which compromises the bishops, the priests, and the believers.

1. On April 11 Rugienis, together with a representative of the government from Moscow, forced the Ordinaries to write this deplorable letter.
2. This letter is slanderous because the 17,000 believers did not sign on blank sheets of paper but under the text which is known throughout the world.
3. This letter insults and compromises the finest sons and daughters of the Catholic Church in Lithuania who had the courage to sign this memorandum.
4. This letter irrevocably compromises the Ordinaries themselves.
5. Priests are bound to obey their bishops only within the bounds of the *Codex Juris Canonici.* No one can obligate a priest to read slander.
6. Conscientious priests will not read this letter regardless of whatever consequences they may have to suffer.

"Father, we appeal to your priestly conscience; being a messenger of Him who called Himself the Truth, do not yield to lies and coercion, do not betray the cause of the nation and of the Church for a mess of porridge."

***

On the aforementioned Sunday, special persons were sent from the *rayon* offices to the churches to monitor which priests would read the letter and which would not.

The atheists made use of the "pastoral" letter of April 11 for their propaganda. For example, even before April 30, at a parents' meeting at the secondary school in Aukš-toji Panemunė, representatives of the authorities decried to the parents those persons who sign various papers, often without knowing themselves why they were doing so. To confirm the veracity of their words, they read the appropriate thoughts from the bishops' letter: "If you don't believe me, here's what your bishops say."

Only an insignificant number of the clergymen read aloud the entire letter: some did so because they did not grasp the significance of the situation, others—to appease the civilian authorities. Some of the clergymen read only the parts that dealt with churchly matters, leaving out the falsehoods. The others preached a sermon as usual on the above-mentioned Sunday.

After April 30 the KGB tried to obtain more precise information about the reading of the letter, even making use of the priests who were loyal to them in these efforts.

Even though the bishops' letter was sent out very late —some priests had received it but a few days before April 30—and there was no time for consultations, yet the challenge had been met successfully. The government organs have become convinced that they would not be able to make use of the majority of Lithuania's clergy for their designs.

EVENTS IN KLAIPĖDA

In 1945, as the war was ending, Hitler's army mined and blew up the masonry church of the Catholics in Klaipėda. The local residents testify to this fact.

After the war, the number of Lithuanians in Klaipėda grew rapidly. In present-day Klaipėda, there are 85,000 Lithuanians and 43,000 Russians (1970 census data). The majority of the Lithuanians are believers. For example, in

1972, during the Lenten retreat alone about 8,000 persons received Holy Communion.

After the war, the Soviet government allowed the Catholics to make use of a small German sectarian church on Bokštai Street. During services it would become extremely congested, and people would faint; and the Catholics began demanding permission to build a larger church.

In 1954, the pastor of the parish in Klaipėda (now Bishop Povilonis) received permission to build a new church. At that time the head of the USSR government was Malenkov; the persecution of the believers in Lithuania had abated somewhat. Believers were being urged to join in the preservation of peace throughout the world. The permit for constructing the church in Klaipėda, no doubt, was also granted for propaganda purposes, since many foreign seamen come to Klaipėda.

"Build it so the steeple could be seen even from the sea," said the representatives of the authorities.

Even though at that time there was a great shortage of construction materials in war-ravaged Klaipėda, the government permitted the use of stockpiled materials in building the church. As construction began, no evil intent was apparent on the part of the authorities to later take over the finished church and use it for profane purposes.

On June 30, 1957, Bishop P. Maželis, the ecclesiastical administrator of the Diocese of Telšiai, blessed the foundation of the Catholic church of Klaipėda, which was under construction. A document with the following contents was placed in the cornerstone: "Submitting themselves to the motherly care of Mary, with their offerings the Catholics of Klaipėda, as well as of all Lithuania are building in Klaipėda the Queen of Peace Church, whose foundation was blessed on June 30, 1957, by the administrator of the Diocese of Telšiai, H.E. Bishop Petras Maželis."

"We are building a church in honor of the Queen of Peace," stated the parochial committee of the Catholic parish in Klaipėda in its proclamation to the Catholics of Lithuania. "By this action we want to emphasize that we never again want to see the fires and devastation of war on the shores of the Baltic."

Offerings for the construction of the church were collected throughout Lithuania. The Catholics of Klaipėda rejoiced and enthusiastically joined in the actual building of the church. Although the selected plot of land was in a very marshy area, within a few weeks the people had filled in the marsh by hauling dirt in small carts and even by lugging it in baskets. After returning from work, the believers would hasten to volunteer their services and would work until nighttime. In their free time, drivers brought the materials needed for the construction of the church and gathered loose-lying bricks from the ruins throughout the city. Even the auto-inspectors "failed to notice" the drivers with vehicles who were assisting in the building of the church. Even public officials sometimes came to the assistance of the faithful. Among the ranks of the voluteer workers could also be seen those who previously had never gone to church.

The believers contributed about three million rubles for the construction of the church. Even poor Catholics cheerfully contributed their savings for the building of the church. One worker who brought a rather large sum of money said: "Brick up my heart along with the bricks in the walls of the church." It turned out that this worker, who had to support a large family, had contributed one month's wages. Whenever people sold anything, they would allocate a part of the money for the church.

Construction was completed in the summer of 1960, and the consecration ceremonies were planned for the feast of the Assumption of Mary. Unfortunately, a second "explosion" occurred, similar to that of the Hitlerites. The faithful who had gathered for the consecration ceremonies found the church's gates boarded up.

"The government forbids the opening of the church!"
"The atheists are taking away our church!"
Such shouts flew from lips to lips causing anguish

among the believers. They all felt they had been trampled upon and deceived.

Why had the church been closed?

Some Party workers explained it this way: When Nikita Krushchev found out that a church had been built in Klaipėda, he shouted in a rage, "I forbid its opening!" This prohibition was transmitted to the LSSR government, and the opening of the church was called off.

No doubt the atheists' complaints to Moscow also contributed to the closing of the church. They had been afraid that the success of the atheistic propaganda would have been impaired.

The atheists dealt visciously with the new church. Using tractors, army units knocked down the church steeple at nighttime .They smashed the valuable plaster statues of the Stations of the Cross and heaped them into the dirt. The people's sole weapon against the self-will of the army and the police was their tears. Police officials tried to apprehend the bystanders and carted them off to jail. Some of them were taken up to forty or fifty kilometers out of town by trucks and were mockingly ordered to return home on foot. Such viscious treatment of the church and of the believers cannot even be imagined in any state which respects human rights. The faithful, whose contributions and sweat enabled the church to be built, felt that they had been grievously wronged.

"So this is the true face of a godless government," spoke the people through their tears.

"We must protest to the higher-ups. . ."

"Who is there to protest to when the believers are beyond the bounds of the laws? The atheistic government won't defend our rights."

Fearing a riot by the faithful, the authorities sent in about 200 policemen.

In the early part of 1961, two priests from Klaipėda were arrested—Povilonis and Burneikis—and sentenced to prison. Father Talaišis was exiled from Klaipėda.

At the present time a people's philharmonic hall has

been established in the new church of Klaipėda. In the beginning, the believing public, Lithuanians and Russians alike, would not attend the concerts. There were times when fifty artists were performing on stage and only five spectators were to be found in the hall. The Russians used to say: "We don't go to church..."

* * *

And so the Catholics continue to languish in the little church. During the services on Sundays and holy days, one can constantly see people who have fainted being carried out. In the early part of the year, after listening to the atheists' persistent talk that the rights of believers are not being restricted, that people of every conviction should be respected, the Catholics decided to appeal to the government of the Soviet Union requesting the return of their church. For several months signatures were cautiously collected, but because of persecution by the KGB, the collecting had to be curtailed.

Before Easter a petition with the following contents was sent to Moscow from somewhere in the Russian Soviet Federative Socialist Republic (so that the KGB of the LSSR would not confiscate it):

"To: L. Brezhnev, General-Secretary of the CPSU, Moscow

A Petition from the Catholics of the City of Klaipėda, the LSSR

"During the years 1956-1961, a Catholic church was built and completely furnished in Klaipėda with funds provided by the believers and with the permission of the Council of Ministers of Lithuania. The authorities, however, did not permit its use and made it into a philharmonic hall.

"The building in which Catholic services are now held is unsuitable, in poor condition, and small; and during holy days the faithful are forced to stand in the street.

Just the fact that permission had been granted for building a church in Klaipėda indicates that the present structure in which services are being held is not suitable.

"We believers appeal to you, asking and hoping that you would understand our aspirations and would soon normalize the situation by correcting the injustice inflicted upon the believers and returning the church built with our funds.

"This appeal is supported by the following signatures. . . .

Klaipėda, the LSSR
March 19, 1972"

The petition was signed by 3,023 believers.

So far only the KGB has responded to the appeal from the residents of Klaipėda. Because the petition to Moscow was sent with Jonas Saunorius' return address, the KGB summoned him as many as three times in their desire to find out who had initiated-organized the petition. For similar reasons Commissioner Rugienis summoned Saunorius to Vilnius.

* * *

On Easter Sunday in 1972, during the services, KGB agents apprehended two amateur photographers, who wanted to photograph the throng of believers praying outside the church. The photographers were accused of allegedly taking pictures to be sent abroad. "They're waiting with outstretched arms for these pictures over there," said the security officials, upbraiding them.

The people of Klaipėda are once again planning to appeal to the USSR government asking for the return of their church.

VARĖNA RAYON

The parents from the parish in Valkininkai appealed to the *rayon* administration in regard to the discrimination students experience for their religious convictions. The complete text of their petition is presented below:

*A Petition to the Chairman of the Varèna Rayon Soviet
of Working People's Deputies Executive Committee*

"In September of this year, after returning from
school, our children complained that they had been interrogated in school as to whether they attend church and who
else does; and they were threatened that their conduct grade
would be lowered for attending church and that the fact
would be noted in their personal records.

"I, J. Griežė, state that my daughter was questioned
at the secondary school in Valkininkai by the teachers
[Miss] Kliukaitė and [Mrs.] Butkienė, and by the principal, as to whether she and her younger sister attend
church, and when do they go to confession? A year ago she
had been reminded that if she attended church she would
not be permitted to take the examinations.

"I, [Mrs.] S. Andriuškevičienė, state that my daughter
was threatened at the eight-year school in Urkionys by
teacher [Mrs.] Saulėnienė and she was asked when she
had received First Communion and whether she goes to
church. She was also threatened that her churchgoing
would be noted in her personal records and that as a result
she would be unable to find a job.

"I, [Mrs.] J. Kazlauskienė (Plekštorė Village), state
that both of my sons were questioned by teacher Kliukaitė,
by the principal, and by officials from the *rayon* headquarters as to whether they had received First Communion,
which of the boys and girls went to church, and under
whose care they had received their First Communion.

"I, [Mrs.] J. Blažulionienė (Užperkasė Village), state
that both my son and my daughter were questioned by
teacher Butkienė, by the principal, and by officials from
the *rayon* headquarters as to when they had received First
Communion, who had prepared them, and which girls had
gone.

"During a parents' meeting at the school in S. Naniškės, demands were made that the parents would not take
their children to church. I, Jurgelevičius (Mištūnai Vil-

lage), state that my son told me after returning from school that the teachers had said that if 'you children go to church, the pastor will get two years in prison.'

"There were also others who were questioned for an hour or more.

"It seems to us that no one may question our children without our presence as to whether they attend church, or attempt to intimidate them. The children cry and cannot sleep nights. The questioning alone frightens the children and is a violation of the freedom of conscience and our parental rights. If our child had committed an offense, then we would be blamed and punished. It is our sacred duty to nurture our children. We, the believing parents, feel and understand that our faith is a great help in nurturing our children properly. The children are altogether different after returning from attending services in church. The children see and hear so much that is good there.

"Do the above-mentioned teachers have the right to behave in this fashion with our children—to interrogate and intimidate them solely because they attend church and participate in services at the altar? They go to church because we take them and oblige them to go. Our very nature and the constitution gives us the right to take our children to church and the duty to raise them in a proper manner. Why is there such disregard of the parental rights of us believing parents?

"We would like to ask you, Honorable Chairman, to inform us whether our children can be interrogated in this manner and to help us in order that such events would not recur.

Valkininkai
October 10, 1971"

* * *

This was signed by nine parents. The chairman of the Varėna *Rayon* Executive Committee sent back the following reply after ten days:

"After examining your petition, we did not reach the conclusion that your children were interrogated. The teachers were questioning the children about how they spend their free time and what they do outside of school, and this is natural because teachers should know how their students are occupied and should constantly be concerned about their upbringing.

"Furthermore, you have no right to demand that the teachers propagate the faith since you know perfectly well that the church is separated from the state and that the atheistic education of the students is being conducted in all the schools according to the demands of present-day knowledge.

> November 9, 1971
> Z. Voroneckas,
> Chairman of the Varėna *Rayon*
> Executive Committee"

This reply to the students' parents by the chairman of the Varėna *Rayon* Executive Committee clearly reveals how devoid of rights Catholics are and also the arbitrariness of government officials.

* * *

And now let us consider another complaint written four months later by believing parents from the parish in Lukšiai. At that time the LSSR government was already aware that signatures were being collected for the memorandum from the Catholics in Lithuania.

ŠAKIAI *RAYON*

The Persecution of Students in Lukšiai

In November, 1971, the teachers, especially the homeroom teachers and the principal of the secondary school in Lukšiai started a crude campaign against the pupils who serve mass, strew flowers, participate in adorations and processions, and in general, against all churchgoers. Those who would serve mass were summoned to the principal's office and interrogated. Attempts were made to intimidate them, and to force them to keep away from the altar. They were shamed before the entire class, mocked in newsletters posted on bulletin boards, and were the subjects of caricatures. Even their parents would be told to come to the school and were ordered not to permit their children to assist during mass or during other religious rites. After New Year's Day in 1972, two believing parents, G. Krikštolaitis and [Mrs.] N. Didžbalienė, went to see Principal S. Urbonas and asked that the children who serve mass and those who attend church would not be terrorized. The parents reminded the principal what the Soviet Constitution and the laws say about this.

The principal sternly declared: "We've harried them and will continue to harry them, and even more forcefully than before. The authorities of Šakiai *Rayon* harry us, and we will harry your children; and you may complain to Moscow itself if you wish."

"As for us, we have been taking and will continue to take our children to church," stated the parents in parting.

The servers and the participants of processions did not cease going to church; only one or two had been frightened away. For a long time the believing parents endured patiently and waited, hoping the teachers might see reason; but they did not stop humiliating, mocking, or intimidating the children. Then the parents wrote a complaint to the Procurator's Office of the LSSR. Here are its contents:

"To: the Procurator of the LSSR

"Copies to:

The Ministry of Public Education of the LSSR
The Department of Education of Šakiai *Rayon*
The Chairman of the Šakiai *Rayon*
Executive Committee

*A Petition from the Believing Parents of the Parish
in Lukšiai, Šakiai Rayon*

"A booklet published in Vilnius in 1970 by the Mintis Publishing House and authored by J. Aničas and J. Rimaitis entitled *Tarybiniai įstatymai apie religinius kultus ir sq-*

žinės laisvę [Soviet laws concerning religious cults and freedom of conscience] states that 'every citizen may profess whichever religion he wishes, or none at all. The denial of any rights whatsoever because of the profession of some particular religion or the nonprofession of any religion at all has been rescinded' (p. 17).

"'The requirements of the principle of freedom of conscience are: (1) the right of every citizen to profess any religion he wishes; (2) the right to perform the rites of the cult; .... (6) the equality of the citizens before the law irregardless of their religious affiliation' (p. 15).

"'The Soviet government wages a constant battle against those citizens or workers within the governmental apparatus who infringe upon the rights of either religious organizations or of believers. In the criminal codes of the Union Republics special articles prescribe the liabilities in case of criminal violation of the principles of freedom of conscience of believing citizens' (p. 24).

"'Both the Communist party and the Soviet government have also indicated the necessity of strict adherence to those Soviet laws which guarantee to religious communities and to the clergy the freedom to function within the limits of church canons and dogmas, and to believers every opportunity to fully enjoy their constitutional right of religious freedom. The socialist state forbids any kind of administrative measures, rudeness or tactlessness in regard to religious cults, their ministers, and the believers. Any type of interference with the performance of religious rites when they are performed without violating the laws regarding religious cults is considered a punishable offense. In accordance with Article 145 of the Criminal Code of the LSSR, any interference with the performance of religious rites which do not disturb the public peace or interfere with citizens' rights is punishable with the loss of up to one year's freedom, or with forced labor for the same period, or with a fine of up to 100 rubles' (p. 31)."

(See the decree of the Presidium of the Supreme Soviet of the LSSR 'Dėl Lietuvos TSR Baudžiamojo Kodekso 143 str. taikymo' [Concerning the application of Article 143 of the LSSR Criminal Code], *Tarybų Socialistinės Respublikos Aukščiausios Tarybos ir Vyriausybės Žinios* [News of the Supreme Soviet and of the Government of the Soviet Socialist Republic], May 20, 1966, no. 14, pp. 183-184.)

"In its declarations, Vatican Council II—on whose basis the bishops of Lithuania, in concert with the commissioner for the cult, published at the Vaizdas Printing House the *Liturginis maldynas* [Liturgical prayer book] in 1968—urges and instructs the faithful to participate as actively as possible in religious rites. Therefore while in church, we parents, together with our children, kneel, sing hymns, pray silently or give various responses aloud, and walk in processions carrying ritualistic articles. Our children kneel or stand at the altar, and we parents do so beside them, etc. Our children are not any sort of ministers of the church. They are ordinary churchgoers and participants in the services.

"Yet it is with great sadness that we believing parents are having to bear grievous injustice and discrimination. Because our children participate in religious rites together with us, their parents, the administration and the teachers of the secondary school in Lukšiai tend to persecute them in various ways, to behave rudely with them, to make fun of them, intimidate them, and discriminate against them:

a) Because first-class student Juozas Naujokaitis had gone to church and participated in the services, his teacher, [Mrs.] Vaišvilienė, ordered him to pull off his pants in the presence of all of his classmates (boys and girls) and to lie down; and she said:

"You'll get a licking for going to kneel at the altar."

Frightened by such words from the teacher, the boy began to cry.

b) The head of the science department, teacher [Miss] Martišiūtė, instructed Rolandas Tamulevičius, a student in class 6B, to perform a deed evil in nature by ordering him to drink up the church wine which the priest uses during mass and to refill the container with water.

c) Teacher [Mrs] Vanagienė came to see the parents of R. Didžbalis, a sixth-class student, and explained to them that even if their child were to commit a rather serious offence, this would still be a lesser offence than kneeling at the altar.

d) Teacher [Mrs.] Urbonienė told second-class student Vitas Pavalkis to choose one or the other: either to go to church or to school.

e) Teacher [Miss] Martišiūtė, who had brought some artistic religious pictures to class, asked student Virga Mikelaitytė: 'Why did God drive Adam out of paradise?' When the girl did not answer, she said to [Miss] Vita Maceikaitė: 'You're from a religious family, your cousins are altar boys, so why don't you answer this question?' Afterward, while mocking religion, she questioned the students [Miss] Liutvinaitė and [Miss] Alytaitė.

f) Teacher [Miss] Skirskytė visited the parents of the student Krikštolaitis and whined that if their child will go to kneel at the altar, her pension would be adversely affected.

g) Teacher [Mrs] Sakalauskienė, without determining who was at fault, assailed a completely innocent student from class 7A, Rimas Didžbalis, saying: 'Didžbalis, stop it! You're not at mass now.' After this remark from the teacher, the boy stood up and started to cry.

h) Children who go to church to kneel and pray are rudely interrogated and they are made fun of and shamed before their classmates.

i) On January 22, 1972, caricatures of the following students were included in the newsletter posted on the school's bulletin board: Krikštolaitis, a student in class 5B, shown kneeling in the sacristy and holding a rosary; R. Tamulevičius, a student in class 6B, shown as his mother is driving him to church in the family car, and he is saying: 'I'm going to church. It's fun there. When the priest drinks his wine, I ring a little bell.' The Didžbalis brothers were ridiculed in a similar fashion.

"In addition, in the same issue of the newsletter there is an article by the editorial board which states: 'There is no shortage of those who worship God in our school. Such students degrade themselves, lose their dignity, and discredit the name of the school. These are two-faced persons, hypocrites, who by their actions try to adapt themselves both to the church and the school, to be both Pioneers and altar boys, and who get a few kopeks from the priest's hand for their chameleonlike activities. Such chameleons are class 9A student [Miss] Alytaitė, class 6B student Alyta, class 5B student Krikštolaitis, and class 7A student Didžbalis. Besides these pawns of the church, there are also those in this school who go to church and perform the religious rites like sanctimonious grannies; these are class 9A student [Miss] Liutvinaitė, tenth-class student [Miss] Staugaitytė, eleventh-class student [Miss] D. Bacevičiūtė. Let us give them and their activities a suitable retort.'

"The first such concrete 'retort' was perhaps when ninth-class student [Miss] Janina Alytaitė, fourteen years of age, who had worked as a cleaner at the restaurant in Lukšiai, was promptly dismissed from work after a conversation with her mother about churchgoing children even though the teachers had been aware of the fact that she worked in the restaurant but had never said anything and had tolerated it.

"Finally, is it not a 'retort' when a young person is called a chameleon—that is: an animal? Are not intimidation and threats a 'retort?' Is not punishment and terrorization because of one's religion a 'retort,' because a child attends church with his parents? Is it not a 'retort' to humiliate churchgoers before their classmates by creating the impression that churchgoing is a terrible, shameful offense?

"Furthermore, does not such conduct by the teachers in regard to the students debase their position of authority? Even a child knows that there is freedom and equality of all the faiths. But what are they given to understand by the actions of the teachers? We parents want our children to respect both us and their teachers, to learn, and to be virtuous.

"The teachers of the secondary school in Lukšiai call believing parents backward and stupid. For example, teacher Genys and teacher [Miss] Martišiūtė said to [Mrs.] Ona Alytienė: 'You parents are fools for going to church and for taking your children along.' How can a child refuse to go to church if his father or mother takes him along or tells him to go there by himself? After all, it is the parents who have the greatest responsibility in the upbringing of their children. Is it wise or pedagogical, therefore, to ask a child every Monday during classes 'Did you go to church yesterday?' and again on Saturday to ask him, 'Will you be going to church tomorrow?' How can a child not go? How can he disobey his parents! What an effective means of alienating a child from his parents! In many cases a child will be incapable of making the distinction. He will say to his parents: 'You're a fool, you're backward. Don't try to tell me what to do.' When a child misbehaves, he is told to bring his parents, but when we parents teach them religion and take them to church, the children are told to disregard their parents. Where is the logic in this, where is the respect due the parents and teachers?

"Thus, greatly distressed by these matters, we believing parents are appealing to you and asking you to take action in order that our children would not be punished, persecuted, derided, or discriminated against for professing the faith and for participating in religious rites. We parents have tired of the constant pushing around, the intimidation, and the mockery of our children; we're tired of their tears, their sudden awakenings at night. We do not want our children to have to be afraid of a school in which terror, derision, and humiliation prevail against a child who believes in God.

"We want our children to go to school with joy and to return in a happy mood. We want the school to be a second home to them, and the teachers—a second set of parents, who, noticing a student's mistakes or tactlessness, would be capable of educating the student in a pedagogic and parental manner, of providing him with the access to knowledge, and of developing a highly cultured person.

"We believing parents want the law regarding freedom of religion to be not merely pretty words of propaganda but a reality.

"We ask you, Honorable Procurator of the Republic, to remind the principal and the teachers of the secondary school in Lukšiai that they too are bound by the Soviet laws, and that they should not continue making these and similar mistakes.

Lukšiai
February, 1972"

The petition was signed by fourteen parents.

* * *

When the principal and the teachers found out that a petition had been written, they tried to stop it from reaching any agency of the Republic. Class 9B student [Miss] J. Alytaitė was questioned as to whether her mother had collected signatures and who else had collected them, etc. The student had answered that she knew nothing.

The teachers turned to the chairman of the Lenin Collective Farm and deputy to the Supreme Soviet, K. Glikas, so that he would intercede for them. The enraged chairman assailed the believing parents for slandering the teachers of the secondary school in Lukšiai and for publicizing this matter throughout the Republic.

At a meeting of one of the collective farm's brigades, Glikas stated that the complaint had been shown to him in Vilnius, that he had had to suffer much unpleasantness because there was such disorder in his collective farm.

"We'll show them! We'll twist off the fangs of those who are aggravating our teachers!" said the agitated deputy. He threatened among other things to have the parents who had signed denounced in the newspaper. Glikas went to the home of G. Krikštolaitis and angrily reproached him, asking why the parents had slandered the teachers. "They are scholars; they must be respected, and you should not quarrel with them." The chairman stated that life would be made miserable for the parents who had signed the petition.

Glikas told [Mrs.] Tamulevičienė through the agronomist, that if she would not "change her tune," she would be kicked out of her position as accounting clerk. He also threatened that if the Tamulevičius family would have to move to a settlement, they would get but little money for their old farm.

The intervention of Chairman Glikas disheartened the parents. Rumors began to circulate among the people that the church in Lukšiai would be closed, that the pastor would be transferred, etc. To many it seemed that there was no need for so much unpleasantness which results from having children serve mass. Some were even angry with the parents who had signed the complaint. The more courageous persons consoled themselves with the belief that God would not abandon them. During his sermons the pastor would remind them of the need for self-sacrifice. The more fervent Catholics prayed: "O Lord, retain at your side the little children whom You love best."

On March 9 a commission from Vilnius arrived at Lukšiai to investigate the facts brought to light by the complaint. The members of the commission stated that they were from the Ministry of Education. The commission remained in Lukšiai for three days; children, parents, teachers, and uninvolved persons were questioned.

They asked first-class student J. Naujokaitis:

"Did the teacher scold you very much because you serve mass?"

"She did."

"Did the teacher really try to frighten you by telling you to 'pull down your pants?'"

"That's what happened," confirmed the boy.

The commission members explained that the teacher had no right to do so, that there is freedom of religion, and whoever wants to attend church may do so while those who do not, don't.

The members of the commission explained to Vitas Pavalkis:

"If you like, you may go to church and serve mass; no one will punish you for this or expel you from school."

The boy returned from school in a happy frame of mind, convinced that no one would make fun of him anymore.

They asked seventh-class student R. Didžbalis:

"Was a caricature of you included in the newsletter on the school bulletin board?"

"Yes, it was."

They explained to the boy that no one can ridicule a child or place caricatures of him in a newsletter because of his faith; it is only permissible to say that there is no God. The boy was asked whether there was anything else that he wanted.

"The freedom to go to church!"

They asked [Miss] Alytaitė why she had been dismissed from the restaurant.

"For going to church."

"Were you written about and caricatured in the newsletter posted on the school bulletin board?"

"Yes."

"What is it that you want? " she was asked by the commission.

"That the teachers would not scold me for going to church, and that they wouldn't put me in the newsletter."

The members of the commission again explained that students may not be insulted for attending church; they promised to warn the principal and the teachers not to use such an approach.

The commission asked R. Tamulevičius:

"Who told you not to go to church and not to serve mass?"

"The teachers and the principal."

The boy related how once he had been summoned by three teachers. They were laughing as they told him to put on a red tie and then see whether the priest would let him serve mass or not.

"Did your teacher, [Miss] Martišiūtė, tell you in jest or in all seriousness to drink the priest's wine and refill the container with water?"

"I don't know, but that was what she said."

"You may go to church if you want to; if you like, you may serve mass, but read more atheistic books and don't join the priesthood."

Pijus Didžbalis explained to the visiting commission:

"I don't have anything against the school. There is only one thing wrong, and that is that the teachers tend to greatly harass the children who go to church. Those children are afraid—they don't even want to go to school. Our faith is such that on Sundays we must go to church and take our children along. The teachers started to intimidate our children, to write about them in the newsletter which is posted on the school bulletin board, to make fun of them in class, and so on."

The commission members explained that the teachers should not have behaved this way, and that they would amend their ways.

One commission member explained to [Mrs.] Ona Alytienė that teachers were not allowed to insist that a child would not believe in God or go to church; they were not allowed to ridicule children because of their faith or to write about them in the newsletter to be posted on the bulletin board. The commission member also reminded her that the principal and the teachers would be punished for their misdeeds. The commission members also explained to G. Krikštolaitis that children may not be scolded, interrogated, or written about in the newsletter for attending services. One of the commission members recommended that the children be kept in the middle of the church during services, but if their parents allowed them to serve mass, they had the right to do so.

One could only rejoice if complaints were always handled in this manner, but, unfortunately, this was perhaps the first such response during the postwar years.

In 1969 the Scientific Research Institute of the LSSR Ministry of Education published a book by B. Bitinas entitled *Religingi mokiniai ir jų perauklėjimas* [Religious students and their re-education]. Here is what is written therein:

"Some assert that in the atheistic nurturing of students satirical criticism should not be used in regard to those students who practice religious rites. The data we have compiled indicates that this contention cannot be accepted categorically when one is confronted with young religious adolescents. In some cases the expression of an atheistic public opinion in satirical form actually helps the religious adolescent to accept the goals of an atheistic education more readily than other forms of atheistic influence..." (p. 122).

This book by B. Bitinas can be found only in the methodology sections of public education departments, and it is being recommended as instructional material to be used in the re-education of religious students.

The question arises—which should be believed? The words of the commission members or the written instructions?

That is something the future will reveal.

IGNALINA *RAYON*, 1971

"To: The Chairman of the Presidium of the
Supreme Soviet of the LSSR
The Secretary of the Central Committee
of the Lithuanian Communist Party

The Chairman of the Council of Ministers
    of the LSSR
The LSSR Commissioner of the Council
    for Religious Affairs
The Curia of the Archdiocese of Vilnius

*A Petition from the Parochial Committee and the Believers
of the Parish in Ignalina*

"The Constitution of the Soviet Union guarantees freedom of religion and of conscience. Practicing Catholics need churches, but we believers of Ignalina do not have one.

"A church was built in Ignalina during the difficult years when the area was under occupation by bourgeois Poland and during the especially difficult days of occupation by the Germans. The believers contributed much toil and money into its construction, often while they themselves wanted for bread. Much construction material had been readied, but construction work was halted by World War II. In the postwar years the local government deceived us grievously. Because the church building had not been completed, the authorities promised to complete it, and we would just have to pay for the labor. The building was confiscated from the parish, however, and turned into a cultural center.

"The present five-year plan provided for the construction of a new cultural center because the church building is plainly unsuitable for this purpose: it is too small, the columns obscure visibility, the acoustics are poor, etc. Despite all these shortcomings, a new cultural center is not being built, but instead, major repairs have been undertaken on our former church. Already the presbytery has been demolished, and the foundation for an addition is being built right next to our present house of worship, which is an ordinary little shack.

"People at prayer have already been disturbed by music, orchestras, noisy programs, and even by not infrequent incidents, such as, for example, when a few years ago the director of the cultural center himself had broken windows with rocks during the services. When the addition will be built, the distance between the cultural center and our house of worship will decrease by five or six meters, and the noise and the music will interfere with the believers' prayers even more.

"Today, with aching hearts we gaze at the overturned cornerstone of the church and our sanctuary, which is being ravaged. It's the same as if they were ravaging our very hearts.

"Our present house of worship is very small, uncomfortable, and cannot accommodate all the faithful. It can accommodate only two to three hundred persons. In winter the ceiling and the walls freeze over, and on Sundays, when the people gather in great numbers for the services, condensation of vapors occurs, and it literally rains from the ceiling. Thus the place is damp and stuffy. In addition, it is not only the believers from the parish in Ignalina who gather to pray here, but also the people from neighboring parishes who have come to the marketplace or on other businesss and hope to fulfill their religious obligations at the same time. As a rule, however, during the services a majority of them are forced to stand outside in foul weather and in the cold.

"Seeking the return of our church, we have appealed twice to Comrade Vaitonis, vice-chairman of the *rayon* executive committee, who replied rudely to us: 'It's useless. Don't expect anything—I won't return anything! You should have brought this matter to my attention in 1950. Now it's too late.' Is this the sort of answer one would expect from a responsible official? And is it truly too late now? for the wounds of the war have been healed everywhere during this lengthy period of time. Why was it a possibility in 1950 when accommodations truly were a problem for everyone, but today—after so many years of progress and achievement—our last hopes are being taken away.

"In the summertime many vacationers and tourists from various corners of the Soviet Union pour into Ignalina. They are amazed at the wrong that has been inflicted upon us! Why haven't we the right to have suitable conditions for praying? Is it really too late to heal this grievous wound of ours?

"Putting our trust in the humane laws and the constitution of the Soviet government, which guarantees religious freedom, we trust that you will grant our request for the return of our church, and that we shall not need to turn to higher authorities concerning this matter.

Ignalina
March 14, 1971"

This petition was signed by 1,025 believers.

A short time later an unknown representative of the government arrived at Ignalina and, summoning the chairman of the Ignalina Parochial Committee, an old man of eighty, inspected the exterior of the little church and paced off the area it occupies. It was later learned from *rayon* officials that this had been Rugienis, the commissioner of the Council for Religious Affairs. After this visit by the commissioner, the parochial committee once again appealed to the authorities of the Republic.

"To: The Chairman of the Presidium of the Supreme
      Soviet of the LSSR
   The Central Committee of the Lithuanian
      Communist Party
   The Chairman of the Council of Ministers
      of the LSSR
   The LSSR Commissioner of the Council
      for Religious Affairs
   The Curia of the Archdiocese of Vilnius

A Petition

"In response to our petition of March 14, 1971, a representative of an unknown agency arrived from Vilnius on

March 29 of this year to acquaint himself with the condition of our house of worship.

"The Ignalina Parochial Committee wants to find out why the aforementioned individual failed to meet with all the members of the parochial committee but contented himself with a talk with one old man.

"In our opinion and according to the old man's assertion, he familiarized himself with the situation only superficially. He did not go inside our house of worship but only paced off its exterior dimensions (20 x 8). That would amount to 160 square meters, whereas the interior of the structure occupies considerably less (17x6). In addition, the usable space for the believers is even smaller. The presbytery takes up about 30 square meters; the catafalque, the confessionals, the stairs, the space for a small choir, the pews, the benches, and the remainder also take up usable space—from this one can form a picture of how much space is left for the believers.

"We are most concerned that an erroneous decision based on the above-mentioned individual's misleading data would not result.

"We therefore request that you ascertain the opinion of the entire parochial committee and not just that of one person who does not constitute the entire committee and cannot speak in its name.

"Because we do not know which governmental agency the aforementioned individual represented, we are therefore sending our petition to all the agencies to which we sent the previous petition.

Ignalina
April 7, 1971"

The petition was signed by seven members of the parochial committee. Four representatives of the committee delivered the statement to each of the agencies. When they came to the office of the commissioner of the Council for Religious Affairs, Rugienis, he upbraided them, called them saboteurs, and angrily retorted: "If I grant you this, you'll be wanting something else. Don't ask for anything; you won't get it!"

After several weeks had passed, Rugienis sent his reply through Vaitonis, the vice-chairman of the *rayon* executive committee. The members of the parochial committee and several believers went to see him. Vaitonis did not want to admit the believers but was forced to give in. Vaitonis read the memorandum from Rugienis, which he would not allow anyone to look at, even from a distance. The basic idea of the note was: no one is pulling down your church, no one is interfering with your prayers, and you have sufficient space; as for the cultural center— no one will ever give you the cultural center.

MOLĖTAI *RAYON*

"To: the Chairman of the Council of Ministers
of the USSR

A Petition from the Believers of the Parish in Stirniai and in Molėtai Rayon

"Admonitions by readers constantly appear in the press concerning various shortcomings in cultural and existential services, to which the Soviet government always responds. In our religious life we believers constantly experience not only shortcomings but restrictions as well. Since we believers cannot speak out about these restrictions in the press, if we remain silent, one can form the impression that we do not feel these restrictions. That is why we are appealing to you, Chairman of the Council of Ministers.

"To a nonbeliever religion appears to be worthless or even harmful, but to us believers it is a matter of great importance. Restrictions placed on the practice of our religion are more painful to us than material wrongs.

"Priests are essential to the practice of religion. Because the government limits the number of candidates that can be admitted to the seminary, the number of priests that are ordained is several times smaller than the number that die every year. Already there are several parishes without a priest, and because of this the religious life of thousands of believers suffers. Despite the shortage of clergymen, more and more priests are being sentenced to prison because they taught children the tenets of the faith in church at their parents' request. In September of last year (1970), Father Antanas Šeškevičius, the pastor of the parish in Dubingiai, which is in Molėtai *Rayon*, was sentenced to prison; and in November of this year, two more priests from other dioceses were convicted, whereas the Rev. A. Šeškevičius, who has served his sentence, is not being allowed to work in a parish.

"Basing our request on the Soviet Constitution, which guarantees freedom of conscience, we ask that the above-mentioned violations of religious freedom be corrected, and that they not be allowed to recur in the future, namely:

1. that Father Šeškevičius be allowed to work in a parish.

2. that the sentenced priests be released from prison.

3. that there would be no interference with the teaching of religious truths to children in church by the clergy.

4. that the seminary administration would not be hindered from accepting all those who want to become priests.

"We trust that the Soviet government will adhere to its Constitution and satisfy our requests.

January, 1972"

This petition was signed by 190 believers, and in early April they sent it to the chairman of the Council of Ministers of the USSR. The following address was enclosed with the petition for the reply:

Jonas Lipeika
Mindūnai Village, Stirniai Post Office
Molėtai *Rayon*, the LSSR

ZARASAI *RAYON*, 1971

On December 17, 1971, Bezusparis, the interrogator of the Zarasai *Rayon* Procurator's Office, and police Lieutenant Bagdonavičius came to the eight-year school in Aviliai during class time.

They interrogated the following students one at a time in the faculty room in regard to their preparation for First Communion in the summer of 1971: Bakutis, [Miss] Razmanavičiūtė, and the two Jezerskas sisters. The students were asked these questions: Did the pastor teach you? For how long did he teach? What did he teach? Did the pastor give you a catechism? Did he give you a prayer book? What did the pastor talk about?

Each child was interrogated for about an hour; before being released, he had to sign a written report. After returning to class, Bakutis cried through the entire lesson.

Other children were called to the physics room, and the interrogator wrote on the blackboard: "To the Procurator of Zarasai *Rayon*." The children had to write how many times they had gone to see the pastor and who had taught them about the faith and how? They had to sign their papers. The interrogator took with him these testimonials writen by eighteen children. The children had been deeply upset during the interrogation, and some even returned home crying. After her young daughter returned home in tears, [Mrs.] Pupeikienė went to see the principal to express her anxiety over the interrogation of children without their parents' knowledge regarding their First Communion. On the following day, [Mrs.] Mažeikienė came to see the principal, complaining that that night her child had even started from his sleep because of his fright.

On Dec. 20 several women set out for the Zarasai Procurator's Office to protest the interrogation of children without their parents' presence, because in that case the children write down whatever the interrogator commands them to, out of fear. The women presented a written protest to the procurator. Then they were all questioned by the procurator and the interrogator.

At the same time that the women were being interrogated in the Procurator's Office, the children, with teachers keeping watch so that they would not run away, were again being questioned regarding First Communion.

Several mothers whose children had not returned home on time after classes hurried to the school. Forcing their way into the office, they found their children undergoing interrogation. A police officer and one teacher were also in the office. A tape recorder hidden under a desk was recording. Protesting that their children were being interrogated without their knowledge and were being detained all day without having eaten, the mothers collected their children and took them home. The children who had not been questioned yet were allowed to leave with them. As the officials from the Procurator's Office were leaving, they promised to return again.

When the parents came across the principal, they assailed him severely for allowing their children to be interrogated and intimidated so that they cannot sleep at night and tremble whenever they see an automobile in their fear that perhaps the interrogator is coming again.

What a pity that little children eight to ten years of age are being interrogated because of First Communion as if they were thieves or hooligans.

For unknown reasons criminal proceedings were not begun against the pastor of the parish in Aviliai, Canon B. Antanaitis.

AKMENĖ *RAYON*

On January 13, 1972, the People's Court of Akmenė *Rayon* had sentenced seventy-year-old [Miss] Kleofa Bičiušaitė to one year in prison for teaching religious truths to children in the parish of Kruopiai. Four days later, the convicted woman was transferred from Akmenė to the prison in Šiauliai. The Supreme Court of the LSSR changed the penalty to a fine of 100 rubles. Bičiušaitė spent one month at the prison in Šiauliai. She returned home on February 17.

Kleofa Bičiušaitė had been punished for teaching religious truths to children once before. She had been dismissed from work at a kindergarten and was given neither another job nor a pension; her brother helped support her.

JURBARKAS *RAYON*

On April 20, 1972, the administrative commission of the Jurbarkas *Rayon* Soviet of Working People's Deputies Executive Committee, chaired by [Mrs.] H. Tamošiūnienė, deliberated in an open session the administrative case of Father Viktoras Šauklys, MIC, the pastor of the parish in Girdžiai. The pastor was accused of having "used underage students from the school in Girdžiai to carry banners and scatter flowers in church, thereby violating the decree handed down on May 12, 1966, by the Presidium of the Supreme Soviet of the LSSR." The commission imposed a fifty-ruble fine. Father Šauklys, MIC, appealed this decision to the People's Court of Jurbarkas *Rayon*.

* * *

An administrative fine of fifty rubles was also imposed upon the organist of the parish in Girdžiai because she had organized a procession.

* * *

Because the pastor of the parish in Vadžgirys, the Rev. Gustavas Gudanavičius, allowed children to serve mass, he was fined fifty rubles by the administrative procedure. Father Gudanavičius appealed the above decision of the administrative commission to the People's Court of Jurbarkas *Rayon*.

KAUNAS

On April 16, at the cathedral-basilica of the Kaunas Archdiocese, H.E. Bishop J. Labukas ordained six theology students who had completed their fourth-year theology studies. (N.B. Last year twelve priests died in Lithuania.) Next year, another six seminarians are expected to be ordained.

With the departure of six neopresbyters from the seminary, at present only thirty-three seminarians remain:

Philosophy Course	11
Theology Course I	9
Theology Course II	7
Theology Course III	6

* * *

At the halfway mark of the past academic year, the commissioner of the Council for Religious Affairs visited the seminary's library to check on the literature the seminarians were reading. He was displeased that they were not reading the classical authors of Marxism.

* * *

In midyear the commissioner of the Council for Religious Affairs wanted to expel several seminarians from the seminary. His reasons were unclear. Most people are guessing that it was a case of ordinary blackmail, in order to maintain among the seminarians a constant atmosphere of fear.

ŠILALĖ

After having been tormented for half a year by not being permitted to carry out his clerical duties, the Rev. A. Šeškevičius was appointed to the position of curate in Šilalė. The registration certificate was issued temporarily, however—for three months.

At present the commissioner of the Council for Religious Affairs is issuing temporary registration certificates for priests to all "anti-Soviet priests." All priests who do not defer to the oral instructions of the authorities but are instead zealously carrying out their clerical duties are considered such.

ALYTUS *RAYON*

In February the curate of the parish in Simnas, Father S. Tamkevičius, was summoned to the Procurator's Office of the LSSR in Vilnius. The procurator reproached him for slandering Soviet reality in his sermons and instructed him to be loyal to the Soviet government and to desist from the teaching of religious truths to children. Otherwise, criminal prosecution would threaten, with up to two years' loss of freedom.

At the end of April, a "high-level warning" was arranged for Father S. Tamkevičius. Six representatives of the government and the following witnesses took part:

Father Grigaitis, the dean of Alytus; Father Turčinskas, the dean of Daugai; and Father Matulevičius, the pastor of the parish in Simnas. Father Tamkevičius was accused of passing information abroad, of slandering the Soviet schools, and of engaging in other anti-Soviet activities. He was not allowed to explain himself.

* * *

KAUNAS

The apartment of Father Šalčius, a retired priest in the parish of Aleksotas, was searched in April. During the search *"samizdat"* literature was sought.

PRIENAI

In March a thorough search was made in the rectory of the parish in Prienai. Prayer books and *"samizdat"* literature were sought.

VILNIUS

On March 13, Fathers Laurinavičius and Žemėnas were summoned to the office of the commissioner of the Council for Religious Affairs. The commissioner berated Father Žemėnas for signing the petition sent to the Soviet government demanding that Bishop J. Steponavičius be allowed to perform his duties, and that a large edition of prayer books for Catholics be published, etc. (see *Chronicle of the Catholic Church in Lithuania*, no. 1). The agitated commissioner called Father Žemėnas "Satan," claimed he was being insolent, and declared that he would probably like to see clericalists sitting in the Kremlin!

* * *

On April 4, 1972, the KGB summoned the Rev. V. Merkys, who in 1959 had been forcibly expelled from the seminary by order of Rugienis and had been ordained illegally in 1960. The interrogator declared that Father Merkys would receive work in a parish (he presently works at the Vilnius arboretum), if he would describe in great detail in writing who had ordained him, where he had said Mass and preached sermons, etc.

KAPSUKAS *RAYON*

During the months of April and May Commissioner Rugienis and the Kapsukas *Rayon* administration tried to force the pastor of the parish in Liubavas, Father V. Už-kuraitis, to banish from the altar the children who served mass. Rugienis had even summoned the Liubavas Parochial Committee. He threatened that, if the children were not stopped from serving mass, the parish would be left without a pastor. The pastor refused to banish the children, basing his refusal on the fact that the children were not his, but their parents', and that he did not have the right to interfere in the affairs of other people's children.

* * *

While Father P. Bubnys was serving his sentence at the strict-regime prison camp in Kapsukas, it was suggested to him that he write an appeal for clemency. Father Bubnys refused to do so because of his feeling that he had been convicted though innocent, for it is the duty of every priest to teach the tenets of the faith to children.

* * *

On April 27, 1972, [Miss] Ramanauskaitė, a homeroom teacher at Kapsukas Secondary School No. 5, brought to class a questionnaire sent by the Ministry of Education and told the students of class 9B to fill it out. In answer to the question "Which shortcoming do you want to get rid off?" the teacher ordered the students to reply "Religion." "Even if you're a nonbeliever," explained the homeroom teacher, "write in 'religion' anyway."

Not one student answered "religion"; instead, they wrote down "laziness."

VILKAVIŠKIS *RAYON*

On April 12, 1971, [Mrs.] Miknevičienė, a teacher of class 10C at the secondary school in Kybartai, told the students who had been to church on Easter to write an essay on the topic "The nearer the church, the farther is morality." The other students were allowed to write on a topic of their choice. The best students in the class, [Miss] L. Šalčiūnaitė and [Miss] T. Menčinskaitė, did not write the atheistic theme. For that the teacher gave them a failing grade. Afterward they had to go to see the head of the science department to explain themselves.

The parents of the persecuted students wrote a complaint to the LSSR Ministry of Education, which was forwarded to the Vilkaviškis *Rayon* Department of Education for consideration. After a few months, this reply arrived:

"In reply to your complaint to the LSSR Ministry of Education, the Education Department of Vilkaviškis *Rayon* would like to inform you that the matters brought to our attention were investigated on the scene. The accusations made against teacher [Mrs.] Miknevičienė have not been confirmed because the topics for the Lithuanian language and literature essays were found to have been selected from a prescribed program." It was signed by the head of the education department, J. Šačkus.

The complaint to the Ministry of Education of the LSSR had not been sent in regard to the program, but because the teacher was discriminating against the churchgoers and forcing them to write statements contrary to their convictions, thus forcing them to be hypocrites.

IGNALINA *RAYON*

On March 16, 1972, [Miss] Dalgėdaitė, the principal of the eight-year school in Paringys, together with the teachers Milašius, Šadrecovas, [Miss] Misiūnaitė, and Vaitulionis, summoned three fifth-class students—A. Bivainis, B. Gaižutis, and Č. Patiejūnas—to the faculty room and through intimidation forced them to sign a statement the adults had composed, at the same time demanding that the students would stop going to church. The teachers said that for every child that goes to church the priest will have to pay a fifty-ruble fine.

KAUNAS *RAYON*

Father J. Żdebskis is at present completing his sentence at the regular-regime prison camp in Pravieniškės. Although the convicted priest carries out his assigned work very conscientiously, the camp's administration does not intend to release him before his term is up because "he is incorrigible."

* * *

A poem dedicated to Father Zdebskis' mother has been circulating widely among the Catholics of Lithuania:

Don't cry, oh, dear Mother, for the reason your son
Once again has been shackled with chains.
He's accepted his irons as though they're God-sent,
For the youth, for our entire nation!

Though his hands cannot rise in the altar's sacrifice,
Nor distribute the heavenly bread—
On the heights of Golgotha together with Christ
They pour forth redemption and light.

And at nighttime, please, Mama, don't wail like the sea
In your grief—like the tempest-tossed Baltic.
Heed the hearts of the children, heed how they pray
They're resolving to live life with honor!

Behold how the seed that was scattered now sprouts,
Sown once by his generous hand.
He's brought honor to the Church; he's her truest of
A beacon most bright for our journey!   *{sons,*

Unimportant are Caiphas and Pilate to him,
And all unjust judges and kings,
Both the thorns, the portentuous way of the cross—
He serves the Almighty alone!

He stands like the stones in the fields of his land,
Like the frost-covered mountain ash, grasses.
He will never betray Church or Country—his choice
Is obeying the will of the Highest.

Up in heaven the angels all wonder and pray;
With their fortitude martyrs attend him.
He has lived not for self, but for others always.
For this reason alone are his hands bound!

In the joy of the saints, Mama, seek consolation
And feel happiness near for a moment:
In our history his illustrious name will remain
Inscribed with honor forever!

Therefore cry not, dear Mother, for the reason your
Cannot draw near to the altar—   {son
He suffers with Christ behind bars for us all
And inflames our entire nation!

The children, 1971

THE SOVIET PRESS ON THE PRESENT SITUATION OF THE CATHOLIC CHURCH IN LITHUANIA

The journal *Nauka i Religiya* [Science and religion] 1972, no. 3, devoted twenty-three pages to Lithuania.

The head of the propaganda and agitation department of the Central Committee of the Lithuanian Communist party, P. Mišutis, presents therein a review of atheistic propaganda and Catholicism.

Lithuania has been a part of the Soviet Union for over thirty years already. The atheists have been waging a campaign against religion with "strict adherence to the Soviet laws," and they "treat the believers with respect as equal Soviet citizens" (p. 27).

The council coordinating atheistic propaganda, which is attached to the Central Committee of the Lithuanian Communist party, has now been functioning for eight years; atheistic councils or commissions function alongside the Republic's Council of Trade Unions, the Central Committee of the Young Communist League, the Ministries of Culture and Public Health, and the committees for the propagation of television, radio, the press, and films; etc. Similar councils and commissions function alongside the city and the *rayon* Communist party committees. Atheistic activities are headed by the Central Committee of the Lithuanian Communist party.

In 1970 alone, about 40,000 lectures were given on atheistic, philosophic, and natural science topics. Every year there are larger editions of atheistic literature. Radio and television have been a great help to atheism.

In spite of all these means at their disposal, P. Mišutis regretfully states that "comparatively speaking there are still many religious persons" (p. 30).

Mišutis classifies priests into three groups:

1) those who have left the priesthood

2) those who have become secularized

3) those who violate the Soviet laws and oppose the Soviet form of government.

"Party organizations are carefully monitoring that atheistic propaganda would not make use of administrative measures or tactlessness, or violations of the believers' rights" (p. 34).

***

Nota Bene

Radio Vatican broadcasts in Lithuanian are as follows: daily—at 9:20 p.m. at the frequencies of 25 m, 31 m, and 41 m.

***

Readers of the *Chronicle of the Catholic Church in Lithuania*, please help us in collecting accurate facts about present-day life.

The readers are asked to guard the *Chronicle* from falling into the hands of the KGB.

The *Chronicle of the Catholic Church in Lithuania* will be able to acquaint many readers with the present situation of Lithuanian Catholics if it will be passed from hand to hand.

no.3

THE CHRONICLE
OF THE CATHOLIC CHURCH
IN LITHUANIA

No. 3   August 20, 1972

THE ROLE OF THE KGB IN THE
THEOLOGICAL SEMINARY

On April 14, 1970, an interview of Rugienis, the commissioner of the Council for Religious Affairs, by the journalist E. Baleišis was published in the newspaper *Vilnis* [Wave]. Here is what he had to say about the theological seminary in Kaunas:

"An interdiocesan theological seminary functions in Kaunas. Its administrators and instructors are appointed by the Lithuanian Ordinaries. A candidate to this school must obtain a recommendation from the pastor of his parish. The seminary administration decides whether to accept the youth into the seminary, taking into account this note of recommendation, the diploma the candidate submits, and the youth's personality. The candidates who have been chosen to be admitted are then reviewed by Dr. Viktoras Butkus, rector of the seminary, in conjunction with the sponsor of the seminary, H.E. Bishop Juozapas Labukas, the Apostolic administrator of the Kaunas Archdiocese. The curriculum of the seminary, like that of all Catholic universities, is determined by the Congregation of Seminaries and Universities in Rome. The course of studies here lasts five years. All living expenses of the seminarians are gratis and nonrefundable and are covered by contributions from the faithful..."

Since Rugienis failed to mention the role he himself and the KGB play in the seminary's affairs, his interview must be supplemented.

Already at the secondary-school level attempts are made to influence youths whose intention to enter the theological seminary becomes apparent, to choose another profession. The school administrators and sometimes officials of *rayon* executive committees advise him to enter another institution of higher learning. They even promise to help. If agitation does not work, sometimes attempts are made to cause difficulties with the pregraduation examinations, so that the future candidate would have to retake the exam, and he would be delayed at least one year. At times the school administrators do not want to hand over the diploma, volunteering to forward it with a recommendation to some institution of higher learning. When the administrators fail to dissuade the youth, they sometimes ask him to enter the seminary from some other institution after a few years have passed, hoping in this way to vindicate themselves before the agencies of the *rayon* and the Republic because of their "poor educational work."

In order that the enrollment of youths into the seminary be delayed for several years, since 1954 seminarians have been required to complete military service first. It has happened that the military commissariat postpones a candidate's induction into the army for several years, and the candidate does not have the right to enter the seminary.

By order of the KGB the seminary administration must report to the organs of state security as soon as a candidate crosses the seminary's threshold. There has been more than one instance of government agencies beginning to harass candidates right after a visit to the seminary, although they had not even filled out an application for admittance.

Rugienis has indicated to the seminary administration which candidates' applications are not to be accepted. To this category belong the so-called anti-Soviet elements, that is, persons who for one reason or another have fallen into disfavor with the KGB, for instance, if their parents were exiled to Siberia, if one of their relatives had been a freedom fighter in the postwar years, etc. This means that the first screening of candidates must be performed by the seminary administration itself.

KGB agencies become especially active when the seminary administration sends out its list of candidates to Rugienis for his approval. Using all possible means, the KGB gathers information about the candidate: in school, in his place of employment, in the community. The security organs are particularly interested in finding out whether this youth, once ordained, would harm the cause of atheism and thereby the Soviet regime, or whether he would be only an innocuous opponent.

While the seminarian pursues his studies at the seminary, KGB officials sometimes visit his parents; pretending to be good friends of their son, they discuss religion and inquire about the books he reads and the priests he knows, etc.

The summer before the candidate enters the seminary, he receives a visit from the KGB, sometimes many visits. So that the security workers would have enough time, the seminary administration must present its list of candidates to Rugienis very early in the year, for example, this year (1972) the deadline was June 26.

In their desire to meet with a candidate, KGB officials sometimes travel secretly to his homestead, or they summon him to the military commissariat, or to the personnel department at his place of work. It is strictly forbidden to tell family members, or the pastor, or anyone else about these discussions with the secret police. During these meetings KGB officials first try to talk the youth out of entering the seminary; they offer to help him enroll in some other school of higher education. When dissuasion fails, *the KGB officials try to recruit the candidate to become an agent of the security organs.* Their arguments run as follows: "If we were to become friends, there would be no obstacles to your entering the seminary. We won't interfere with your clerical duties; we'll only meet once in a while and talk. Should the need arise, we'll provide material assistance or help in some other way, and no one will know about our meetings."

If it happens that the candidate, sensing the duplicity of the KGB officials, declares he is unwilling to work as an agent of the state security organs, then the threats begin: "You're a fanatic! You won't be able to enter the seminary. It's all in our hands. You probably don't like the Soviet government. Think it over, so you won't have to regret it!"

As they conclude this discussion, the security officials sometimes even make the candidate sign a statement that he will not reveal to anyone what had been discussed, under threat of criminal prosecution.

If in his discussion with KGB officials the candidate appears strongly principled, his candidacy is rejected at once; the secret police draw the conclusion that such a person cannot be allowed to study at the seminary, for once he becomes a priest, he will be completely intractable.

For the sake of truth it must be admitted that KGB officials succeed in recruiting certain youths. This occurs because of imprudence or due to some priest's unwise advice: "Don't be afraid to sign, everyone does so. Afterward you don't have to work for the secret police." Unfortunately, the organs of state security have sufficient means to force service on their behalf, and only men with a strong spirit of self-sacrifice are capable of resisting.

What does the KGB hope to accomplish by recruiting seminarians as security agents?

State security organs require accurate information about seminary instructors, the administration, the seminarians, and about events in the life of the Church. A. Barkauskas, the secretary of the Central Committee of the Lithuanian Communist party, stated at the Sixth Plenum of the CC of the LCP on July 6, 1972: "The intensification of the ideological struggle compels us to be especially alert and to act deliberately and purposefully, so as to securely bolt the door against any sort of enemy influence. We must react appropriately to every diversion our enemies organize, perceiving and foiling them in time."

No doubt the KGB is aware that no conscientious priest will work wholeheartedly for the security organs. But even in this case, the recruiting of security agents serves a purpose. Mutual distrust is sown among the seminary students; the recruited seminarian is afraid to appear devout and avoids any serious discussions, etc. Sensing his duplicity, the recruited youth inevitably becomes morally corrupted. Thus these efforts by the KGB to recruit seminarians and priests as security workers are a flagrant violation of human rights.

Within the seminary as well as beyond its boundaries, it is clear to everyone who is a serious candidate and who "has a Party ticket."

The recruited seminarians differ. Many of them are men of good will and do not want to harm the Church. They avoid meeting with KGB officials, avoid priests' gatherings so that they would not have to relate to security officials what had been spoken there. Having lost their priestly and human dignity as well as their conscience, a few of the recruited agents carry out everything that the KGB officials demand of them.

Rugienis, the Commissioner of the Council for Religious Affairs, usually deletes several youths from the candidate list sent to him by the seminary administration, often declaring that these can never become priests. So that Rugienis would not cross out too many candidates, the seminary administration is forced to send in for approval only as many candidates as do not exceed the limit set by the government. (At the present time ten candidates may be admitted annually. A few years ago, barely five were allowed to be admitted.)

For the seminarians, Christmas, Easter, and summer vacations are especially worrisome. Seminarians must report beforehand where they intend to vacation, so that KGB officials could find them in case of need, and a need always turns up: to urge the unrecruited ones to become agents, and to get the recruited ones accustomed to working for the KGB, for example by telling about their friends, which of them are devout, and which are not; about what is happening in the seminary; about the seminarians' attitudes, their topics of conversation, the books they read; about what they bring back from the city on Wednesdays, etc.

Upon returning to his homestead, many a seminarian, finds a letter from the state security organs. In it are holiday greetings and a reminder to come to a meeting, for instance, to a certain bus stop, or the post office, or to call a designated Kaunas telephone number. In order to avoid having to meet with security officials, during vacations the seminarians try to travel more, but for this they are rebuked.

The security officials' meetings with the seminarians are carried out in a most conspiratorial manner, for if it became evident to the populace that this or that seminarian was meeting with KGB officials, then he would be unsuitable as a security agent since everyone would be on his guard against him.

The seminarians are advised not to vacation with "reactionary" priests. (All who sincerely labor in the Lord's vineyard are considered such, especially those who do not adhere to the Soviet government's secret instructions restricting the religious life.) It is very desirable that seminarians vacation with "loyal" priests, who are either recruited security agents or who, toadying to the government, neglect their clerical duties and live a secular way of life. In this way the KGB seeks to destroy the idealism of seminarians so that, seeing inappropriate priestly models, they themselves would become accustomed to such a way of life.

Because of the intrusion of the KGB into the internal affairs of the seminary, an atmosphere of fear and suspicion prevails there. To intensify it Rugienis visits the seminary from time to time and threatens that one or another seminarian should be removed.

These difficult conditions created by the KGB tend to

depress the seminarians' spirits and undermine the health of many. During the past several years, a disappointing phenomenon has been noted: the health of the majority of seminarians has been very poor.

If the secret police fail to break a seminarian's spirit, then once ordained, the young priest is assigned to a "loyal" pastor, in order that while taking the first steps of his clerical life he would be without the example of an ideal priest.

The KGB strives to recruit both young priests and those of the older generation; however, they have been winning over only certain ones, those who have compromised themselves morally before the faithful.

These efforts by the KGB to involve the clergy directly in the attempts to destroy the Church are a crime against human rights and the freedom of conscience. This crime has been perpetrated throughout the entire postwar period and with particular intensity recently.

N.B. This information concerning the role the KGB plays in the seminary has been collected from those whom the state security organs attempted to recruit as their agents.

THE PERSECUTION OF O. BRILIENĖ, A TEACHER

In October, 1969, photographs of the First Communion of teacher [Mrs.] O. Brilienė's children fell by chance into the hands of [Mrs.] Kerušauskienė, a teacher at the secondary school in Vilkaviškis. Kerušauskienė handed them over to Čekanavičius, the principal of the school. Immediately, a closed meeting of the school's Party members was called, after which teacher Brilienė was ordered to present a written explanation. The teacher confirmed that these were her family photographs; and basing her stand on Lenin's ideas, she suggested that they should not interfere in internal familial matters. Harassment began: daily cleanliness inspections of Brilienė's classroom and of how she conducted her classes. It all made a bad impression on the inspectors, although until then Brilienė had not once been reprimanded.

One day a hearing was organized.

"Well then, Brilienė, do you believe in God, or don't you?" asked the principal.

"Yes, I do believe," she calmly answered.

The members of the commission began to explain that it was not fitting for a college graduate to believe in God, that one should resign from school if one is unwilling to renounce his faith, etc. They threatened the teacher with a review by the education department in front of all the teachers of the *rayon*, and so on.

"For a teacher to publicly profess his faith is a terrible thing," spoke the principal.

"How undignified it is for a teacher who has worked in the school for twenty-one years to be a believer! Where is your conscience!" thus spoke the teacher [Mrs.] Blažaitienė, wanting to ingratiate herself with the principal.

They tried to humiliate teacher Brilienė: "So, do you also believe in life after death?"

The teachers had been very disgusted with teacher Kerušauskienė's action in informing about the photographs, but after they were upbraided by the principal for being "incognizant," their attitude began to change.

The photographs were returned after Brilienė sent a written complaint to the USSR Ministry of Public Education.

In May, 1970, a special faculty meeting was convened, during which teacher Brilienė's behavior was to be considered.

"I have always been and remain a deeply religious person. I go to church because that is my duty. I have always gone to church, but secretly. Now I have no reason to hide my actions since this matter is known to all," spoke Brilienė at the meeting.

In their statements the teachers stressed that Brilienė was a good person and teacher, but because of her faith, she was unfit for pedagogical work. After the meeting some of the teachers apologized to teacher Brilienė. It was evident—many had spoken out of fear, having been forced to do so. At the conclusion of the meeting, the principal moved that they vote that teacher Brilienė was not suited for pedagogy. Several of the women teachers did not vote, and because of that they were berated by the principal.

In June, 1970, at a meeting of the school's local committee of the teachers union there was a discussion of the fate of teacher Brilienė. Chairman Girdauskas read a memorandum from the head of the Education Department of Vilkaviškis *Rayon* asking the committee to approve the dismissal of teacher Brilienė from work. All of the participants declared that the religious teacher Brilienė could not work in the school. She explained: "By deliberating about me because of my convictions, you are violating the laws of the Soviet Union." To this the principal replied that, by believing in God, she was offending her Communist teacher colleagues, that she was unsympathetic to the Soviet system. In addition, he stated regretfully that it would be necessary to note in the school records of teacher Brilienė's children after they completed the eleventh grade that they believe in God. He suggested she inquire at the *rayon* administration, and she would be provided with work. As the meeting was ending, they voted to dismiss teacher Brilienė from work.

During a teachers' conference which took place in August, while speaking about ideological matters, Vyšniauskas, the head of the propaganda department, called teacher Brilienė a sanctimonious granny and reminded his listeners that she should not be working in a school. The principal said that the schools were neglecting the cause of atheism and ordered the teachers to warn their students that they are not to walk behind a priest and a crucifix no matter whose funeral it might be. (Recently, during the funerals of a student and Father Valaitis, many students carried flowers and wreaths.) The principal scolded the teachers because they had seen their students carrying flowers and wreaths and had not pulled them from the ranks of the procession. "The believers throughout the *rayon* have become emboldened, and for its part, the Party will take vigorous measures to suppress this tide," said the enraged principal.

When the persecution of Brilienė began, the teachers who were Party members openly expressed their animosity: they did not speak with her; it seemed that they did not even want to look in her direction. Incited by someone, the teachers constantly kept suggesting to Brilienė to change jobs voluntarily. They were particularly displeased with the Brilius family's public attendance at church.

On September 14, 1970, the Education Department of Vilkaviškis *Rayon* ordered the dismissal of teacher Brilienė from work. The principal implored her not to complain anywhere, for that would make things even worse.

During her last lesson, as teacher Brilienė was saying farewell to her students she explained that she was being dismissed because of her faith. This incensed the school administrators.

In the final days of September, Brilienė appealed to the People's Court of the *rayon* requesting that she be returned to her position. The trial took place on October 14. Šačkus, the head of the education department, explained to the court that Brilienė was a believer, that she attended church, and then added untruthfully that during her lessons she had taught the students to believe in God.

Brilienė confirmed that she believed in God and went to church, noting, however, that this was not forbidden by Soviet laws.

The procurator asserted that a person of such low moral character could not work in a school.

In general, the hearing was more like atheistic propaganda than an effort to clear up a violation of legal procedure.

Noticing this incessant persecution of the teacher, the students' parents appealed to the Procurator General of the USSR with this petition:

"To: The Procurator General of the USSR, Moscow
"From: The parents of students from the Salomėja
          Neris Secondary School in Vilkaviškis,
          Vilkaviškis, the LSSR

A Petition

"Teacher Ona Brilienė has worked in our secondary school for many years. We all came to know her as a good person, teacher, and educator of youth.

"On September 15 of this year she was dismissed from her teaching duties. The children returned from school with eyes reddened from crying. We learned that teacher Brilienė had been dismissed because of her religious convictions. We, the parents of students from the secondary school in Vilkaviškis have been greatly offended by this. Can it be that in the Soviet Union, whose Constitution's Article 124 guarantees the freedom of conscience to every citizen, persecution because of an individual's religious convictions continues to occur even now without even taking into consideration that the teacher is a college graduate in pedagogy and has taught successfully for over twenty years!

"We ask you to clear up this deplorable occurrence and to reinstate our highly esteemed teacher, O. Brilienė, in the school.

Vilkaviškis
October 15, 1970"

This petition was signed by forty-six parents.

On November 10, 1970, the Supreme Court met in session. Teacher Brilienė was not permitted to read her statement; she then requested that her written statement be attached to the documents of the case.

At the beginning of her statement, teacher Brilienė set forth the course of events: how the photographs were taken, how she had appealed to the USSR Ministry of Public Education regarding religious persecution, and how she had further been persecuted.

"Soviet laws," she wrote in her statement, "guarantee USSR citizens total freedom of conscience and, at the same time, the freedom to profess a religion. The LSSR Criminal Code even specifies the sanctions to be imposed against those who would attempt to restrict these freedoms. The issue of defending the freedom of conscience has also been discussed in the press. In his article 'Už visišką sąžinės laisvę' [For total freedom of conscience], published in the July 10, 1970, issue of *Tiesa* [Truth], no. 158, Docent J. Aničas has written: 'In Soviet Lithuania today, freedom of conscience has been fully developed, embracing the right of citizens... to profess any religion and to practice religious rites without interference.'

"In the periodical *Mokslas ir gyvenimas* [Science and Life], 1966, no 9, in his article 'Marksistų ir katalikų dialogas' [Dialogue between Marxists and Catholics] V. Niunka wrote: 'In its proclamation-letter of February 4, 1938, the Central Committee of the Lithuanian Communist Party had declared: "Although we have nothing in common with any religion, we support the freedom of conscience and we oppose religious persecution of any sort." ' After the Soviet form of governnment was proclaimed in Lithuania, this asserted principle was legitimized in the Soviet Constitution and in other laws in the attempt to block the way completely and finally against any attempts to discriminate against believers by one means or another. Recently the Presidium of the Supreme Soviet of the LSSR has ruled that certain actions must be considered a violation of the laws and be subject to criminal prosecution, such as refusing to employ citizens or preventing their enrollment into educational institutions; or dismissing them from work or from an educational institution; or depriving citizens of the privileges and preferences prescribed by law; or any other restrictions of citizens' rights which are carried out as a result of their views on religion.

"J. Aničas and J. Rimaitis wrote in their booklet 'Tarybiniai įstatymai apie religinius kultus ir sąžinės laisvę' [Soviet laws concerning religious cults and the freedom of conscience] (Vilnius, 1970), p. 37 : 'Religious freedom is understood to be the right of every citizen to profess any religion without interference. It is the freedom to choose one's religion and to change one's religious convictions, the freedom to practice religious rites.' Further, on p. 54 they wrote: 'The freedom of conscience necessarily includes the freedom to practice religious rites, the freedom to believe, the freedom of the Church to function in fulfilling the religious needs of its faithful.'

"By persecuting me publicly because of my religious convictions, the Vilkaviškis Public Education Department and the school administration failed to conform with Soviet laws, interferred with my normal work, arousing a mistrust of Soviet laws.

"Thus, on July 28, 1970, I again appealed to the USSR Ministry of Public Education, asking once more that they would influence the LSSR Ministry of Public Education to compel the Education Department of the Vilkaviškis *Rayon* and the school administration to comply with Soviet laws and to cease persecuting me because of my faith and my performance of religious obligations. The USSR Ministry of Public Education, however, once again referred my petition to the LSSR Ministry of Public Education, from which I received a reply on September 24, 1970 (already after I had been dismissed from work), stating that my application had been denied.

"On September 15, 1970, I was summoned to the public education department of the *rayon*, where without any ruling by the local committee of the teachers' union or the local collective committee, I was dismissed from work in accordance with Article 47, Item c, of the Work Statute. I consider this dismissal unlawful, however in two respects:

1. In dismissing me without the consent of the local collective committee, the head of the public education department violated the dismissal procedure established by the Work Statute Code.

2. Dismissal from work because of religious convictions and the practice of religious rites is contrary to Soviet laws.

"Therefore, on September 28, 1970, I appealed to the People's Court of Vilkaviškis *Rayon*, so that, after ascertaining the violation of the dismissal procedure, it would reinstate me in my place of employment in accordance with the decision handed down on June 30, 1964 by the Plenum of the Supreme Court of the USSR, without even considering the reasons for my dismissal. The People's Court ignored my appeal and, without delving at all into the violation of the dismissal procedure, at once began to deliberate on my religious convictions and my performance of religious obligations as the basis for justifying the reasons for my dismissal. This was also reflected in the verdict handed down by the People's Court, which stated: 'The plaintiff was dismissed because she is religious.' Although the decision of the People's Court stated that I had been reviewed many times by the pedagogic collective because I attend church, and because I fail to support the atheistic cause at school and for other reasons, however, the last review held on June 23, 1970, could not have taken the place of the local collective committee's approval to dismiss me from work on September 15, 1970. All the more so because to this day I have not been informed of any decision that had been reached at the deliberations concerning my dismissal from work.

"Dismissing me from work because I am a believer is contrary to the freedom of conscience which Soviet laws guarantee. Soviet laws assure the right of citizens to choose any religion and to perform religious duties. No one has the right to even ask which religion one professes or whether one professes none at all. All the more so, no one can dismiss anyone from work because of his religion or the performance of his religious obligations."

Teacher Brilienė explained in the conclusion of her statement that she had worked conscientiously as an educator for twenty-one years, and no one had found fault with her work; nor had she made a show of her religious convictions at the school. It was only after the school administration had appropriated her family's photographs of a religious nature and had publicly announced her religious convictions that she had begun the public practice of religious rites. The charge that she had taught religion to children was a fabrication.

The judicial questioning began.

"Do you believe in God, and do you attend church openly?"

"Yes, I'm a believer, and I go to church openly. I've had enough of concealment—I've concealed this for twenty-one years, and now that my religious convictions have been made public, I see no more reason for concealment."

"What did you tell the children during your last lesson?"

"I told the children I would no longer be teaching them, that I had been dismissed because I believe in God."

Addressing the court, teacher Brilienė asked: "If the education department had the right to dismiss me from work for my faith, don't I have the right to explain why I was dismissed after having worked for twenty-one years? Was it for drunkenness?"

"You also told the children something else?"

"I said that a person has to have firm convictions, that it is better to die standing up than to live a life of groveling."

"What studies have you completed?"

"I graduated from the Pedagogic Institute in Vilnius with a major in geography."

Šačkus, the head of the Education Department of Vilkaviškis *Rayon* spoke next, reminding the court that teacher Brilienė was a believer, that she hindered atheistic work with children, and that she attended church openly. She had even gone to court to publicize this affair.

As he was being questioned by the judge, Šačkus constantly kept blundering, making a pitiful impression on everyone: "Well then, it looks as if you don't know anything. You don't even know how to dismiss a person from work," the judge noted.

While the judges conferred, there were lively discussions in the courtroom. The procurator was saying:

"A teacher like you should not teach children. You are a hypocrite, a corrupter of children. You don't even have the right to raise your own children. We'll take your children away from you so they can grow up to be true Soviet people, and not be ruined."

"In other words, you can't convey the faith to your children, because they're pupils; later they'll be students—and again they are not permitted to believe; so when can a person believe? When he has retired? Is that what is meant by freedom of religion?" one man questioned the procurator.

The procurator continued in the same vein:

"We'll get rid of one teacher, and then another, if anyone else dares to show he's a believer, and you'll see. . ."

"So you don't abide by your own laws!"

"We have our own faith and our own laws, and according to them, such teachers will not be allowed to work in a school."

At that point, another man interrupted: "Although I'm a nonbeliever, this teacher has been unjustly dismissed from work. This is a violation of the laws. Soviet laws guarantee the freedom of conscience, but what kind of freedom is this if they deliberated and deliberated and then fired her because of her religious convictions?"

At that moment the judges returned from their conference and read their verdict that the teacher was to be reinstated. The enraged procurator declared: "I won't permit this!"

The head of the education department spoke disconsolately: "Now the entire atheistic cause will collapse. . ."

After the Supreme Court's decision to reinstate Brilienė, the parents who had written the complaint in October were asked to come to the Vilkaviškis Procurator's Office and were given a statement to sign to the effect that O. Brilienė had been reinstated.

But teacher Brilienė had not been reinstated. When she arrived at the school with an enforcer from the court, the head of the education department retorted irritably to the enforcer: "I won't receive you! Come back at 3 p.m."

Apparently the matter had yet to be discussed with someone. In the afternoon, Šačkus signed the document and ordered her to go to the school.

The judge from the People's Court of Vilkaviškis *Rayon* advised teacher Brilienė to write a letter of resignation from her teaching position, otherwise she would be unable to find work in Vilkaviškis.

At school the situation was unbearable. The teachers would not greet her or speak with her. Each day the principal would announce: "Today there will be no classes. You are free to do what you want!"

Most probably it was not entirely on his own initiative that the principal did not allow the teacher to meet her classes. Someone must have been afraid that the religious teacher might "ruin" some Soviet students.

In December, a meeting of the local committee of the teachers' union was held, in which the case of teacher Brilienė was again considered. Teacher [Mrs.] Urbonienė, the secretary of the school's Party organization, spoke with particular vehemence. As the meeting was ending, everyone voted to dismiss O. Brilienė from work, which in fact was done on December 23.

Almost imperceptibly the question arises—who had masterminded teacher Brilienė's dismissal from work? Throughout the whole time, one could sense that the head of the education department, the principal, and the others were only tools in someone's hands. Finding themselves in a delicate situation, they would even go to Vilnius to confer with someone. There is no doubt that after the Supreme Court's decision, the principal had not acted on his own initiative in forbidding teacher Brilienė to do her work. Someone had also advised the Procurator's Office of Vilkaviškis *Rayon* to fool the students' parents into signing that teacher Brilienė had been reinstated.

After being dismissed from work, teacher Brilienė attempted to find work elsewhere; however, in Vilkaviškis she was unable to find work even as a cleaning lady. For teacher Brilienė's husband, Jurgis Brilius, who worked as an operations administrator at the Prienai MSV, working conditions were made intolerable, and he was forced to resign his position.

In May of this year, after the memorandum of Lithuania's Catholics had resounded throughout the world, Rugienis arrived in Vilkaviškis and summoning Jurgis Brilius (his wife, who had just given birth to their fifth child, could not come) expressed his regrets, saying that he had not known of teacher Brilienė's persecution, and he promised to help her find a good job, only not at a school. Rugienis reminded Jurgis Brilius that he too would probably have to resign from his new place of employment because the manager was an ardent atheist and would not tolerate an engineer who was as deeply religious as J. Brilius was.

* * *

In the September 16, 1971, issue of *Valstiečių laikraštis* [Newspaper for tillers of the soil] appeared an article entitled "Vatikano radijo nuodėmės" [The sins of Radio Vatican]. It stated that Radio Vatican "regularly wages a campaign of slanderous propaganda against Soviet Lithunia," that "Lithuanian clerics shamelessly lie," by "whimpering about the discrimination against the believers in Soviet Lithuania." The newspaper continued: "Article 96 of the LSSR Constitution guarantees to the citizens of our Republic the freedom of conscience and, at the same time, the freedom to practice religious rites. But we do not limit ourselves only to declarations. The citizens' rights and freedoms, among them the freedom of conscience, are protected also by other laws. Article 145 of the LSSR Criminal Code prescribes the penalties for interfering in the practice of religious rites. And in the interpretation of Article 143 of the same code... it is pointed out that open to criminal prosecution are actions such as... dismissing someone from work or expelling someone from an educational institution ... as well as other substantial limitations of the rights of citizens, which are carried out because of their views on religion."

"As we see," the newspaper continues, "the rights of believers in socialist Lithuania are strictly guarded by criminal law, and everyone knows perfectly well that every citizen of Soviet Lithuania, no matter which religion he might profess, may freely practice the rites of his religious cult. Or can perhaps the gentlemen from Radio Vatican present us with facts as to when and which citizen experienced discrimination because of his religious convictions— whether by demotion, dismissal from work, expulsion from an institution of higher learning, or similarly?"

LAZDIJAI *RAYON*

Right by the Polish border is the small parish of Kučiūnai. A small, temporary wooden church was built here already before World War I. In 1939, the faithful of Kučiūnai began to build a brick church, but a new war interfered—the roof and the interior were not finished.

In 1951 workers sent by the *rayon* administration began to tear down the brick walls, but the faithful chased them away using canes. Then soldiers were sent from the garrison, but they too were compelled to retreat by the people.

During 1957-59, the Kučiūnai Parochial Committee applied a total of three times to various agencies of the Republic requesting permission to complete the brick church. In 1959 a commission headed by [Miss] Dziržinskaitė inspected the small wooden church and sent back their reply: "Repair the old church!"

In May, 1970, eight hundred believers from Kučiūnai sent a petition to the Council of Ministers of the LSSR once more requesting permission to construct a roof over the brick church. Rugienis replied: "There is no sense in building a new church in Kučiūnai. Repair the old one!"

In December, 1971, a petition was again sent to Leonid Brezhnev, the General-Secretary of the Central Committee of the CPSU, signed by 700 believers and six deputies. It read: "We, the faithful of the parish in Kučiūnai, want to repair an unfinished brick church which is located near a small wooden church that is no longer suited for prayers. This hut-church was built without a foundation for temporary use. Now its walls have begun to rot from contact with the ground. In addition, the wooden church was damaged during the war, and the walls lean from the perpendicular about half a meter, therefore it is impossible to repair. By using the roof, ceiling, and wooden floor of the old church, we can easily repair the brick church, which has good, five-meter-high walls."

In January, 1972, Rugienis summoned first the pastor and later the parochial committee and asked them to calm the people. Later, the chief of the Lazdijai *Rayon* State Security Committee summoned the pastor. The pastor was accused of inciting the faithful. The security chief declared:

"In these times no one will give you a permit for building a brick church. If anyone starts writing petitions or collecting signatures, we'll put him behind bars, because we have the power to do so... We'll blow up the brick walls of the church; overnight only a pile of rubble will remain. When the firemen arrive, they'll close down the wooden church, and the parish will be liquidated."

The people awaited the return of their pastor impatiently, but great was their disappointment when they heard what had been said by the chief of the security committee.

Officials of the Lazdijai *Rayon* Executive Committee called together a general meeting of the kolkhoz workers from the K. Požela Collective Farm and urged the people to present the brick walls to the collective farm to be used in constructing a clubhouse. During the voting, the believers expressed their will unanimously—we won't give them away!

In March representatives of the Executive Committee and the Party committee of the Lazdijai *Rayon* arrived in the locality of Kučiūnai and, summoning the pastor and the parochial committee, urged them to present the brick walls to the collective farm to be made into a restaurant or to let the people themselves tear down the walls; there'll be bricks for their chimneys.

After this visit by *rayon* officials, a great commotion arose in the parish. People were saying: "The government not only refuses to permit us to finish the brick church, but also mocks us! Drunkards will be vomiting in the corners of the church!"

In May the Kučiūnai Parochial Committee appealed to the General-Secretary of the Central Committee of the CPSU. Their statement said that the suggestion made by the Lazdijai administration of tearing down sound brick walls and repairing the rotting church was ludicrous, while the suggestion of giving away the brick walls to be used in the construction of a restaurant—that was scandalous.

VILNIUS

On July 16 of this year, the Catholics of Lithuania again sent a petition to Moscow demanding freedom for the Catholic Church in Lithuania:

"To: The Central Committee of the CPSU

A Petition from the Catholics of the LSSR

"We, the faithful of the LSSR, appeal to the highest authority of the USSR asking to set right certain irregularities in our lives.

"The Constitution of our land guarantees the freedom of religion and of conscience, but our children find it impossible to study religion. We have no religious textbooks, and we ourselves know little about religion, but when we ask that our children be taught by those who do know about it, they are punished, for example, the court recently sentenced priests from Prienai and Girkalnis to prison for teaching religion to children. Recently the priest from Valkininkai was on trial for this, and somewhat earlier, the priest of Dubingiai.

"The Constitution assures freedom of worship, but we are not allowed enough priests: candidates who wish to enter the seminary are hampered, while many parishes are served by old, invalid priests. There are quite a few parishes without any priests. Our children are forbidden to go near an altar—to serve Mass.

"There are no such restrictions in other neighboring countries—Poland or the German Democratic Republic.

"We observe with apprehension how the cancer of amorality is gnawing at our society—alcoholism, divorces, juvenile delinquency. These did not exist previously. Such are the fruits of a nonreligious upbringing: when religion is taken away and nothing of higher worth is provided in its place, for atheism does not encourage the uplifting of morality.

"We believers work equally with nonbelievers, but we do not feel that we have equal rights—our religious needs are being restricted. And this is distressing to us. It is even more distressing to note how the moral standards of people are gradually becoming lower and lower, which is something only religion can halt. Therefore we request that no one be punished for teaching religion, and that whoever wants to, could enter the seminary.

July 1, 1972"

This petition was signed by 1,100 believers from Lithuania, most of them from the Vilnius Archdiocese. For a reply the address of the Vilnius Archdiocesan Curia was provided: Vilnius, Kretinga Street, No. 14.

KLAIPĖDA

In July the faithful of Klaipėda again appealed to Leonid Brezhnev, the General-Secretary of the Central Committee of the CPSU. In the petition of the people from Klaipėda is written:

"On March 19, 1972, the Catholics of Klaipėda sent a request to Leonid Brezhnev, General-Secretary of the Central Committee of the CPSU, which was signed by 3,023 believers. After some time, the sender of this appeal, Jonas Saunorius, residing in Klaipėda, Soviet Army Street 41-5, received a notification from the post office that the appeal had been presented to the addressee. After a few days, however, a KGB official visited J. Saunorius and took from him the postal notification. Afterward, no official response was received from Moscow.

"Thus the suspicion arose that the petition with the signatures had not reached Moscow—that someone had arbitrarily withheld it in Lithuania hoping to conceal from the Soviet government this petition from the citizens of the LSSR.

"In view of these circumstances, we are once again sending the petition with copies of the 3,023 signatures.

"We await the reply at the following address: Klaipė-da, Mituva Street 8-2, [Mrs.] Gražienė, Vanda, daughter of Antanas."

KAPSUKAS *RAYON*

On June 19, 1972, several individuals from the Kap-sukas *Rayon* office arrived at the church in Šunskai, where children had gathered for catechization, and listened to what the pastor was telling the parents and children.

On June 22, four officials from the *rayon* administration arrived: Markevičius, the vice-chairman of the *rayon*; Karkockas, the head of the financial department; the secretary of the Šunskai Young Communist League; and apparently, a KGB official. Father Petras Dumbliauskas, the pastor, met the officials at the door of the church, but their purpose was not to chat with the pastor, but to check on how the children were being catechized.

The officials counted fifty-eight children and eighteen parents in the church. They draw up a report on the spot, which the pastor signed.

On the following day, the pastor was summond by the Executive Committee and Vice-Chairman Markevičius ordered him to provide a written explanation. Father Dumbliauskas wrote that he had been performing his priestly duties by teaching the tenets of the faith to the fathers, mothers, and to the children which these parents had brought along. Now that he had been warned by representatives of the government, he would remind the parents to prepare their children for First Communion themselves.

"Will I be able to test them?" the pastor asked the vice-chairman of the *rayon*.

"You may not test them."

"But even Rugienis allows this."

"Neither Rugienis nor the bishop is the law," Markevičius retorted, categorically.

All week long the children of the parish in Šunskai went to the rectory to be tested on the tenets of their faith. Every day KGB officials stood guard at the church, watching what the pastor was doing. They photographed the people entering and leaving the church, and the arriving autos.

The Procurator of Kapsukas *Rayon* and the secretary of the I. Laukaitytė Collective Farm Party organization visited people questioning them as to how the children were being taught the truths of their religion. People reacted in various ways: some became frightened, but others said, "Don't meddle in other people's affairs. We are Catholics and want to raise our children as Catholics."

The people were also interrogated by KGB officials.

These events only served to show people the weakness of atheism, for it needs the support of *rayon* and state security officials.

"Now we'll attend church for sure, if this is what the government is doing," spoke those people of Šunskai who had never been known for their piety.

In July Father Dumbliauskas, the pastor of Šunskai, was transferred on orders from Rugienis to the parish in Liubavas, which is near the border.

When he had been working in the parish of Šunskai, Father Dumbliauskas had committed yet another "crime," which had upset the *rayon* officials. While cleaning up the area around the church, the pastor had noticed a sizeable rock by the churchyard gate, and, to keep it from getting in the people's way, he had buried it right there. It turned out that Kapsukas had once given a speech while standing on this rock. The *rayon* administration had promptly given the order to have the rock dug up and put back in its place.

The Rev. P. Dumbliauskas fell into disfavor with the Soviet authorities in 1969, when together with the Rev. J. Zdebskis, he had sent in January a declaration to Moscow in which he indicated that government officials had interrogated him and had threatened to put him on trial.

When he was pastor of the parish in Garliava, he had constantly been cautioned by government officials to observe the Soviet laws. In 1970 Bezdžinskas, the vice-chairman of Kaunas *Rayon*, warned the Rev. P. Dumbliauskas that he had grossly violated Soviet laws, because in the summertime he had taught the tenets of the faith to about 200 children.

In the summer of 1971, Rugienis had ordered Father Dumbliauskas to be transferred to the parish in Šunskai, but he was not permitted to work here either for very long.

BIRŽAI *RAYON*

For more than ten years, H.E. Bishop Vincentas Sladkevičius has been living in exile within the parish in N. Radviliškis, which is by the Latvian border. At present he is performing the duties of pastor of the parish in N. Radviliškis since Rugienis does not allow the appointment of a pastor for this parish.

On July 21 of this year (1972), about thirty children who wanted to receive their First Communion assembled in church. As the bishop was testing the children, three women entered the church and observed everything that was taking place there.

One teacher and a policeman were standing guard by the church, waiting for the children to leave. They asked every one of them for his name and surname. Some of the children attempted to run away, but the policeman caught up to them and draged them back to the teacher, who wrote down the child's name.

After Bishop Sladkevičius had calmly concluded the testing of the children, one of the women who had arrived presented herself at the sacristy:

"We are from the Procurator's Office of Biržai."

The bishop explained that he had been merely testing the children and that the women who watched should have become convinced of this. The woman from the Procurator's Office declared that she would decide what had been going on here and would then enlighten the bishop.

On July 23 there were ceremonial services at the church in N. Radviliškis—the children received their First Communion and Bishop Sladkevičius solemnly administered to them the sacrament of Confirmation.

Last year H.E. Bishop Sladkevičius was also set upon by Biržai *Rayon* officials as he was testing children prior to their First Communion.

He had been testing the children on June 24, when the *rayon* procurator, a correspondent, a policeman, the chairman of the locality, and several teachers entered the church. In the church there were about thirty children, who had come together with their parents. When the bishop addressed the new arrivals asking how he might be of assistance to them, the procurator muttered abruptly:

"We're not bothering you, sir."

As the children were dispersing, the officials detained them in the churchyard: the correspondent was photographing them from all directions, and the procurator was asking them their names. Seeing that the children were very frightened, and some were even crying, Bishop Sladkevičius declared:

"Don't terrorize the children. I'm here, the children's parents are here—ask us."

The *rayon* officials drew up an official report at the office of the locality and brought it to the bishop to sign. Since it was noted in the document that twenty-eight children carrying catechisms had been found in the church and the fact that their parents had been with them had been omitted, Bishop Sladkevičius entered into the document the remark that he disagreed with the unobjective contents of the document.

Later, the bishop was interrogated at the Procurator's Office in Biržai. In concluding the interrogation, the procurator stated: "Whether charges will be brought against you or not, I can't say. That will become apparent later on."

After a few days, Karosas, the vice-chairman of the *rayon*, explained to the bishop: "Although by catechizing children you have committed an offense, and in one way or another we could have put together a case against you, but because you're a bishop and everyone is taking an interest in you, starting with N. Radviliškis and ending with the Vatican, we'll consider this matter closed."

Bishop Sladkevičius declared that the *rayon* officials were causing a commotion when it was unnecessary and remained silent when they should have reacted energetically. When a few years ago a student had had his shoes stolen at the school in N. Radviliškis, the event had gone unnoticed, but when some children had actively participated in Holy Saturday services, then security officials and other functionaries from the *rayon* office had come flocking.

"We're not concerned about shoes, but about people," replied Vice-Chairman Karosas. "You can make new shoes, but not people."

JURBARKAS *RAYON*

The Trial of Father Viktoras Šauklys, MIC

On May 16, 1972, the People's Court of Jurbarkas *Rayon* considered the complaint by the Rev. V. Šauklys concerning an unjust fine imposed by the administrative commission of Jurbarkas *Rayon*.

The court's decision reads as follows:

"The plaintiff, V. Šauklys, indicates in his complaint that in the decision handed down on April 20, 1972, by the administrative commission of the Jurbarkas *Rayon* Soviet of Working People's Deputies Executive Committee he was unjustly fined fifty rubles because on April 2, 1972, he had not indicated to underage citizens that they should participate in a procession and he had not seen that the participants in the procession were underage. Participation in the bearing of church standards and the strewing of flowers is the practice of religious rites—the public worship of God. From the explanation by the plaintiff V. Šauklys and the testimony of the witnesses [Mrs.] E. Mockienė, and [Mrs.] Br. Bakšienė, it is evident that underage children participated in the procession conducted on April 2, 1972. Thus, the regulations stipulated by law were violated by organizing a procession and also involving them in work which is not related to the practice of religious rites. In the presence of such circumstances, the decision handed down on April 20, 1972, by the administrative commission of the Jurbarkas *Rayon* Soviet of Working People's Deputies Executive Committee to fine V. Šauklys fifty rubles is lawful. . ."

Since the court rejected his complaint, Father Šauklys then appealed on May 30 to the Chairman of the Supreme Court of the LSSR to have the decision of the People's Court of Jurbarkas *Rayon* nullified. We present some of the thoughts expressed in Father Šauklys' complaint to the Chairman of the Supreme Court:

"The administrative commission based its fine on the grounds that I had used underage students from the school in Girdžiai for carrying standards and strewing flowers in church.

"[Mrs.] E. Mockienė, and [Mrs.] Br. Bakšienė testified that they themselves had brought their own daughters to the procession. Others had acted similarly. The pastor had not pressured anyone to take part in the procession. The people had organized themselves spontaneously in accordance with an old custom.

"It was not proven in court that I had personally organized the procession or had instructed the girls. Easter processions have been held in all churches for ages. The parishioners know how they are conducted and take care of the arrangements themselves...

"The court indicated in its decision that 'underage children were involved in work which is not related to the practice of religious rites...'

a) Canon 1290 of Church law and the Book of Rituals for Lithuanian dioceses, Vol. II, 1966, consider the Easter procession a religious rite and decree it as compulsory. Therefore, not only is it related to the practice of religious rites, but it itself is a religious rite—the public worship of God.

b) That girls held the ribbons of the standards which were being carried, or that they strewed flowers—this is not work, but the participation in the rites of a cult, just as participating in an organized march is not considered work. The 'work' of those who carried a prayer book during the procession and of those who held the ribbons of the standards or a bouquet of flowers in their hands was identical. If one is not punished for holding a prayer book in one's hands during a procession, then why should one be punished for holding ribbons or scattering flowers?

c) The lawyers claimed that they did not know of any law forbidding underage girls to carry ribbons or strew flowers, all the more so I, who am not a jurist. Even if there were such a law, it would be difficult to enforce. Passports would have to be checked, since the girls who are so eager to participate in processions like to think of themselves as being of age.

"Taking advantage of their privileged position, the atheists of Jurbarkas *Rayon* are exhibiting an unhealty zeal. And here is why:

"P. Mišutis, the chief of the propaganda and agitation department of the Central Committee of the Lithuanian Communist party, has written in the atheists' organ *Nauka i Religiya* [Science and religion] no. 3, 1972, p. 34: 'At this time, the Party organizations are attentively observing that there would be no recourse to administrative measures, no restrictions of believers' rights, no rudeness or tactlessness in regard to them.'

"Then why is it that the officials of Jurbarkas *Rayon* resort to coercive means instead of fighting with ideological weapons? Perhaps they want to show thereby that the atheistic idea is inferior and that they cannot win solely through persuasion without the use of canes.

"The administrative measures and rudeness censured by the atheists' organ were resorted to in regard to the ministers of the cult in Girdžiai: the pastor and the woman organist were each fined fifty rubles. This produced great dissatisfaction among the faithful. To the surprise of the organist, they brought her a receipt, indicating that they had already paid the imposed fine to the bank. On this occasion one is reminded of the assertion to be found on page 119 of Marx and Engels' book *Apie religiją* [Concerning religion]: 'Persecutions are the best means of strengthening undesirable convictions.'

"In the Soviet press one reads that the religious sensibilities of believers should not be offended. But is it not an offense that at the school in Girdžiai the newsletter posted on the bulletin board contained caricatures of those students who had participated in this year's Easter procession? Five exemplary female students from the upper classes were drawn kneeling with rosaries and underneath were their names and the caption: 'They are praying for the sins they committed during the year.' Is this not rude pressuring?

"We are used to seeing caricatures of hooligans and drunkards on street bulletin boards, but to ridicule sacred convictions in this manner—is this pedagogical and permissible?

"Decree no. 97 of May 20, 1966, by the Presidium of the Supreme Soviet of the LSSR, regarding the application of Article 143 of the Criminal Code states that anyone interfering with the practice of religious rites is to be punished. And when the officials from Jurbarkas *Rayon* fined me and the organist, was that not interference with religious rites? Perhaps only God will apply the above-mentioned article?"

The verdict of the People's Court of Jurbarkas *Rayon* was left in force.

The Trial of Father Gustavas Gudanavičius

On May 19, 1972, the People's Court of Jurbarkas *Rayon* reviewed the complaint by Father Gudanavičius regarding the nullification of an administrative penalty. (see the *Chronicle of the Catholic Church in Lithuania*, no. 2). The verdict of the People's Court reads as follows:

"The plaintiff, the Rev. G. Gudanavičius, indicates in his complaint that on March 23, 1972, he was unjustly penalized with a fifty-ruble fine by the administrative commission of the Jurbarkas *Rayon* Soviet of Working People's Deputies Executive Committee for a violation of the decree handed down on May 12, 1966, by the Supreme Soviet of the LSSR regarding the 'administrative responsibility for violating laws concerning religious cults,' because he had not violated this decree. From the plaintiff's statement and the data collected in this case, it is evident that underage children assisted in church, and for this, although not regularly, they nevertheless received compensation. Assistance in church by underage children is work and is not related to the practice of religious rites, therefore, the Administrative Commission of the Jurbarkas *Rayon* Soviet of Working People's Deputies Executive Committee penalized the plaintiff justifiably. . ."

The complaint of Father Gudanavičius was rejected. Prior to the hearing, Rugienis had summoned Father Gudanavičius and requested him not to take legal action against the administrative commission. Rugienis had promised not to create any obstacles if the bishop should want to transfer the priest to any other parish.

Father Gudanavičius appealed the court's decision to the chairman of the procedural review board of the Supreme Court. The priest's complaint reads as follows:

"The Administrative Commission of the Jurbarkas *Rayon* Soviet of Working People's Deputies Executive Committee in its decision handed down on March 23, 1972, penalized me with a fifty-ruble administrative fine. I consider that fine unlawful and therefore appealed to the People's Court to have it nullified; however, the court's verdict was to leave it in force.

"When I was penalized with this fine, my explanations were not heard because my bus was late, and I arrived fifteen minutes late. It was pointed out to me that everything had been decided already, that everything was self-evident, that such cases are decided in three minutes by an administrative commission. . .

"I have been punished because several children served mass, that is, dressed in their own surplices, they knelt behind the altar railing and rang the bell during mass. (These children do not yet know how to serve mass properly.) Praying in church at the same time were the parents of these children. . .

"I had never been warned previously and did not know that children sent by their parents may not serve mass. As far as I know, children do serve mass in other churches.

"The church is not mine, but belongs to the parish, and now the parishioners are reproaching me for chasing their children from the altar. They demand that I point out to them the law which forbids children to serve mass. But not only do I know nothing of such a law, but neither could the lawyers point it out to me.

"In its decision the court indicated that underage children had assisted in church, that is, they worked, and for this work they had received compensation, and therefore I had been justly penalized.

a) Serving mass is not work, but merely participation in the rites of worship. As the witnesses in the case demonstrated—the mothers of those very children— they themselves send their children to church to serve mass because they are religious, they themselves teach the

children prayers and the servers' responses since some
of their close relatives are clergymen.

I consider that participation at mass, just as at any
other services, is not work.

b) If the parents are religious, it is natural that they themselves pray and teach their children to do so. It would
be better if atheists fought with ideological weapons
and not with administrative, coercive means. If they
would succeed in convincing the parents, then not even
children would go to church.

"It is not indicated in the decision what kind of work
the children had performed in church. 'Assisted in church'
can be understood variously; that could really be work if
the children had been tidying up in church or performing
other chores. But it has been established in this case that
this assisting in the church was the serving of mass, which,
as I have indicated, cannot be regarded as work. For this
the children received no compensation, and this was proven
by the testimony of witnesses. If I have sometimes given
some child candy or a ruble, it was not as compensation for
participating in the rites of worship, but as a gift on the
occasion of his name day or some holyday. This is very
fashionable today...

"Therefore, I request that you protest the unjust decision of the People's Court of Jurbarkas *Rayon*.

The Rev. G. Gudanavičius' appeal was rejected.

The Administrative Commission of the Jurbarkas
Rayon Soviet of Working People's Executive Committee
penalized Father Gudanavičius a second time for the same
"offense" and declared that criminal prosecution would be
initiated for a third such violation.

ALYTUS *RAYON*

We present the declaration of the Rev. Sigitas Tamkevičius, the curate of the parish in Simnas, to the Procurator's
Office of the LSSR:

"On April 29, 1972, I was summoned by the Alytus *Rayon* Executive Committee. The members of the commission had gathered in the office of the *rayon* chairman: the *rayon* chairman, two deputies, the chief of the propaganda and agitation department, and a correspondent from the Council for Religious Affairs. Summoned as witnesses were Father Matulevičius, the pastor of the parish in Simnas; Father J. Grigaitis, the dean of Alytus; and Father Turčinskas, the dean of Daugai.

"For about an hour, Comrade Jančauskas, the vice-chairman of the *rayon*, sternly accused me of things I had not even dreamed of. I was not allowed to explain at all. When I attempted to speak, Comrade Jančauskas declared: 'We haven't gathered here for discussions!' And when I tried to explain myself in regard to a certain slander, the representative from the Council for Religious Affairs snapped at me: 'You can explain yourself at the Procurator's Office!' Thus, while listening to the gravest accusations, I had to remain silent. Murderers and robbers have the right to speak in defending themselves, but I, being a priest, was not permitted to do so. As if that were not enough, Comrade Jančauskas called this performance a 'high-level warning,' asserting that 'we're very humane' and 'in the postwar years, nobody would have bothered to speak to you like this. . .'

"Since the accusations that were propounded are slanderous, I feel the need to reply; because in addition to the government officials, three other priests participated in this talk and the deans were obligated to report the given warning to the ecclesiastical administration, I am sending copies of my reply to the deans and curias referred to.

"First of all, I was accused of slandering Soviet schools and Soviet life in my sermons. This is untrue. There were instances when I brought to light in my sermons certain evils in connection with violations of the freedom of conscience. This was not slander, but reality. If need be, I am ready to illustrate with concrete and numerous facts that I had not lied. If need be, I can present witnesses who can clearly testify that I had spoken the truth.

"It is totally incomprehensible to one who has grown up in the postwar years that government officials fear the truth. After all, truth must be the foundation on which the state rests. In my opinion, those who criticized me mercilessly should have thanked me for having called attention to existing evils. One must respect citizens who tell the truth, and one must fear those who, while pretending to be ardent patriots, toady to the government hoping to ingratiate themselves and conceal from its sight shortcomings which neither benefit anyone nor bring honor.

"I was charged with organizing the writing of complaints in Simnas and Santaika to various government agencies...

"When accusing someone, one must have proof, for to use various speculations as a basis does not bring honor to the officials of the Executive Committee.

"I was further accused of informing the foreign press about teacher [Mrs.] Brilienė, about the first warning given by Comrade Jančauskas, about the funeral of teacher [Miss] Babarskaitė.

"Had I no conscience, I could with no less firmness assert that Comrade Jančauskas kad passed on the abovementioned information to the foreign press, or someone else of the higher-ranking government officials. Since when do Soviet laws permit the public accusation of a citizen regarding offenses of one sort or another without any proof? It seems to me that with the expansion of ties with foreign countries, one should not be surprised if news widely disseminated in Lithuania also reach the foreign press. And in Lithuania, seemingly, speaking about the present times is not forbidden. Even when Comrade Jančauskas presented his first warning, he did not order me to say nothing. If that had been a state secret, then the pastor of the church in Simnas and the chairman of the town of Simnas would not have participated in the talk, and the secretary of the locality would not have been sitting just outside the open door.

"I was charged with fabricating the speech Father Juozas Zdebskis gave during his trial, with disseminating it throughout Lithuania, and with passing it on to the foreign press. Only a completely irresponsible official could have accused me in this manner. Can it be that the experts do not have the means to determine who wrote the statement referred to: the Rev. S. Tamkevičius or the Rev. J. Zdebskis?

"I was also accused of organizing children to serve mass. I was given some sort of memorandum from Kuroyedov, the chairman of the Council for Religious Affairs, and ordered to banish the boys from the altar and the girls from the processions.

"I stated to the members of the commission that I would sign Kuroyedov's memorandum when it would be published in *Vyriausybės žinios* [News of the government] and when it would be legally binding.

"I did not organize or teach the children. The parents themselves send them to serve mass. Let Comrade Jančauskas ask the children's parents about this, and then let him bring charges, but he did the opposite: first he accused, and now probably, he will look for proof.

"As for chasing children away from the altar, I can assert that I did not become a priest in order to chase away children when they are worshipping God. They have the right to pray where they please: by the altar or by the door, and not where some official would prefer.

"Having heard all of the charges, I realized why the deans had been summoned and why I had not been permitted to explain myself. Comrade Jančauskas had even ordered that this procedure be reported to the curias. In other words, the ecclesiastical administration and the clergy are to begin talking about me like about some terrible criminal. Could it be that at times there is an adherence to the folk proverb, 'If you want to shoot a dog, you should announce that he is rabid'?

"I therefore protest against the slanderous campaign being conducted against me and request the Procurator's

Office to take measures so that government officials would cease persecuting me because I am a priest, that they would cease reminding me of the postwar time of terror, whose burden even the most loyal Communists experienced." (N.B. This rebuttal is abriged.)

This declaration was mailed in early May, but the Procurator's Office has not sent any reply.

MOLĖTAI *RAYON*

On June 8, 1972, the faithful from the parish in Stirniai, located in Molėtai *Rayon*, sent a petition to the Chairman of the USSR Council of Ministers concerning discrimination against believers (see the *Chronicle of the Catholic Church in Lithuania,* no. 2).

In May, Rugienis summoned the pastor of the church in Molėtai, the Rev. Jonas Zubrus, and reprimanded him, charging that he had organized this petition from the faithful. Shortly thereafter, Rugienis ordered Father Zubrus to be appointed pastor of the parish in Dubingiai.

In the middle of May, a reply from Moscow concerning the complaint by the faithful arrived at the address of [Miss] V. Šapkauskaitė:

"Your petition addressed to the Chairman of the Council of Ministers of the USSR was reviewed by the Council for Religious Affairs.

"We hereby clarify that the Rev. A. Šeškevičius works at the church in Šilalė; individuals wishing to enter the theological seminary may realize their wish in accordance with the admission regulations established by the seminary.

"Regarding the demand 'not to interfere when priests teach religious truths to children in church,' this is contrary to our laws, just as is the demand to release the priests who had been sentenced for gross violations of the laws concerning religious cults."

The reply was signed by E. Tarasov, a member of the Council.

Immediately upon arriving at the parish in Dubingiai, Father Zubrus was summoned by the Molėtai *Rayon* Executive Committee. Four officials accused him of not complying with Soviet laws, of engaging in charitable works, of giving children religious books to read, and of conducting retreats without receiving permission from the authorities. Father Zubrus was informed that he would not be allowed to register in Dubingiai.

After a few days, orders from the Kaišiadorys Curia arrived assigning Father Zubrus to the position of curate at the parish in Širvintos, although formerly no curates were assigned to this parish. Meanwhile, the parish of Dubingiai was preparing to remain without a permanent pastor, for it would only be served by priests from a neighboring parish.

KAUNAS

On June 23 of this year, [Miss] Jadvyga Stanelytė was called to the office of the Security Committee in Kaunas. A year earlier, her purse containing the book *Visi mes broliai* [We are all brothers] had disappeared. Stanelytė was interrogated about where she had obtained that book and who had organized the memorandum.

Then they took her back to her apartment and, without presenting a warrant, searched it. During the search the following were taken: A. Maceina's *Bažnyčia ir pasaulis* [The Church and the world], *LKB Kronikos Nr. 1* [The chronicle of the Catholic Church in Lithuania, no. 1], *The Chronicle*, (in Russian), and a notebook.

On the following day she was summoned for interrogation. The interrogators were especially interested in who was reproducing books with the Era photocopying machine and where. J. Stanelytė explained that she did not know this.

Having found several addresses in her notebook, the security officials examined the books in the homes of [Miss] O. Sereikaitė and [Miss] S. Kelpšaitė.

* * *

On June 29, two KGB officials visited the home of Dr. Mikšytė and looked through her books. Having found nothing of interest to them, they asked:

"Don't you have anything of yellow journalism?"

"What?"

"That which is forbidden by the Soviet government," explained the security officials.

The KGB officials continued to question her, asking whether Dr. Mikšytė had signed the memorandum, whether she had solicited signatures for it, and which priests visit her.

On July 14, documents were checked at several houses on Maironis Street. "We're checking on the sanctimonious-granny nests,' declared the persons who had been sent by the KGB.

* * *

The self-immolation of the youth R. Kalanta on May 14, had apparently been mainly nationalistic in nature; however, during the demonstration, not only national but also religious slogans could be heard.

VILNIUS

In recent times Rugienis has been explaining what is permissible in the sphere of religion and what is not. Rugienis has been trying very hard to prevent minors from serving mass. When he calls in an "offending" priest, he reads to him this memorandum:

"In connection with your inquiry as to whether it is an offense when priests invite minors to assist at mass, during religious rites, processions, and other ceremonies of the cult, the juridical department of the Council for Religious Affairs has determined that these actions must be regarded as a violation of the laws because the church may not engage in special work with children.

"The Council for Religious Affairs has already made it clear that for violating the regulations established by the decrees of the Presidiums of the Supreme Soviets of Union Republics, concerning religious assemblies, processions, and the performance of other rites of the cult, and also for violations in connection with special church activities, the ministers of the cult draw upon themselves administrative responsibility.

"In those cases when the participation of minors in rites of the cult is a concealed form of religious instruction (the systematic singing of psalms and hymns by children during cult rites, the conducting of collective discussions with children on religious topics, the organizing of activities for children in preparing them for their confirmation, etc.), the violators are subject to criminal prosecution according to Article 143 of the LSSR Criminal Code.

[Signed] Kuroyedov
Chairman of the Council for Religious Affairs"

* * *

A. Barkauskas, the Secretary of the Central Committee of the Lithuanian Communist party, speaking at the Sixth Plenum of the CC of the LCP, also touched upon the question of the Church:

"The Church and its ministers of the cult are beginning to participate more actively in the ideological struggle. A number of their actions also have a nationalistic coloring. Now that the nationalist propaganda has intensified and the Vatican has become more active, the members of the Catholic clergy with reactionary tendencies have also become more active. Therefore, the spirit of militancy must be increased in working for the atheistic cause, and those who, under the guise of religion, fail to conform to the norms of our Constitution must be publicly unmasked. No one may be permitted to violate the laws concerning the cults. . ."

NEWS IN BRIEF

ŠILALĖ

The Rev. A. Šeškevičius continues to be subjected to discrimination. He is not permitted to test children who are preparing for their First Communion; he does not have the right to travel alone outside the boundaries of his parish; he was not allowed to conduct a retreat for the clergy at the church in Šilalė. When Father Šeškevičius appealed to the Council for Religious Affairs in Moscow, he was told that he was not being discriminated against.

VALKININKAI

A motorcyclist slightly grazed the car of the Rev. A. Keina, the pastor of Valkininkai. There was no crash, and no one was hurt. The local atheists called in the Varėna auto-inspectors, who revoked the pastor's driver's license for three years.

In 1970, when Father Keina had started to put a new roof on his church, he was called to serve in the army for twenty days. When he started to lay down a new floor in the church this year—they revoked his driver's license for three years.

LUKŠIAI

Because Father Montvila, the pastor of Lukšiai, did not banish from the altar the children who served mass (see the *Chronicle of the Catholic Church in Lithuania*, no. 2), he was transferred, by order of Rugienis, to the parish in Vištytis, which is located near the border.

no.4

```
┌─────────────────────────────────────┐
│         THE CHRONICLE                │
│    OF THE CATHOLIC CHURCH            │
│         IN LITHUANIA                 │
│                                      │
│  No. 4                      1972     │
└─────────────────────────────────────┘
```

THE TRUE SITUATION OF THE CATHOLIC CHURCH IN LITHUANIA

On August 12, 1972, in the newspaper *Sovietskaja Litva* [Soviet Lithuania] appeared an article by Rimaitis entitled "Bažnytininkai prisitaiko" [Churchmen adapt]. It stated that in the struggle against religion "irreparable harm can be caused by various administrative attacks or affronts to the sensibilities of believers. The use of incorrect methods in the struggle against religion not only fails to destroy the basis of the propagation of the faith, but, on the contrary, leads to a strengthening of religious fanaticism and to secret forms of the cult and of rites, arousing mistrust and discontent among believers and irritating them."

Rimaitis repeated the old atheistic principle which demands an uncompromising struggle against religion. In the event of a strong reaction by the faithful, this principle permits a retreat—allowing the faithful to calm down—then after determining the best means of attack, to strike again.

The reaction of the Lithuanian clergy and the faithful to the restrictions of religious freedom, which began in the summer of 1968, reached its culmination in early 1972. After the arrests of the priests Juozas Zdebskis and Prosperas Bubnys, a flood of written protests from the faithful appeared, describing the persecution of believers. The Soviet authorities ignored these protests by the populace and did not react to them, acting similarly as they had with the protests of the clergy in 1968-1971.

The first of the more significant conflicts between believers and government officials occurred on the day Father Zdebskis was tried, in Kaunas, on Ožeškienė Street. Only the use of force enabled the police to disperse the crowd which had gathered near the courthouse to honor the priest on trial.

Causing especial anxiety to the authorities was the news that signatures were being collected on a memorandum to the Soviet government. Government functionaries were intending to ignore this appeal by the faithful on this occasion as well; however, this memorandum of the Catholics caused one unexpected event after another. The document, signed by 17,000 believers and sent to the General-Secretary of the Central Committee of the CPSU through Kurt Waldheim, the Secretary-General of the United Naitons, immediately became known throughout the world. Public opinion hailed the brave action of the faithful and condemned the existent restrictions of human rights in the Soviet Union.

The Soviet authorities decided to remedy the situation, which was becoming more and more complicated, by forcing Monsignor Č. Krivaitis, the administrator of the Vilnius Archdiocese, to declare to all foreign countries in April that there is freedom of religion in Lithuania. The faithful of Lithuania learned of this interview with the ELTA News Agency only from foreign radio broadcasts. There have been rumors that what administrator Č. Krivaitis told the reporters differed somewhat from what was made public.

On April 11 all officially functioning bishops and ecclesiastical administrators were invited to the Curia of the Kaunas Archdiocese. Compelled by government representatives, they signed a so-called pastoral letter through which the government tried to compromise the organizers of the memorandum and the believers who signed it. Although on April 30 some priests read the above-mentioned letter from the pulpit, whether in modified, shortened, or complete form, nevertheless, the expected results were not forthcoming: some listeners did not understand who was being condemned in the letter, and others were outraged and deeply distressed at the government's attempts to involve our spiritual leadership in actions that would benefit atheism. Soon, news of this shameful act of coercion appeared in the columns of the foreign press.

The security officials who were searching for the organizers of the memorandum and the channels through which accurate information about the Catholic Church in Lithuania reaches the free world, were then taken unawares by the tragic events in May. On the 14th day of that month in the city park of Kaunas, the youth Romas Kalanta immolated himself as a protest against the persecution of freedom in Lithuania. Deeply moved, everyone discussed this tragic protest against coercion, the lack of national rights, and the Soviet government's tyranny toward nationalities. The interrupted funeral turned into a spontaneous demonstration demanding national and religious freedom. The army and police dealt roughly with the demonstrators, but government officials were disturbed— apparently, not only priests desired freedom, but also "their very own," that is the youth brought up communistically from the time they were Little Octobrists. Among those arrested were members of the Young Communist League, who had been born and grew up during the years of Soviet rule.

In the summer of 1972, an ebbing of tension could be felt. Children preparing for their First Communion were set upon by Soviet officials in only a few places: N. Radviliškis and Šunskai. A few priests were punished by administrative measures for failing to banish children from the altar. J. Rugienis, commissioner of the Council for Religious Affairs, almost ceased persecuting the clergy.

No doubt this was a deliberate step taken by the atheists in order to restore tranquility in Lithuania and, at the same time, to repair somewhat their own fallen prestige in world opinion, or perhaps even to convince the world and the Vatican that the disturbances had been stirred up by the tactlessness of one or another official. Thus, all is quiescent at present. Currently the lives of the faithful proceed in a normal fashion.

How does the present situation of the Catholic Church in Lithuania appear to the clergy and the faithful?

Everyone is very concerned that *the Soviet government is increasingly trying to strangle the Catholic Church in Lithuania with the hands of the clergy and faithful themselves.*

How is this being accomplished?

I. The Church Leadership Is Being Subjugated to the Interests of the Atheists

Wishing to conceal from the world its treatment of the Catholic Church in Lithuania, and nurturing the hope of deceiving the Vatican in order to obtain there decisions favorable to itself, the Soviet government has more than once forced certain Lithuanian bishops and ecclesiastical administrators to publicize to the world incorrect information. For example, the interview of H.E. Bishop J. Labukas published by the newspaper *L'Humanité*; the interview of Monsignor Č. Krivaitis, the administrator of the Vilnius Archdiocese, by Jokūbka, the editor of *Vilnis*, and his 1972 interview with the ELTA News Agency; the interview granted by H.E. Bishop Pletkus for radio transmission to Lithuanians abroad; and others. In these interviews the following has been maintained: that the present state of the Catholic Church in Lithuania is normal, and that the faithful are not being persecuted by the government. It is unclear whether the persons referred to really made such statements because many instances are known of interviews being intentionally distorted, altered, and arbitrarily supplemented.

Knowing that the clergy and the faithful of Lithuania lack the conditions and possibilities for informing the world about the true state of the Church, a most lamentable situation has developed over the years. When the Vatican conferred the title of monsignor on certain priests "loyal" to the Soviet government, thus apparently indicating approval of their behavior, when it nominated as bishops candidates selected by the government, when it remained silent about the distressing situation of believers in Lithuania—then voices began to be heard: *"The Vatican has been deceived!* The Chekists have penetrated the Roman Curia! We have been betrayed!"

At such a difficult time, all that the Catholics of Lithuania could do was to trust in Divine Providence and search for ways by which the correct information might find its way to the Vatican and the world, namely, that the most disastrous threat for the Catholic Church in Lithuania is not its persecution from without, but the noose being tied by hands within it.

Desiring to weaken the influence of the priests on the believers, the government has more than once forced bishops to restrict the rights of priests. In 1968 H.E. Bishop J. Labukas, compelled by Rugienis, prevented the Rev. S. Tamkevičius, curate of the parish in Prienai, from preaching for several months; in July, 1970, he revoked the power of jurisdiction over the Vilkaviškis Diocese and the Kaunas Archdiocese from the Rev. Br. Antanaitis, pastor of the parish in Alksninė, formerly chancellor of the Panevėžys Diocese, who had been exiled in 1960 to the Vilkaviškis Diocese. A circular sent to priests on March 30, 1971, restricted the rights of priests regarding the hearing of confessions and preaching of sermons—priests from one diocese were not allowed to preach sermons or hear confessions in another diocese without the consent of the Curia. This prohibition aroused protests from the clergy, for under conditions of persecution, the rights of priests should be expanded, not restricted. The bishops had to proclaim all these restrictions of clerical rights in their own name while the chief perpetrator—Rugienis, the commissioner of the Council for Religious Affairs—remained in the shadows.

The bishops are allowed to appoint only some of the priests to parishes themselves; Rugienis often specifies which priests are to be transferred, and all that the bishop has to do is to put his signature on the appointments. It is not by accident that the most diligent priests are scattered throughout small and remote parishes, but those who are lax, physically feeble, or have even compromised themselves before the faithful, not infrequently occupy the most important posts of ecclesiastical work.

Rugienis himself suggests to which parish the priests who curry favor with the government or who have fallen into disfavor should be appointed, and without his consent, a bishop may not transfer a priest even in case of necessity. For example, in September, 1972, under compulsion by Rugienis, Bishop Labukas forced the pastor of the parish in Juodaičiai, Father Pesliakas, under threat of suspension to take over the duties of curate in the parish of Viduklė. Whenever a diligent priest improves the state of spiritual matters of a parish and becomes familiarized with the people and the conditions of his work, Rugienis tries to have him transferred and lets the bishop appoint a negligent priest, so that everything in the parish would fall apart again.

Rugienis forbids the bishops to mention that he controls the appointment of many priests. Thus, priests know absolutely nothing about their appointments in advance. They are pushed around like billiard balls in accordance with Rugienis' whims. When people want to find out why a priest is being transferred, Rugienis sends them to the bishop, who gives them to understand that he is powerless to do anything.

Seeing that the bishops are coerced by government officials, sometimes the priests attempt to appeal to Church law: "This transfer is uncanonical; therefore, please do not assign me to a new parish."

Under direct or indirect compulsion, H.E. Bishop Labukas obtained a dispensation from the Holy See on November 19, 1970, enabling him to assign priests without complying with Canon Law. In the opinion of all the priests, this dispensation has made the bishop even more subservient to Rugienis' plans. Previously the bishop could have opposed Rugienis: "I can't transfer a good pastor to a small parish because Church law doesn't allow me to do so," but now the representative of the government can reply to the bishop's objections: "You have the pope's dispensation, so please transfer this priest from the parish."

The bishops were forced to cover up Rugienis' arbitrary interference in clergy appointments with the circular of March 30, 1971, in which was written: "Desiring to improve the ministry of the spiritual needs of the faithful, the Ordinaries have decided to reorganize the system of appointing priests to parishes. It has been decided in the future to assign priests who are young, diligent, and suitable for such duties as pastors where there is much work; whereas the elderly priests who cannot cope with the work will be transferred to smaller parishes, where it will be easier for them to serve as pastors." As one reads the circular, one forms the impression that the Ordinaries in Lithuania act with complete freedom, assigning priests wherever they wish. In practice, however, the matter has been and remains otherwise. Immediately after the publication of this circular, the young and enthusiastic Father P. Dumbliauskas was transferred from the parish in Garliava to the small parish in Šunskai; and the pastor of the parish in Šunskai, the Rev. I. Pilypaitis, born in 1903, was appointed to the Aleksotas Parish in Kaunas.

Bishops are also being forced to interfere with the struggle waged by the clergy and the faithful for freedom of religion in Lithuania. In December, 1970, the Rev. A. Jakubauskas, the curate of the parish in Kėdainiai, was threatened with suspension if he left the boundaries of the parishes in Kėdainiai and Apytalaukis. At that time, the above-mentioned curate had been preparing to solicit signatures on a petition asking that bishops would not be subjugated into participating in the attempts to destroy the Church.

On April 11, 1972, those who had collected signatures and those who had signed demanding freedom of religion in Lithuania were condemned in a "pastoral letter."

The bishops are forced to keep in check the congregations of religious sisters working underground so that they would not "step out of line" and draw upon themselves the government's attention. It is no wonder then that some of them have not fully given their share to the religious life of the nation but have been content to only pray. Meanwhile, like a storm, atheism has been raging and destroying the life of the Church.

In an attempt to prevent the government from subjugating the leadership of the Catholic Church in Lithuania to its interests, the Lithuanian clergy addressed an appeal to the bishops and ecclesiastical administrators of Lithuania in September-October, 1970, in which they indicated which concessions must not be made. This appeal was signed by fifty-nine priests from the Vilkaviškis Diocese and fifty priests from the Vilnius Archdiocese.

II. Involvement of the Clergy in the Atheistic Cause

Priests are forbidden to teach religious truths to children. They have been left only with the right to test them. Since parents are most often incapable of preparing children well for First Communion, many priests, especially in the larger parishes, allow them to receive Communion with little or no preparation. For example, at the Aušros Vartai Shrine in Vilnius children have been receiving their First Communion for some time without even having been taught their prayers properly. They come in droves from Byelorussia, where there are no priests. Their parents are not able to prepare them because the printing of catechisms or other religious literature is forbidden. Since the priests decline to teach the children, *the faithful form the impression that if the priest is afraid then they should fear the authorities all the more.* That is how people begin to easily excuse their children when they begin to neglect religious practices for trivial reasons: "The teachers will scold; they'll note it in the school record; the child won't be able to enter a school of higher learning, etc."

The government pressures the pastors to keep children from serving at the altar and from participating in processions. Uncompliant priests are punished. Priests are especially being coerced in these matters at present. Some, who have resolved to bear all the necessary hardships, do not forbid children to participate in religious ceremonies, but others, currying favor with the government and valuing their good position or their peace and wanting "no unpleasantness with the government," do not permit children to take part in processions or to serve mass. Thus, in place of children at the altar, one frequently sees old men.

No doubt a most negative effect concerning this question resulted from the circular written under duress on May 31, 1961, by Dr. J. Stankevičius, the administrator of the Kaunas Archdiocese and the Vilkaviškis Diocese: "According to a decree by Rugienis, the commissioner for Religious Affairs, public participation in liturgical rites is permitted to those who are eighteen years old. Younger children cannot serve mass, cannot sing in the choir, cannot carry banners or scatter flowers. Children are to participate in liturgical-religious practices only with their parents." So reads the circular referred to. After receiving this circular, certain priests began to justify their behavior all the more readily, but lately in many parishes children have again begun to participate in religious rites. Because children participate in the rites in so many places, it is most difficult for Rugienis to fight against this.

The secret police try to recruit certain priests into becoming their agents. Wanting to draw them into this despicable work of undermining the Church, security officials both entice and threaten the clergy, promising them, in exchange for signing to become a security agent, permission to work in a choice parish, to be made deans or perhaps to attain even higher positions, or to let them leave for studies in Rome or to travel around the United States. Sometimes they promise an outright monthly wage. Priests who have sinned against morality are blackmailed by security agents: if they do not sign up to collaborate, all their vices will be dragged out into the open. Security officials have succeeded in recruiting a few amoral priests and are forcing them to carry out assignments for the Soviet government.

It is true that the recruited priests never work all that seriously for the State Security agencies, but sensing their inner duplicity, they ultimately become demoralized, unstrung, and take to drink. Such priests try to justify themselves by claiming that they are not destroying the Church but merely seeking "dialogue" with the Soviet government. *The Vatican, it appears, does not understand what this "dialogue" means. It is total capitulation. The complete betrayal of the Church's cause.* The postwar experience of the clergy testifies to this truth. Foreigners often consider priests recruited by State Security forces as knowing how to adapt to conditions of persecution. This shows total ignorance of the situation in our country.

In the assignment of the more active priests, bishops are being forced by the government to place them under the "tutelage" of pastors who are timid or who have been recruited by the secret police. State Security agents threaten such pastors by claiming that they will have to answer for any of their curate's "excesses." They are ordered to watch that their curates would not deliver any "anti-Soviet" sermons, that they avoid traveling too much, etc. For example, Father Berteška, the pastor of the parish in Prienai, was even ordered to report on every trip outside the parish by his curate, the Rev. J. Zdebskis. At present, more than a few of the more diligent priests are already forced to suffer more from their own people than from government functionaries. In this manner the government alienates the clergy, setting them against each other, the clergy against the curiae, and conversely. Priests who work for the security police label their diligent colleagues as hotheads, ex-

tremists, and revolutionaries who want to "bang their heads
against the wall"; but they look upon themselves as wise
and capable of "plowing deeply"; but as they do so, only
a handful of old men and women tend to remain within
their church.

The secret police try to involve recruited priests in
Soviet propaganda. For example, in the publication intended only for abroad, by J. Rimaitis, *The Church in
Lithuania* (in English and Italian), and also in J. Aničas'
book *Socialinis politinis Katalikų Bažnyčios vaidmuo Lietuvoje 1945-1952 metais* [Socio-political role of the Catholic
Church in Lithuania, 1945-1952], can be found untrue statements by certain priests that minimize the extent of persecution of the faithful throughout the entire postwar
period. No doubt the government may also be successful
in compelling even priests who have not signed up to work
for the secret police into making statements about the
"freedom" of religion in Lithuania.

The special duty of recruited priests is "to take care
of," in an ideological sense, the tourists visiting from a-
broad, especially priests. They present an erroneous picture
of the actual situation of the Catholic Church, declaring
that there is freedom of worship, that whoever wants to,
may pray, that the parishes are adequately provided with
priests by the seminary, that some of the clergy are but
hotheads. If it weren't for them, the bishops would be
able to obtain even more privileges from the Soviet government, and so forth.

In order to demonstrate how well the Soviet government treats the clergy, foreigners might be shown the villa
of the ecclesiastical administrator Monsignor Č. Krivaitis
on the banks of the Neris River or the rectory of the Rev.
St. Lydžius, pastor of the Immaculate Conception Parish
in Vilnius, or others. The foreigner will not be able to visit
out-of-the-way places and will not see that at times the
priests lack even the basic necessities. For example, Father
A. Lukošaitis, the pastor of the parish in Valakbūdis, lived
in a tent pitched in the churchyard during the summer of

1972 because the government refused him permission to purchase a residence. Meanwhile, the nursing home for the aged, which had been confiscated from the parish, stands practically uninhabited.

To understand the actual truth, to get a feeling for the capably masked duplicity, hypocricy, and deceit, it is necessary to live for some time in Lithuania. Hence it is not surprising that even the Vatican has been misled for a long time. Seen through the eyes of those of us who live in Lithuania, a number of its decisions have been disadvantageous to the Catholic Church in Lithuania. Even now the priests and believers of Lithuania are distressed that the Holy See, while defending those who are being discriminated against throughout the world, only mentions in passing the "Church of Silence and Suffering" and does not bring up the question of persecution in the Soviet Union or condemn it.

No one in Lithuania believes that dialogue is possible with the Soviet government. The atheistic authorities need it only in order to get into a better position to destroy the Church the more successfully from within. In Lithuania it is plain to all that the Church will not be destroyed if the priests are imprisoned, or if school children are forced to speak and act against their beliefs, or if there is no Catholic press and no officially published prayer books or catechisms; but the Catholic Church in Lithuania will lose the people if it should lose their confidence because of bootlicking the Soviet government. Something similar to this has already happened to the Russian Orthodox Church.

III. Involvement of the Faithful in the Atheists' Designs

According to the program of the Communist Party, all intellectuals—teachers, physicians, agronomists, and others—should be ideologically "enlightened" and prepared to "enlighten" others. In the hospital at Švenčionys, an order from the chief physician was posted year-round to the effect that every physician, not excluding even physicians known to be believers, was obligated to be prepared at a moment's notice to present a lecture on one medical topic and one antireligious topic. In the schools, more than once teachers known to be believers have been assigned to sponsor atheistic groups. In factories and offices even believing workers are assigned to atheistic councils. This is done to make them speak and act agaist their convictions. Because they do not wish to lose their jobs, or at the least, experience some unpleasantness, even educated persons give in at times, becoming accomplices of the atheists. It is impossible to even make a rough estimate of the numbers of believing teachers, who, terrorized by the atheists, have spoken against the faith; or of how many students they have enrolled into the atheistic Pioneers and the Young Communist League or into outright atheistic groups. It is not by chance that in Lithuania one can often hear it said that it is the teachers who have contributed the most toward turning our nation into a godless one, and thus to its assimilation.

Terrorized by the atheists, indifferent Catholic parents also often undermine their children's faith. When a child doubts whether or not to join the Young Communist League, more than once religious parents, fearing that their child might be harassed otherwise, advise him to join: "Join, child. What can one do? Such are the times. . ." Thus they push the child onto the path of hypocricy and spiritual lameness. The majority of such children lose their faith, and their parents fail to understand that they themselves have destroyed their children's religious life, due to fear of persecution by the atheists.

There are parents who, from fear of reprisals or simply from imprudent behavior, are afraid of defending their children when they are being compelled to act against their faith. There are also, however, some very resolute parents who declare: "Don't terrorize my child, or I'll be forced to keep him out of school."

The atheists try to involve even believing students in atheistic activities. In school it happens more than once that a religious student must speak against the faith, draw antireligious caricatures, or ridicule a friend for publicly practicing his religion. Acquiring an attitude of obsequiousness usually from their elders, the children conceal their faith and look down upon those classmates who practice their faith openly.

Soviet pedagogy encourages such behavior by religious students, calling it "a positive effect of the collective."

* * *

Let us compare the facts we have stated with atheistic propaganda:

That "the Soviet state and its governmental organs do not interfere in the Church's internal affairs" is stated in a booklet by J. Aničas and J. Rimaitis, *Tarybiniai įstatymai apie religinius kultus ir sąžinės laisvę* [Soviet laws concerning religious cults and freedom of conscience], Vilnius, 1970, p. 21.

"The Party fights for complete freedom of conscience and regards with respect every sincere conviction in the area of religious beliefs," has written A. Balsys in the brochure *Kur susikerta ietys* [Where lances cross], Vilnius, 1972, p. 58.

THE ARCHDIOCESE OF VILNIUS

ADUTIŠKIS

On March 13, 1972, the Rev. B. Laurinavičius, pastor of this parish, was summoned by J. Rugienis, the commissioner of the Council for Religious Affairs, who "responded" to the petition sent by the clergy from the Archdiocese of Vilnius on November 24, 1971, to Leonid Brezhnev, the General-Secretary of the Central Committee of the CPSU (see the *Chronicle of the Catholic Church in Lithuania*, no. 1).

The commissioner accused Father Laurinavičius of insolence, of anti-Soviet inclinations, and advised him "to concern yourself more with pastoral work." Since it was not possible to respond to the government representative's accusations during the discussion, the pastor sent a detailed written reply on July 20, 1972. What follows is a selection of some of the ideas and facts from the above-mentioned statement which clearly illustrate how the Catholic Church in Lithuania is being persecuted.

" 'You write to the bishops and priests who "are working within the boundaries of the Soviet Union's legal system." ' "

Father Laurinavičius did not deny this charge by Rugienis because it was necessary to write. For example, on April 11, 1972, Lithuanian bishops and ecclesiastical administrators sent out a pastoral letter condemning collective complaints by the faithful to representatives of the Soviet government. "Brotherly admonitions are acceptable within the Church. That is a sign of the democracy within the Church. Every pastor may state his opinion of the bishops' decrees," wrote the Rev. B. Laurinavičius.

The priest recalled further that the atheists especially tend to write many letters of complaint against the clergy.

"On January 16, 1968, the commissioner showed me about thirty declarations accusing me. Where did these declarations come from and how? It turned out that Z. Baranauskas, the principal of Švenčionėliai Secondary School No. 1, did not let a group of little children leave until they had written down those dictated statements. These statements obtained through coercion have affected the health of some of these students.

"At the funeral of K. Valadzka in the cemetery of Jakeliai Village in 1971, I spoke of God, death, and eternal life. That is the most innocent of themes, but the director of the Jakeliai State Farm was scandalized: 'This is not the place for propaganda.' There were rumors that the director had even written a complaint against me. When relatives and acquaintances asked the accusers, 'What have you charged the pastor with?', one of them replied: 'I don't know, since I signed on a blank sheet.' Others said: 'I signed because I was afraid they would dismiss me from work.' Complaints are often signed because 'they won't give me a horse, or hay, or other goods essential for life.' Nonbelievers write scores of accusations against priests..."

Father Laurinavičius wrote that Lithuanian priests want to work within the bounds of the Soviet Union's legal system, but the Soviet government itself does not observe its own laws. "On January 16, 1968, Commissioner J. Rugienis told me frankly: 'If you don't leave Švenčionėliai, you'll have to choose another profession.'

"On January 3, 1971, V. Sauliūnas, the vice-chairman of the Švenčionys *Rayon* Soviet of Working People's Deputies Executive Committee, haughtily asserted that in 1968 he had dismissed me from my duties at the parish in Švenčionėliai.

"Church law requires each priest to teach religious truths to children and the youth. After all, conditions are not always favorable for parents to teach the tenets of their faith: on weekdays they work, and on Sundays some of them are afraid to come to church. At the Jakeliai State Farm caricatures are drawn of those faithful who choose to attend church and these drawings are then posted on the disciplinary bulletin board. If a priest visits someone out of necessity, he is accused: 'You visit homes in order to agitate.' That is how I was rebuked on January 11, 1972, by V. Sauliūnas, the vice-chairman of the Švenčionys *Rayon* Executive Committee.

"If the Church is still permitted to exist in the Soviet Union, then it is clear that the faithful must be allowed to live according to its laws. If believing citizens under eighteen may not take part in common services, such as processions and the singing of hymns, then why are little children under the age of reason enrolled in the Little Octobrists and the Young Communist League?

"I have not forced anyone to go to church. If I would do so, I would violate the Constitution of the Soviet Union, which guarantees freedom of conscience. Hence, on what laws did [Mrs.] Turlienė, the teacher of Lithuanian at the secondary school in Adutiškis, base her action of making the children leave the church on April 14, 1972?

"Article 124 of the USSR Constitution states: 'The school is separated from the church' and 'the church is separated from the state.' It is unheard-of that a priest would have gone into a Soviet school! It is unheard-of that a priest would have come to a Party meeting; however, atheists and their assistants come to church very frequently. They come to spy out what the priest teaches. The abovementioned V. Sauliūnas stated candidly on January 5, 1971: 'Your sermons are known to us; we can disclose them at any time.'

"One of the laws of the Church orders the faithful not to feast or make merry during Lent. After I explained this law to the believers, A. Laurinavičius, the chairman of the Adutiškis locality, came and warned me: 'Pastor, don't meddle in leisure-time activities!' This is what we have come to—a pastor does not even have the right to explain the commandments of the Church concerning fasting and self-control!

"Actually, the state is very closely connected to the Church. It practically thrusts its way into our internal affairs: priests are forced to chase children away from the altar and the choir; they must forbid the singing of hymns; they must take away all banners from the faithful; they must not provide a Catholic burial according to the ritual of the Church; they must not teach children.

"You charge: 'You write anti-Soviet tracts!'

"On March 13, 1972, I replied to the commissioner that I have not written any anti-Soviet tracts. In the petition of December 24, 1972, from the Vilnius Archdiocese addressed to Leonid Brezhnev, the General-Secretary of the Central Committee of the CPSU, there were no anti-Soviet attacks. It was only a listing of facts:

1. Enrollment into the Kaunas Theological Seminary is not free from hindrances.
2. Neither a catechism, nor a hymnal, nor the Bible has been printed during the Soviet period. Some prayer books have been published but only for propaganda

purposes. If as many as are necessary were published, the believers would not be offering thirty rubles for one. Only selected individuals were able to receive a prayer book: choir members and those who were fortunate when lots were drawn.

3. We did not try to return H.E. Bishop Julijonas Steponavičius and H.E. Bishop V. Sladkevičius to their posts by force. We are not the first to petition for or to show concern over the injustices committed against our rightful superiors. Dear to us are our brethren in ideology—our Ukrainian brothers; also dear to us are Zdebskis and Bubnys, who have been imprisoned for the Faith. Before the war, the Communists were also concerned about their comrades. They wrote, pleaded, and solicited signatures. Please refer to *Jaunystės atradimas* [Rediscovery of youth] by A. Venclova (Vilnius, 1970).

After World War II, the commissioner of the Council for Religious Affairs edited a most disgusting document against His Holiness Pope Pius XII and demanded that the clergy sign it.

Lietuvos pionierius [Lithuanian Pioneer], no. 34, April 22, 1972, published the following: 'The Pioneers of Kėdainiai Secondary School No. 2 have collected 1,600 signatures for a protest and contributed 150 rubles to the Peace Fund.' In the Soviet Union children are allowed to solicit signatures under protests and to collect contributions, but when priests petition Soviet agencies, that is regarded as something malicious and anti-Soviet.

We had requested that the Ukrainian priests be allowed to work because the believers of the Ukraine give us no peace—they bid us to come work among them. We have asked that their priests be permitted to work, because they have not been convicted in court.

On March 17, 1964, a session of the People's Court of Švenčionys *Rayon* was held, during which the judge did not allow me to answer my opponent's slander. He did not grant me a final word even though I requested and demanded it. He did not permit me to appeal his decision to a higher court. Yet Article 2 of the LSSR Code of Criminal Procedure states: 'The tasks of the Soviet criminal court are to ascertain crimes speedily and thoroughly, to incarcerate the guilty and to apply the laws appropriately so that every person who has committed a crime would be justly punished, and that no innocent person would be subject to criminal prosecution or punishment.'

H.E. Bishop J. Steponavičius has been punished for more than ten years without an explanation of his offense.

Article 4 of the LSSR Code of Criminal Procedure states: 'No one may be prosecuted in any other way than on the basis and procedure established by law.'

The imprisonment of H.E. Bishop Steponavičius was not based on any law.

Article 11 of the LSSR Code of Criminal Procedure states: 'Justice in criminal cases is executed only by a court. No one may be judged guilty of committing a crime and punished as a criminal otherwise than by judgment of the court.'

H.E. Bishop J. Steponavičius was not punished by a court. That was why we had requested that he, not having been judged guilty by a court, should be reinstated to his proper post, because the Archdiocese of Vilnius needs an Ordinary in the true sense of that word."

Further are listed facts as to how arbitrarily *rayon* and local government officials act with regard to priests:

"a) Some years ago Telyčėnas, the vice-chairman of the Švenčionys *Rayon* Executive Committee, assigned the same Sunday for a day of recollection to all the clergy of the Švenčionys Deanery. When he was reminded of how could there be a retreat without assistants, he ironically replied: 'How could it be that your neighbor would not come to you if you ask him?'

b) The police ordinarily take care of traffic in the streets, but on January 5, 1971, V. Sauliūnas, the vice-chairman of the Švenčionys *Rayon* Executive Committee, demanded that I should forbid the believers to sing hymns or carry banners in the street during a funeral procession. What mockery! The priest must forbid the faithful to pray and carry banners!

c) On Christmas Eve, 1971, I treated some guests who had come to visit me to some candy. Christmas Eve for us believers is not an ordinary time. Everywhere that evening especially great hospitality is shown. But I was rebuked for this by the government. V. Sauliūnas even drove twenty-nine kilometers to do so. What insolent interference in the private life of a priest!

d) On January 11, 1972, V. Sauliūnas demanded that I collect from the villages all the banners of mourning which the faithful carry during funerals. You see, that which they dare not do themselves due to fear of God or a sense of embarassment before the people, they force a priest to do.

e) On March 10, 1971, [Mrs.] J. Valadkienė, the chief of the Financial Department of Švenčionys *Rayon*, demanded that I show her the Baptismal Records book, because it was needed for tax assessment purposes. Later it became evident that she had wanted to find out whether certain persons had had their children baptized or had married in the church. Fortunately, not all of these had been noted down.

f) On April 5, 1971, [Mrs.] Kluonienė, the secretary of the Adutiškis Locality, declared: 'Pastor, if you trust me, give me the baptismal and matrimonial books, if you don't trust me, take them to the office of the locality yourself.' 'But why do you need them?' I asked. 'Two strangers have come demanding them." I suggested they check with the CBAIB. I did not show the books, since the faithful would have suffered, and I would have been a betrayer.

g) In 1966 V. Bukielskis, the chairman of the Švenčionėliai Executive Committee, exclaimed: 'If you want to take part in funerals, to go to the cemetery, then get in the rear of the people!'

From these facts we can see into whose hands we have fallen.

4. We have requested that the unjust application of Article 143 of the LSSR Criminal Code, which is contrary to the USSR Constitution, be rescinded.

5. We have requested that the secret instructions unknown to us concerning the religious life be abolished. Instructions according to which the lives of citizens are regulated must be known to all. The principle 'An unpromulgated law does not bind' is in force everywhere.

6. We have requested that the cases of individuals sentenced because of their faith be reviewed and that they be exonerated, for they functioned within the limits of Articles 124 and 125 of the USSR Constitution in carrying out their primary duties.

"You have accused me of being 'by nature anti-Soviet in orientation.'

"In saying this the commissioner is mistaken. If I had been anti-Soviet in orientation, then I would have withdrawn to the West in 1944. At that time I was living with my parents and had no official duties. While many were hurrying westward, I turned east, to Švenčionys.

"You have said that 'Laurinavičius has convinced himself that he cannot be curbed.'

"The commissioner did not shout at me on March 13, 1972, the way he did on January 16, 1968. This year he spoke, one may say, in a muffled tone of voice, elliptically.

"The laws and courts are at your disposal, also de-

crees, secret instructions, force, and the keys of prisons, but
on my side there is only ageless truth, for which you have
no regard.

"You have said, 'You're insolent!'

"If I were insolent, I would have reminded you of the
following: when on January 16, 1968, you compared me
to a tomcat; when you called me a fanatic; when you unlawfully tried to hound me from Švenčionėliai; when you
pestered me repeatedly concerning the construction materials left over from the building of the church in Švenčionėliai—all those times I was silent.

"To clarify who was really insolent, let us recall a few
things from the past.

"The commissioner, I believe, remembers well how
the church in Švenčionėliai once looked, for in the spring
of 1957 you arrived to look it over. Nine months of driving
around, petitioning, demanding. How much worry there
was over obtaining the permit! You cannot even imagine
the whole story, since at that time you did not occupy your
present position. At the office of the Švenčionėliai Executive Committee they had replied: 'Don't even think about
a permit. Nobody will give you one!' K. Dudlauskas, the
chairman of the Soviet of Working People's Deputies Executive Committee, had threatened: 'If you want to sit in
Švenčionėliai, sit quietly!' J. Paleckis, the chairman of the
Supreme Soviet of the LSSR, who had received us very
pleasantly the first time, acted very rudely during the
second time.

"After the permit was obtained, it was necessary to
find supplies. The first year, we received a permit only to
buy the lumber. Money was needed. The commission you
formed in 1957 guessed almost exactly. They forsaw the
estimate—a million rubles! Specialists had to be found,
transportation obtained. When I was unable to arrange for
transport, I brought one ton of cement from the store to
the building site by bicycle. I toiled on the construction of
the building for four years.

"With God's blessing and the assistance of kind

people, the work was finished. 'Well-done"—that was how the state commission evaluated it.

"During construction, the parochial committee of Švenčionėliai did not pay me for my work since there was often a lack of money. When the church was finished, the committee paid me with the materials left over from the construction, with which I built myself a house after buying ten tons of cement. I didn't build it just anywhere but right next to the church in Švenčionėliai. Having begun construction, I drew up a will at the notary public of Švenčionys *Rayon* to the effect that when I am gone, in that house would live the priests who work at the church in Švenčionėliai. I invested my own savings and those of my parents into the building of this house because they wanted to live in a more spacious home and to be benefactors of the parish in Švenčionėliai. Usually parishes remember their benefactors. I had also borrowed from friends in order to build this house. We lived peacefully for two years. In 1962 a certain Sprindys from Vilnius visited me. He turned out to be a representative of the State Security agency. After our talk he suggested to me that I go to see H.E. Bishop J. Steponavičius and certain friends. He even promised to provide transportation. The purpose of my trips was to be, as he said, 'to help clear up certain questions.' Declining to take part in any kind of bargaining, I answered that I would not be an Antanavičius." (In the Soviet press Father Antanavičius is called a spy of the Tsarist government—ed.)

"First of all I was ridiculed in *Šluota* [Broom]—a satirical periodical. Then you summoned me on June 24, 1962, and 'explained' that any leftover materials from the construction of the church belonged to the state. When I explained to you that the parochial committee had repaid me for four years of hard labor in building the church with the leftover materials, you replied that the committee had no such right. How odd: the committee had no right to compensate those who had worked on the construction of the church, *but it only has the right to pay taxes.* On June

24, 1962, you said: 'You shouldn't have worked!' I had the right to work. The parochial committee had elected me chairman of the parochial committee, and on March 19, 1957, (Memorandum no. 2429) you confirmed this with your signature. Even though that time when you made fun of me I had not been insolent and did not exhibit any insolence, insolence was actually spouting from you in my direction. After calmly listening to your mockery, I returned home and wrote the Švenčionėliai Parochial Committee and you a statement that I had returned to the parochial committee the construction materials received from the parochial committee for four years of hard labor, and that I had kept the sum which I had invested myself into the construction of the house.

"I wrote everywhere. To all my petitions I received the reply: 'Such was the verdict of the court. There is no basis for complaint.' Yet how could the court have ruled without hearing both sides! Three of my petitions addressed to Rudenko, the Procurator General of the USSR, were forwarded to the LSSR Procurator's Office. From here they would answer every time: 'There is no basis for protesting the decision of the People's Court of Švenčionys *Rayon*. My fourth petition addressed to the Procurator General of the USSR reached the hands of a *human being*. This person directed A. Kirijenko, the LSSR Deputy Procurator to protest the decision handed down on March 17, 1964, by the People's Court of Švenčionys *Rayon*."

Father Laurinavičius then presents the decision handed down on June 3, 1965, by the Supreme Court of the LSSR, which reads as follows: "Since the building materials were purchased by the parochial committee, they are thus its property, and the committee could have presented them to anyone. A gift is not considered income from work. Moreover, it is evident from the explanations of Citizen Laurinavičius that his personal income, which was obtained from the performance of religious rites, was also used for the construction of the house. The stated circumstances have not been denied, nor has it been proved that the house had been built as a result of abuse by Citizen Laurinavičius.

"The juridical board decided 'to nullify the decision of March 17, 1964, by the People's Court of Švenčionys *Rayon*.

"The case was transferred to the People's Court of Ignalina *Rayon*, whose judge had the audacity to write into its decision whatever she wanted. When court was in session S. Janulis had declared that he was not a member of any commission, but she recorded that he was. The house was built smaller than the permit allowed, yet the judge, contrary to my documentation, accused me of having enlarged the house. In an effort to cover up the judge's fabrications, when I was thrown out of the house, in 1966 a small room was finished in the attic.

"The judge of the People's Court of Ignalina *Rayon* allowed the decision of July 7, 1965, to be appealed at the Supreme Court of the LSSR. A day was assigned for the hearing, but the court never considered the case because it became apparent that the judge had had no right to allow her decision to be appealed.

"If the judge had not understood whether her decision was appealable or not, then how could she have judged the case?

"This comedy was played out in the twentieth century, in which much is said about how men should be friends and brothers to one another. Now everyone can conclude that atheistic morality exists on paper, but not in life.

"What crime have I committed? What was I punished for? On what grounds did they take away my compensation for four years of hard work? Why was my parental inheritance seized?

" 'What about the children's choir? The acolytes? The strewing of flowers during processions?'

"On March 13, 1972, I replied that at the church in Adutiškis everyone sings the hymns. There are no acolytes. There are only worshippers and children who scatter flowers because a procession is an inseparable part of the services. The faithful worship God as best they know: some sing hymns, others carry banners, and still others scatter flowers."

In regard to Rugienis' advice to become more involved in pastoral work, Father Laurinavičius answered thus:

"How pleasant it was to hear such words from your lips.

"When we were studying in the theological faculty at the University of Vilnius, it was explained to us that the concept of the term 'pastoral duties' is very broad and meaningful. I shall mention at least several meanings here: (1) The pastor must visit his parishioners; (2) He must visit the sick; (3) He must teach morality and religious truths to children, the youth, and all believers; (4) He must catechize children and teach them hymns; (5) He must bury the dead according to the ritual established by the Church.

"In reality, a pastor today does not have the right to perform his pastoral duties:

1. Not only is he not permitted to visit the homes of the faithful and to bless them there, but he also does not have the right to bless those who come to church. I recall very well how, summoning me on June 24, 1964, you gave me a tongue-lashing simply because I had blessed some little children after devotions on the Octave of Corpus Christi.

2. The pastor does not always get permission even to visit the sick. On November 17, 1971, I wrote you that even the dying request of V. Stakauskas had not been granted—he died without receiving Extreme Unction because his sister was not permitted to call a priest. I am certain that you received my note since I sent it by registered mail. I never did receive a reply from you. Strange! Whenever government agencies summon a priest, he must come at the appointed time, but he waits in vain for a reply to his letter.

3. A pastor does not have the right to teach little chil-

dren, not only in school, but also in church. For this work, these priests have been made to suffer severely: A. Šeškevičius, J. Zdebskis, P. Bubnys. And to teach them on other occasions—even to think of it is impossible.

4. On December 23, 1971, the children sang some hymns together with the adults. Two weeks later, V. Sauliūnas strewed many angry and sharp words in my direction.

5. To bury the dead in accordance with the ritual of the Church is forbidden. Thus how can one perform one's priestly duties? How can one do pastoral work? If it is impossible for a priest to do all that he is meant to do, why do you make fun of us?

"On January 16, 1968, you called me a fanatic. I understood the word, but after returning home, I glanced at the dictionary, where it was stated: 'fanatic—a person of extremist convictions, noted for his great animosity toward people with differing convictions.' Although in my life I have met people who thought differently than I do, I did not act with hatred toward them. It was only because of my opponents' fanaticism that I was driven out of Švenčionėliai and thrown out of my home. All this you have done, not from love for one who thinks differently, but only from hatred.

"When Father Laurinavičius was in the Polish Army, they wanted to recruit him into disrupting the solidarity of his compatriots. For this they even promised 'to make him one of the gentry.' When he complained to a Polish colonel, the latter stated: 'Laurinavičius is a Lithuanian. It is forbidden to try to persuade him to harm his own nation!' The Polish gentry did not wrong the priest.

"If the atheists, the apologists and propagators of modern atheistic morality, proclaim their morality to be above all others, then they ought to show at least some tolerance toward everybody! Therefore return the house which was unjustly confiscated, in which not I shall reside now, but according to the will I have made, here will reside those who will work at the church in Švenčionėliai. Furthermore, do not exhibit an incomprehensible animosity toward those who think differently; provide at least the minimal conditions for existence, and then no one will need to write any more petitions.

"The commissioner had urged me to 'concern myself' with pastoral work, but the locality and the *rayon* offices continue to interfere. On July 14, 1972, A. Laurinavičius, the chairman of the Adutiškis Locality, in the presence of witnesses forced Father Laurinavičius to sign an indictment regarding his pastoral work. 'Faster, faster,' urged the chairman, 'I have to take it to the *rayon* office.'

"That a priest would have incited the populace through his pastoral work is unheard-of and yet, how often is he so accused! And even turned over to the State Security agency. The actual agitators remain unpunished.

"For instance, in 1969 in the cemetery of Davaisiai Village an unknown evildoer knocked over all the tombstones and crosses. People went around cursing the evildoer, the government, and the times. It would seem that the officials in charge of order and security should have taken an interest in that deed. Not at all—to this very day no one has bothered his head about it.

"In December of 1971, arriving at the cemetery of Jakeliai Village, two policemen and the chairman of the locality together with a number of workers tore down a shrine which had stood for centuries in the cemetery. The faithful were scandalized. They gnashed their teeth, especially since the bricks were loaded and taken away to be used in building stables.

"It is events such as these that disturb the peace among the citizenry, cause dissatisfaction, and make the people hostile.

Adutiškis
July 20, 1972
The Rev. B. Laurinavičius"

A PETITION FROM THE PARENTS FROM
THE PARISH IN ADUTIŠKIS

On April 20, 1972, fathers and mothers from the parish in Adutiškis appealed to the Soviet government. The complete text of the petition is presented below:

"To: Comrade L. Brezhnev, the General-Secretary
　　　　of the CPSU
　　　Comrade Furceva, the Minister of Public
　　　　Education of the USSR
　　　Comrade Kuroyedov, the Chairman of the
　　　　Council for Religious Affairs

*A Declaration—Petition by the Fathers-Mothers
of the Roman Catholic Parish in Adutiškis,
Švenčionys Rayon, the LSSR*

"Very often we and our children experience difficulties just because we are believers.

"In 1971 the administration of the secondary school in Adutiškis banished our children from the altar. This year, they created a great uproar because some children went up to the choir loft to sing with everyone else. Lately they have created a great uproar because our children wear white garments.

"The interrogation of our children and our "re-education" tax our health and that of our children. Sometimes it even ends in tragedy. One mother, Aleksandra Stasiūnienė, residing in Adutiškis, was called in to the school because her son Julijus goes to church. After the meeting in the school on April 7, 1972, she was so aggravated and agitated that shortly she was stricken and died on April 9, 1972. How haggard she had looked when she came out of the school can be attested to by [Mrs.] Birutė Juknienė, residing in Adutiškis, who had spoken with her.

"[Miss] M. Skrickaitė, a pupil who is very quiet and polite, received a grade of four in conduct. Her mother inquired for which offense the conduct grade had been lowered. She received the reply: "She got a four in conduct because she goes to church."

"Hoping to request that those who disturb our and our children's peace and interfere with matters of conscience be restrained, we contacted the Education Department of Švenčionys *Rayon* on April 13, 1972. We were informed that the affairs of the faithful are administered by Comrade Sauliūnas, the vice-chairman of the *rayon* Executive Committee. The vice-chairman did not want to speak with us, even though we had gone to see him during office hours when he was in. Comrade Sauliūnas told us that up to the age of eighteen children do not have the right to take part in religious rites. If so, then why do children participate in all sorts of outdoor demonstrations, for example, during the May Day and October holidays? If the children may not dress in white garments, then why are red kerchiefs tied on them? If one may not pin a cross, which he loves, on a child, then why are stars pinned on them? Why are they enrolled in the Little Octobrists, the Pioneers, and the Young Communist League and taught to lie to their parents? Why are children forbidden to utter "Jesus, I love You" in church, when cursing and reviling are not prohibited as strictly?

"We, the parents, are responsible before God and society for the upbringing of our children. Experience has proved that Soviet schools can teach children only to read and write, but as to educating them how they should live —they are incapable. A few facts follow. A couple of years ago Kazlauskas, a student from the secondary school in Adutiškis, left home for school, but he never got to school; instead he hanged himself. Jasiulionis, a former student from the secondary school in Adutiškis, has stolen and tends to beat his mother. Former student Jukna was publicly tried for assaulting and robbing a soldier in 1970. [Miss] Trečiokaitė, who was fifteen-sixteen years old and a schoolgirl of the eight-year school in Svirkos, went to "spend the night" with the locality's chairman, who was much older than she.

"Therefore, the school ought to pay more attention to children who commit immoral and criminal offenses, and not to ours, who do no wrong.

"We kindly ask you to instruct the appropriate agencies and the administration of the secondary school in Adutiškis, that they should not interfere with our children so that they could be members with equal rights of both the school and the Church, so that they might go without fear to listen to the teachings of the Church, which are as essential to man as daily bread. We want our cildren to hear, not only the truths of the atheists, but also to know the true God and the Church which He founded.

"It is understandable that [Mrs.] A. Stasiūnienė died before her time defending her own rights and those of her child. Do not think that we shall fear death or cease defending our children's rights. No!

"We request freedom of conscience for our children, basing our request on Article 124 of the Constitution of the Soviet Union, which guarantees to all citizens the freedom of conscience.

Adutiškis
April 20, 1972"

This petition was signed by eighteen fathers and mothers.

On July 13, 1972, "the twenty" from the parish in Adutiškis were summoned to the locality's administrative office. V. Sauliūnas, vice-chairman of the Švenčionys *Rayon* Executive Committee, spoke to them:

"Comrades, we have invited you here to explain what is permissible for believers ... You are allowed one priest, an organist, a sacristan, and a bell-ringer. You cannot have a curate since there are not enough priests. Everything must be managed by the parochial committee. The priest may not collect contributions, but only the treasurer...

"Children are forbidden to serve the priest at mass, to participate in processions, to scatter flowers; children are not permitted to say together with the priest 'Jesus, I love You!'; children may not sing hymns in the choir loft or be taught hymns...

"Explain to the priest what is permissible to him: to say mass, to visit someone who is ill, to participate in a funeral procession that begins at the church. A priest is forbidden, however, to participate in a funeral procession that begins at the home of the deceased or to pray in the homes of believers. Tell the priest to direct his people not to sing hymns as they walk in a funeral procession. A priest may not prepare children for their First Communion but can only test them..."

V. Sauliūnas asked the men of the parish:

"Who gave you permission to build a cross in the churchyard? Who let you repair the churchyard fence? You didn't ask anyone."

"I had come to see you," spoke Bičelis, a member of the parochial committee. "I asked for bricks and cement, but you replied: 'There are none for the church. We lack materials for construction projects.'"

During the entire conversation, the bearing of the people from the parish was courageous. Povilas Burokas even pulled out from his pocket a copy of the USSR Constitution and was preparing to read to V. Sauliūnas about the freedom of conscience, but the representative of the government did not let him.

The chairman of the locality presented "the twenty" with a statement to sign which indicated that children in the parish serve mass, strew flowers, sing in the choir, etc. No one signed.

THE ARCHDIOCESE OF KAUNAS
KAUNAS

Ten seminarians enrolled in the philosophy course of the Kaunas Theological Seminary. Rugienis rejected two candidates. This year the KGB officials were less active in regard to those who were entering the seminary; nevertheless, they all had to have a talk with the security people during registration.

ŠILUVA

On September 8 - 15 crowds of people stream in to participate in the Festival of the Nativity of the Blessed Virgin Mary. The authorities take active measures to reduce the number of worshippers. This year the police guarded the roads. Here is what one worshipper has related:

"We went by bus, sixty-one of us. Most of them were elderly. The police stopped us 8-10 km. from Šiluva, drew up a list of people, and led off the driver. After some time he returned with an order to withdraw. After riding for several kilometers, the people began asking the driver to wait so that they could walk to the festival on foot. Once again the group of pilgrims had to pass the police. The women reproached them: 'You're shameless. Is it nice to trouble old people like this? Over the radio and in the newspapers you keep lying that there is freedom of religion in Lithuania, but how do you act? Christ was tormented. We'll also suffer our share for Christ. It doesn't matter that you're standing here with your red caps. We'll reach Šiluva anyhow.' When the festival ended, we walked back 11 km. Only then were we able to return home on the bus."

Another pilgrim related the following:

"We were riding the bus from Kaunas. Halfway between Raseiniai and Šiluva, we were stopped by the police. They led off the driver and spoke with him for a long time about something. One civilian, probably a security agent, looked over our vehicle, expressing surprise that it contained mostly young people. The driver was ordered to allow no one out of the bus and to drive everyone back to Kaunas. The police kept the driver's license and other documents. We were all very upset. Going on foot to Šiluva, we prayed the rosary for the policemen and all atheists, so that they would come to their senses and stop persecuting the Faith. Near the church in Šiluva stood many passenger cars. I saw one official copying down the license numbers of the cars—most probably not for a commendation. As we were passing a car 'on guard,' the Soviet officials within it laughed at us: 'God's lambkins are going to the festival.' "

MEŠKUIČIAI

For a long time the parish in Meškuičiai has been famous for its Hill of Crosses, on which stood not less than three thousand crosses, and it was almost impossible to count the small ones. Each cross had its own history.

Here is what one priest has recounted: "Once I was going to the Hill of Crosses to bless a newly-built cross. At that moment, a military vehicle drove up to the hill. Two Russian pilots who had brought a cross asked me to bless it. I carried out their request. One of the pilots described how his jet plane had once caught fire while he was flying. It is almost impossible to save yourself in such situations. Suddenly he had recalled some remarkable tales about the Hill of Crosses, and he had resolved that, if he survived, he would erect a cross there. It is uncertain why the plane caught fire, and just as unexpectedly it stopped burning."

Many people would come here on foot carrying crosses and erect them. Quite a few of them had been brought from Latvia, Estonia, Byelorussia, and the United States. The people say that so much suffering, so many illnesses have been brought to this hill. How, one wonders, does it bear so much suffering? It is a Lithuanian Golgotha.

Early in the morning on April 5, 1961, some automobiles drove up to the Hill of Crosses. Strange men began to pull down the crosses. The Hill of Crosses was being destroyed by the army, the police, and some prisoners. They burned the wooden crosses right on the spot, whereas the ones made from stone and concrete they smashed into pieces and hauled off to Šiauliai. It is said that they used them as gravel for a highway. They hauled two truckloads of crosses to Būbniai and burned them, and the others, they sank. In one day, all the crosses were destroyed.

At the nearby crossroads stood policemen keeping watch that people would not head in the direction of the Hill of Crosses. Not far from the hill stood armed guards; they remained for a few more days, to prevent people from putting up crosses anew.

During this barbaric operation, Rugienis was "visiting" Šiauliai. After the crosses had been destroyed, he summoned the Rev. Mažanavičius, pastor of the parish in Šiauliai, and asked him:

"Did you hear what happened to Meškuičiai Hill?"

"No, I didn't."

"The crosses have gone up to heaven in smoke," explained Rugienis and ordered the pastor to use his influence with the people so that there would be no incidents.

On September 14, 1970, walking on bare and bleeding feet Father Algirdas Mocius carried a wooden cross 65 km from the parish in Lauksodis to Meškuičiai and on the Feast of the Exaltation of the Holy Cross, erected it in the area ravaged by the atheists.

THE DIOCESE OF TELŠIAI

KLAIPĖDA

In February, 1972, the faithful of Klaipėda sent to Leonid Brezhnev, the General-Secretary of the CPSU, a petition that the Soviet government return a church confiscated from the faithful (see the *Chronicle of the Catholic Church in Lithuania*, no. 2). Security officials were the only ones who reacted to the believers' request. They even conducted a search of the apartment of [Mrs.] Kudirkienė, a resident of Klaipėda, and of her daughter's apartment.

In July, 1972, the believers in Klaipėda once again sent a petition to the General-Secretary (see the *Chronicle of the Catholic Church in Lithuania*, no. 3). [Mrs.] Gražienė, who had sent the petition, was summoned on August 25 to the office of the city's Executive Committee. Rugienis, the commissioner of the Council for Religious Affairs, who had arrived from Vilnius, showed Gražienė the petition of the faithful with 3023 signatures and said:

"You won't get the church back, since the building is needed by both believers and nonbelievers. You have a church, so pray there. No one is bothering you. It's not the church you need so much as you're interested in passing information abroad. If all the people can't fit into the church on Easter, that's not our fault."

Gražienė was questioned as to who had organized the petition and who had collected the signatures. The government officials rebuked her for getting mixed up in "politics," and promised to turn her over to the security agencies.

PLUNGĖ

During Holy Saturday services in 1972, two youths, atheists, came into the church in Plungė and began to cause a disturbance. Since they ignored the requests of the faithful to stop their racket, the sacristan asked them to leave the church.

At night, about 2 a.m., as the people were participating in the devotions of the Stations of the Cross, these youths took down the crucifix from the wall, carried it out beyond the churchyard, and smashed it into pieces. In his Easter sermon, the pastor said that he who profanes the flag of a nation insults all the citizens of that country, that the crucifix is the flag of the faithful, and that today it had been desecrated. The entire congregation wept.

The culprits were apprehended by the police, but no one has heard anything about their being punished. Greatly distressed by this desecration of the crucifix, people have been saying: "Such are the fruits of an atheistic education of youth."

PALANGA

In the summertime, before religious services, at the church in Palanga religious music would be played over loudspeakers and numerous vacationers of various nationalities would gather to listen to it.

In early August, 1972, everyone was astonished at the sudden cessation of these programs of religious music. It turned out that the vice-chairman of the city's Executive Committee had summoned the pastor of the church in Palanga and had demanded that there be no further programs of religious music. The excuse was that they do not constitute a part of Church ritual. The people are waiting to see whether before long the Soviet officials will perhaps begin telling them what hymns to sing in church or how many candles to burn on the altar .

MAŽEIKIAI

During the night of Holy Saturday, 1970, (about 3 a.m.) twelve members of the Young Communist League with their leader Miknius on their way home from a dance stopped by at the church in Mažeikiai and caused a disturbance by mocking the people praying at a casket that symbolized the coffin of Christ. Scandalized by the behavior of the League members, the people drove them out of the church. Before long, several of them returned, took down the crucifix from the wall, carried it outside, and smashed it into pieces. The parochial committee informed the police of this event, declaring that this action had offended all believers, and they demanded that the culprits be punished. Unfortunately, at this time Soviet laws are being zealously applied only to the faithful, but atheists may mock the most sacred sentiments of believers without being punished. In this case it was also inconvenient to punish the culprits because the son of Kerpauskas, a former secretary of the Party, had participated in the "nighttime expedition."

KARKLĖNAI
(Kelmė rayon)

During 1970, J.J., a student at the secondary school in Karklėnai would play the organ during services at the church in Pašilė. For several years everything was peaceful, but then complaints began to flow into the school. After the first complaint, [Mrs.] Irena Saunorienė, a teacher, declared during a history lesson: "There are some degenerates amongst us who do not belong in a Soviet school." After another complaint, the principal summoned J.J. and ordered her to stop playing the organ in church; and Irena Saunorienė, the head of the Education Department, took the girl and several of her classmates to the chemistry laboratory and declared that they would be the school's atheists. [Miss] Aldona Butkutė was elected president, and J.J. —vice-president; however, both pupils began to protest vigorously that they would not participate in such an organization. Jadvyga was told to go to the principal's office, where Telyčėnas, the chairman of the Kelmė *Rayon* Executive Committee, and some stranger from Vilnius were waiting for her. This individual, who was probably a security official, began to speak, saying that he had heard that J.J. played the organ in church, that her way to higher education would be blocked, that there was no room for such as she in a Soviet school. In her misery the student began to cry and asked what had she done wrong? The interrogator said to J.J. that she probably did not believe in God but only went to play for the fun of it. "No, I do believe, and I play there gladly," declared the girl. "But child, think of your future... and make sure that this has been the last time," the government representative lectured and threatened. "Take care that you wouldn't have to bid farewell to school." Meanwhile, Irena Saunorienė, the history teacher, was threatening Jadvyga's class, saying that those who serve the ministers of the cult would have their conduct grade lowered, that they would no longer be free to choose a profession, and that they would receive poor characterizations in their school records.

As the school year was ending, Algis Vilkas, the principal, summoned J.J. and told her: "I don't know what to do with you. You're a fanatic! What kind of character reference will you get?" The principal kept his promise: it was noted in her character reference that J.J. had grown up in a religious family, that the parents maintained contact with priests, that she had played the organ in church, and that she had done all this with fanatical stubborness. After completing the secondary school, J.J. tried to enter the Medical Institute of Kaunas, but during her interview with the admissions commission, one instructor read her character reference and asked in amazement: "A fanatic? Girl, you came here in vain!" Later she enrolled in another school of higher learning.

ŠILALĖ

In the summer of 1963, [Miss] Nijolė Siekytė, a fifth-class student living in Rubinavas Village, used to come to church with her mother. At the beginning of the school year, her teacher [Mrs.] Statkevičienė, upbraided Nijolė for going to church, saying that by doing so she had dishonored her school uniform. She ordered the girl to explain in the presence of all the students why she had attended church and to denounce herself. Having climbed onto the stage, Nijolė began to cry. Teacher Statkevičienė and several other teachers ordered Nijolė to go home and not to return to the school anymore. Nijolė returned home weeping, threw her books into a corner, and told her parents she would not be going to school anymore. Later, at the urging of other teachers, she began to attend school once again. The atheistic teachers, nevertheless, did not cease to bother her. That was why the girl transferred to an evening school for youth.

THE DIOCESE OF PANEVĖŽYS

ŠEDUVA

On August 27, 1972, Canon P. Bakšys, the ecclesiastical administrator of the dioceses of Panevėžys and Kaišiadorys, administered the sacrament of Confirmation. The government had permitted only two priests to assist him. About 3,000 were being confirmed. Exhausted from the strenuous work, having scarcely finished delivering a sermon, the Rev. Juozas Ražanskas (b. 1910), dean of Šeduva and pastor of the church in Pakruojis, died in the sacristy.

That same day in this town, some hooligans using a brickbat beat up an old woman who sold devotional articles, as she was on her way home. The assailants kicked her repeatedly after she fell down and, grabbing her rosaries and her money, fled. The old lady died in the hospital.

JONIŠKĖLIS

Here, on August 13, 1972, took place the Festival of the Assumption of the Blessed Virgin Mary. Afterward,

Stapulionis, the vice-chairman of the Pasvalys *Rayon* Soviet of Working People's Deputies Executive Committee visited this locality and summoning Father B. Jareckas, the pastor, together with the treasurer of the parochial committee reprimanded them angrily: "Why had so many priests and seminarians been invited? Why had the pastor allowed a priest from another *rayon* to deliver the sermon? Why had the pastor permitted the girls to wear the national costume in the procession?" In fact, only three priests and as many seminarians took part in the festival. Stapulionis insisted that the priest promise not to give out national costumes to the girls again. When he refused to do so, the vice-chairman forced the members of the parochial committee to sign a statement saying that they would banish the national costume from the church. The "uninvited guest" even wanted to confiscate the national costumes, but he could not find the church keys.

In the entire Pasvalys *Rayon* it is forbidden to wear the national costume in the churches during processions.

KRIKLINIAI

Toward the end of 1971, the Rev. P. Masilionis, pastor of the parish in Krikliniai, requested permission from the Pasvalys *Rayon* administration to visit family members residing in the United States. In June, 1972, he received a negative reply.

Nobody was surprised at such action by the Soviet government. Apparently, neither was Father Masilionis, for at this time only priests who are completely trusted by the government and who deal more or less with the KGB are permitted to leave in order to visit capitalist countries. The The pastor of the parish in Krikliniai has not earned any "merits" with the Soviet authorities. He had hardly arrived at his parish when Stapulionis, the vice-chairman of the Pasvalys *Rayon* Executive Committee, warned him sternly: "Stay put in the church! Don't go touring the parish." Neither do the *rayon* officials like Father Masilionis' sermons, which touch upon questions relevant to the lives of the faithful. For example, the administration of the Krikliniai Collective Farm pays double wages to those who come to work on Sunday: ten rubles for the day. Prior to the Festival of the Visitation (July 2) an announcement was made to the collective-farm workers to the effect that those who would work during the festival would each get a wagonload of hay. Since it is hard to obtain hay, more than one worker succumbed and worked during the festival. In his sermon the pastor reminded the faithful not to sell their Sundays. Moreover, the parishioners were reminded that Catholic parents do wrong to celebrate the wedding of their children who refuse to receive the Sacrament of Matrimony: "There is nothing to rejoice about when a child begins an unauthorized wedded life." Father Masilionis said that a great error is committed when ceremonious funerals —with an orchestra and a large procession of children and youths—are held for suicides. The pastor recalled one driver's funeral. He had killed a man while drunk; later he hanged himself and was buried with much pomp.

At the end of July, 1972, Father Masilionis was summoned to the State Security office in Pasvalys. Its chief rebuked him for the excesses committed by some priests during their sermons. Among the hotheads he mentioned were Fathers Buliauskas and Nykštus. The pastor of Krikliniai was also supposedly acting-up too much. The security agent reminded him that there were enough prayer books for the faithful. He added that the Soviet government had agreed to publish a Catholic newspaper, but the clergy have been unable to form an editorial staff. He also said that there were enough priests, but a better selection of more suitable candidates to the seminary should be made.

Father Masilionis explained that atheistic propaganda had begun to bore everyone, that it was full of fabrications and pornography. It was a priest's duty to tell the truth to the faithful.

"Why do you priests write collective petitions, such as the one in regard to Canon Žiukelis?" asked the security agent.

Canon Žiukelis, you see, under orders of Rugienis, was being assigned to the out-of-the-way parish in Šimoniai. Defending their dean, the clergy of Pasvalys *Rayon* had objected in their petition to the ecclesiastical administrator Canon P. Bakšys that such a transfer contradicted Church law. The security agent also reminded him that petitions sent abroad, such as the memorandum of the 17,000, would serve no purpose. "If you need something, write it down and send it to Rugienis," advised the security agent.

At the end of the meeting, the chief expressed regret that the State Security Committee which had been founded for the struggle against counterrevolution, must now concern itself with priests.

THE DIOCESE OF VILKAVIŠKIS

PRIENAI

On July 26, 1972, the faithful of Prienai traveled to the Pravieniškės Prison Camp to greet the about-to-be-liberated curate of Prienai, Father J. Zdebskis; however, he had already been released. That was because the camp administration had been ordered to release Father Zdebskis the previous evening in order to prevent a "political demonstration." The government officials were apprehensive about what would happen if many people were to come to welcome the priest.

The parishioners greeted Father Zdebskis with ceremony on Sunday, August 27. Little children scattered flowers as the priest was returning to the sacristy after mass. In the churchyard children and adults congratulated the former prisoner. There were so many flowers that the priest could not hold them all in his arms, and the people covered the ground with them.

Rugienis would not allow H.E. Bishop Labukas to appoint Father Zdebskis to the Vilkaviškis Diocese. Two months later, Father Zdebskis was appointed curate of the parish in Šilutė. This is a "civilized" kind of exile: if you want to work in a parish, then leave your diocese!

KALVARIJA

The Sacrament of Confirmation was being administered here on July 22-23, 1972. The previous evening, officials of Kapsukas *Rayon* ordered the pastor of the parish in Kalvarija to take down the loudspeakers that were set up outside. On July 22 no sermons were even delivered so as not to "anger the authorities." About 4,000 children were confirmed.

METELIAI

On September 24, 1972, the 150th jubilee of the church in Meteliai was celebrated. Rugienis permitted the bishop to come, but he did not allow him to administer the Sacrament of Confirmation.

* * *

The Catholics in Lithuania are becoming increasingly aware of their duty to pray for their homeland. The following proclamation has been passing from hand to hand among the believers:

LET US COME TO THE AID OF OUR NATIVE LAND!

During the postwar years the material wounds of our country have healed over, but even more grievous ones have been opened: the persecution of believers, godlessness, cursing, drunkenness, dissoluteness, murder of the unborn, mockery of the most sacred national and religious traditions. In their concern over their own fate, many of our compatriots are forgetting the fate of our native land. That is why it is necessary to pray for our homeland every day. Let us urge those dear to us to pray also. For this intention let us often dedicate our rosaries, our masses, our Communions, and our other religious acts. For the sins of our compatriots let us offer to God all our deeds and hardships and all that we have to suffer.

The homeland is as dear to every human being as is his mother, as is his birthplace. Only a degenerate cannot love his homeland. Therefore let us come to the aid of our native land through sacrifice and prayer.

Prayer for the Homeland

O God, cast Your glance upon Lithuania, which today is travelling a dolorous way of the cross.

May its arduous lot bring, not ruin, but the resurrection of the nation.

May our voice of apology reach You, O heavenly Father, through the cloudiness of our sins, for grave transgressions have oppressed our nation, which is as if shackled.

Many of its children are no longer aware of You, Father, nor of their eternal purpose.

May this cup of suffering soon pass from our nation.

Until You draw near to Your suffering children, O Lord, help us to bear patiently and with perseverence this burden of oppression, which dims the sun for us and pains our hearts.

We ask this through Christ our Lord. Amen.

Our Father. Hail Mary. Glory be to the Father.

no.5

- *Deceptive tranquility during which, however, the campaign against religious youth is intensified; instances of heroic resistance increase*

- *Petition upon petition by 1,709 believers of Ceikiniai to Leonid Brezhnev, to the government of the LSSR, to the Lithuanian commissioner of the Council for Religious Affairs, and to the rayon administration with facts upon facts of discrimination against the faithful*

- *Man is sent to a psychiatric hospital for constructing a cross*

- *"Shortage" of paper for the works of Bishop Valančius*

- *Priest is released from prison camp (Father Bubnys)*

- *Burglarization of churches increases*

- *Priest is transferred and demoted (Father Pesliakas)*

- *Woman struggles against the destruction of her parents' cemetery monument with the words "Save us, O Lord!"*

- *Pastors are forbidden to participate in funeral processions (Father Balaišis and Father Raščius)*

- *Priest is warned to find work other than priestly duties (Father Zdebskis)*

- *Pastor is warned not to involve youth in religious rites (Father Matulaitis)*

A GLANCE FROM THE THRESHOLD
OF THE NEW YEAR

The second half of 1972 was comparatively calm for the Catholic Church in Lithuania: the brazen persecution of the faithful and the clergy had decreased. Not even once was legal action taken against priests for the so-called illegal teaching of religious truths to children, although by making use of their "juridical" methods, the representatives of the Soviet government could have convicted more than one priest with little difficulty.

Government officials received the priests Juozas Zdebskis and Prosperas Bubnys rather politely upon their return from a prison camp, permitting them to perform their priestly duties for a time in their own parishes.

It was completely otherwise one year ago. In the fall of 1971, when Father A. Šeškevičius left the Alytus prison camp, he was told that for having committed crimes against the government he would not be allowed to perform his priestly work and would have to change his occupation. Only after great efforts by Father Šeškevičius did the commissioner of the Council for Religious Affairs, Rugienis, permit him to work as the curate of the parish in Šilalė in the Telšiai Diocese.

In 1972, for the first time in the history of the Catholic Church in Lithuania, the Soviet government began to tolerate retreats for the priests of an entire deanery. H.E. Bishop J. Labukas and H.E. Bishop J. Pletkus were permitted by Rugienis to travel to the retreats for the clergy and speak on topics concerning the inner life of the clergy. Some bishops even let it be known that deanery conferences regarding pastoral matters would be permitted.

At the beginning of Advent the first edition of a new translation of the New Testament was to appear, and somewhat later, a Catechism.

The security agencies showed more restraint in seeking agents among theological seminary students.

No efforts were spared in disseminating propaganda to prove the humaneness of the Soviet government in regard to religion and believers. "The Soviet state and its governmental organs do not interfere in the internal matters of the Church, i.e., in its canonical and dogmatic concerns.... it is important to enforce Soviet laws which grant religious communities and believers their rights" (interview of J. Rugienis by the editorial board of *Tarybu darbas* [Work of the Soviets], 1972, no. 9, pp. 17-18).

"To defend the rights of believers is one of the requirements of socialist legality... Persons who discriminate against believers must undoubtedly be punished severely," wrote V. Kuroyedov, the chairman of the Council for Religious Affairs, somewhat earlier (*Religija ir įstatymai* [Religion and the laws], 1971, pp. 24-25).

Regretfully, government agencies forget or do not want to hear that catechization is commanded by Church canons of the Code. The cases of the priests A. Šeškevičius, J. Zdebskis, and P. Bubnys show the government's brazen interference in canonical matters of the Church and belie their mendacious interviews and statements.

The Party leaders have remembered Lenin's words which he spoke long ago at the first congress of Russian workers: "One must fight religious superstitions with extreme caution: those who contribute insults against religious feelings to this struggle cause much harm. One must fight by propagating and enlightening. By imparting harshness into the struggle we may anger the masses" (Lenin, *Raštai* [Writings], vol. 28, p. 158).

Lenin condemned the flagrant persecution of religion and of the faithful, calling it "cavalry charges." After the memorandum signed by 17,000 Lithuanian believers and the events of May in Kaunas, the authorities realized that their "cavalry charges" had already considerably "angered the masses."

As the Soviet government was celebrating the fiftieth anniversary of the USSR on December 21, 1972, a new problem was encountered—the acute question of nationalism. Causing great concern are not only the Baltic nations and the Ukraine, but also the Moslem Asian republics, whose population increase is the largest, and which have preserved their customs and religion.

The well-informed member of the Žinija [Knowledge] Society, A. Balsys, wrote: "The Communist party tries very diligently to study and remove the causes that may arouse nationalistic remnants, for there can be no trifles in national relations" (*Kur susikerta ietys* [Where lances cross], 1972, p. 34). The aforementioned propagandist affirms that "mistakes and excesses in the fight against religious vestiges in a certain republic" *may support nationalism* (ibid., p. 33).

In its June 8 editorial, "The Most Precious Feeling," *Tiesa* [Truth] tried to convince Lithuanians that their homeland is the Soviet Union, which was not and will not be a stepmother, and thus should be loved like a mother.

Soviet propaganda asserted that Lithuania was not being Russified, that only Czarism tried to throttle its captive nations and incite Great-Russian nationalism (compare A. Balsys, *Kur susikerta ietys* [Where lances cross], p. 35).

Our active emigration, faithful to the ideals of its native land, has publicized throughout the world the distressing persecution of the Catholic Church in Lithuania. The world's major newspapers and radio and television stations have often commented on events in Lithuania. All this has harmed the prestige of the Soviet Union. All the more so, since it is "fighting" even for the rights of Catholics in Ireland.

Soviet propaganda has attacked and assailed the Lithuanian emigration as never before. Perhaps doubting their own authority, they tried to "invite" even priests to their aid. Articles signed by certain priests appeared in overseas newspapers, reviling the emigration, the history of Lithuania, while exalting the present (*Laisvė* [Freedom], 1972, nos. 67, 68, 69).

The present "tranquility" in the Catholic Church of Lithuania is temporary and deceptive. Its purposes are the following:

1. To calm the growing dissatisfaction in the nation regarding religious and national injustices.

2. To compromise the emigration's efforts and work, which are vitally necessary for the Church and the homeland.

3. To repair throughout the world the Soviet Union's prestige, which has been shaken because of its persecution of the Church. This is especially urgent in the face of the preparations for the Helsinki Conference.

4. It seems likely that the deteriorating economic situation in the Soviet Union influenced the appearance of this "tranquility"—the necessity of buying huge quantities of wheat abroad. It is worthwhile to recall certain sentiments in the U.S. Congress. Senator Jackson is preparing legislation which is now supported by seventy-five senators to the effect that the United States must not sell wheat to the Soviet Union as long as it does not implement the Universal Declaration of Human Rights. In Senator Jackson's words, the USSR was the first to sign the declaration and has remained to the present the only state in the world which has completely avoided implementing it.

5. Having softened their administrative attacks, the atheists hope that the Catholics of Lithuania will forget and stop demanding the most elementary rights and means for their religious life. Even some sects in the Soviet Union are in a better situation than Lithuania's Catholics. The

chairman of the Council for Religious Affairs, Kuroyedov, has written: "Many churches and religious groups have been founded and registered (the sects—ed.); the Bible and a collection of hymns have been published in editions numbering thousands of copies; the journal *Bratski Vestnik* is published regularly; two-year Bible study courses function alongside VEKBS" ("Religija ir įstatymai" [Religion and the laws], p. 51).

The Catholics of Lithuania have no calendar, no newspaper, no catechism, no religious literature, nor other essential requirements.

The superficial calm has not prevented the atheists from striving against the Catholic Church in Lithuania covertly but methodically this year also. A whole series of facts testify to this:

Atheistic propaganda was greatly intensified. It mercilessly assailed active priests and believers. "Desiring to maintain the influence of religion, the most fanatically-inclined ministers of the cult and believers are fighting for the abolition of laws concerning religious cults, so that a completely unrestricted propagation of religion might be assured thereby. Such elements of extremist bent impudently violate the laws governing matters of religion and the Church, which the fanatics interpret very erroneously." These thoughts by Kuroyedov, the chairman of the Council for Religious Affairs, were widely propagated by the atheists of Lithuania.

Teachers were particularly coerced into educating students in a godless spirit. "It is the noble duty of the schools to protect children from religious influence and to educate the students to be militant atheists" (*Tarybinis mokytojas* [The Soviet teacher], February 13, 1972).

During the first half of the 1972-73 school year, students were even forcibly compelled to join the Pioneers and the Young Communist League.

Rugienis, the commissioner of the Council for Religious Affairs, complained that public commissions were working alongside *rayon* and city executive committees and were not monitoring the enforcement of laws concerning religious cults. He suggested including in them a wider circle of the most active members. "Thus, it would be useful to review the composition of these commissions, bringing in more people" (*Tarybų darbas*, [Work of the Soviets], 1972, no. 9, p. 18). There was especially intensive jamming of the 7:45 a.m. Radio Roma broadcasts. Since they are broadcast at an inconvenient time—in the morning—and have been severely jammed, the Catholics could make little use of them. Radio Vatican could be heard better, and many believers gladly listened to its broadcasts at 9:20 p.m.

In April, 1972, H.E. Bishop J. Steponavičius appealed to the government in Moscow, demanding that he be allowed to perform his pastoral duties. Rugienis explained to him that, for now, he could not be assigned a position.

In the summer of 1972, H.E. Bishop V. Sladkevičius requested a transfer to another parish, where he might more easily avail himself of medical help. Unfortunately, his request was not granted.

The publication of a catechism, it appears, has been forgotten. Besides, the Catholics of Lithuania would not be satisfied at present with the *Tikybos pirmamokslis* [A primer of the Faith] by Bishop K. Paltarokas. If the Lithuanian émigrés were able to publish in Rome in 1960 a 256-page catechism prepared by the Rev. P. Manelis, then it would be appropriate for Lithuanians in the homeland, where there is "complete religious freedom," to publish a catechism that is no smaller.

Although the New Testament will soon appear, the Catholics in Lithuania regret that the Soviet government has already, before publication, managed to compromise its translator, Father C. Kavaliauskas, by forcing him to write a whole series of articles for a Lithuanian Communist newspaper in the United States, in which the Lithuanian emigration, together with active priests and believers in Lithuania, and Radio Vatican programs are reviled and the "good and flourishing" life in Lithuania is extolled.

After Father J. Zdebskis had returned from a prison camp, Rugienis wanted to exile him quietly from the Vilkaviškis Diocese to the Telšiai Diocese. Since this plan fell apart, the Prienai police ordered Father Zdebskis to register for work somewhere within fifteen days.

How successful were the atheists, not just in the persecution of the faithful, but in their primary objectives? During 1972, thirty-three schools for atheistic lecturers functioned in Lithuania, in which 750 lecturers studied. The periodical *Religija ir dabartis* [Religion and the present] was published for atheistic propagandists; besides which, publication of *Atsakymai tikintiesiems* [Answers to believers] was begun.

"As last year's practical experience of the republic's school for atheistic lecturers demonstrated, not all of the Žinija [Knowledge] Society's organizations were sufficiently attentive to this form of study for lecturers. Some of them apparently did not send the most suitable people to the school. *Hence, a considerable percentage of the students* (editor's italics) stopped attending the school after one or two lessons" (*Laikas ir įvykiai* [Time and events], 1972, no. 23, p. 11).

"People sent from the organizations in Druskininkai, Ukmergė, Joniškis, Telšiai, and elsewhere were not utilized at all in the *rayons*, as they themselves have admitted," (ibid., p. 12).

Pranas Beniušis, a lecturer from the Central Committee of the Lithuanian Communist party, complains that the atheists of Šilalė *Rayon* have been very inefficient, and that the organization Tėvynė [Fatherland] of Panevėžys showed little interest in atheistic subjects, etc." (ibid., no. 21, p. 19).

The atheists also had little success in popularizing godless ceremonies. "However, it must be candidly admitted that in many places some admirable initiatives have begun to die out. The storks who strut around announcing the celebration of a newborn infant's name day, are beginning to disappear, not because times have changed, but evidently because good intentions are dying out, because these intentions are supported less and less by concrete action, initiative, and ingeniousness, because there is a lack of creativity and a course of the most common banality is followed." (*Tiesa* [Truth], January 14, 1973). Just what would be the results of the atheists' efforts if the Soviet government did not support them and the faithful were given freedom of action!

Religious Students in an Atheistic School

In Lithuania, the majority of the children receive a religious upbringing. The following facts testify to this: Every year a large number of children prepare for their First Communion. For example, each year about 150 children prepare themselves in Anykščiai, about 200 children in Švenčionys, about 300 children in Prienai, about 500 children in Marijampolė. In the larger non-*rayon* parishes approximately 100-120 children prepare for their First Communion every year. In the smallest parishes, 15 - 30 children receive First Communion.

The atheists themselves concede that a substantial number of children and adolescents are still under the influence of religion. The newspaper *Lietuvos pionierius* [Lithuanian Pioneer] published the following in 1971: "This summer a number of students from the school in Valkininkai attended church and performed religious rites. Some even assisted the priest during mass. Among these students there were even Pioneers and members of the Young Communist League... Even the most active Pioneers and members of the Young Communist League had become so placid, that they 'saw nothing wrong in that'... Others, unfortunately, themselves began asserting that they 'believe in God' and will not cease going to church. Most distressing is that among the 'others' were Pioneers and members of the Young Communist League" (V. Grublikas, "Skaudi pamoka" [Painful Lesson]).

The constantly intensifying struggle for nurturing an atheistic world view among students indicates that a majority of students are religious. In 1972 the importance of an atheistic upbringing was particularly stressed. A. Bar-kauskas, the secretary of the Central Committee of the Lithuanian Communist party, wrote in the February 26, 1972, issue of *Tiesa* [Truth]: "It is the task of the schools to ensure that the facts presented during the educative process become firm convictions. The fostering of militant atheists is the duty of every pedagogical collective and every teacher."

The Minister of Education of the LSSR, M. Gedvilas, affirms: "Taking into consideration the ongoing ideological struggle in the world, we must continually search for ways and means to foster even more successfully well-rounded and spiritually rich personalities with a materialistic world outlook, Communist convictions, and a strong civic consciousness" (*Tiesa* [Truth], August 18, 1972).

By what methods are atheistic convictions instilled in believing students?

Students are forcibly taught atheism. Teachers in all fields are coerced into propagating atheism when they teach their subjects, e.g., physics, astronomy. Even mathematics classes must have atheistic elements. *Mokslinis-ateistinis auklėjimas mokykloje* [Scientific-atheistic education in the schools], a booklet by [Mrs.] A. Gulbinskienė and V. Petronis intended for teachers, states: "For example, in classes 3-4 one may ask the pupils to calculate the unnecessary expenses of people needed for maintaining churches and priests . . . It is absolutely essential to demonstrate how this money might be employed for improving the life of the working people" (Kaunas, 1959, p. 33). History, literature, and social science teachers especially are supposed to undermine their students' faith. Homeroom teachers must plan and conduct atheistic lectures at class meetings. Atheistic lectures, discussions of atheistic books, evening programs with question-and-answer sessions and demonstrations of "miracles" are organized in the schools. The proponents of atheism consult neither parents nor children as to whether they wish to be atheists, instead *they forcibly intrude upon the consciences of people* and dare to proclaim: "Total freedom of conscience has been implemented in the Soviet Union" (J. Aničas and J. Rimaitis, *Tarybiniai įstatymai apie religinius kultus ir sąžinės laisvę* [Soviet laws concerning religious cults and freedom of conscience], 1970, p. 17).

The most elementary truth is entirely disregarded in the atheistic upbringing of children. The most brazen slander is resorted to in depicting the Church as the greatest disseminator of superstitions and the clergy as criminals. For example, the textbook for class 6, *Vidurinių amžių istorija* [History of the Middle Ages], ridicules the Church, the popes, and convents and monasteries. Regarding St. Ignatius Loyola, it states that he taught the following: "The Pope must be obeyed without question, even in the case of sin, and one must commit a sin if a superior demands it" (1972, p. 226).

In the text *Senovės istorija* [Ancient history] it is asserted that Christianity originated from legends about Christ, and that these had come from the myths about Osiris, etc. (1971, p. 225). Whereas Tacitus, a historian of the first century, writes in the fifteenth book of his *Annals*: "The originator of their name, Christ, was condemned to death in the reign of Tiberius by the Procurator Pontius Pilate" (P. C. Tacitus, *Rinktiniai raštai* [Selected writings], Vilnius, 1972, p. 224).

The eleventh-class textbook *Visuomenės mokslas* [Social science] states: "The ranks of the ministers of the Church are supplemented by parasitical elements, spongers, and morally decadent subjects" (1971, p. 212).

Seeking to discredit miracles, the propagandists of the Soviet school affirm: "Churchmen often deceive the faithful by turning water into 'blood.' Churchmen also employ the following trick—in the church the candles ignite spontaneously at night" (A. Gulbinskienė and V. Petronis, *Mokslinis-ateistinis auklėjimas mokykloje* [Scientific-atheistic education in the schools], p. 28).

Carried away by their lies, the propagators of godlessness transform even Galileo, Copernicus, and other scientists into "atheists" (ibid., p. 64).

On December 25, 1971, in the secondary school of Prienai, [Mrs.] Vaškienė, the history and social science teacher, "enlightened" the tenth-graders by telling them that Mary was a whore and Joseph a dolt, etc.

Students who attend church diligently *are threatened* that their faith would be noted in their school records and, therefore, they would be unable to enroll in a school of higher education. Throughout the postwar period the practice has been to note in school records that: "The student has not rid himself of religious superstitions."

Lenin once wrote: "Any distinctions among citizens which affect their rights and are made on the basis of their religious convictions are absolutely inadmissible. Even any sort of references to one or another religious belief of citizens in official documents must be completely eliminated" (Lenin, *Raštai* [Writings], vol. 10, pp. 65-68). It cannot be assumed that teachers would note the religiousness of secondary school graduates in school records on their own initiative. If this were not encouraged by the highest echelon of the government, no teacher would dare do so under the conditions of the Soviet system. Unfortunately, teachers know that many have suffered for religious convictions, but not one among those who violate the freedom of conscience of the believers!

Religious students are forced to join the atheistic organizations of the Pioneers and the Young Communist League.

Students in the lower classes are enrolled in the Octobrists and the Young Pioneers without even consulting either the children or the parents. The children are simply told to buy their stars and red neckties. Quite a few teachers purchase the stars and neckties themselves and then order the students to bring the money. Having enrolled them into the Pioneers by force, the teachers tell the children to stop dissembling, to stop attending church, since a true Pioneer must be an atheist. Most often the teachers do not coerce the children on their own initiative, but are themselves coerced by the Ministry of Public Education. In the majority of Lithuania's schools, the wearing of a red necktie is unpopular, and the children avoid doing so.

"The religiosity of the parents and of the children themselves is the fundamental, if not the sole, reason why students do not want to join the Young Pioneers organization. Consequently, in those cases when a young adolescent refuses to join, one may assume he is being raised in a religious family, and he himself is religious to a greater or lesser extent," thus reasons Bitinas, who is an expert at turning students into atheists (B. Bitinas, *Religingi mokiniai ir jų perauklėjimas* [Religious students and their reeducation], 1969, p. 128).

In connection with the fiftieth anniversary of the USSR, upper-class students were particularly pressured to join the Young Communist League in the first half of the 1972-73 school year. Students were told it would be harder for nonmembers to be admitted to schools of higher education. In truth, there are quite a few instances of students being rejected because they are not members of the Young Communist League. In some schools, during 1972 homeroom teachers would keep students after class for three to four hours, constantly urging them to join the League. Lately, the students' reluctance to belong to this organization has become increasingly apparent. Some do this for patriotic and others for religious reasons, since they do not want to betray their convictions, but the majority see no use in the Young Communist League.

Homeroom teachers must report the number of League members to the *rayon* education department. If few in the class are members, the education department concludes that this teacher does poor work in educating the class. The careerists try to show off at least thus: my class is one-hundred-percent enrolled in the Young Communist League.

In the autumn of 1972, many students enrolling in schools of higher education were not members of the League. Evidently, the more time goes by, the harder it will be to implement the "one-hundred-percent" dream.

Registering a student in the Young Communist League

is considered an important part of his atheistic education. "The decision to become a member of the Young Communist League is at the same time a decision to finally renounce religious views" (B. Bitinas, ibid., p. 108).

When a student is registered in the League, he is not asked whether he believes in God or not, but later is severely criticized more than once. A schoolgirl from the secondary school in Čedasai has remarked: "I remember how ashamed I was when a Young Communist League meeting discussed my churchgoing." Having joined the League and not wanting to have unpleasant experiences in school, many Catholic students begin to avoid the church, going somewhere farther away to practice their religion so their friends and teachers would not find out, and thus gradually stop practicing their religion. At present, it is becoming more and more clear to the Catholic youth of Lithuania—*joining the Young Communist League is a great mistake.*

In the secondary schools, alongside all the other groups must function an atheistic group. There are very few who join, therefore, *the teachers force believing students to participate in the atheistic group's activities.* Several representatives from each class are usually assigned to this group. Occasionally all the members of the Young Communist League are registered in the atheistic group, as in the secondary school in Punia, and sometimes even students who actively practice their religion, so they would be "re-educated" by taking part in atheistic activities. Certain teachers even resort to deceit in order to register religious children in an atheistic group. During the first half of the 1972-73 school year, [Miss] Dainauskaitė, a teacher in the secondary school of Krosna, invited some students to enroll in a group whose members would make excursions, "visit churches," etc. Failing to see the deception, the believing children registered for the atheistic group, but when they discovered the deception, they withdrew.

The unpopularity of atheism among the students is borne out by the fact that the atheistic groups in nearly all the schools of Lithuania are moribund: they function only to the extent it is "required."

Registering a religious student in an atheistic group is the most flagrant violation of a child's and his parents' convictions.

An even more widespread violation of a student's conscience involves *compelling a religious student to speak out on atheistic subjects, to answer questions during atheism classes, to write atheistic compositions and writing tests, and to participate in atheistic activities afer school.*

B. Bitinas has written: "We shall touch on certain methods being utilized to involve students in atheistic activities. One of these is a public statement by a religious student on an atheistic topic (in a discussion, during a reader's conference, while discussing a film, a newsletter to be posted on a bulletin board, etc.). . . . What is most important is that such a statement encourages the student to make a decision. Now he must act the way he spoke, for otherwise, his classmates will consider him a hypocrite. An adolescent is usually very sensitive to such a charge" (ibid., p. 165).

Are any comments necessary after these words stated by an underminer of the spirit of Lithuanian youth testifying to the complete disregard of the students' freedom of conscience? It remains only to add that the book cited is published by the LSSR Ministry of Public Education and is recommended for teachers as a guide for turning students into atheists.

Art teachers very frequently tell believing students to draw something atheistic. A failing grade is given for refusing. Such coercion of believing students is considered humane and in accordance with the programs established by the Ministry of Public Education.

Students who attend church are quite often ridiculed and upbraided in class meetings, in newsletters on bulletin boards, etc. In April, 1972, [Miss] Lina Galinskaitė, a tenth-class student of the secondary school in Aštrioji Kirsna went to a neighbor's wake and, kneeling down, prayed for the deceased. The chairman of the teachers' trade union [Mrs.] Lukoševičienė, and [Mrs.] Valiukonienė, the secretary of the Party organization, became very indignant when they saw the schoolgirl praying at the wake. The next day an emergency meeting was called in L. Galinskaitė's class. The homeroom teacher publicly rebuked Lina for "kneeling and making the sign of the cross."

"I have knelt and will continue to kneel. I have crossed myself and will continue to cross myself. You won't forbid me this because you have no right to," the religious girl courageously retorted.

"You can crawl around if you want, but for that you may have to be expelled from school or receive a failing grade in conduct."

Lukoševičienė and Valiukonienė then resolved to have Lina's behavior discussed in the presence of all the students. The members of the Young Communist League would have to condemn her behavior.

"We ourselves go to church and pray, so how can we condemn our friend," said the students, declining to do so.

Then Lukoševičienė called a production meeting; she wished that at least the cleaning women would condemn the religious girl; however, the women defended her unanimously.

Generally teachers avoid mocking religious students themselves (although even such instances occur), but they encourage the students to do so. The book *Religingi mokiniai ir jų perauklėjimas* [Religious students and their re-education] states: "Some assert that in the atheistic nurturing of students satirical criticism should not be used in regard to those students who practice religious rites. The data we have compiled indicates that this contention cannot be accepted categorically when one is confronted with young religious adolescents. In some cases the expression of an atheistic public opinion in satirical form actually helps the religious adolescent to accept the goals of an atheistic education more readily than other forms of atheistic influence. The adolescent does not want to appear ridiculous before his peers, and this often exerts a stronger influence than does urging by parents to perform religious rites" (p. 122). "A student feels uneasy when he is being scolded for practicing religious rites, particularly if he is a Pioneer" (ibid.).

Especially persecuted are those students who assist at mass and participate in processions (see the *Chronicle of the Catholic Church in Lithuania,* nos. 1, 2, 3, 4). Teachers rebuke the students so they would not take part in religious rites and try to convince parents not to allow their children near an altar; while government functionaries threaten the priests with fines, transfers to smaller parishes, etc. The atheists fear that active participation in religious rites might foster conscientious Catholics, and in particular, that candidates to the theological seminary might appear among the boys who assist at mass.

Student E. of the secondary school in Karklénai would at times assist at mass. The principal, A. Vilkas, called him in and asked:

"Do you really assist at mass?"

"Yes, really."

"What does the priest pay you for it?"

"I get paid from above."

"You'll have such a bad school record that you won't be accepted by any school."

"And those members of the Young Communist League who loaf around drunk at the cultural center and are up to their necks with failing grades, will they have good records and be accepted at schools of higher education?"

"You're a sanctimonious granny!"

P., another student, was also persecuted for his faith. Summoning him to his office, Vilkas asked whether he attended church.

"I not only go to church, but I also play the organ."

"I know, I know about your little activities. I'll tear apart this nest of fanatics," shouted the principal.

"We're all fanatics in our own way. I believe in God; you also believe... And what's wrong with that? After all, there is freedom of conscience."

"We'll see how you sneeze when you'll have to go into the army because of your poor school record," threatened the principal.

Atheistic teachers and government officials are especially anxious when they learn that students visit priests and read the literature obtained from them. Contacts between priests and students are even prohibited by Soviet laws.

If teachers see that a student might enter the theological seminary, they make special efforts to influence him so that his aspirations might be turned in another direction. More than once, a student is even indulged just so as to gain his sympathies. There are also entirely contrary cases —attempts are made to especially pressure such a student during the school year and during examinations.

For attending church, the grades of students are quite often lowered, especially the conduct grade.

[Miss] Aurelija Račinskaitė, a first-class student at the eight-year school in Rageliai (Rokiškis *Rayon*), received a grade of five in all her subjects [the higest grade—tr] during the second trimester in 1972, but her conduct grade was only satisfactory [poor in Soviet schools—tr.]. A note at the bottom of her report card read: "... conduct grade in the second trimester is satisfactory because she attends church.

Teachers often take away crucifixes and medallions from religious students. For instance, [Mrs.] Rimkienė, principal of Kaunas Secondary School No. 2, is particularly experienced in this work. After tearing off a small medallion from a girl's neck in January, 1973, she declared: "I have a whole drawer full of such scraps of metal!"

There are instances where even parents have been persecuted at work for their children's religiosity. At meetings they are reproached for harming Soviet youth by interfering with the efforts of Soviet schools to foster confirmed propagators of the Communist cause.

How Do Religious Students React to Such Discrimination?

A considerable number of students adapt to these conditions of persecution and, currying favor with the teachers and wishing to avoid unpleasantness in their lives, join the Pioneers and the Young Communist League and avoid attending church. They cannot be called atheists because they have not entirely broken off ties with the Church.

Some students yield to the one-sided atheistic propaganda. Unfamiliar with the faith, encountering only its ridicule and coercion, students, especially in the upper classes, begin dissembling and try to avoid revealing themselves as believers; some become atheists. A common trait is noticeable among students of this category—an indifference to ideological questions: both to atheism and the faith; they show an interest only in sports, television, and—later —drinking and erotic matters. Thus it is not surprising that in Lithuania's prison camps atheistic youths make up the largest number of criminals.

When they join the Pioneers or the Young Communist League, quite a few students fail to notice one evil. Growing up in the atmosphere permeated with lies and dishonesty that appeared during the postwar years in Lithuania, students are unable to comprehend the harm in hypocricy and lack of principles.

Many students who are compelled to answer questions during atheism classes or to write atheistic essays do not perceive any moral wrong in this. The disorientation in matters of faith and morality, together with the distressful coercion, are the fundamental reasons why students demonstrate great abhorrence regarding the faith and cannot avoid entirely inexcusable mistakes. Especial responsibility for mistakes of this type and for lapses by the students falls on the parents' consciences. Some of them are negligent in religious matters, others are afraid to defend their children when they are coerced in matters of the faith, still others erroneously advise: "Join the Young Communist League, child. The important thing is that you don't renounce God in your heart!"

Some of the students dare to resist and actively defend their convictions.

During the first half of the 1972-73 school year, the students in classes 9-11 of the secondary school in Griška-būdis were given three questions to determine their convictions. Ninety percent answered that they believe in God.

On September 15, 1970, at the eight-year school in Salininkai, one schoolgirl wrote down entirely contrary ideas during an atheistic writing exercise in class. Although there were no mistakes, the principal gave the girl a failing grade.

In February, 1972, at the secondary school in Klaipė-da, the following conversation took place between a teacher and N., a schoolgirl in class 7:

"I'm ashamed that you're a good student and still not a Pioneer."

"But I'm not ashamed at all."

"Why do you want to be different from the whole class?"

"I don't want to pretend. I want to be the way I really am."

The teacher spent the entire class explaining about the Young Pioneers organization. Concluding, she said:

"There is such an organization. If you're told to join, you join without any deliberations."

When girl members of the Pioneers wanted to forcibly tie a necktie around her neck, the schoolgirl would not give in: "My neck is my own to do with as I please."

In 1971 one girl's letter was published in *Lietuvos pionierius* [Lithuanian Pioneer]. She wrote: "I myself am a Pioneer, but I donned the Pioneer's necktie only because my homeroom teacher insisted . . . I attend church. And not because my grandmother, grandfather, or parents make me, but willingly. Like nearly all the other students of our class, I go to communion. I am firmly convinced that God exists."

In the Klaipėda Medical School, the director of the Klaipėda Theater, B. Juškevičius, gave the atheistic lectures in 1969. To obtain credit for these, several philosophical questions had to be answered in writing. The instructor of atheism became very upset when he found the following thoughts in one girl's essay:

"It is asserted that the various religions originated out of human helplessness and ignorance, but this is untrue. The origin of religion is much grander ... Scientists discover the most varied principles, and does this not compell one to consider who created these principles? Man discovers only that which God has already created long ago. Man is more than just a hunk of meat and a pile of bones. Man has an immortal soul. Christ really existed. The years are counted from His birth ... If everyone was a true and firm Catholic, how ideal and beautiful life would be—like paradise. No army, no police, no prisons would be needed, whereas now ... I think that the Catholic religion is the only true religion. I have thought so for a long time but became even more firmly convinced during these lectures..."

Lately, the desire among students to defend their convictions and not to submit to coercion is becoming ever more apparent. Believing students find their chief support in their religious parents.

N., a girl at the secondary school in Kapsukas publicly professed her faith in class. The teacher told her to bring her father. The latter courageously defended his daughter:

"Is it possible that you want a person to sell his convictions for a mess of porridge?"

One mother from the parish in Karklėnai discovered that her children would have to perform in a play and sing during Lent. The resolute mother went to see the principal and declared she would not permit her children to act and sing during Lent.

"You're only concerned about somehow pushing a child through a class, but I'm concerned about the child's entire life and eternity. I don't want my children to be hooligans."

At a parish in Samogitia one set of parents found out that their children were learning some sort of atheistic play after returning from school. The next day the mother visited the principal and declared:

"My children will not act in something that is against God. If you force them to act, they won't come to school tomorrow!"

The children did not have to perform in the atheistic play.

One mother wrote to the editors of *Lietuvos pionierius* [Lithuanian Pioneer]: "Why is it that now, when there is so much scientific enlightenment, people no longer see the greatest light—God? I pity those mothers who do not teach their children to know God. As for myself, I truly believe in God and want my children to believe too. It seems to me that if I were ever to hear my children saying that God in unnecessary—I'd rather they died now."

The atheists call the parents who defend their children's faith fanatics. In reality a fanatic is one who hates those who think otherwise than he. Does not the present persecution of believing students arise from fanaticism?

In the course of the past few years parents have even begun to collectively defend the children who are persecuted for their faith. One may mention the following collective complaints by parents: the petition of October 10, 1971, by parents from the parish in Valkininkai to their *rayon* administration (see the *Chronicle of the Catholic Church in Lithuania*, no. 2); the petition of August, 1971, by parents of the parish in Simnas to the government of the USSR; the petition of February, 1972, by parents from the parish in Lukšiai to the Procurator of the LSSR (see the *Chronicle of the Catholic Church in Lithuania*, no. 2); the petition of April 20, 1972, by parents from the parish in Adutiškis to Leonid Brezhnev (see the *Chronicle of the Catholic Church in Lithuania*, no. 4). All these collective complaints cite cases of persecution against students and demand that the situation be corrected. The collective declarations demonstrate the growing consciousness of the

Catholics and that, in the future, parents will defend their children more and more energetically against all who violate their freedom of conscience.

THE ARCHDIOCESE OF VILNIUS

CEIKINIAI

On September 5, 1972, the faithful of the parish in Ceikiniai, which is in Ignalina *Rayon*, sent to Leonid Brezhnev, the General-Secretary of the Central Committee of the CPSU, the following petition:

"It is very regrettable that we must appeal as high as to Moscow for such a trifle as the repair of a church storehouse. This trifle reminds us of a whole series of other painful matters which we would like to forget.

"Near the churchyard in Ceikiniai stand a decrepit parochial woodshed and a dilapidated storehouse. In their place we would like to build one orderly storehouse. We requested a repair permit in the beginning of 1971. After many trips and appeals, Vaitonis, the vice-chairman of the *rayon* Executive Committee, stated on May 27, 1971, that if we wanted to obtain a repair permit for this storehouse, we would have to apply to Vilnius to the commissioner of the Council for Religious Affairs. We went there. The commissioner again referred us back to the *rayon* office. And there is no end to it—nearly two years have now passed. We made numerous trips ourselves, desiring to obtain a permit for these alterations, and *rayon* officials visited us a number of times. The vice-chairman of the *rayon* Executive Committee came to see us with an interrogator, also the chief of the financial department, the police, the *rayon* architect (as many as four times), and, on several occasions, the locality's chairman and the secretary of the Party ... The documents concerning the materials purchased for the repairs were inspected as many as three times —as if they were capable of multiplying themselves.

"On June 30, 1971, we wrote to the Council of Ministers of the LSSR. Finally, on August 30, 1971, the *rayon*

Executive Committee gave us permission to repair this building. One noted builder from the *rayon* advised us to buy a house from people who had to move from their farmstead because of land-reclamation work and transport it here to be used as the storehouse. We did not want to ruin the timber, so we began to construct a storehouse that was 80 cm. wider but considerably shorter. In addition, we shifted the storehouse one meter away from the churchyard toward the garden.

"For this reason, on July 21 of this year the *rayon* authorities ordered us to tear down the structure we had begun to build. Even our appeal to the commissioner of the Council for Religious Affairs was to no avail. We were accused of building illegally.

"In a rural area at some distance from the road, is it really that important whether this structure will be 80 cm. wider or narrower? Apparently the cause is not to be found here. The people have a saying: 'He who wants to strike will find a cane.' In this case the violation of building regulations is merely a pretext. On June 30, 1972, the Executive Committee of our religious community was summoned to the *rayon* office. There the commissioner of the Council for Religious Affairs told us: *'Banish the children from the altar so they wouldn't assist at mass, so they wouldn't scatter flowers in processions; see to it that priests who come from elsewhere would not assist in the church—then we'll allow you to repair the storehouse.'*

"But does the Mass really have any connection with the repair of a storehouse?

"In 1965 the *rayon* administration pulled down a cross in Ceikiniai that was dear to us, arguing that it supposedly interferred with traffic. Now shrubbery grows and an electric power line pole stands in place of the cross.

"On December 2, 1966, we were fined 59.76 rubles for 'violating' the environmental protection laws by chopping down in our cemetery some rotten birch trees, which were threatening to fall over and smash some grave markers. Are rotten birch trees also included among the objects under protection? If so, why do the responsible agencies let them fall over and rot completely? Where is the logic? The reason is clear: we are believers.

"We have written many times in regard to similar wrongs.

"On May 10, 1964, and on March 16, 1965, we wrote to the commissioner of the Council for Religious Affairs.

"On December 19, 1966, and on April 16, 1967, we wrote to the chairman of the Council of Ministers of the LSSR.

"On March 25, 1968, we asked the commissioner of the Council for Religious Affairs to indicate which laws or decrees prohibit children from serving mass. He has not indicated any as yet.

"On March 3, 1969, we wrote to the Ministry of Public Education.

"On May 30, 1971, on December 9, 1971, and on June 20, 1972, we wrote to the commissioner of the Council for Religious Affairs.

"On June 30, 1971, and on July 27, 1972, we wrote to the Council of Ministers of the LSSR.

"We also appealed many times to the *rayon* administration.

"On June 24, 1968, the commissioner of the Council for Religious Affairs called in the parochial committee and told them not to write any more petitions. But he who feels pain complains.

"On June 30, 1971, we enumerated the following troubles of ours to the Council of Ministers of the LSSR:

"1. Since 1940 not once has the sacrament of Confirmation been administered in our church, that was why we requested that Bishop Steponavičius be permitted to come to Ceikiniai at least once to administer the rite of Confirmation.

"2. For a long time the *rayon* administration did not allow us to install electricity in our church. In 1965, the vice-chairman of the *rayon* Executive Committee said: 'Six old ladies will light up the place with candles, and you

won't need electricity.' And last year, the *rayon* administration cut off the three-phase electric current so that it
would not power the organ, supposedly because electricity
had to be conserved. But we use so little in the church—in
1970 the total was only 457 kw.

"3. Collective volunteer help is often organized in our
country: the volunteers come from the city, other villages,
even from other Republics. But we are forbidden to call
even neighboring priests to our assistance. When on March
14, 1965, we appealed to the commissioner of the Council
for Religious Affairs regarding this matter, he rebuked us
angrily: 'You're men, and yet you concern yourselves with
church affairs! Aren't you ashamed of yourselves?'

"On June 8, 1966, before the Feast of St. Anthony,
[Mrs.] Gudukienė, the chairman of the *rayon* Executive
Committee, who did not even accept our petition, treated
us similarly.

"4. On May 7, 1967, Jadzevičius, the head of the *rayon*
education department, arrived and called our pastor out
of the church, interfering with the services, and questioning him as to why the priest from Švenčionys was assisting
here without permission.

"5. In 1966 [Mrs.] Šiaudinienė, a teacher at the Ceikiniai school, punished Martinkėnas, a sixth-class student,
by ordering him to wash the classroom floor for a whole
month because he would park his bicycle near the churchyard.

"6. On December 9, 1968, P. Juršėnas, a student at the
Ceikiniai school who had died in an accident, was buried
in Ceikiniai with religious burial rites. The funeral took
place after classes, yet the students were purposely not allowed to leave the school. Even his classmates could not
accompany the deceased to the cemetery in a funeral procession.

"7. On April 16, 1964, the head of the Ignalina Education Department together with other individuals called
B. Laugalis, a student at the secondary school in Ignalina,
out of class and threatened him because he was living with

the priest of Ceikiniai; they promised to give him a poor character reference: 'You won't get into any schools'; they threatened to expel him from school and ordered him to sign a statement against the priest, saying: 'We'll take care of him.' Scarcely had he turned sixteen, when the Ignalina police took away his birth certificate and fined our pastor because the student was living with him without registering and without a passport. But how could he have obtained a passport if the police had not returned his birth certificate?

"Similar things also happen to other students if they attend church and do not join the Young Communist League. In 1971 a Ceikiniai resident, an eleventh-class student at the secondary school in Ignalina stated the following when pressured to join the League: 'We are free to either join or not join the Young Communist League. Besides, I don't see any good examples in the Young Communist League. League members Ručenko and Dervinis are even sitting in jail for their activities. That's why I won't join.' On another occasion the secretary of the League, Šuminas, shut the same youth in a room and stamping his foot angrily on the floor demanded that he 'obey his elders.'

"8. On the evening of April 5, 1971, while driving the pastor of Daugėliškis an Ignalina taxi also carried several students from Ignalina Secondary School No. 1. This was noticed by Jadzevičius, the head of the education department. It seemed to him a 'great crime' that the children were travelling together with a priest. Immediately he threw everybody into an uproar. He forced the children to write 'explanations' at the school. That was not enough. So that he would be able to acuse the priest, after reading those papers the principal himself ordered the students to 'correct' them by writing in untrue facts; namely, he told the students to write that they had returned home after 10 p.m., although in fact they had returned at about 9 p.m.

"9. At the end of May, 1971, in Ceikiniai, while the teacher [Mrs.] Daukšienė dictated, [Miss] Rakštelytė, a fourth-class student, wrote down a 'declaration' stating that the pastor of Ceikiniai was preparing children for their First Communion. Then the teacher frightened some little children (R. Miklaševičius, Z. Maskoliūnas) into copying that note and signing it. The parents of the students went to the school and demanded: 'We must know what our children are being forced to write.' No one even showed the parents those papers.

"10. On May 31, 1971, we drove to Vilnius to see the commissioner of the Council for Religious Affairs and asked him to refer the matter of the storehouse to the *rayon* architects for a decision. Unfortunately, we gained nothing by this. We are amazed that nonspecialists interfere in and direct the work of highly-skilled specialists. It would appear that vice-chairmen of *rayon* executive committees and commissioners of the Council for Religious Affairs are electrical engineers, architects, artists, and finally, the chief sacristans who administer all matters connected with the church and pressure the faithful.

"11. When we started to repair the church's leaking roof, a *rayon* representative arrived on June 22, 1971, and began questioning us whether we have a permit and where we were able to buy the materials. He badgered the workers, interfering with their work. One volunteer was even made to stop working because... his wife was a teacher.

"12. The Feast of St. Peter is one of the most important of our religious feasts, during which a Solemn High Mass is celebrated. This has been approved by all government agencies. On the morning of June 29, 1971, however, the chairman of the Ceikiniai Collective Farm, incensed that the pastor was saying mass in church, began to defame him before the collective-farm workers, calling him a bandit who should be shot or turned over to the secret police, and so on.

" A girl member of the Young Communist League recounted how once the wife of the chairman of the collective farm was collecting signatures for some sort of declaration accusing our pastor. 'All kinds of nonsense was written there,' she candidly explained. 'I didn't sign it. N.N. didn't sign it either.' But, of course, there will always be those who will sign even under untrue things to curry favor with their superiors.

"During 1971 certain students from Ceikiniai who were studying at the secondary school in Ignalina were called out of class even during their lessons regarding such declarations, grilled, and forced to confirm by their signatures such charges directed against the pastor, about which they had not even heard anything.

"These matters, which are set forth in our June 30, 1971, note to the Council of Ministers of the LSSR are recurring in many places.

"Therefore, we request that all these wrongs be abolished.

Ceikiniai
August, 1972

"As we were writing this petition, on August 11, 1972, *rayon* authorities informed us through the Ceikiniai Locality office of its written decision of July 21 to demolish the storehouse we had begun to construct. After signing that he had been informed of such a decision, the chairman of our parochial committee added this remark: 'Until a final decision arrives from Vilnius or even Moscow, please do not hurry to execute this decision.'

"On August 14 of this year, we sent another separate memorandum regarding this question to the *rayon* administration: 'Since this is a disputable question, we are appealing to higher authorities and ask you not to hurry with the execution of your decision until we have received a reply from the higher authorities.'

"On August 24 of this year (while everyone was still asleep), two policemen arrived with eight men at approximately 4:30 a.m. and, with the chairman of the Ceikiniai Collective Farm participating, demolished the structure we had been repairing. They broke and sawed up the timbers and even dug up the entire foundation with some kind of machine. Now the place looks as if there has been a bombardment—one cannot even walk through it. What is the purpose of this senseless destruction of the people's labor and property? Does such action increase the Soviet government's authority in the eyes of the people?

"It seems as if the *rayon* Executive Committee has been granted supreme authority, and there is no point in appealing to higher levels of government. For instance, when we went to Vilnius to see the commissioner of the Council for Religious Affairs with our complaints on March 14, 1965, he referred us to the *rayon* administration: 'Everything will be taken care of over there.' Afterward, Vaitonis, the vice-chairman of the *rayon* Executive Committee, told us: 'Well then, did you gain much in Vilnius? I'm not changing my mind.'

"Our petition of 1971 addressed to the Council of Ministers of the LSSR, which was also referred to the *rayon* Executive Committee, bore no fruit.

"On September 5 of this year, the commissioner of the Council for Religious Affairs informed us: 'Regarding your petition addressed to the Council of Ministers of the LSSR and referred to us, we are informing you that the question of constructing the storehouse must be settled in conformity with the procedure set down by the laws.'

"But does the *rayon* administration itself observe the laws which guarantee all citizens equal rights and freedom of conscience?

"Therefore we, hundreds of the faithful, are appealing to Moscow.

"We are enclosing three photographs of the buildings under repairs and after demolition.

"A reply may be sent to: Juozas Maldžius, Didžiasalis Village, Post Office of Ceikiniai, Ignalina *Rayon*, the LSSR."

This petition was signed by 1,709 believers.

Four months after this petition was mailed to Moscow, on December 29, 1972, the vice-chairman of the Ignalina Executive Committee, Vaitonis, summoned J. Maldžius, in whose name the petition of the believers from the parish in Ceikiniai was sent to Moscow. At the Executive Committee's office, four officials of the civil administration questioned the seventy-four-year-old man for over two hours, asking who had written the petition, scolding, and even threatening him with prison. Finally, they said: "Your declaration to Moscow didn't do any good. The church buildings are ours. We only let you use them. Withdraw the children from the altar, and then we'll permit you to repair the storehouse."

NAUJOJI VILNIA
In accordance with the order of October 15, 1972, given by Lauraitis, chief of the Interrogation Office of the Ministry of the Interior, Vytautas Lažinskas was brought to the Naujoji Vilnia psychoneurological hospital.

On the night of July 21, 1972, he had erected a metal cross that was five-and-a-half meters high near Klaipėda Road on the outskirts of Ariogala. Government officials pulled down the cross the next day and the "offender" was interrogated.

The court's psychiatric commission headed by Glauberzonas determined that V. Lažinskas was lucid and of a good disposition except for a slightly weakened memory, that his intellect corresponded to his education and experience in life, that he showed no deviations of a physical or neurological nature.

The court's psychiatric commission pronounced V. Lažinskas to be suffering from paranoid psychopathy since *he does not admit to having committed a crime and had recounted "systematized delirious ideas of a religious nature"*; thus, he was irresponsible and in need of medical treatment in a psychiatric hospital.

VILNIUS
As 1972 was ending, the Vaga Publishing House put out a two-volume edition of the writings of Bishop Motiejus Valančius.

Literary works are published in large editions of from 10,000 to 30,000 copies; however, there was a "shortage"

214 THE CHRONICLE / 5

of paper for the writings of Bishop Valančius, which are permeated with religious ideas—scarcely 5,000 copies were printed. Most Lithuanian bookstores did not receive this two-volume work at all.

Every book of better quality is immediately sold out, particularly if it contains religious or national ideas, whereas the "classics" of Marxism and atheistic literature lie on bookstore shelves for years on end.

THE ARCHDIOCESE OF KAUNAS

GIRKALNIS

On Nov. 10, 1972, at about 3 p.m. the Rev. Prosperas Bubnys was released from the Kaunas strict-regime prison camp after having been sentenced a year ago for teaching children the tenets of their faith. Priests and a group of believers greeted the prisoner. Some members of the prison administration were even able to see a scene unusual for this place—a bouquet of roses in the hands of the priest-prisoner.

On November 15 the choristers of Girkalnis organized a reception for Father Bubnys. The choir sang during mass, and the church was full of people even though the faithful had not been informed of the reception in advance. Everyone felt that the year spent in the camp was not just a victory for Father Bubnys alone, but for the entire Church in Lithuania.

The Raseiniai *Rayon* administration declared to Father Bubnys that it had no claims upon him and would not prevent him from performing his priestly duties.

After a few months had passed, Father Bubnys was appointed pastor at the parish in Lygumai.

KAUNAS

On December 12, 1972, H.E. Bishop J. Labukas sent to the clergy of the Kaunas Archdiocese and the Vilkaviškis Diocese a circular which stated: "We direct you to take the Blessed Sacrament into the sacristy and place it in a suitably prepared place for the night in those churches where there are no night watchmen. "No Church vessels are to be left in church at night. They must be kept in the sacristy or, it would be even better, if they were to be kept in the rectory." The circular appeared in connection with increased burglaries of churches and desecrations of the Blessed Sacrament.

JUODAIČIAI

The Rev. V. Pesliakas, pastor of the parish in Juodaičiai, underwent medical treatment in June, 1972. When he returned home, he learned that the Raseiniai *Rayon* administration had been searching for him since the middle of June, demanding that he pick up his registration certificate and assume the duties of curate in Viduklė as soon as possible. H.E. Bishop Labukas explained to him that Rugienis had demanded his transfer to Viduklė, and H.E. Bishop Krikščiūnas told him: "You did your work well, but you should realize that Bishop Labukas will not leave two dioceses and travel to Žagarė on your account." (Žagarė is the residence of the exiled Bishop Steponavičius—ed.)

H.E. Bishop Labukas directed Father Pesliakas to assume the duties of curate of Viduklė or be suspended: "If you don't start work as the curate of the church in Viduklė by September 20, 1972, inclusive, you will be *ipso facto suspensus a divinis.*" (The performance of priestly duties will be prohibited—ed.)

Realizing that the bishop was transferring him to Viduklė and demoting his position only because of pressure by Rugienis, Father Pesliakas refused to go to his new assignment.

On September 26, 1972, three officials from Raseiniai came to Juodaičiai Locality and declared to the executive body of the Church: "Your pastor is disobeying the bishop. He is being removed from his position..."

The aforementioned fact surprised all the people very

much—how greatly the civil authorities were interferring in the internal affairs of the Church.

In his memorandum of Oct. 10, the Rev. V. Pesliakas wrote to the bishop: "Taking into consideration the cited facts and the common opinion of a majority of the clergy, I am firmly convinced and truly regretful that someone forced Your Excellency into writing such letters on my account. For this reason, I consider them false and void." H.E. Bishop Labukas lifted the suspension, and the Rev. Pesliakas went away for medical treatment.

In December Father Pesliakas was appointed to the church in Viduklė as a retired priest.

THE DIOCESE OF TELŠIAI

PALANGA

During the postwar years, the members of the Astrauskas family were exiled to Siberia, where they suffered for eleven years. After returning to Lithuania, they found their homestead destroyed and their parents dead. As 1971 was ending, they erected a monument for them in the Palanga Cemetery. Next to their parents' grave the Astrauskases reserved two places for themselves, inscribing on the monument their birth dates. A talented artist designed the expensive monument. The monument failed to please only the Palanga city administration since its design reminded them of their deeds: the artistic bronze statue of Christ which had been overturned in the city park by a tractor and handed over to a scrap heap, the two destroyed statues of Mary on the Hill of Birutė, etc. On the Astrauskases' monument were depicted broken crosses and a Lithuanian girl with clasped hands praying: *"Save us, O Lord!"*

Sofija Astrauskienė was informed in writing that according to a decision reached on April 13, 1972, by the Palanga Executive Committee, the Municipal Works Department was charged with demolishing the monument. The woman appealed to the Palanga Executive Committee, to the police, but she was told there that the monument was designed improperly, that the words "Save us, O Lord" had to be struck off, that her and her husband's inscriptions had to be eliminated. Astrauskienė disagreed:

"The proper place for a monument without the name of God is only beside a tavern and not in a cemetery. I am a Catholic. I live and will die with the name of the Lord. If you're atheists and don't believe in God, why do you fear His name?"

"That inscription is anti-Soviet," the officials upbraided her. "All you would have to add is: 'Save us, Lord, from the Communists!' Change the inscription, or we'll tear down the monument!"

Astrauskienė wrote a complaint to the Council of Ministers of the LSSR, which referred it to the Ministry of Communal Farms, but the latter remained silent. The Council of Ministers of the LSSR replied negatively to a repeated complaint. Then Astrauskienė appealed to the Council of Ministers of the USSR but obtained from them merely a postal receipt, to the effect that the complaint had been received.

On October 11 Astrauskienė learned that government officials had gone to the cemetery to demolish her monument. When she arrived at the cemetery, she found there officials from the Palanga Executive Committee and many policemen and security agents. Workers had been brought here forcibly from construction sites and ordered to tear down the monument. Many of the younger workers resisted:

"We won't do this kind of work—tear it down yourselves!"

"If you won't tear it down, we'll dismiss you from work," threatened one official.

"We'll find a better job," retorted the workers and began to disperse.

Astrauskienė resolved to defend the monument. She stepped in front of it declaring: "As long as I'm alive you won't tear it down. Shoot me first."

"You're under arrest. Get away from the monument!"

Four secret policemen forcibly dragged Astrauskienė away from the monument, shoved her into a police car, striking her head severely in the process, and took her away to their headquarters, where Astrauskienė fainted. Only after a physician pronounced Astrauskienė to be in poor health, did the police allow her to return home. The monument was pulled down using a tractor and taken away.

THE DIOCESE OF PANEVĖŽYS

SALOČIAI

In December of 1972, Stapulionis, the vice-chairman of the Pasvalys *Rayon* Executive Committee, visited Saločiai. Failing to find the pastor at home, he himself began "taking charge" in the church and removed explanations about the season of Advent from the bulletin board.

Later, he rebuked Father Balaišis, pastor of Saločiai, for supposedly alarming people by predicting the end of the world to be at the end of this century. The explanation about Advent which Stapulionis stole from the bulletin board had mentioned that the second coming of Christ would be at the end of the world.

Stapulionis ordered the pastor of Saločiai not to accompany the deceased to the cemetery in a funeral procession.

KRINČINAS

On January 5, 1973, Stapulionis, the vice-chairman of the Pasvalys *Rayon* Executive Committee, summoned Father Raščius, pastor of the parish in Krinčinas, and indicated to him the following:

1. Priests are forbidden to accompany the deceased to the cemetery in a funeral procession since this interferes with traffic. The cemetery is 400 meters away from the church.

2. Participation in a church procession while wearing the national costume is prohibited, since nationalism is

thus allegedly propagated within the Church.
3. Priests are strictly forbidden to collect contributions in church.
"You priests pounce upon money like dogs!" shouted Stapulionis hysterically.

THE DIOCESE OF VILKAVIŠKIS

ĄŽUOLŲ BŪDA

In the summer of 1972, a girl helped the parishioners of Ąžuolų Būda prepare children for their First Communion. On August 3 this girl was apprehended by the principal of the secondary school in Ąžuolų Būda and the secretary of the Party organization of the Šviesa [Light] Collective Farm and turned over to the secret police in Kapsukas.

After being interrogated, the "offender" was handed over to the school authorities for "re-education." It is unclear how this "re-education" is being accomplished.

PRIENAI

On January 8, 1973, the Rev. J. Zdebskis was summoned to Prienai police headquarters, from where he was transported under police guard to an outpatient clinic for a medical examination to determine if he were capable of physical labor.

On January 26, 1973, Father Zdebskis was presented with a strict warning to find some kind of work within fifteen days other than priestly duties, for otherwise he would be provided with work at the discretion of the police.

The civil authorities permitted Father Zdebskis to carry out his priestly duties only in the Telšiai Diocese. What was this ruling based on since Father Zdebskis has not been sentenced to exile by a civil court? Church laws do not include banishments; besides which, Father Zdebskis has not violated any Church laws. According to Church law, he belongs to the Vilkaviškis Diocese and is under no obligation to work in another diocese.

THE DIOCESE OF KAIŠIADORYS

NEMANIŪNAI

On May 15, 1972, K. Černeckis, the vice-chairman of the Prienai *Rayon* Executive Committee, warned the Rev. J. Matulaitis, pastor of Nemaniūnai, that he was not observing Soviet laws and forced him to sign the following warning: "It is known that in the parish church of Nemaniūnai children and adolescents assist in religious rites. This is a violation of Soviet laws. We are warning you not to involve children and adolescents in religious rites.

"In addition, you leave your parish without a permit and perform religious rites in churches of other parishes. We are warning you that this must not happen again."

A lecturer from Prienai came to the school in Nemaniūnai to "enlighten" the students on atheistic topics. The children were warned not to participate in processions. The more timid vanished from the processions, but the others continue to attend church diligently and participate in religious rites.

* * *

ANNOUNCEMENTS

The *Chronicle of the Catholic Church in Lithuania* thanks everyone who helped collect material about the situation of the persecuted Church in 1972, and asks for even more diligent help in the future.

The *Chronicle of the Catholic Church in Lithuania* needs the assistance of all conscientious Catholics in order to acquaint many people with the true situation of the Church.

The *Chronicle of the Catholic Church in Lithuania* has been published since March 19, 1972.

no.6

- Complaints are signed by 14,284 and 16,498 believers; texts and aftermath
- Atheistic indoctrination and forcible ethnic assimilation of students
- Official Soviet instructions concerning the compiling of data on Catholicism in Lithuania
- State security organs take an interest in typewriters
- The new edition of the New Testament appears
- Tumėnas replaces Rugienis as commissioner of the Council for Religious Affairs
- List of Lithuanians from Vilnius who were interrogated by the secret police in 1973
- Atheistic public debates on love, friendship, and the family
- Priests are being denied access to dying hospital patients
- Inspection of churches by the commissioner of the Council for Religious Affairs or his representatives
- Some data on the clerical situation in Lithuania
- Arrests in Kaunas
- Students are made to answer a religious questionnaire
- Father Zdebskis is appointed pastor of a parish near the border
- Churches are burglarized
- Believers in Lankeliškiai petition Leonid Brezhnev
- Teachers threaten students not to attend church

THE CHRONICLE
OF THE CATHOLIC CHURCH
IN LITHUANIA

No. 6   May, 1973

COMPLAINTS SIGNED BY 14,284 AND 16,498 BELIEVERS

In mid-May, 1973, the believers of Lithuania sent to the Presidium of the Supreme Soviet of the USSR a complaint and two petitions which had been signed by thousands of believers. These petitions originated because discrimination against believers has not ceased.

How the Signatures Were Collected

The texts of these petitions passed from hand to hand, spreading throughout Lithuania. On each sheet that the believers were to sign was the complete text of the petition with which the signers were to familiarize themselves. There were very many persons who, motivated by a profound faith and grievously affected by the restrictions imposed on the rights of their homeland and the Church, *devoted much time and effort until they collected a total of 30,782 signatures.* All this had to be done in their spare time at the constant risk of falling into the hands of the security police. Someone who has never solicited signatures under our conditions will never understand how much heroism and self-sacrifice was exhibited by those who collected the signatures.

How did believers react when asked to sign? Many signed enthusiastically, without hesitation, particularly if they were certain of the character of the one collecting signatures. When the collector was an unknown person, many found themselves wondering whether this might prove to be a provocation by the government, and whether the Church and the faithful would be harmed thereby. Because of such fears, some parents did not permit their children to sign the petition.

It was evident that it would be careless to collect signatures near the churches, thus almost all the signatures were collected in the homes of believers. The gathering of signatures took about one-and-a-half months. A number of sheets with the petition fell into the hands of dubious persons who, either through dishonesty or evil intent, ruined them, and thus some of the signatures had to be deleted.

The organs of state security quickly became aware that signatures were being gathered and began to hunt down the collectors. In Kaunas a search was conducted at the home of [Miss] V. Grincevičiūtė, since someone had informed that she had collected signatures. She was summoned for interrogation several times. The interrogators were mainly interested in learning who was organizing the collecting of signatures.

Within the parish in Kapčiamiestis, in Lazdijai *Rayon*, security agents were looking for a certain woman who, according to their information, had been gathering signatures. They apparently did not succeed in apprehending her.

The secret police of Panevėžys confiscated the sheets containing the petitions and signatures from [Mrs.] Rudienė, a resident of Steponiškis Village. The woman was interrogated as to where she had obtained the texts of the petitions and also threatened with the loss of her parental rights.

Certain priests in Ignalina *Rayon* were interrogated because someone had informed the secret police that signatures were being collected.

Tumėnas, the commissioner of the Council for Religious Affairs, ordered Lithuania's bishops and ecclesiastical administrators to persuade the clergy through their deans that priests would not only not take part but even hinder the gathering of signatures near churches.

In many places in Lithuania, for instance, in Klaipėda, Kapsukas, and elsewhere, government officials warned local pastors that signatures must not be collected.

After such reaction by the secret police, the question naturally arose: what is the sense of sending petitions with signatures to Soviet agencies? Is it solely to enable them, once the signatures are in their posession, to interrogate the signers, threatening them with dismissal from work, from school, and similarly? Aside from that, once the signatures are in their hands, the security workers could then slander the believers by insisting that the signatures were forged, that so many thousands had not actually signed, etc.

Some people wonder whether it would not be better instead of appealing to agencies of the Soviet government to attempt to break through the Iron Curtain and direct our appeal to the conscience of the entire world.

* * *

The complete texts of the complaint and the two petitions by the believers of Lithuania are presented below:

"To: Presidium of the Supreme Soviet of the USSR
"Copy: K. Tumėnas, Commissioner of the Council
for Religious Affairs

A Complaint by the Believers of Lithuania

"In the decree handed down on April 12, 1968, by the Presidium of the Supreme Soviet of the USSR, 'Concerning the Procedure for Examining Suggestions, Petitions, and Complaints by Citizens,' it is written: 'Under the present developmental conditions of Soviet society, complaints are usually the form through which a response is made to instances of violation of citizens' rights and those of their interests which are protected by law... They also demonstrate that serious shortcomings still exist in the functioning of many state and public agencies.'

"V. Kuroyedov, chairman of the Council for Religious Affairs, has written: 'It is necessary to be especially responsive to complaints by believers that their rights are being violated. All complaints must be examined and settled in strict compliance with the April 12, 1968, decree of the USSR Presidium of the Supreme Soviet' (*Religija ir įstatymas* [Religion and the law], 1971, p. 24).

"In early March, 1973, it occurred to us, the faithful of Lithuania, to appeal to the Soviet governmental agencies in Lithuania requesting that the discrimination of religious students would be stopped, that they would not be compelled to speak and act against their convictions, that history would be taught objectively in the schools, and that the publication of the most essential religious literature would not be restricted. In order that the Soviet authorities would know the opinion of Lithuania's believers, signatures were collected under the complaints addressed to the LSSR Ministry of Public Education and to K. Tumėnas, the commissioner of the Council for Religious Affairs. If the Soviet press were to be believed, all those who inform governmental organs about existing evils and demand their elimination are strengthening social justice, participating in the governing of the state, and are decent people worthy of respect (cf. *Švyturys* [Beacon], 1973, no. 6, pp. 8-10).

"However, scarcely had officials of the state security organs learned about the collection of signatures when a 'witch hunt' was begun: searches of innocent people's homes, interrogations, and threats of imprisonment. This is how the secret police of Vilnius, Kaunas, Panevėžys, Lazdijai, Ignalina, and other places acted. K. Tumėnas, the commissioner of the Council for Religious Affairs, ordered the bishops and ecclesiastical administrators of Lithuania to make use of the deans and the clergy to disrupt the collection of signatures. The secret police managed to confiscate some of the signed sheets.

"Despite this 'responsiveness to the believers' complaints,' 14,284 believers signed the petition addressed to the LSSR Ministry of Public Education and 16,498 believers signed the petition addressed to the commissioner of the Council for Religious Affairs.

"Since officials of the state security organs regarded the believers' appeals to the Soviet government as a political offence and are terrorizing those who collect signatures, we have refrained from sending the original petitions bearing the signatures to the above-mentioned establishments. This will be done only when the faithful will become convinced of the good will of the Soviet government and when officials from the state security organs will cease to interfere in the religious affairs of the faithful.

"The Presidium of the Supreme Soviet of the USSR has expressed the desire for expressions of opinion regarding a draft of the principles governing the laws concerning public education, which was proposed by the USSR Council of Ministers in early April. This draft completely disregards the rights of believing parents and their children. It is contrary to Article 5 of the December 14-15, 1960, Paris Convention Against Discrimination in the Field of Education, which requires that parents be guaranteed 'a religious and moral upbringing of their children in accordance with their convictions.' The petition we believers have sent to the LSSR Ministry of Public Education will adequately acquaint the Soviet authorities with the kind of education and upbringing for children of religious parents that is desired in Lithuania.

"Enclosures: The text of the petition addressed to the LSSR Ministry of Public Education; the text of the petition addressed to K. Tumėnas, the commissioner of the Council for Religious Affairs.

May 14, 1973"

"To: Ministry of Public Education of the LSSR

*A Petition from the Students of Lithuania
and Their Parents*

"We, students and parents, who fully comprehend the purpose of the school and its obligations to the younger generation, are often disillusioned because students are not provided with what is truly necessary.

"In the textbook *Visuomenės mokslas* [Social Science] it is written: 'Patriotism is one of the best manifestations of human nature... It finds expression in love for the land in which we were born and raised, in love for its history...' How can students learn about the past of Lithuania if J. Jurginis' *Lietuvos TSR istorija* [History of the LSSR] is too brief—barely 100 pages—and biased, and [Miss] A. Gaigalaitė's *Lietuvos TSR istorija* (148 pp.) tells only about the revolutionary movement and the postwar years? On the other hand, the *TSRS istorija* [History of the USSR] is composed of four parts—a total of 650 pages. Thus, although students know much about Pugachiev, Peter I, and others, they know almost nothing about the honorable past of Lithuania.

"The greatest evil is the attempt to foist atheism upon students. It is said that in the Soviet Union religion is the private affair of every citizen, that the USSR Constitution guarantees everyone the freedom of conscience, but practical experience says otherwise.

"At times, religious students are ridiculed and upbraided for practicing their religion; their caricatures 'adorn' newsletters on school bulletin boards. Medallions and crucifixes are taken away from students. Sometimes teachers even make believing students leave the church, for example, during funeral services.

"Religious students are compelled to speak and write against their convictions and to draw antireligious caricatures. Those who refuse to be hypocrites are given the grade 2 or 1 [failing grades—tr.].

"Teachers force religious students to join atheistic groups and organizations, and consequently, many are encouraged to become hypocrites.

"Some of the teachers turn their lessons into atheistic propaganda. Atheism is even propagated both within the school and beyond its walls by utilizing deception, for instance, by demonstrating 'miracles,' by deriding and consciously distorting the Catholic faith.

"Occasionally the conduct grade is lowered to 'satis-factory' solely because of church attendance. The convic-tions of believing students are noted in their school records, thus making it more difficult for them to enroll in schools of higher education.

"Students must frequently fill out questionnaires with questions touching upon their religious convictions. It is incomprehensible to us why there is such forcible encroach-ment upon their consciences. Not wanting to reveal their convictions, a number of students answer these questions hypocritically. Who benefits from this?

"We have mentioned only certain instances of coercion against a student's conscience, but they lead us to think that Soviet schools are primarily concerned, not with teach-ing or educating, but with atheistic indoctrination. This sort of 'educating' undermines the school's authority and causes students irreparable harm.

"We have tired of such forcible atheistic indoctrina-tion, and this has provoked a reaction—to turn our backs upon ideas being foisted upon us. Why is this happening in our schools when the USSR Constitution proclaims that there is freedom of conscience?

"Therefore we ask the Ministry of Public Education to put an end to these harmful occurences in the schools so that no one would hinder students from enjoying the freedom of conscience.

March, 1973"
14,284 signatures

N.B. Approximately twenty-five percent of the signa-tures were those of students.

"To: K. Tumėnas, Commissioner of the Council
for Religious Affairs

A Petition from the Believers of Lithuania

"We have read the statement by Bishop R. Krikščiūnas in the March 1, 1973, issue of *Gimtasis krastas* [Native land]:

" 'The Catholics in Lithuania publish any books they need. Recently we printed *Romos Katalikų Apeigynas Lietuvos Vyskupijoms* [Book of Roman Catholic rituals for the Dioceses of Lithuania], *Maldynas* [Book of Prayers], *II Vatikano Susirinkimo Nutarimai* [Decisions of the second Vatican Council], and other books. Here, still smelling of printer's ink, is a very significant publication—*Šventojo Rašto Naujasis Testamentas* [New Testament].'

"We believers also felt the desire to obtain this New Testament. Unfortunately, our local priests explained to us that they had received only from a few to a dozen copies —about one book for every 300 believers...

"If the Catholics in Lithuania publish any books they need, then why have they not published in the postwar years the most essential book, the catechism? Why were only 10,000 copies of the New Testament published? Why have we not seen with our own eyes the book on the decisions of the Second Vatican Council? Why couldn't we obtain the *Maldynas*, even though every Catholic must have a prayer book? As if this were not enough, why is it that although we are unable to obtain copies of the New Testament, we have heard that someone has been sending thousands of copies to Lithuanians abroad? Are we going to have to ask our relatives abroad to send us the New Testament which was printed in Lithuania?

"Since it has become evident to us that religious books are published in very small editions, not by the Catholics, but by the Soviet government at the Bishop's request with you, Commissioner, as a go-between, we therefore ask you to see to it that the New Testament and the *Maldynas* are reprinted in order that there would be enough so that each Catholic family could obtain at least one copy. In addition, we request permission for the publication of a comprehensive catechism. Otherwise, it will be difficult for us to believe in any talk concerning the publishing of the most essential Catholic books in Soviet Lithuania.

March, 1973"

16,498 signatures

(to be continued)

ATHEISTIC INDOCTRINATION AND FORCIBLE ETHNIC ASSIMILATION OF RELIGIOUS STUDENTS

A Survey of Soviet Propaganda During January-April, 1973

In recent times, the Communist party has become especially interested in the education of school children and academic youth. The pages of the press are aglitter with articles urging more concern for the fostering of a materialistic world view among the youth and their indoctrination with the principles of "Soviet patriotism" and "proletarian internationalism."

1. Negation and belittlement of Lithuania's past

"During lessons dealing with the history of the LSSR, anything through which in one way or another is expressed the idealization of reactionary manifestations of the past must be resolutely eliminated. In explaining historical events that occurred in Lithuania, concrete examples must be used to prove that the true creator of history was the populace and not the grand dukes, those representatives of the exploiting class" (*Tarybinė Mokykla* [The Soviet school], 1971, no. 3).

A. Sniečkus, First Secretary of the Central Committee of the Lithuanian Communist party, spoke as follows at the March meeting of the Republic's Party activists: "There is cause for concern in that during studies of the historical past there is at times the tendency to succumb to its idealization of sorts... For instance, instead of investigating present-day subjects, certain workers at the ethnography department of the Institute of History began to analyze nearly exclusively the problems of the past... Publishing houses shoud also evaluate their work critically. Occasionally in their undertakings obvious concessions could be noted toward the exaggerated, usually artificial fascination of certain individuals with the days of yore..."

Tiesa [Truth] demanded obstinately: "It is absolutely necessary to fight against each occurrence of the tendency to idealize the past" (March 27, 1973). *Lietuvos TSR istorija* [History of the LSSR] by J. Jurginis and V. Merkis, which comprises barely 105 pages and also distorts many Lithuanian historical facts, was criticized in *Tiesa* because it had raised too few "ideological questions" and because "in the textbook the class viewpoint of historical events is sometimes overwhelmed by secondary matters" (March 10, 1973).

2. "Patriotic" and "internationalist" education of students

The Soviet press is particularly concerned about fostering the spirit of "internationalism" among students. "In the entire educative system, first place within the complex of the means useful in influencing ideology is occupied by Soviet patriotism and socialist internationalism" (*Tarybinis mokytojas* [The Soviet teacher], March 21, 1973).

What, in fact, is this "patriotism" and "internationalism" mentioned in Soviet propaganda?

A. Snieckus stated at the meeting of Party activists that "the ties between Lithuanians and Russians in the schools are being strengthened *through the languages being taught*" (emphasis ours—ed.).

"A very important means in trying to instill in students the spirit of friendship is to have them *study the Russian language*. All the nations and nationalities of the USSR consider Russian their second native tongue.... the study of Russian fosters the students' love and respect for this language, and develops the sentiments of Soviet patriotism, internationalism and friendship among nations. Hence, the need arises to constantly keep perfecting the instruction of Russian. (*Tarybinė mokykla* [The Soviet school], 1973, no. 3).

Tarybinis mokytojas [The Soviet teacher] praised S. Lokit, the principal of the secondary school in Kalesninkai, and the Russian language instructors L. Supron and V. Voitkun for making special efforts and using all possible means to instill the love of the *Russian language* in students (February 14, 1973). For this purpose, Russian-language concerts of revolutionary songs are organized in this school and Russian works are committed to memory, etc.

Military training *in Russian* has been established in all schools. Its purpose is the fostering of "patriotism" in students. "With great devotion the schools' military advisors are instilling feelings of patriotism in our youth" (ibid., March 21, 1973).

3. Atheistic education of students

Speaking at the meeting of Party activists, A. Sniečkus demanded an intensification of efforts in the atheistic cause: "We cannot reconcile ourselves with the fact that individual Party organizations have recently noticeably decreased their efforts in the atheistic cause. Our times demand not only comprehensive but also constant and profound atheistic propaganda."

Tiesa urged that "all Communists, all members of the Young Communist League, and all intellectuals would work for the atheistic cause" (March 4, 1973).

Why has so much attention been devoted lately to atheistic propaganda?

Doctoral candidate in philosophy I. Galickaya indicates that handwritten religious literature is being disseminated among the youth, that priests discuss religious topics with young people and visit their parents, that the youth has an excessive interest in the early days of the Church, and that they collect holy cards and crosses (In her article "Jaunimas ir religija" [Youth and religion] published in various newspapers of the Republic).

In *Tarybinis mokytojas* it was printed that: "The clergy is becoming increasingly active among the believers. . . . they organize the preparation of children for catechization, for assisting at church services during religious festivals, and they even make a practice of joint excursions of children with parents. . ."

To the question of why a struggle against religion must be waged in Lithuania, A. Sniečkus was perhaps the one who answered the most truthfully: "Religious superstitions very often are closely associated with nationalist prejudices. Recently, the obscurants have even attempted to depict church traditions as being nationalist."

New tasks are being assigned to atheistic propaganda:

a. To conduct sociological studies about man's religiosity and its causes (*Tiesa* [Truth], March 4, 1973).

b. To work individually with each believing student (*Tarybinis mokytojas* [The Soviet teacher], March 30, 1973).

c. To convince parents that they should not interfere with the atheistic indoctrination of youth (ibid.).

The petition from Lithuania's believing parents and children to the Ministry of Public Education of the LSSR appeared as a response to this intensified atheistic indoctrination and attempted ethnic assimilation of students.

INSTRUCTIONS FOR SOVIET AGENCIES
(for official use)

"Concerning Data under the Heading 'Catholicism in Lithuania and the Present'

"The Procedure for Collecting Information:

"Data for the above subject are to be collected for scientific purposes in order to become better acquainted with the dynamics of present-day Catholicism as well as of other confessions. The data are to be collected in a composite manner by investigating the following: the clergy's sermonizing and other forms of pastoral work, the role played in the religious community by those who are the most active within the church and their influence on the activities of the ministers of the cult, the material basis (churches, appurtenances of the cult, choirs, etc.) of religious propaganda; and by observing how the cult is modernized.

"*Sermonizing:*

"To be selected for listening to sermons are those active atheists who have sufficient education. Without participating in the religious rites, yet behaving in a civilized manner, the atheist is to listen attentively to sermons and subsequently reconstruct their contents without adding anything on his own. The description of the sermon must include the following data: (a) the location at which the sermon was delivered (*rayon*, church), the time (date, hour), the name and surname of the preacher and where he is from; (b) the contents of the sermon. The gospel is to be briefly recounted. The contents of the sermon are to be reconstructed in detail, as completely and accurately as possible by strict adherence to the principle of objectivity. It is absolutely impermissible to insert one's own comments or conclusions into the contents of the sermon. After the contents of the sermon are described, one's observations, comments, and conclusions may be presented and designated as 'remarks'; (c) the form of the sermon: whether it was read from notes or an outline was used or whether he spoke without notes and without an outline; the duration of the sermon; the consistency of the stated ideas; other means used by the preacher to influence the believers.

"How many believers participated in the services (including men, women, youths, school-age children) must be specified in the remarks. Also to be indicated is who assisted in the services (adults or children). The religious rites are to be described and their solemnity and emotionalism (organ, choir, orchestra, soloists, etc.); the extent of the participation by believers (whether they sing hymns, pray from prayer books, make responses to the priest, and similarly); and who collected the contributions made during the services (whether a clergyman or one of the more active members of the church).

"*Other Pastoral Work of Clergymen*:

a) *The clergyman and the believers*. Is the clergyman active in pastoral work? If so, how is this activity expressed? Does he differentiate his activity according to separate groups of believers (men, women, youths, children)? Does he comply with Soviet laws concerning religious cults? If not, concrete instances of violations of the law should be specified. What pecularities are present in this clergyman's pastoral work? What do the believers think of their clergyman?

b) *The clergyman and children*. Does the clergyman attempt to make the religious parents feel more responsible for the religious upbringing of their children? If so, then by what means? How are the children of believing parents prepared for catechization and the sacrament of confirmation?

c) *The clergyman's existence and his personal life*. What are the clergyman's relations with the local intellectuals? Describe the cultural life of the clergyman (television, radio, telephone, the newspapers he subscribes, the books he reads, his outings to the theater, concerts, etc.).

"*The Most Active Members of the Church*:

"The basic demographic data must be specified for the religious community's "council of twenty," its executive body, the members of the auditing commission, and those who participate in the church choir: *sex*—men, women; *age*—18 to 25, 26 to 30, etc.; *education*—primary, whether completed or not; secondary, whether completed or not; higher, whether completed or not, etc.; *social position*—blue-collar worker, collective-farm worker, white-collar worker, pensioner, or homemaker; *occupation*: the duties of able-bodied active church members in production collectives are to be specified; *participation of the most active church members in public life*: the most active church members who participate actively in public life—amateur cultural activities, political clubs, etc.—are to be pointed out.

"In addition, the relationship of the most active church members with the pastor and other clergymen must be described. Does the executive committee of the religious community and the auditing commission make use of the rights granted them by Soviet laws concerning religious cults? Or has the pastor usurped these rights? What is the role of the unorganized active church members (devout little old ladies and existing nuns) in the parish.

"The Material Basis of the Religious Community:

a) *The house of worship.* The condition of the exterior and the surroundings (the churchyard) of the house of worship must be described (whether it is in good repair or not, whether the churchyard is neat or not, whether there are flower beds, rock gardens, etc.). The interior of the house of worship is to be described (whether it has been painted, decorated, electrified, and whether it has a public-address system, etc.). Perhaps there are features of modernism in the arrangement and decoration of the church interior?

b) *Appurtenances of the cult.* The bells and their use; liturgical vestments, their condition (whether orderly and clean, or worn and neglected); the attributes of religious processions (baldachins, lanterns, portable altars, banners, and others; their condition).

"The believers' opinion regarding modernization of the cult:

"What do believers think of the introduction of their native language into the services? What do they think of the shortening of the time for fasting before receiving communion to one hour? What do they think of other liturgical innovations?"

TYPEWRITER TYPEFACE SAMPLES
ARE REQUESTED

Early in 1973, some of the *rayon* and city executive committees demanded all offices, farms, and organizations, as well as religious communities, to send them typeface samples from all their typewriters. Here is an example:

"Please send to the Executive Committee by March 22 of this year typeface samples from the typewriters to be found in the office (plant, farm, or organization) under your management and from those possessed by private individuals. Two original copies of the enclosed text are to be typed on a standard sheet of paper.

"In addition, please inform us of any other typewriters in your possession whose typeface samples you are unable to send us because they have broken down or are undergoing repairs, or for other reasons."

When the typeface samples are sent, the serial number and brand name of the typewriter must be specified.

It is clear to everyone that the typeface samples are needed by the secret police. Why have the state security organs taken an interest in typewriters?

Over the past few years the Catholics of Lithuania have sent many complaints to various governmental agencies. It must not be forgotten that every complaint to Soviet governmental agencies in regard to restrictions of religious freedom is considered slander and an "ideological diversion." That is why the state security organs want to ascertain just who has been inspiring and organizing this "anti-Soviet" action.

Aside from that, in Lithuania typewriters are used to produce multiple copies of religious literature, which is then used by people of varied professions. In this manner Soviet citizens are being "harmed"... It must be assumed that the secret police want to ascertain just how multiple copies of this literature are being produced and especially— to intimidate everyone.

These efforts by officials of state security organs to control even private typewriters is reminiscent of the Stalinist period when all typewriters had to be registered with governmental agencies.

THE ARCHDIOCESE OF VILNIUS

VILNIUS

As 1972 was ending, approximately 10,000 copies of the Bible—the New Testament—were printed. In February, 1973, priests were able to obtain them from the curias. Pastors of smaller parishes received only a few copies. Larger parishes received ten to twenty copies. It is said that an average-sized parish received ten copies. Two copies of the New Testament were allotted to each parish church, two to each priest, and as for the rest, the pastor had the right to distribute them at his own discretion among the more active Catholics. On the average, each Catholic was entitled to one page of the New Testament!

People say that when the New Testament was being printed at the Vaizdas Printing House, workers for the project were selected only from Party members. Despite their "loyalty" to the authorities, a substantial number of copies of the New Testament disappeared from the printing house.

When the New Testament came out, certain atheists in Vilnius, pretending to be Catholics, attempted to buy it from the pastors so that as few of them as possible would be left for believers.

Some Catholics were happy with the New Testament, others criticized the translation, and still others said: "We won one ruble's worth but lost ten rubles' worth." After all, such a limited edition of the New Testament will be of little practical use, but the Soviet government will utilize it for propaganda purposes—see what freedom of the press there is in Soviet Lithuania!

The Central Committee of the Lithuanian Communist party took a great number (we lack exact information) of copies of the New Testament. For propaganda reasons, many New Testament books were sent to Lithuanians abroad, to dignitaries of the Catholic Church, and others. Many copies of the New Testament went to non-Catholic Christians, and several hundred were reserved for the theological seminary.

Speaking at a plenary election meeting of the committee for cultural ties between Lithuania and Lithuanians abroad, H.E. Bishop R. Krikščiūnas explained that "Catholics in Lithuania publish any religious books they need... Here, still smelling of printer's ink, is a very significant publication—*Šventojo Rašto Naujasis Testamentas* [New Testament]. The Bishop's statement produced the following reaction by Catholics: "We have no religious books!" That was how the petition from Lithuania's Catholics to K. Tumėnas, the commissioner of the Council for Religious Affairs originated.

Numerous letters from various corners of Lithuania began to pour into the Books by Mail Bookstore, requesting, "Send us the New Testament." Unfortunately, everyone received a negative reply.

VILNIUS

In February, 1973, K. Tumėnas replaced J. Rugienis as commissioner of the Council for Religious Affairs.

J. Rugienis, a long-time KGB worker, had frequently behaved like a Chekist in carrying out his duties as commissioner: he abused, rebuked, and intimidated priests.

Kazimieras Tumėnas is a Party worker, a doctoral candidate in the field of history, who completed the Social Science Academy in Moscow in 1964 and subsequently headed the lecturers' group of the Central Committee of the Lithuanian Communist party.

This change bodes no good for the Church in Lithuania. It seems as though K. Tumėnas will be more tactful; however, like Rugienis, he will continue to work for the destruction of the Church.

VILNIUS

In 1973, the following Lithuanians were interrogated by the Vilnius secret police:

1. Andrašiūnaitė, [Miss] Birutė, engineer (March 28)
2. Božytė, [Miss] Marytė, fourth-year student of Lithuanian studies at Vilnius State University (March 28)
3. Burauskaitė, [Miss] Birutė, engineer (April 2)
4. Eigminas, Kazimieras, a graduate of Lithuanian language studies at Vilnius State University (April 6)
5. Eimaitytė, [Miss] Elena, a graduate of German language studies (March 27)
6. Jakučionytė, [Miss] Rėda, engineer (March 28)
7. Jakučiūnas, Zenonas, a graduate of the music conservatory
8. Janulevičiūtė, [Miss] Veronika, a member of the Ethnographic Ensemble of the Young People's Theater (March 28)
9. Jasukaitytė-Ašmontienė, [Mrs.] Virginija, student of Lithuanian studies at Vilnius State University
10. Juška, Alfonsas, biophysicist (March 27-28)
11. Kanevičiūtė, [Miss] Donatė, mathematician (April 3)
12. Kaukėnas, Danas, correspondent for *Vakarinės naujienos* [Evening news] (April 4)
13. Labanauskas, Kęstutis, employee of the Landmark Restoration Institute (March 28)
14. Matulis, Rimas, a graduate of English language studies (March 28)
15. Misius, Kazimieras, engineer (March 27)
16. Norvaišas, Egidijus, postgraduate student in physics (March 27)
17. Petrauskas, Algimantas, engineer (March 28)
18. Povilaitytė, [Miss] Teresė, a graduate of Lithuanian language studies (March 28)
19. Ramonas, Alfonsas, physicist-mathematician (March 27)
20. Simokaitis, Albinas, instructor at the sanatorium for contagious diseases
21. Stankevičius, Edma, journalism student
22. Trinkūnas, Jonas, postgraduate student in history-philosophy (March 28)
23. Vanagaite, [Miss] Zita (April 3)

The KGB questioned them about excursions to the Ural Mountains and Siberia. Why had they associated with Lithuanian exiles during the excursions? Why had former prison camps been visited? The interrogators charged them with trying to establish ties with nationalist elements among the Armenians, Georgians, and other nationalities during excursions to the Caucasus Mountains.

Those being interrogated were reproached because during excursions to the Sambija region of East Prussia they had taken an interest in and called attention to the destruction of cultural monuments from the past and had burned candles on fortress mounds.

The secret police showed an interest in the Folk Song Club at the Trade-Union Hall; in Romuva, the Vilnius State University students' club which had been disbanded two years ago; in summer expeditions; in the Rasa Festival at Kernavė; in the archeological expedition to the Šventoji River.

The persons being interrogated were rebuked for taking an interest in the past and in idealizing it, for by such means nationalist sentiments are disseminated. "Why are only Lithuanian songs being sung? Why are songs of freedom fighters sung? Why is information being collected about the struggle that had been waged by the freedom fighters? Why are nationalist sentiments being propagated at meetings with Latvians? Why is there cameraderie with Byelorussian Lithuanians? Why are books taken to them, newspaper subscriptions presented to them? Why are their children urged to attend Lithuanian schools in Lithuania?"

The secret police wanted to know by what means large numbers of youths are attracted to programs presented by ethnographers.

R. Matulis was ordered to sign a statement that he would not organize or participate in any gatherings if they did not conform to the policies of official agencies.

VILNIUS
Toward the end of March, 1973, the LSSR Landmark Preservation and Ethnography Society held in Vilnius its

fourth convention, which summarized the etnographers' activities. V. Uogintas, chairman of the society's council, stated that "at every step of his work each ethnographer must follow Marxist-Leninist methodology and its class criteria," that "it is essential to struggle against any encountered tendencies of idealizing the past" and against "demonstrations of nationalism." Particular attention should be devoted to the preservation, care, and popularization of monuments honoring labor, the revolutionary and partisan movements, and the battles fought by the Soviet Army.

"By gathering ethnographic data that is not all-inclusive but only that which savors of the past, we turn away willy-nilly from the most pressing problems of life. . . The ethnographers' immediate task is to record everything that concerns today's worker and what the Soviet government has granted him," spoke J. Jarmalavičius, the chairman of the society's Vilnius city chapter.

[Miss] L. Diržinskaitė, vice-chairman of the LSSR Council of Ministers, requested that our ethnographers collect data on the participants of the revolutionary movement and that they concern themselves with the nurturing of man in a Communist society (*Tiesa* [Truth], March 27, 1973).

VILNIUS

As 1972 was ending, two public debates on the topics of love, friendship, and the family were held at the Museum of Atheism. Prof. K. Daukša stated that love is an animalistic, transitory feeling, that there can be no families who are faithful. What is important, is that the other half does not find out, but if it does, it should be forgiving. The professor admitted having been in love half-a-dozen times in his life. . .

The participants of the debate put many questions to the professor:

"Is it normal for young people to start a sexual life before marriage?"

"Is sexuality normal? It is normal! So what kind of question is this?" replied the professor.

"What is your opinion of a girl's virginity?"

"It's an obsolete religious custom. A man who seeks a virgin for a wife is an egoist."

"Professor, perhaps you are in favor of free love?"

"There is freedom in a Soviet country: you may live in legal wedlock, or you may simply reach a mutual understanding to love one another."

"Then perhaps you are in favor of houses of prostitution?"

"There could be such, only their form would perhaps be different—socialist."

A voice from the hall: "Free of charge!"

"Professor, you have turned everything into banalities: art, poetry, love. Then what's the purpose of life?"

"Purpose? Who knows? There's an inclination to live —so we live, and when this inclination weakens, we hang, poison, drown, or shoot ourselves. Whoever overly ponders the meaning of life will end up in a psychiatric hospital. . ."

To more than one of those present at the debate occurred the question: on whose initiative was prof. Daukša trying to demoralize the capital city's youth? Perhaps atheists no longer believe they can turn youth away from God without first undermining their morality?

VILNIUS

At the beginning of February, 1973, the movie theaters of Vilnius began to show the historical motion picture *Herkus Mantas*, which portrays the struggle Prussians waged against the knights of the Teutonic Order in the thirteenth century. The film is atheistically biased. The film-makers were not as concerned about historical truth as they were about propaganda. Herkus Mantas, the main character in the film, reasons using our atheists' concepts. Even *Tiesa* [Truth], in its review of this film emphasized that "religious fanaticism is somewhat overdone in the film" (February 22, 1973). Even though a great tribute to atheistic propaganda was paid by this film, it aroused nationalist sentiments in its viewers.

DRUSKININKAI

When Novikas became the chief physician at the city hospital, priests were forbidden to set foot inside in order to administer religious rites to dying or critically ill patients. In mid-April of 1973, a patient named Petras Kalinauskas, who was ill with cancer, requested that a priest be called for him. When the patient's wife went to ask for permission, Novikas, the chief physician, berated and ridiculed her and then drove her out of his office. The dean of Druskininkai had appealed to the commissioner of the Council for Religious Affairs and to Kleiza, the minister of Public Health, regarding such interference in ministering to the religious needs of the sick. Although these dignitaries had assured him that no such prohibitions are allowed, as we have seen, at the hospital in Druskininkai the situation has not changed.

VARĖNA

The wooden columns in the vestibule of the church in Varėna should have been repaired long ago so the parochial committee decided to replace them with new ones. This matter was discussed with a Varėna architect and several artists, oaken timbers were obtained, and work was begun, but in April, 1973, the vice-chairman of the *rayon* executive committee ordered all work to cease.

In the summer of 1972, the rotting roof of the Varėna church had been undergoing repairs. The roofer, who was a Party member, was ordered by the authorities to abandon this work.

In 1972, the Varėna Parochial Committee had requested executive committee Vice-Chairman J. Visockis for permission to hook up to the town's waterworks to obtain water for the flowers in the churchyard. The vice-chairman did not grant them permission, explaining that there was a shortage of water. Later, water was obtained from the railroad station. The sanitary engineer, who was a Party member, was rebuked for installing the water supply system.

IGNALINA

In 1973, after the commissioner of the Council for Religious Affairs was replaced by K. Tumènas, the churches in Ignalina *Rayon* were inspected on April 2-8 by either the commissioner himself or his representatives, together with functionaries from the *rayon* executive committee. They examined the church interior, its altars, organ, electrical wiring, liturgical vessels, vestments; they scrupulously checked the account books and electric meters; and they asked questions. Who kept the money collected by the church? How did the parochial committees get along with the pastors? Do children serve mass? Wherever children did serve, they rebuked the parochial committee chairmen and ordered them not to allow children near the altar. When they visited the schools, they questioned certain students about priests and about the children's relations with the Church.

Most likely they were carrying out the instructions issued to Soviet agencies concerning the gathering of all possible information about the Catholic Church in Lithuania (cf. pp. 233-36).

VALKININKAI

On February 16, 1971, the Valkininkai Parochial Committee informed the locality office about the need to supplement the parish council of twenty, for several members had died or resigned. The locality office informed the *rayon* administration about this note, and the latter demanded that the letters of resignation of the members who had resigned be sent to them, otherwise forms on which all committee members would have to be listed would be sent out. After the *rayon* administration received the letters of resignation, it summoned the chairman of the Valkininkai Parochial Committee and the chairman of the auditing commission and demanded that new committee members be elected. During the elections, *rayon* representatives would be required to participate. The committee members were astonished, since new members had been elected long ago, and the *rayon* administration had been informed of this through the locality office. Why must the parochial committee be re-elected? Why must a government representative be present during this election? After all, the Soviet government "does not interfere" in the internal affairs of the Church!

KABELIAI

In the school records of some students who were graduating from the Kabeliai eight-year school remarks were added to the effect that that they are believers and attend church or are children of believing parents or that "their education was influenced by factors external to the school."

One Saturday in November, 1970, a resident of Kabeliai Village named Adolfas Galčius, a pensioner, was repairing the fence around the church. Jonas Kazlauskas, the manager of the State farm, drove him away saying, "I don't want to see you near the church again!"

CEIKINIAI

On April 13, 1973, a retreat and a religious festival were being held at the parish church in Ceikiniai. Near the church doors a certain elderly lady was selling rosaries, medallions, crucifixes, and photographic holy cards. A policeman with two officials from the executive committee, who arrived from Ignalina, took away the old woman's merchandise and wanted to apprehend her, but she quickly slipped into the church, which was full of people. The police did not dare to search for the old lady inside the church so they waited several hours for her outside, but in vain, for the old woman had walked out unnoticed.

THE ARCHDIOCESE OF KAUNAS

KAUNAS

On April 17, 1973, H.E. Bishop Labukas ordained five fourth-year theology students at the Cathedral-Basilica in Kaunas. The ordination of one seminarian was postponed because of illness.

We present some data on the situation of the clergy in Lithuania:

In 1962 the authorities permitted five candidates to enroll into the seminary; in 1963—five; in 1964—four; in 1965—five; in 1966—eight; in 1967—seven.

Year	Died	Number of admissions allowed	Ordained
1968	19	6	6
1969	15	10	3
1970	18	10	8
1971	12	10	4
1972	19	10	6

This is why several parishes in Lithuania are left without a priest each year.

KAUNAS

At the end of March, 1973, four persons were arrested in Kaunas:

1. Povilonis, Vidmantas, engineer
2. Sakalauskas, Antanas, instructor at the Civil Engineering Department of the Polytechnical Institute
3. Žukauskas, Šarūnas, sixth-year student at the Medical Institute
4. Rudaitis, physician.

In mid-April Juozas Rugys was arrested. Type was found during the search.

Viktoras Kruminis, a fourth-year student at the Polytechnical Institute, was expelled from the Institute.

The mother of V. Povilonis appealed to the secretary of the Central Committee of the Lithuanian Communist party requesting the release of her son. The LSSR Procurator's Office informed her that V. Povilonis had been arrested and was being prosecuted for committing an especially grievous offense. He had allegedly belonged to a group anti-Soviet in nature and in February, 1972, had distributed anti-Soviet proclamations in Kaunas.

KAUNAS

With the approach of the 1973 Easter holiday, it was announced in the schools of Kaunas that on April 22 would be held a Communist bee. The students rebelled. They offered to work on other days, only not during Easter. In some schools this bee was moved to an earlier date, but in others—

On April 20, 1973, [Mrs.] Stanionienė, a teacher at Kaunas Eight-Year School No. 2, threatened the children: "Don't any of you go to church on Easter Sunday because policemen will be standing there and will arrest all of you." One girl answered: "I'll go to church with my mommy and daddy—they'll protect me from the police!"

On Easter morning, 1973, a Leninist bee was organized in the schoolyard at the A. Mickevičius Secondary School in Kaunas. The children were forced to dig in the school's garden and to clean up the area around the school. Believers coming back from Resurrection services, tried to shame the teacher: "Aren't you ashamed of forcing children to work on such a day? If you don't respect our holydays, then at least honor your Lenin. After all, today is his birthday."

At Secondary School No. 25, not one pupil from the eighth class showed up at the Communist bee on Easter.

In the showcase at the Young Communist League School No. 1, an announcement was displayed for an entire week to the effect that a bee was scheduled for Sunday, April 22. When teachers and students objected, the bee was moved up to Holy Saturday.

Flowers were not taken to the Lenin Monument from Eight-year School No. 2 on April 22 since very few students showed up.

At Salomėja Nėris School, the teachers who had dismissed students early from the bee were rebuked by the principal.

When it was announced at Secondary School No. 12 that a bee was to be held on April 22, the upperclassmen said they would not come; thus only students of classes five to seven had to "assist" during Easter. In some classes teachers threatened the children that those who would not come to the bee would be turned over to the authorities, that they would receive Unsatisfactory as their conduct grade, etc. Those who did not participate in the bee on Easter Day had to bring written explanations from their parents. The teachers tried to excuse themselves by saying that the order to organize the bee on April 22 had come from higher up.

At Secondary School No. 30 teachers and students objected to the bee that was being organized for Easter Day. The principal explained that the order had come from the Department of Public Education. At first she threatened to "deal with" recalcitrant students, and when this failed to help matters, she asked them in a friendly way to show up at the bee. A remark was entered in students' daily journals to the effect that the son or daughter had to be present at the bee on Sunday. Those who did not take part in the bee had to present written explanations, and their parents were asked to come and explain why they had not let their children participate in the bee.

Stašaitis, the inspector of the Panemunė District Department of Public Education, retorted to those teachers who had suggested changing the date for the Communist bee: "What? Are we going to accommodate ourselves to their holidays? Let them accommodate themselves to ours."

The committee of the Kaunas city Party organization sent pedagogues-spies to observe the students who came to church on Easter and to record the sermons of the priests. The observers had to make written reports.

This tactless organizing of a Communist bee during Easter once again demonstrated how powerless atheists are and made the students reflect on the values of ideas which are urged upon them in such a manner.

KAUNAS

As the first anniversary of the tragic death of Romas Kalanta neared, uneasiness could be felt in Kaunas. The streets are full of policemen and civil patrolmen. Security officials are constantly on guard at the city park. Students have been ordered not to be seen on the avenue Laisvės Alėja on May 14. Plans are afoot to send a number of students out of Kaunas during the anniversary.

KAUNAS

On December 19, 1972, a parents' meeting was called at Kaunas Secondary School No. 12. A lecturer from the Polytechnical Institute presented an atheistic lecture in which he rebuked parents for teaching religion to their children. Unable to bear the tactlessness of the lecturer, some parents declared out loud that the lecturer should stop lying and speaking nonsense. A commotion arose in the hall. The lecturer continued to speak, saying that some parents hold backward views and are incapable of raising their children properly. He praised the children who "come to their senses" and consider their parents ignorant and mistaken. A storm of indignation arose in the hall.

"Who gave the school administrators the right to set children against their parents?" asked one father.

"I don't believe in God, but I was filled with disgust upon hearing a speech like that," spoke one mother.

The lecturer continued to "enlighten" the parents, telling them that husbands find it impossible to live with believing wives, and wives, with believing husbands. Once again a great uproar arose in the hall. Principal V. Kamaitis could endure this no longer and suggested that anyone who did not like what he was hearing could leave. When the commotion would not subside, the "enlighteners" had to depart from the hall. As the principal was leaving, he declared that in the future he would continue his all-out efforts to turn the students into atheists. If he found it impossible to re-educate some of the students, then he would note in their school records that they were atheistically unenlightened.

In this school the students are "enlightened" in other ways also, for instance, Mačys, the art teacher, gave his students the assignment to draw something antireligious, such as priests blessing soldiers going off to Vietnam or collecting contributions from pensioners, etc. During his next lesson with these students, he gave nearly all those students who had not drawn something illustrating this topic a failing grade, but a prize was promised for the "best" drawings.

During a lecture to sixth-class students [Miss] M. Babeckaitė, a teacher, recounted that Christ was a legendary person and that in the past priests used to frighten children by threatening them that God might pull out their tongues through the top of their heads if they would not obey the priest.

Here are the results of the upbringing provided by the secondary school headed by Principal V. Kamaitis: a pregnant eighth-class schoolgirl was expelled from school. In that same year, one evening in November after classes, the parents themselves discovered an entire group of sixth-class students—boys and girls—behaving indecently in the art room. Similar instances are nothing new in this school.

Parents are greatly concerned and wonder whether such teachers should be entrusted with the education of their children.

VIDUKLĖ

The Rev. V. Pesliakas received a reply from one bishop to his letter which had been sent to H.E. Bishop J. Labukas and several other bishops.

This reply is presented here, but the bishop's name will not be publicized:

"Dear Father Vytautas,

"I received a copy of your declaration to Bishop J. Labukas on October 10 of this year. I am convinced that you, as an exemplary priest and faithful son of the Church, are not reproaching your Bishop or expressing your disobedience to him with this declaration but are only seeking to elucidate the distressing situation of our bishops, ecclesiastical administrators, priests, and the faithful because of the flagrant interference by governmental organs, namely by Rugienis, the commissioner of the Council for Religious Affairs, in the internal life of the Church in our country and into its administrative matters.

"In his articles and statements, which of course are mostly intended for foreign countries, the commissioner of the Council for Religious Affairs attempts to portray himself as an innocent lambkin. According to him, the hierarchy of the Church handles the clerical appointments, and he does not interfere in this at all.

"Your case is new and supplementary proof that all such statements by him are only propagandistic lies and hypocrisy.

"By whose will, if not Rugienis' was Father Šeškevičius, who worked in the Kaišiadorys Diocese, banished to the Telšiai Diocese? Father Juozas Zdebskis of the Vilkaviškis Diocese is also being banished to the Telšiai Diocese, not because the bishops will it, but due to Comrade Rugienis' ominous ruling that he would not be permitted to work anywhere else.

"It will be interesting to see how Comrade Rugienis will try to justify himself in his desire to cover up his brazen interference in the internal matters of the Church now that the facts of Fathers Šeškevičius' and Zdebskis' banishment are evident and Bishop Labukas has clearly affirmed that 'Rugienis demanded that you be removed from your duties and appointed to Vidukle.' Bishop Krikščiūnas has also confirmed this: 'You do your work well, but you should realize that Bishop Labukas will not leave two dioceses and travel to Žagarė on your account.'

"Dear Father Vytautas, it can be argued whether you should or should not have written this declaration, but I think it serves the cause of the Church at least insofar as it reveals the unjustifiable interference of government organs in the internal life of the Church. These things are very painful for us all, and especially for you since they affect you personally. But let us not lose heart. Let us continue to hope the time will come when they themselves will realize that in this manner they are harming themselves and thus deign to normalize their relationship with the Church, as has happened in Poland, Hungary, and in other socialist countries.

"I pray for you. I wish you spiritual perseverance, strength, and every possible grace from the Lord.

November 2, 1972"

THE DIOCESE OF TELŠIAI

TAURAGĖ

On April 18, 1973, the Tauragė *Rayon* procurator summoned [Miss] Agota Savickaitė, the church vestment launderess, and confronted her with the following accusations: that she catechizes, that she dresses girls for processions, that she even distributes churchly veils out on the street and invites people in to worship. "If this continues in the future, we'll see that you're provided with governmental bread for the rest of your life," threatened the procurator, and he forced her to sign a pledge that she would reform.

VAITIMĖNAI

On April 14, 1973, the English-language instructor at the Vaitimėnai eight-year school summoned all the students to a meeting. Although she had said she would tell them about spring work in the fields, nevertheless, when the students had gathered, she began to speak against God and the faith. After she finished speaking, she told students to raise their hands if they attend church. All the students raised their hands except for the forester's daughters. The atheistic teacher flushed and was at a loss for words, but one student spoke up: "Your God is Lenin—go to Moscow, but we have been going to church and will continue to go."

KLAIPĖDA

On December 24, 1972, when the eleventh-class students at Klaipėda Secondary School No. 4 were forced to come to class in the daytime on Christmas Eve (a Sunday), each one of them placed a little Christmas tree on his desk. Learning about this, the school administration ordered the Christmas trees to be removed immediately. The students were upbraided and called ignorant and backward. After the administrators had left, the students again pulled out the little Christmas trees from their desks and, as they were leaving for home, asked their friends from the second shift not to touch them.

KRETINGA

In February, 1973, in the parish of Kretinga one J. Daukša died. The children of the deceased decided to bury their devout father with Catholic ceremonies, however, Kecorius, his son-in-law, head of the Kretinga education department, wanted an atheistic funeral and denounced his own relatives to the Kretinga city authorities. Summoning the pastor of the parish in Kretinga, the Party committee forbade him to participate in the funeral procession to the cemetery.

THE DIOCESE OF PANEVĖŽYS

N. RADVILIŠKIS

On March 27, 1973, Kalkys, chairman of the Auksinė Varpa Collective Farm, summoned N. Radviliškis Parochial Committee Chairman Petras Šimukėnas, and commanded him to take two other parochial committeemen and go to see H.E. Bishop Sladkevičius, who presently lives in exile in N. Radviliškis, and accuse him of preaching sermons against the authorities, of passing information abroad, of catechizing children, and of administering the sacrament of confirmation. The chairman even threatened Šimukėnas that if he would not carry out this order, he would not be provided any pasture for his animals.

THE DIOCESE OF VILKAVIŠKIS

PRIENAI

In February, 1973, students at the Prienai eight-year school had to answer the following questions:

1. For what do you hold a person in high regard (for his diligence, truthfulness, fairness, friendliness, collectivism, his appearance, for being well-read, for his abilities, his religiousness)?

2. How do you regard adults who attend church (favorably, unfavorably, have not thought about it)?

3. How do you regard students who attend church (favorably, unfavorably, have not thought about it)?

4. Do you agree with the opinion of believers that prayer and faith make one a better person (agree, disagree, don't know)?

5. Some students' parents urge their children to attend church. How do you regard such parents' behavior (favorably, unfavorably, have not thought about it)?

6. It is asserted in school that prayer and faith in God contradict scientific facts. What is your opinion (agree, agree in part, disagree)?

7. Are religious holy days observed by your family (yes, no, sometimes)?

8. Are there pictures of saints in your apartment (yes, no)?

9. Does your family make the sign of the cross before and after meals (yes, no)?

10. Does your family pray (yes, no, sometimes)?

11.Do you eat blessed wafers on Christmas Eve (yes, no)?

12. Does a priest visit your home (yes, no)?

13. Do you believe that God, angels, and devils exist (yes, no, doubt it)?

14. When did you last attend church (5, 4, 3, 2, 1 years ago; recently)?

15. Did you receive your First Communion [yes, no]?

16. Who prepared you for First Communion and confirmation (family members, elderly women from the neighborhood, servants of the church, priests)?

17. Do you like discussions and books on atheistic topics (yes, no, have not come across such questions)?

18. The Church commands you not to do anything

bad and to honor your parents, therefore it is not harmful (agree, disagree, don't know)?

19. Laws of nature are inviolable; therefore, there can be no miracles (agree, disagree, don't know)?

20. Do your parents believe in God (believe, do not believe, are skeptical)?

21. Why do you attend church (out of conviction, parental encouragement, interest)?

After underlining the appropriate answer, students had to write down their surname and hand in the questionnaire to the teacher who had dictated the questions.

Students answer questions on such questionnaires in various ways: some write what they think, but others do not dare write the truth and answer hypocritically.

Why are religious questionnaires necessary? They are "sociological research" carried out in order to ascertain students' convictions. If the majority of students profess belief in God, atheistic propaganda is intensified at the school.

PRIENAI

On February 9, 1973, at the Prienai eight-year school, a parents' meeting was held to which was invited Radionovas, the chief of the Prienai *Rayon* State Security Committee. The security agent spoke of the existing intense ideological struggle, that the Voice of America was slandering the Soviet form of government. According to him, children in Prienai do not want to join the Pioneers or the Young Communist League because their parents are either religious or at one time were associated with the freedom fighters' movement. When the security chief began to talk about the Rev. J. Zdebskis, who had been "justly" punished for teaching children, a din of protest arose in the hall. Disregarding this, Radionov explained that there are certain priests who, in his words, do not perform priestly duties but occupy themselves with propaganda and with the slander of the Soviet form of government.

The security agent rebuked the parents for forcing

children who have enrolled in the Pioneers and the Young Communist League to attend church, thus teaching them to be hypocrites. One women stated the following: "We go to church, and our children go. We're not the ones who are teaching them to be hypocrites, but you are because you force students who believe in God to join the Pioneers and the Young Communist League." Everyone in the hall concurred. Another women wanted to speak, but Radionovas declared he would not involve himself in a conflict and left the hall. A great uproar accompanied the departing security agent. Principal [Mrs.] Jakaitienė wanted to shame the people for behaving discourteously, saying it would have been better to remain silent.

"We have been forcing children to join the Pioneers, and we'll continue to do so," said the principal.

"And we won't let them," responded the parents.

PRIENAI

In April, 1973, Father Zdebskis was appointed pastor of the parish in Kučiūnai. This parish is near the border. Prior to this appointment Father Zdebskis had been registered to work as a watchman at the Kaunas taxi parking lot by order of the Prienai police. Government agents had spread the rumor that Father J. Zdebskis himself had not wanted to work in a parish.

KRIKŠTONYS

On Easter Morning, 1973, a police agent and, apparently, several security agents from Lazdijai confronted the members of the orchestra, demanding the surrender of their brass instruments. The musicians did not obey the order. At that point the pastor intervened, stating that he would complain to higher authorities, and the government officials, who evidently did not want a conflict of greater proportions, withdrew.

ILGUVA

In April, 1973, several unknown persons burglarized the churches in Ilguva, Žemoji Panemunė, and Paežerėliai and took the Blessed Sacrament from two of them.

SKRIAUDŽIAI

On April 25, 1973, [Mrs.] Rinkauskienė, the principal of the Skriaudžiai eight-year school, asked the parents of certain students to come see her to explain why they allow their children to attend church and why their children participate in processions, during which their girls scatter flowers. The first to arrive at the school was [Mrs.] K. Kairiūkštienė. Several teachers and the principal took part in the discussion. They told the mother she should not let her children attend church and especially processions.

"I'll take the children to church because the constitution guarantees the freedom of conscience. Our faith teaches no evil. Your godless students pushed around Pastor Uleckas and demanded money from him, and later they threw stones at the elderly woman [Mrs.] Tamulevičienė. One of your students raped a girl. Answer me, do churchgoing children of believing parents act this way?"

Since the teachers remained silent, the mother spoke of God.

"Go on with that God," teacher Tumaitienė interrupted her.

"An old people's proverb says, 'Don't spit up at heaven, for you'll spit on your own beard," retorted the energetic mother.

The principal threatened to note on her children's school records that they believe in God and then they would not be able to enroll in any schools of higher education.

"All honest work is honorable. They can work on the collective farm as I do. The collective farm accepts even those who believe in God."

As Kairiūkštienė was leaving, she said: "Please don't be angry if you see me going to church with my girls. I'll continue to take the girls just as I've been doing."

The principal was especially angered when the mother recounted one of the girls' conversations: "Mommy, you're not the only one who says there is a God. The teachers tell us about Him, too. If they're fighting against God, then He must really exist. No one would fight against nothing."

LANKELIŠKIAI

In January, 1973, the faithful of the parish in Lankeliškiai addressed the following memorandum to Leonid Brezhnev:

"We, the believers of the parish in Lankeliškiai, must inform you of a regrettable occurrence. Father Kupstaitis, our former pastor, was transferred to work at the parish in Gižai, and the bishop could not appoint a new pastor for us because there is a shortage of priests in Lithuania. At this time Father J. Zdebskis is available, having returned from a prison labor camp, but the local authorities do not allow him to carry out his priestly duties in our diocese. It seems to us that this is unjust as far as believers are concerned.

"Therefore, we request that you direct the appropriate agencies that they would do nothing to prevent our bishop from appointing the Rev. J. Zdebskis as pastor of our parish.

January 21, 1973"

This petition was signed by 149 believers. The address given for a reply was as follows: Vilkaviškis *Rayon*; Bartininkai Post Office; Moliniškiai Village; Raulinaitis, Juozas, son of Jurgis.

On February 2, 1973, the Lankeliškiai Parochial Committee asked H.E. Bishop Labukas to appoint a permanent pastor.

There was no reply from Moscow to the petition from the believers of Lankeliškiai, and the bishop, even had he wanted to, could not have appointed a pastor because there are not enough priests.

THE DIOCESE OF KAIŠIADORYS

ŠEŠUOLĖLIAI

[Mrs.] M. Pakalnienė, a teacher at the eight-year school, visited the parents of certain students before Easter in 1973, demanding that they would not send their children to church during the retreat and on Easter Sunday.

BAGASLAVIŠKIS

In 1972, just before All Saints Day, a teacher in Bagaslaviškis sternly warned his students not to go to church; he threatened them, saying that those who go to church will be expelled from school and will have to request admission into other schools.

ŠIRVINTOS

The *rayon* administration and the teachers of the secondary school in Širvintos have become concerned that students ate attending church in greater numbers. The principal has remarked that formerly students would stammer, indecisively expressing their unwillingness when they were urged to join the Young Communist League, but now they boldly declare: "I can't join the Young Communist League because I believe in God!" Responding to a question concerning their opinion on religion, tenth-class students stated that it is necessary for man and society.

On Easter Sunday, 1973, the principal himself came to the church in Širvintos to spy on his students. The following day, certain students were upbraided for having been in church on Easter. T. Gurskis, a tenth-class student, was a particular target since he had played the violin during the services.

"Don't ruin your life and career; don't disgrace the Soviet school," said one teacher. "Perhaps I should write it down in your school record so as to hurt your chances of getting into a school of higher education?"

T. Gurskis declared that if he could not finish his secondary schooling in Širvintos, he would go elsewhere.

* * *

ANNOUNCEMENTS

The *Chronicle of the Catholic Church in Lithuania* requests that dates, locations, and the given and surnames of persons would be accurately indicated when information is collected. Information that lacks concrete facts will not be included in the *Chronicle*. Names which should not be publicized are to be indicated.

The *Chronicle of the Catholic Church in Lithuania* has been published since March 19, 1972.

May, 1973

no. 7

THE CHRONICLE OF THE CATHOLIC CHURCH IN LITHUANIA

No. 7   1973

LETTER TO A TEACHER

Dear Teacher,

We are both sons of the same Lithuanian nation, both of us bound not only by blood, language, and cultural heritage but also by our concern for the future of our nation. And our nation's future is our children. We both look to them with hope, concern, and with love. I to my children—you to yours, to mine, and to those of many others, who gather in your classroom each school day. It is from what we shall present to these children and from how we shall prepare them for life, into what sort of people we shall mold them—that is what the future of our nation depends on. A great responsibility for their future therefore rests upon our shoulders.

Being aware of this great responsibility and knowing well the duties of a parent, I try to instill in my children from their very infancy those principles which would aid them throughout their lives to be honest, decent, and persons of character. I acquired these principles from my parents, and having tested and confirmed them by my own experience, having examined and pondered them in my own mind, I have committed myself to them according to my conscience. I am conscience-bound to pass on to my children what I consider good and necessary. On the other hand, I have the right to do so. We parents brought our children into this world. We rear them, dress and feed them, and nurse them when they are sick. No one forbids me to clothe my children in one way or another; no one hinders my feeding them the food which, in my opinion, they need. Therefore, no one has the right to forbid, to hamper, or to prevent me from transmitting to my children those intellectual or moral values which, I am convinced, are essential for a human being! I know that one should not lie, or steal, or cheat, or murder. I endeavor to instill these convictions also in my children. I know that it is good to behave decently, to be honest, to love one's neighbor—I want to convince my children of this also. I know further that to persevere as an honorable person, one must strive against one's weaknesses, one's faults, and against worldly temptations. I am preparing my children for this struggle. From my own experience, I am convinced that such a struggle is most successful when a person feels responsible not only to people, but also to God; when he is convinced that his actions and conduct have not only a temporary, a passing, but also an eternal worth; when he heeds not only the laws but also the voice of his conscience. Therefore, I consider it my essential duty to bring my children up religiously, and I do not want anyone to interfere in my performance of this parental obligation. Besides, you, the teacher, have also affirmed that parents have the duty of nurturing their children.

I do not educate my children alone. I send them to school. There I entrust you with their education.

But I want you to continue my work at the school and not to attempt to destroy it. I want you to arm my children's minds with learning, want you to teach them to use their knowledge. In my opinion, that should be the purpose of the school. Yet it is very distressing to me that you try to demolish rather than build. Instead of objectively providing educational information, the basics of its various areas, you begin to belittle mine and my children's convictions. You call my beliefs religious superstition and my nurturing, coercion; but the atheism you forcibly thrust upon children, you consider to be the way of freedom and normality. You do not value my convictions—leave them in peace, the way I neither attack nor ridicule yours. Teach my children to read and write, explain the principles of mathematics and the laws of physics but do not slant these subjects tendentiously against those principles which I and my child respect. I am not afraid of the objective facts of education, but I do not want you to present them in a distorted and tendentious way solely for the purpose of inducing a foreign world view within my child. When you attack mine and my child's convictions, you do not content yourself with the use of only purposely slanted subject matter; even in extracurricular activities you search for the means to uproot from my child's consciousness that which I have instilled there. Disregarding my wishes, you force him to join the Pioneers or the Young Communist League, or an atheistic group. You ridicule his beliefs in newsletters posted on bulletin boards, in showcases, and during atheistic affairs and lectures. You compel him to answer various questionnaires and intrude upon his conscience.

Should my child be weak, or should I have been unable to harden him in every way, you will warp his mind, teaching him to be a hypocrite and to disbelieve his parents or his teachers, most likely both. Will not my child begin to lose his equilibrium? Will he not begin deceiving you and me? Will he not seek out suspect pastimes and shallow pleasures and end up where neither you nor I want him to go? Will he cherish noble ideals? Will the future of his nation concern him? The good of his people? Perhaps he will simply turn into an egoist, without any lofty aims, without any higher goals, concerned only with his personal pleasure? Will there then be much joy for you and for me from such a youth? Will this benefit the nation and its people? Our nation is small, so each member is precious and needed, especially each youth. Each unfolding bud of the nation should be healty and beautiful!

Yes, dear Teacher, our children are our future, the future of our nation, and we should seriously consider how we are dealing with this future. True, you will try to excuse yourself by saying that such are the orders, that you are carrying out someone's directives, someone's will. Perhaps you yourself are against it and wouldn't be doing this if it were up to you. I can well believe that. But still, remember that the child is *mine* and does not belong to those who have ordered you to educate him contrary to my teachings. Keep in mind your great responsibility to your nation. Its future, its existence should also impose a duty upon you. Would you be unafraid to stand before a tribunal of the nation? Would you be able to testify with a clear conscience that you never exchanged the matters most sacred to man and nation for higher wages and a secure tranquility?

Finally, money. The money which you receive for your work has been earned by me and the parents of other pupils. Yet you do not want to consider the parents' wishes concerning the education of their children.

I do not want to be telling you, a teacher, how to do your job. That is your task as an educator. Truly, working with the young is not a simple matter. To educate a child or a youth, to mold his character is indeed a great responsibility and a difficult task. That is why in this work there should be no place or time for tearing down what I have already accomplished. Rather, we should both cooperate in this work, helping each other and working together very closely. This is demanded of us by our duty—that of father, teacher, and the duty of both of us as sons of the small Lithuanian nation!

The father of one of your students

THE RESPONSE TO PETITIONS BY THE FAITHFUL
PANEVĖŽYS RAYON

On April 6, 1973, to the home of Julius Rudys in Steponiškis Village arrived Ilicevičius, an agent of the Miežiškiai Locality police, [Mrs.] R. Smetonienė, chairman of the locality, and Glebavičius and P. Drilinga, workers from the Nevėžis Collective Farm, and one unidentified official.

Smetonienė and Ilicevičius demanded that Rudienė surrender the signed petitions in her possession (see the *Chronicle of the Catholic Church in Lithuania*, no. 6) threatening that if she did not give them up they would ransack the house. Hoping to avoid a search, Rudienė surrendered the petitions bearing forty signatures, among them those of the Rudys family. The uninvited "guests" presented Rudienė with a summons to appear at the Panevėžys security committee office on April 7. Here she was interrogated by the same "unidentified" official who had been present during the raid at her home. Rudienė was questioned as to who had given her the texts of those petitions. The interrogator told her that this was all nonsense because it interfered with the nurturing of children. He threatened to revoke her parental rights and to make her children wards of the state. Showing her the signed petitions, the interrogator asked Rudienė to name the signers whose signatures were illegible.

A week later Rudienė was again questioned by the security committee about the source of the petitions. The interrogator threatened to start criminal proceedings against her for defaming the Soviet government if she did not reveal where she had obtained the texts of the petitions.

To the office of the locality's Soviet of Working People's Deputies were summoned eleventh-class students from the secondary school in Miežiškiai [Miss] E. Skrebytė and [Miss] J. Rudytė. Their signatures were checked. Skrebytė was asked whether she was a friend of Rudytė, whether strange priests ever visited the Rudys home, and whether they prayed together. Rudytė was asked who had given her mother the petitions, whether strange priests visited their home, whether Father K. Balsys, pastor of the parish in Miežiškiai, had been there recently, and what priests say during confession. They explained to Rudytė that her mother was a fanatic and that she, her daughter, must re-educate her, and ask her to admit who had given her those petitions.

On May 23 J. Vilutis, the interrogator from the LSSR

Procurator's Office who handles the most important cases, with Ilicevičius, an agent of the police, and two security men, made a search of the Rudys home. The search lasted three hours, during which time holy pictures of the statue of the Blessed Mother of Šiluva and those commemorating the first mass of Father Sungaila, together with the addresses of relatives of the Rudys family were seized. Following the search, Rudienė was taken away to the security committee building. During her interrogation, samples of her handwriting and signatures were taken while she was sitting, standing, and even stooping. Interrogator Vilutis asked her where she had obtained the petitions and whether she had any acquaintances among the monks or nuns. She was again threatened with prison and told that her daughter would not be allowed to complete the secondary school or else would receive a bad characterization in her school records if she failed to divulge the desired information.

Also questioned were Rudienė's husband and even their eleven-year-old son, Stasys. The lad was asked whether any strange men called at their home, whether he believed in God, whether he knew his prayers, and why he hadn't joined the Pioneers.

Valaitis, manager of the local state farm; [Mrs.] J. Kalačiovienė, third secretary of the Panevėžys *Rayon* Communist party; *Tėvynė* [Fatherland] editor Kancė; and several other people called at the homes of those who had signed the petitions addressed to the LSSR Ministry of Public Education and to K. Tumėnas, commissioner of the Council for Religious Affairs. The callers upbraided the people for having signed the petitions and asked to be shown any prayer books or rosaries in their posession. If they saw religious pictures hanging on the walls, they asked where and how their owners had obtained them. The signers were also asked whether they attend church and whether they perform their Easter Duty. The persons who answered in the affirmative, they called uneducated and backward to their faces.

A. Šukys, chairman of the Miežiškiai Parochial Committee, was censured for failing to see what was going on in the church, and for failing to report to the authorities that signatures were being solicited. [Mrs.] Gritenienė treated the callers to some snacks. "Why do you offer us refreshments, for we are your enemies?" "Our religion teaches us to love even our enemies," the woman replied. The Turauskas children were asked whether they knew the tenets of their faith. The children gave an excellent recital of everything they knew. The officials then tried to shame the parents by saying they were backward. "As long as we are alive our children will be the same. All of us will fulfill our religious obligations," the Turauskases declared.

The officials wanted to carry off *Misijų metraštis* [Missions Annual] from one of the homes, but the son, a recent graduate, chased after the departing visitors and took it back. [Mrs.] J. Pinigienė was questioned for a long time concerning the signatures and was repeatedly forced to sign her name—while seated, while standing, and even with the paper placed on the floor—for the officials wanted in the worst way to prove that most of the signatures were forgeries.

PANEVĖŽYS

The apartment of [Mrs.] E. Svirelienė, an inspector of the finance department of the city of Panevėžys, was raided on May 24, 1973. Since the lady was undergoing treatment at the Druskininkai Sanatorium at the time of the raid, her daughter Irma was asked to be present during the two-hour search. The raiders took with them a leaflet listing the intentions of the Living Rosary Society, Tihamér Tóth's book, *Jaunuolio būdas* [The character of a youth] produced by a copier, and a photograph of Svirelienė. [Miss] Svirelytė was questioned. Does she read religious books? Who visits her mother? To what religious organizations does her mother belong? Do they go to church often? Had she seen the petitions with the signatures? Had her mother asked her to sign? She was threatened that criminal charges would be brought against her mother. A search was also made at Svirelienė's place of employment, but the searchers found nothing incriminating. On May 25, Interrogator J. Vilutis went to Svirelienė's room at the Druskininkai Sanatorium and searched through her belongings, confiscating several letters. After she returned from the sanatorium, E. Svirelienė was questioned by the security committee, who was trying to determine where she had obtained the petitions and to whom she had given the signed copies. The interrogator tried to frighten her by saying that she would be dismissed from her position and sentenced. In the beginning of June, Svirelienė's case was considered by the executive committee, and she was charged with attending church and taking part in processions. The "accused" was ordered to "voluntarily" resign from her position, but the courageous woman refused.

KAUNAS

In March, 1973, [Miss] V. Grincevičiūtė, a member of the Kaunas cathedral choir, showed some sort of petition to several persons. A security officer called at her apartment on March 29 and began to search it even though he had no warrant from the Procurator's Office. He was looking for the text of the petition which Grincevičiūtė had shown to several people. When he did not find such a text, Grincevičiūtė told him that she had personally written the petition requesting that more copies of the Bible be published. The security committee questioned Grincevičiūtė concerning a number of people and threatened to start criminal proceedings against her.

On another day, again without a search warrant, Grincevičiūtė's apartment was raided and the book *Ieškau Tavo veido* [I seek Your face] was taken. The occupant was again interrogated as to where she had obtained the text of the petition and on other matters.

A third "examination" of Grincevičiūtė's apartment was performed by security officials on April 2.

On May 11, this time with a search warrant, another meticulous search was made of Grincevičiūtė's living quarters and at her place of employment. Even the bathroom tissue was examined. The search was directed by J. Vilutis, the interrogator from the LSSR Procurator's Office who handles the most important cases. Its aim was to confiscate any literature criticizing the Soviet government and the texts of the circulated petitions. To their consternation, the searchers could not find any petitions nor any literature vilifying the Soviet government. They did take all the addresses, notes, letters, and postcards that they found, together with several publications, among them *Tragedija Dainavos Šalyje* [Tragedy in the land of Dainava]. During the interrogation Grincevičiūtė was confronted with cathedral organist Beinorius, who testified that she had shown him the text of the petition addressed to the LSSR Ministry of Public Education. Grincevičiūtė denied the validity of this testimony.

After numerous interrogations, attempts at blackmail in her place of employment, and threats that she would be convicted, Grincevičiūtė was finally summoned to the Republic's Procurator's Office and advised that a case was not being brought against her, but that the matter might be renewed if she dared to teach religious truths to children.

How much time was wasted, how much malaise had to be endured simply because a citizen had decided to ask the government to publish more copies of the Bible!

CATHOLICS OF LITHUANIA WRITE

"To: Presidium of the Supreme Soviet of the LSSR

A Petition by a Group of Believers

"Scathing antireligious propaganda is being waged in the press, at meetings, in schools, on the radio and television, in motion pictures and the theater, which does not hesitate to use distorted facts, unjust accusations, and the ridicule and debasement of believers. Under the guise of antireligious action, even the disparagement of the nation occurs. This is done in the motion picture *Herkus Mantas*, in which, while propagating atheism, a grievous, historically unconfirmed accusation is made: that Prussians offered human sacrifices to their gods. To degrade and belittle religion in the eyes of the people even vile means are used without hesitation.

"Religion is being condemned while atheism is foisted upon everyone by force. What are the results of this?

"Lenin taught that the truth of ideas, theories, and science is confirmed by practice. It has been almost thirty years since the young generation and the entire population has been educated and directed in the spirit of atheism. In schools during lessons and all extracurricular activities atheism is being propagated, and religion is scorned. Caricatures ridiculing believers are put in showcases in the schools. Students who attend church are interrogated, intimidated, occasionally even punished, as happened to [Miss] Aurelija Račinskaitė, whose deportment grade was lowered and the entry added, 'for attending church.' What has this not overly brief practice of atheistic nurturing shown?

"Whereas before the introduction of atheistic education into the schools thievery, banditry, attempts upon a person's life, and sexual incontinence were very rare among the youth of Lithuania, now these are everpresent phenomena. In the war against juvenile delinquency, children's quarters have been set up at police departments. Never before in Lithuania were drunkenness, theft, murder, dishonesty, and dereliction of duty as rampant as in recent years. Laxness of conscience is evident in contacts with employees and officials everywhere: in stores and factories, in administrative, doctors', and other offices. Experience has shown that atheistic training is incapable of fostering strong moral principles in the young, and atheistic propaganda is unable to improve the morality of the public.

"Christian morality, which has withstood centuries of

trial and fosters conscientiousness and encourages self-control, the overcoming of undesirable tendencies, the conscious performance of one's duty, and an inner sense of responsibility for one's actions—it is now being repudiated and hampered.

"Believers are being assailed but are not allowed to defend themselves. Article 123 of the LSSR Constitution, which proclaims the equality of every citizen in all areas of public life, and Article 125, which guarantees LSSR citizens freedom of speech, press, assembly and street processions, are not applied to believers. They cannot defend their beliefs at meetings, or in the press, or on the radio, or by any other means which atheists can use to disseminate their ideas without interference. Books of religious content cannot be published. It is true that *Maldynas* [Book of prayers], *Vatikano II susirinkimo nutarimai* [Decisions of the second Vatican Council], and *Naujasis Testamentas* [The New Testament] were published in Lithuania during Soviet rule. Three books in the period of some thirty years! And even these were published in such limited editions that only very few families of the faithful were able to acquire them. The press and official statements by government representatives often condemn racial and religious discrimination in other lands. Then why is religious discrimination allowed in Lithuania?

"We, the undersigned believers, request the Presidium of the Supreme Soviet of the LSSR to bar religious discrimination and to allow Lithuania's believers:

1. To defend and disseminate their beliefs by means of the media (press, lectures, radio, television)
2. To establish public organizations of and for believers
3. To publish newspapers and religious books
4. To attend church services without fear of persecution or punishment if they are students
5. To enroll an unlimited number of candidates in the theological seminary
6 To be secure from every means of religious discrimination

"We want to believe in the good will of the Soviet government. In Poland and other socialist countries, believers attend church without hindrance, catechize children, and publish religious books. We await the cessation of all religious discrimination in Lithuania also.
Signatures of five hundred and forty (540) believers."

"To: the Presidium of the Supreme Soviet of the LSSR

An Explanation
"We are sending the text of a petition to the Presidium of the Supreme Soviet of the LSSR, which was signed by 540 believers. The original pages of the petition bearing the signatures are not being submitted for the following reasons:

"Sent by the Procurator of the LSSR, Interrogator J. Vilutis, who handles especially important cases, terrorized Catholics in Kaunas, Panevėžys, and elsewhere for several months solely because they had solicited or were only suspected of having solicited signatures for the petitions addressed to the Soviet government concerning discrimination against believers. The signers of the above-mentioned petitions were also harassed. The government of the LSSR thus demonstrated, not its desire to consider the rights of believers, but only its aim of imposing an alien ideology upon Catholics.

"At the beginning of August of this year, the Soviet government forbade the bishops of Lithuania to administer the sacrament of confirmation 'until after the harvest.' This administrative interference by a secular government in the administering of sacraments clearly demonstrates with what kind of "harvesting" the Soviet government is concerned—with the forcible weaning of the people from religion.

"Because of the aforementioned reasons, we shall send the texts of the petitions which bear 540 signatures to the Presidium of the Supreme Soviet of the LSSR only when we are completely convinced of the good will of the Soviet government. At the present we are convinced only of its desire to quietly and quickly, even through inhuman means, to destroy the Catholic Church in Lithuania.

"We would also like to inform the Presidium that four copies of the petition addressed to the Ministry of Public Education of the LSSR bearing 320 signatures and four copies of the petitions bearing 302 signatures addressed to K. Tumėnas, the commissioner of the Council for Religious Affairs, were received late. These signed copies will be added to the previously gathered copies of the petition about which the Presidium of the Supreme Soviet was informed in the declaration dated May 14, 1973.

"Thus, a total of 14,604 believers have signed the petition addressed to the Ministry of Public Education of the LSSR concerning the discrimination of believing students, and 16,800 believers have signed the petition addressed to Council for Religious Affairs Commissioner K. Tumėnas concerning the lack of Catholic publications.

August 31, 1973
Representatives of the Catholics in Lithuania"

THE ARCHDIOCESE OF VILNIUS

VILNIUS

In early August, 1973, Murnikovas, deputy commissioner of the Council for Religious Affairs, informed the bishops and ecclesiastical administrators of Lithuania that because of the "harvesting" in the month of August it would not be possible to administer the sacrament of confirmation on Sundays or on the Feast of the Assumption (August 15).

Not knowing about this prohibition, believers gathered in great number in Šilalė and Alunta on August 15, and great was their discontent, since the bishop had not been allowed to come because of the so-called harvest.

Bishop R. Krikščiūnas informed the priests of Panevėžys Diocese that because of the harvest even the devotional ceremonies had to be postponed. The priests, howver, held the devotions as formerly, and the authorities did not dare to interfere.

On August 15, priests in pulpits informed their parishioners about the postponement of the sacrament of confirmation to some later date. The more courageous priests frankly indicated the true reasons for this prohibition and delay. Murnikovas and other government officials had been mainly concerned with preventing thousands of children from receiving confirmation at the time most convenient to them. This prohibition of administering the sacrament of confirmation is gross interference by the government in the affairs of a religious cult.

* * *

On May 8, 1973, K. Tumėnas, the new commissioner of the Council for Religious Affairs, summoned the acting bishops and ecclesiastical administrators to a introductory meeting. He was very courteous, promising his aid in all matters, promising to grant permission for the publication of a catechism and the manufacture of devotional goods.

Afterward, showing those present a copy of the *Chronicle of the Catholic Church in Lithuania,* no. 5, he expressed his sorrow that this publication "slandering" Soviet reality was aimed for overseas consumption, that some priests have been involved in this, and that someone would have to suffer for it. Another great "evil" found in the Lithuanian Catholic Church, according to him, was the solicitation of signatures for various petitions.

Commissioner Tumėnas expressed similar thoughts to the priests of the Šiauliai and Joniškis deaneries who had gathered for their first postwar conference.

* * *

A group of students from the V. Kapsukas University in Vilnius who had organized a tour through Dzūkija decided to visit the monument to Vytautas, Grand Duke of Lithuania, in Perloja (Varėna *Rayon*). After purchasing some flowers, nine of them went there on May 13.

Arriving in Perloja, they placed the flowers at the monument to Vytautas but did not sing any songs or make any speeches. They had been followed there by a security agent, who telephoned for more security agents and the police. As the students were going home, they were detained and returned to Perloja, where interrogations were begun. The net result: the three most-active students— Eugenijus Banys, Remigijus Kajeckas, and Pranas Grigas— who had already been under suspicion, were expelled from the University.

First of all they were ousted from the Young Communist League for disobedience, and Kajeckas, additionally, for his fickle opinions (a prayer book was found when he was searched).

All three students were expelled from the university for "gross disobedience." Sudavičius, the rector's assistant for educational affairs, and the administrators censured the students for having placed flowers at the monument to Vytautas, without there being any special occasion or reason. According to the university administration, this had constituted a covert commemoration of the anniversary of Romas Kalanta's self-immolation.

Seeking justice and support, the disciplined students even turned to the Central Committee of the Lithuanian Communist party. This was the committee's retort:

"It was sufficient that you placed flowers at the monument to Vytautas—a feudal lord and usurper! This is not compatible with the principles and patriotism of either a League member or of a Soviet man."

This is how the past of our nation is valued by the Soviets!

RATNYČIA

Monsignor Č. Krivaitis, the ecclesiastical administrator of the Vilnius Diocese, administered the sacrament of confirmation at the church in Ratnyčia on July 8, 1973. Although the administering of sacraments is strictly an internal Church matter, it is a matter of great interest to the authorities. Government officials decide where and how many times each year the sacrament of confirmation can be administered and concern themselves with how the ceremonies are organized. For instance, just prior to this ceremony the Rev. A. Andriuškevičius, pastor of the church in Ratnyčia, was summoned to the chairman's office of the Varėna *Rayon* Soviet of Working People's Deputies Executive Committee for a "chat." Here he was ordered to see to it that the diocesan administrator would be greeted only in the churchyard. The chairman of the *rayon* executive committee expressed his desire that the least number of people would accompany the administrator.

Early in the morning on July 8, believers began to head for Ratnyčia on foot and in vehicles. Among the early arrivals were governmental "assistants." Along all the roads to Ratnyčia, auto-inspection posts were set up, where cars were stopped, their drivers' documents were inspected, and not infreqently the travelers were asked why and where they were going.

Collective farms and other establishments were forbidden to provide horses or other means of transportation for this purpose, and if anyone tried to make use of such means, the auto inspectors did not allow them to pass. The chief auto inspector himself, who was on guard at the Druskininkai Bridge, personally took over the reins to turn back a horse and wagon containing several children.

Exacting inspectors kept constant check on all private vehicles. Some drivers were stopped six times on their way to Ratnyčia.

The buses running to Ratnyčia, Druskininkai, and Baltašiškė could not accommodate all those who wanted to attend the rites.

There were as many governmental "assistants" in the vicinity of the churchyard, within the churchyard, and even in the church. Their duties here were different: to record the automobile license numbers, to observe the people, to listen to the priests' sermons, and to apprehend those who were selling rosaries, prayer books, crosses, and holy cards. They tried to perform this last task early in the morning when the sellers had just laid out their wares, and while there were not too many believers present. Their victims related how this had been done. Several civilians would come up in a group (sometimes up to seven at once) and pretend to be choosing rosaries or prayer books, handling and examining them, asking prices. Then suddenly some of them would seize the seller and the rest grab the goods, and they would all dash out of the churchyard. They would try to accomplish all this quietly so as not to cause a commotion, and so that the believers would not rescue those who had been apprehended. If a seller began to explain or to cry in a loud voice, he was ordered to keep quiet. The devotional merchandise would sometimes be desecrated right on the spot—torn up and kicked around.

In his sermon that very day Father L. Kunevičius publicly condemned such dastardly acts. The preacher said that believers have already been forcibly impoverished because they are not allowed a religious press—newspapers, magazines, or books; they cannot make use of the radio or other means of civilization to better know their faith and strengthen it. As though this were not enough, they are not even permitted to acquire rosaries, prayer books, or crucifixes.

Despite all these handicaps, approximately 7,000 persons gathered at Ratnyčia, and 2,700 children and youths were confirmed.

There were long lines at all the confessionals in the church. Especially great numbers of believers came from Byelorussia, since there are very few priests there.

The authorities were displeased with the ceremonial rites of confirmation. The pastor of the parish in Ratnyčia was summoned to the Varėna *Rayon* office, where Visockis, vice-chairman of the executive committee, reproached him for the sermon delivered by the Rev. L. Kunevičius, pastor of the parish in Gerdašiai. The administrator of the sacrament of confirmation himself was also upbraided by Commissioner Tumėnas for the poorly chosen preachers at Ratnyčia.

Also "raked over the coals" was the dean of Gardinas for sending his believers into another Republic. He was ordered to report how many confirmation certificates had been issued in his deanery.

At the present time there is much talk about ending the "cold war," about decreasing tensions, and about useful mutual cooperation even with capitalistic countries. Believers, alas, wait in vain for the day when the Soviet government will renounce its use of cold-war methods against the believing public, the day when this oppressive discrimination will be abolished.

VALKININKAI

Father Algimantas Keina, pastor of this parish, was testing two little girls in the sacristy on July 10, 1973, to see whether they were ready to receive their First Communion. Unexpectedly Šalna, a Varėna *Rayon* official and Daugėla, a correspondent, burst into the sacristy. The latter photographed the little girls, and the other shouted:

"It is forbidden to catechize children or to test their knowledge! In fact, it is forbidden to bring children to church. There is only one official school! ..."

The woman who had brought the two girls courageously defended the girls' rights:

"We have the right to take our children to confession. We ask the priest to test their knowledge of religion. You don't have the right to forbid this. If you don't allow us to do this publicly, we shall go underground and take our children to church in secret."

The government officials badgered the woman to tell them her name. When she refused, a Varėna security officer arrived and took her away to the office of the locality.

Since the Varėna *Rayon* commission had found only two children being tested, they did not penalize the pastor. Apparently they had expected to take by surprise a large number of children in the sacristy of the church.

CEIKINIAI

"To: M. Gedvilas, Minister of Public Education
of the LSSR
The Curia of the Vilnius Archdiocese

*A Petition by the Parents of Pupils from the Parish
in Ceikiniai, in Ignalina Rayon*

"We, the parishioners of the church in Ceikiniai, wrote a petition to the General-Secretary of the CPSU on September 5, 1972, a copy of which was sent to you. On October 10, 1972, you sent us this written reply: 'Replying to your petition, we hereby state that the church cannot interfere in school matters, disrupt the established order, or compel children to perform religious rites. (Signed) M. Gedvilas, Minister of Public Education.'

"We were expecting a more serious answer, particularly from the Minister of Public Education. From all the facts we set forth, it is readily apparent how teachers and even the head of the Department of Education interfere in the internal affairs of the Church, disregarding basic parental rights. But in your response there seems to be the tendency of casting the blame on us, who have been wronged.

"On March 3, 1969, the parents of the pupils from the parish in Ceikiniai wrote to the Ministry of Public Education that [Miss] Kanišauskaitė, a teacher at the school in Valėnai, had expelled Verutė and Onutė, daughters of the Galatiltis family, and [Mrs.] Varnienė's daughter, Alma, because the mothers had taken their daughters to church on Christmas Day. In the same petition we wrote that during a religious festival in May, 1967, Jadzevičius, the head of the Ignalina Department of Education, came to Ceikiniai and, summoning our pastor from the church, interrupted the services for some time.

"In 1969 [Miss] Medeišytė, a teacher in Ceikiniai who wanted to enroll all our children into the Pioneers, assigned her pupils a writing exercise in the Lithuanian language so they would learn how to write an application for joining the Pioneers. After the pupils had writen down such an application as though it were a writing exercise, the teacher collected their papers and told her pupils, 'You are now Pioneers.'

"Late in the evening on January 16, 1967, Ceikiniai teacher [Mrs.] Šiaudinienė drove Algis Sapiega out of the dormitory because he was a churchgoer and would not join the Young Communist League. The lad walked home, a distance of seven kilometers, at night through a blizzard, with the temperature at twenty-five degrees below zero centigrade. He became ill after he returned.

"In our previous petition to you we pointed out the facts about students being forced to write all sorts of declarations without their parents' knowledge to be used in bringing charges against priests, and about teachers punishing students simply because they park their bicycles near the churchyard, and so on.

"It seems to us that teachers would not act in this manner if the Ministry of Public Education did not condone such actions.

"We would like to know how all this can be reconciled with the Soviet Constitution, which guarantees freedom of conscience for everyone.

"We trust that you will seriously consider all these problems and will in the future abolish all these inequities.

Ceikiniai
March 28, 1973"

The petition was signed by 120 parents.

THE ARCHDIOCESE OF KAUNAS

KAUNAS

A state of war could be sensed in Kaunas on the occasion of the first anniversary of Romas Kalanta's tragic self-immolation. Policemen were in evidence not only all over Laisvės Alėja [Liberty Avenue] but throughout Kaunas. There were even soldiers dressed in police uniforms. The policemen kept watch "armored" with "bananas" [riot sticks—tr.] and two-way radios. People from government agencies and schools were assigned to help maintain order in the streets. On May 14 the Laisvės Alėja teemed with people, but the police kept ordering them to keep moving.

During the night before May 14, the Lithuanian tricolor flag was flown atop the City of Kaunas Executive Committee building, but it was soon noticed and taken down. (This information was learned from a security agent.) All persons who dared to place flowers at Kalanta's grave or at the site of his self-immolation were arrested. How many persons were arrested is not known. The youth of Kaunas gathered briefly on the central boulevard to commemorate the anniversary of Kalanta's self-immolation. The anniversary passed without any noteworthy incidents.

The principal participants of the demonstration on this occasion were the soldiers and policemen, who clearly showed how much the Soviet authorities fear freedom of thought. During those days many students were transported out of Kaunas under various pretexts. At some schools the "activities" lasted from 8 a.m. until 10 p.m. so that students would not be free to go out into the streets of the city. In addition, students were ordered not to be seen on Laisvės Alėja on May 14; they were even forbidden to go to the stores there.

* * *

On June 5, 1973, the People's Court of Kaunas *Rayon* considered the case of [Mrs.] Dambickienė, who was charged with burglarizing the churches in Babtai and Vandžiogala. [Miss] Martusevičiūtė was the presiding judge. The court's decision stated that Dambickienė's guilt had been fully proven, for she had burglarized the churches in Babtai and Vandžiogala and had in addition stolen from the cemeteries some decorative linens and candles that were affixed to wreaths. All these items were found in her possession during a search. Because the accused was ill with sclerosis and undergoing treatment at the psychiatric hospital, she was not sentenced. The plaintiff in the case was a plain village woman who couldn't even pose a simple question. The man who had been living with the accused for ten years, one Savickas, took part in the court proceedings, not as one who was guilty, but only as a witness.

This trial was not an exceptional occurrence in Soviet

court proceedings. In the summer of 1964 the church in Kaišiadorys was burglarized. The burglar was apprehended as he tried to break into the church in Vievis. It became apparent that he was "a man of wide-ranging activities"— he had already burglarized a Russian Orthodox church in Riga.

The Procurator's Office unwillingly drew up a case, and during the trial on October 6, Judge Kasperavičius tried in every possible way to vindicate the thief. "He was in straitened circumstances... Noticing the steeples of the church, he thought that perhaps there would be unused monies here..." As though that were not enough, the judge made use of this opportunity to make accusations against the church and the clergy. Unable to put up with this, Father Šalčiūnas spoke up, saying to the judge: "Just who is on trial here: this thief, or we, the representatives of the church?"

The burglar was put on probation and freed immediately. He had been released from preventative custody even before the trial began.

Such court proceedings only encourage thieves to burglarize churches. As an example, in July, 1973, two hooligans broke into Alytus Church No. 2 at nighttime and beat its caretaker with rocks until he was unconscious.

ŠVENTYBRASTIS

In 1973 the Kėdainiai *Rayon* Department of Culture dismissed Head Librarian [Miss] Janina Rutkūnaitė for "a serious crime"—she had gone to church on Easter Sunday!

GIRDŽIAI

Presented below is a report made by the pastor of this parish to H.E. Bishop J. Labukas:

"On May 30, 1973, the husband of Petrė Klimienė hired a car and took me, the pastor of the parish in Girdžiai, to Smalininkai to minister to his critically ill wife, who was in the contagious diseases ward of the hospital. We arrived at 6 p.m. Her husband was permitted to go into the ward to see the sick woman, but they did not allow me, a priest, to enter. The doctor insisted I telephone Jurbarkas and obtain permission from the *rayon* office. I had to return without administering the sacraments to a seriously ill patient.

"When a condemned man asks for a cigarette or some other item, he is granted his last wish. Yet undergoing treatment here was not a criminal but a loyal Soviet citizen, and she was not shown any human kindness. If her husband was allowed into the ward, why was I refused admittance?

"Similar overeagerness by Soviet employees only serves to irritate citizens and set them against the present form of government.

"Should Your Excellency have occasion to talk to the commissioner of the Council for Religious Affairs, perhaps it would be worthwhile to inform him about this.

Girdžiai
June 1, 1973"

THE DIOCESE OF PANEVĖŽYS

UTENA RAYON

Presented below is Father A. Liesis' appeal to the People's Court of Utena and his statement of defense, which the judge did not allow him to read:

"To: The People's Court of Utena *Rayon*
"Copies to: Presidium of the Supreme Soviet
of the LSSR
The Commissioner of the Council
For Religious Affairs
The Curia of Panevėžys Diocese

An Appeal by the Rev. A. Liesis, Residing in Daunoriai
Village, Utena Rayon

"On June 29, 1973, the administrative commission of the Utena *Rayon* Executive Committee stated that on June 12, 1973, I taught catechism to a group of children at the church in Daunoriai. The commission concluded that by doing so I have violated the following resolution of the Presidium of the Supreme Soviet of the LSSR: 'The following actions are violations of the law regarding religious cults: the organization and holding of special meetings for children and youths... that are not related to the performance of religious rites' (See the May 12, 1966, decision of the Presidium of the Supreme Soviet of the LSSR 'concerning administrative responsibility for violating the law regarding religious cults.').

"Upon reading this resolution adopted by the Presidium, we can see plainly that it prohibits only those gatherings of children which are not related to the activities (performance) of the cult. Those which are related to the activities of the cult are not prohibited.

"At the above-mentioned children's gathering, I and the children prayed together. I questioned them about the sacraments, prayer, and God. I preached a sermon to them about God. A sermon (just as are prayer, the celebration of mass, and the administration of sacraments) is an essential part of the Catholic cult. Delivering sermons, administering sacraments—that is all part of the Catholic cult. Which means that only cultic activities were being performed at this gathering. The cited resolution adopted by the Presidium does not forbid assemblies for cultic activities, and Article 96 of the LSSR Constitution specifically permits gatherings at which cultic activities are performed ('Freedom of religious worship is recognized for all citizens of the LSSR.').

"We priests are constantly being accused and punished with harsh prison sentences (for example, Fathers A. Šeškevičius, Zdebskis, Bubnys), on the basis of still another resolution adopted by the Presidium of the Supreme Soviet of the LSSR, namely: 'By violation of the laws concerning the separation of the church from the state and of the school from the church... is understood the following:... the organization and systematic performance of religious educative activities for minor children in violation of the regulations set by law' (See the May 12, 1966, resolution adopted by the Presidium of the Supreme Soviet of the LSSR.).

"It is evident that this resolution concerning the organized, that is group teaching of religion to children also prohibits, not absolutely, nor at all times, but only in those instances when the 'regulations set by law' are violated in teaching religion to groups. When keeping within the bounds of these 'regulations,' the teaching of religion to children in groups is not prohibited. These 'regulations' which priests are supposed to observe when teaching religion to groups of children have not been officially announced anywhere, which means that they do not exist, and if they do not, then what juridical basis do the LSSR courts have for charging priests with the violation of these imaginary resolutions and for punishing them so severely?

"We priests are constantly being reproached with violating the constitutional article 'the school is separated from the church' while teaching religion to children. Dear jurists, let us speak not poetically but juridically. In legal terminology a 'school' is an institution specially designed for education. In the juridical sense, no one has the right to call a house of worship (where people pray), or some establishment or factory a 'school,' because all these places are specifically designed not for teaching but for other purposes, even though there, just as in all of life, people inadvertently learn and specialize. Poetically and pictorially speaking, no doubt, everything, including life itself, could be called a 'school.' I said speaking 'poetically,' not juridically.

"Speaking in legal terms, we do not have the right to call students or teachers a school, just as we do not have the right to call the sweepers, cooks, or diners a restaurant, or barbers and their customers a barbershop. In juridical language a 'restaurant' is a place for eating, a barbershop is a place for cutting hair, and a 'school' is an educational institution and not its guards, nor students, nor teachers.

"Ergo, the constitutional law separating 'the school from the church' calls only the educational institution a 'school' but not other establishments, nor other places, nor its students or teachers.

"Which means that we priests who teach religion to children in places which are not educational institutions (we do not even set foot in them) do not violate in the slightest the aforementioned constitutional law.

"Which also means that the administrative commission of the Utena *Rayon* Executive Committee found me guilty and fined me (fifty rubles) without any legal grounds and, also, immorally, since penalizing a priest for performing his sacred and honorable duties (imposed upon him by Christ and the Church) is a truly uncivilized and genuinely immoral action.

"I therefore request the People's Court of Utena *Rayon* to nullify this decision of the administrative commission."

Father Liesis' Statement of Defense

"The constitutional laws governing speech, the press, and assembly permit the teaching of religion to groups of children. Article 97 of the LSSR Constitution states: 'In conformity with the interests of the working people, and in order to strengthen the socialist system, LSSR citizens are guaranteed by law: (a) freedom of speech; (b) freedom of the press; (c) freedom of assembly, including the holding of mass meetings.'

"We shall examine the meaning of this article. The introduction speaks about the interests of the working people. The welfare of the working people and their interests are the goals of every law. Lawmakers sometimes note this goal in the statement of the law, sometimes they do not. The essence of the law, however, always remains the same, regardless of whether this aim (the welfare of the working people) is noted in the text of the law or not. Article 97 of the LSSR Constitution notes this purpose explicitly within this opening sentence: 'in conformity with the interests of the working people (i.e., welfare of the working people; for their benefit)... are guaranteed...'

"Even should this introductory wording, 'in conformity with the interests of the working people,' have been omitted, the essence of this article would remain the same, namely: 'LSSR citizens are guaranteed by law: (a) freedom of speech; (b) freedom of the press; (c) freedom of assembly, including the holding of mass meetings.'

"Citizens must comply unconditionally with every moral law. Which means that Article 97 of the constitution must also be enforced unconditionally. Its essence, as mentioned is such: All citizens (thus, priests also) are guaranteed freedom of speech and of the press (i.e., all kinds of speech, all kinds of publishing, of all points of view, which also means freedom of speech and publishing of a religious nature), and freedom of assembly (meaning also religious assemblies of children called by priests). The stated word is 'freedom,' which means true freedom, total unrestricted freedom.

"That is the true meaning of Article 97 of the constitution. There are many, however, who interpret this article of the constitution erroneously. They think that this article guarantees not absolute but conditional freedom of speech, the press, and assembly. They say that the LSSR Constitution guarantees only the freedom of such speech, press, and assembly which 'agrees with the interests of the working people,' with their welfare, and which benefits the working man.

"If the constitution would grant the freedom, not of all speech, not of every press, not of every assembly, but only of beneficial speech, a beneficial press, and beneficial (suited to the interests of working people) assembly, then it (the constitution) would also present clear criteria for distinguishing beneficial speech, beneficial press, and beneficial assembly from harmful speech, harmful press, and harmful assembly; I say that the constitution would present standards indicating what speech, what press, and what assemblies are considered 'harmful,' and which are 'beneficial' to the welfare of the working people.

"But the above-mentioned constitutional laws do not

offer any criteria to distinguish beneficial speech from that which is harmful, a beneficial press from that which is harmful, or beneficial assembly from that which is harmful. Without clear standards the constitutional law of freedom of speech, the press, and assembly, if understood according to the second interpretation, becomes absolutely obscure, that is, it is altogether unclear as to which form of speech, press, and assembly the constitution considers beneficial and which harmful to the welfare of the working people.

"An ambiguous law has no juridical value. An unclear law is a juridical flaw. That is why the aforementioned constitutional laws concerning speech, the press, and assembly, if understood according to the second interpretation, would therefore be unclear and become a legal flaw.

"The lawmakers certainly did not want the laws they promulgated to be legal flaws. Therefore, they intended that these laws were to be regarded in the original sense and not according to the second interpretation.

"Thus if Article 97 of the constitution guarantees full, unrestricted freedom, not merely for so-called beneficial speech, so-called beneficial press, and so-called beneficial assembly, but for all speech, of every point of view, meaning also speech and publishing of a religious nature; and for every assembly of every viewpoint (without exception), this means also the religious assemblies of children called by priests.

"Undoubtedly, the framers of the constitution knew that in making use of the constitutionally guaranteed freedoms, citizens may also make many unfortunate mistakes. To the drafters of the constitution, however, it was also plain that the truth would out and that the mistakes would be overcome, not by any one party, nor by the restrictions of its censors (who themselves are not infallible), but only by total freedom of speech and of the press. That is why the framers of the constitution guaranteed this unrestricted freedom of speech, the press, and assembly which is useful for the victory of truth and for the welfare of the working people.

"Which means that we priests also have the constitutionally guaranteed freedom to hold various meetings (of the young, or old) and to express our thoughts during them. Ergo, the administrative commission of the Utena Executive Committee did not have the legal (even more so, the moral) right to censure me and to penalize me because on June 12, 1973, I spoke about God, his commandments, the sacraments, and prayer to a small group of children at the church in Daunoriai. I therefore request the court to nullify this unlawful and erroneous decision of the administrative commission.

"I request the People's Court of Utena *Rayon* to include this statement with the documentation in my case file."

(N.B. The People's Court of Utena found that Father A. Liesis had been justly penalized.)

VABALNINKAS

During a history lesson at the vocational school, [Mrs.] Morkūnienė, who was lecturing, noticed a chain around [Miss] Danutė Kruopaitė's neck, and demanded that the girl surrender it. Because the girl would not give it to her, the teacher herself took off the chain, which had a small religious medal attached. Someone in the lecture hall stated that [Miss] Genė Dovidonytė and [Miss] Viktorija Jurginaitė were also wearing medals. Rushing over to Dovidonytė, Morkūnienė ripped the chain off the girl's neck and kept it. When she saw that the girl had two more small medals, she demanded that the girl surrender them, and when the girl refused, the teacher grabbed her hand and took them away by force. Then, going to Jurginaitė, Morkūnienė ripped the chain from the girl's neck, but she did not succeed in taking away her medal. After the lecture, Morkūnienė chided the above-mentioned girls for wearing religious medals.

During another lesson Morkūnienė ordered Jurginaitė to answer questions. Barely had the girl begun answering when the teacher interrupted her, saying that she had begun incorrectly. Taking up a book the teacher read a beginning phrase and told the girl to relate the rest. When Jurginaitė explained that she did not have that particular book, the lecturer snapped at her, "If God loves you, He could have, plop, dropped that book from heaven for you." As the girl tried to continue her recitation, the teacher said, "God didn't come to your rescue—you get a grade of 2." It was plain to everyone in the lecture hall why their classmate had received the failing grade.

Dovidonytė asked Morkūnienė to return her medal, but the woman laughed: "It'll be a nice little trinket for the [atheistic] museum." Asked whether she would still wear a medal, the girl replied: "I've always worn one and will continue to do so. I'll buy another one and put it on."

Jurginaitė was summoned to the teachers' room, where they insisted that she surrender her medal. The girl was assailed by teachers [Mrs.] Griciūnienė and [Mrs.] Šablinskienė, but they succeeded in obtaining only the chain without the medal.

The teachers decided to take this matter under advisement. Jurginaitė and Dovidonytė were made to leave the school.

MIEŽIŠKIAI

One-half of the eleventh-class students of the secondary school in Miežiškiai were not members of the Young Communist League in 1972-73. When the new year began, the students of the graduating class were especially pressured to enroll in the League. They were often kept two to three hours after school and threatened that unless they joined the Young Communist League they would not be accepted into schools of higher education and would not be able to attain anything worthwhile in life. The most "diligent" were class leader [Mrs.] Kabliūnienė, League Secretary [Miss] Bučytė, and Šakalys, a teacher. The last-named once asked students to answer the question "What do you think of priests who have left the priesthood?" Almost all had answered that such priests were either foolish or lacked character.

The aftermath of such answers by the students was even greater persecution, but finding themselves incapable of influencing the students by force, the teachers began to try to persuade them to enroll in the Young Communist League. Students were told they could attend church elsewhere, not necessarily in Miežiškiai. Hoping to induce one eleventh-class student to join the League, the teachers promised to give him a very good characterization in his school records and said that he wouldn't even have to attend League meetings; however, when after joining the Young Communist League the student failed to attend one meeting, the school administrators confronted him and warned that if he would not attend the League meetings, he would be expelled from the League, and this would be noted in his characterization.

In May, 1973, [Mrs.] Kalačiovienė, secretary of the Panevėžys city Party Committee, visited the secondary school in Miežiškiai. She declared to the students who were not members of the Young Communist League: "We shall strive to see to it that during examinations nonmembers receive the worst possible grades and thus find it imposible to enroll in schools of higher education."

In October, 1972, during one of her classes, teacher [Mrs.] B. Gabrūnienė made the boys leave the room and ordered the girls to unbutton their uniform blouses and show her whether they were wearing crosses. Finding one girl with a cross, the teacher berated her and told the girl to never again show up in school wearing a cross.

* * *

On Palm Sunday, 1973, Party Secretary [Mrs.] Kalačiovienė checked on students atending the church in Miežiškiai and recorded the pastor's sermon.

The pastor's sermons were discussed at a secret meeting of the secondary school faculty on April 20. Although all the participants had been ordered to hold the contents of their deliberations in strict confidence, everyone learned soon after what had been discussed at the meeting. Kalačiovienė interrogated the teachers, trying to find out who had disclosed the subject of the secret meeting. Some students were ordered to spy upon those students who were going to church on Easter. Several Panevėžys Education Department employees arrived to investigate the situation on Easter Day at the church in Miežiškiai.

Government officials from Panevėžys came to the Miežiškiai Locality in the early part of May, 1973, among them Propaganda Department Director Kanapienis, Young Communist League Committee Advisor [Mrs.] Pukienė, [Mrs.] Kalačiovienė, and Dr. Kristutis, representative of the Ramygala atheists. People from the area were summoned to the locality office where they were posed a variety of questions about their personal religious life. Some of the people became frightened and said that they believed but little in God, but others deported themselves very courageously.

One of the officials asked [Mrs.] Gudienė, "Why don't you allow your son to join the Young Communist League?"

"Because I don't see any good examples among the Communists. They are dishonest and liars because they themselves secretly take part in religious rites while slandering others who do so."

Gudienė was berated for this response.

The officials asked [Mrs.] Murmokienė, "Do you truly believe there is a God, and do you teach this to your family?"

The woman confirmed that she truly believes and would always remain a believer.

The *rayon* officials visited believers' homes and asked them what kind of sermons were being preached by their pastor, and who was letting them bring their children to church? The representatives of the government asserted that Soviet laws permitted parents to take their children to church only once a year. Seeing religious pictures on the walls, the officials reproachfully insisted that their presence was a bad influence on students. Kalačiovienė even said: "You've decorated your walls with pictures of Jews!" Pensioners were threatened with having their pensions cut off. Kalačiovienė demanded that people show her their prayer books and rosaries, and when these were brought out, she wanted to confiscate them, but the owners refused to give them up.

The people were astonished that atheism was so powerless that Party representatives had to go around visiting homes and forcibly wage the fight against religion.

Directors of the local state farm began to intensify their attacks on believers. Office workers were warned that they would be dismissed from their jobs for attending church. They were not intimidated, however, and claimed that they hadn't forgotten yet how to milk cows.

Whenever locality Chairwoman Smetonienė would see people going to mass as she was strolling not far from the church, she would point to her temple with her forefinger to ridicule these people as fools.

The Panevėžys *Rayon* Party leaders noted down a reprimand against state farm Director Valaitis for permitting priests to purchase apartments.

The principal of the secondary school in Miežiškiai and the Party secretary of the state farm were censured for neglecting their work for the atheistic cause.

* * *

Father Masiokas, pastor of the parish in Miežiškiai, died on June 27. He had been badgered by government agents for some time. On Kalačiovienė's initiative, the pastor's telephone had even been disconnected without cause. The directors of the state farm ordered their workers to stay away from the pastor's funeral. No one paid any heed to this prohibition, and many adults and students were present at the funeral.

PANEVĖŽYS

In May, 1973, sixth-class students of secondary school no. 5 were made to answer various questions, among them: "What is the purpose of man's life on earth?" Many of the pupils answered with words from the catechism. Upon reading such answers, the teacher ordered the young people out of the classroom.

To the question "What name would you give to a new chapter of Pioneers?" some answered, "The name of St. John because he was the finest man in the world."

THE DIOCESE OF TELŠIAI

KLAIPĖDA

Tarasov of the Moscow Council for Religious Affairs came here in July, 1973. After inspecting the building in which the Catholics worship, he said, "What more do they want? The Catholics in Moscow have a smaller church and are content..."

But can one compare the number of Catholics in Moscow with that of the Catholics in Klaipėda?

ŠILALĖ

On June 15, 1973, at the request of their parents, [Miss] Eidukaitė, an elderly woman (b. 1887) of Vingininkai Village, was teaching the catechism to sixteen children. A commission comprised of collective farm Chairman Mikutis, brigade leader Vidmantas, agronomist Martinkus, and several representatives of the *rayon* administration, suddenly and noisily burst into the room. The commission members grabbed the catechisms, prayer books, and rosaries out of the children's hands. The youngsters tried to hide their catechisms and, sobbing, attempted to run out of the room, but the invaders frisked them and confiscated everything. They also recorded the names of each child and of the mothers who were present. The representative of the *rayon* department of education told the children: "Children, don't listen to your parents and don't study the catechism." The mothers were offended. "These are our children. We've been teaching them and will continue to teach them. We'll get some more catechisms."

The *rayon* procurator interrogated the elderly Eidukaitė and threatened her with imprisonment.

"It's shameful to go to prison for a sinful act, but for teaching the 'Our Father'—I am not afraid!"

The children and their mothers were also interrogated. Terrified by this experience, some of the children had trouble falling asleep that night.

* * *

Many atheistic drawings ridiculing religion and the clergy are posted on the hallway walls of the secondary school in Šilalė. Beside them is nailed a cracked black crucifix representing the approaching end of religion.

Once during class time, teacher [Mrs.] Petvienė and [Mrs.] Bendikienė ordered their students to draw a priest sitting on a devil's lap and surrounded by girls with whom he was drinking whiskey.

Here is what one eighth-class student from Šilalė wrote: "When atheists are unable to drive people out of church with the help of the police, it's as though a worm were gnawing at their souls... Children are forcibly enrolled in The Little Octobrists, the Young Pioneers, and other organizations... How painful it is to think that among our beloved Lithuanians there are such murderers who are destroying the souls of innocent children by leading them astray... In the showcase is the following inscription: 'People seek the way to heaven because they have lost their way on earth.' Those who have strayed from the path on earth are those who go around getting drunk and acting like hooligans. Those who seek the way to heaven are always in control of their passions, always orderly, and cause no harm to others, seeking in this manner eternal life. The persons who put together the showcase clearly reveal their inability to think straight. Ideas must be well thought out to avoid making a fool of oneself."

* * *

Through their unceasing propaganda, atheistic teachers make fanatics of their students. A case in point: Gotautas, an eighth-class student, wore a medal on a chain around his neck. Noticing it, Kurlinkus, a member of the Young Communist League, began to laugh and, calling a friend to help him, tried to take the medal away. Another student shamed them, however, and the two of them withdrew with flushed faces.

Lithuanian language teacher [Mrs.] Balčienė often pokes fun at religious students. During classes, expressions such as the following can often be heard from her: "You, Stasys, should be a priest. Speaking so nicely and softly, you'll be able to grant absolution to sanctimonious grannies."

Of a student with clean hands Balčienė says: "As for you, you'd make a fine pastor. The sanctimonious grannies will enjoy kissing such hands."

The people refer to such teachers as the atheists' "sanctimonious grannies."

* * *

On May 25, 1973, second-class pupils were made to draw cartoons ridiculing religion. Failing to realize that this was wrong, many pupils did so. Others, however, were disgusted at such conduct by the teacher. One girl said: "It was so awful that I couldn't look. I asked permission to go to the washroom and stayed there for a half-hour rather than draw any such things."

VEIVIRŽĖNAI

Balsėnai Village resident [Mrs.] Ona Strumilienė erected a cross on her farmstead under one of her windows. When they noticed the cross, collective farm Chairman Daugėla and Party Secretary [Mrs.] Bielskienė called upon Strumilienė and ordered her to either demolish the cross or to erect it beside the barn on the other side of her house.

"I know how a cross should be venerated and where it should be erected," the lady replied.

"We will force you not only to pull down the cross, but also to destroy it," the officials shouted at her.

Several days later *rayon* police Chief Ruščenkovas arrived and tried to intimidate the sickly elderly lady, demanding that she demolish the cross.

"The cross will stand in its place. As long as I'm

alive I will not allow anyone to destroy it. I didn't erect
it so that you would destroy it."

Strumilienė's son, Pranas, supported his mother. Rus-
čenkovas then ordered him to come down to police headquarters where they tried to intimidate him. He was told
he would be turned over to the security people if he didn't
agree to demolish the cross.

"I can erect a cross, but to tear it down—never!" retorted Strumila courageously.

Party officials kept calling at the Strumila home, constantly demanding that the cross be demolished immediately. Later, executive committee Chairman Karečka arrived
and tried to shame Strumilienė because she wasn't obeying
the officials.

"If you don't tear down the cross yourself, then we'll
demolish it, and you will have to pay the costs," Karečka
shouted.

"I will not tear down the cross; neither will I let you
do so. Show me the law that orders crosses to be demolished."

Hearing this, Karečka was livid with rage.

Unable to bear the constant threats, Ona Strumilienė
wrote a complaint to Moscow, but she never received an
answer. A commission from Vilnius arrived, inspected the
cross, declared that it was not a work of art, and demanded
that it be dismantled because, they said, it was scandalizing
the neighbors.

Two other Balsėnai Village families, those of Antanas
and Ignas Bočkus, were also ordered to demolish the crosses
erected on their farmsteads.

LAUGALIAI

Priests are not permitted to make calls at the nursing
home, thus many inmates die without receiving the last
sacraments, even though they ask to see a priest. For example, ninety-year-old [Miss] Agnietė Brazauskaitė's and
her eighty-five-year-old sister Ieva's requests were rejected
by the directors of the nursing home—they were not allowed to make use of the religious ministrations of a priest.

KALTINĖNAI

Religious students of the secondary school are being coerced—they are being forced to enroll in atheistic organizations. Teacher [Mrs.] Sinkevičienė whacked fourth-class student [Miss] Birutė Buivydaitė's palm with a ruler for not joining the Pioneers. Birutė later related how she had then said three 'Hail Mary's,' and the pain had gone away.

PAJŪRIS

Secondary school teacher [Mrs.] Valavičienė is a noted fanatic of atheism. Once, while deriding girls who kneel in adoration of the Holy Sacrament, she said: "Why do you crawl around on your knees about the pastor?"

At a meeting of parents of the students from the school in Šilalė on April 6, 1973, teacher Valavičienė stated that parents shouldn't "corrupt" their children—that they should not take them to church. The mothers who were present began to call out that they had come to hear about their children's schooling and behavior, and that they would not listen to this kind of nonsense. The lecturer had to give up and leave the meeting.

Teacher [Mrs.] Kulikauskienė notes in the school records of believer graduates that they still have not rid themselves of religious superstitions.

LAUKSARGIS

[Mrs.] Petkienė, a teacher at the eighth-year school, tries fanatically to impose her views on her pupils. She once boasted: "When I get through, not one student will go to church on Sundays!" Once a month all the students are compelled to go to the cultural center, where Petkienė "enlightens" them.

Caricatures slandering religion are posted in the school building—for example, an old woman dragging a resisting child to church. Doesn't Petkienė act similarly by trying to forcibly drag the entire student body in the direction of atheism? Whenever a child doesn't want to join the Young Communist League, Petkienė immediately rushes to see his parents, trying to convince them not to interfere.

THE DIOCESE OF VILKAVIŠKIS

ŠEŠTOKAI

In the summer of 1973, elderly [Miss] O. Merkušytė taught catechism to several children at the church in Šeštokai. To investigate this "criminal act," a commission comprised of Šeštokai Locality Chairman G. Maslauskas, [Mrs.] Šaulienė, principal of the school, and [Mrs.] Junelienė, a teacher, arrived at the church. Finding six children there, the investigators asked whether they were being taught how to pray. Three days later Merkušytė was summoned to the Lazdijai *Rayon* office and fined fifty rubles. In the decision of Administrative Case No. 30 it is written: "The Administrative Commission of the Lazdijai *Rayon* Soviet of Working People's Deputies Executive Committee (Chairman: Baranauskas; Secretary: [Mrs.] Kazakevičienė; members: [Miss] Ruškevičiūtė, Brilius, Šerkšnas, Šulinskas, and Jurkevičius), after deliberating in an open meeting this administrative case, has decided that Citizen Ona Merkušytė, who resides in the town of Šeštokai, has violated the May 12, 1966, order of the Presidium of the Supreme Soviet of the LSSR."

In its decision the commission didn't dare to write down just exactly what offense the elderly lady had committed. When releasing the woman, the commission warned her that no one is allowed to teach children the tenets of their faith, and that if she made one more attempt to teach children, she would be sentenced to two years' imprisonment.

VEISIEJAI

"To: The Curia of Vilkaviškis Diocese

*A Statement by the Rev. Albinas Deltuva,
pastor of the parish in Veisiejai*

"While Bishop L. Povilonis was administering the sacrament of confirmation at Veisiejai on July 28-29 of this year, several incidents occurred which scandalized the believers.

"With the excuse that it was harvest time, the days

on which the sacrament of confirmation was to be administered were declared to be working days in the *rayon*. To local collective farms and state farms was given the order that they were not to provide any means of transportation. On Sunday it rained. The harvesting ceased. Still, inspection points on the roads to Veisiejai permitted only buses and private means of transport to pass through. All other vehicles and wagons carrying people were turned back. That was why only eleven persons from neighboring parishes in Byelorussia who desired to receive the sacrament of confirmation were able to reach Veisiejai.

"The believers have noticed that of the many Saturdays and Sundays occurring during harvest time, only the days during which the sacrament of confirmation was to be administered were declared working days.

"At about 4 p.m. on July 28, just before the bishop was to arrive, I was summoned to the city executive committee office. Soviet of Working People's Deputies Chairman Vaikšnoras and three others, who appeared to be state security operatives, demanded that I would not allow the sale of any devotional objects near the church. On the grounds that there were not as yet any stores selling religious articles and that the faithful had been supplied with such goods only through the churches, I categorically refused to comply with their demands, warning them that any interference in this matter by government organs may result in grievous misunderstandings. Their response was that no one is afraid of complaints.

"Shortly thereafter, during the welcoming of the bishop, Petras Rėkus, an auxiliary policeman, assaulted one woman and forcibly snatched her devotional objects out of her hands and fled with them when a commotion began. Some people assert that the rosaries were being torn apart and crucifixes were being trampled underfoot, but I have not as yet found any eyewitnesses to this.

"Early in the morning on Sunday, July 29, policemen Leonovas and Morkevičius seized one woman's devotional objects and arrested her.

"Somewhat later, before 10 a.m., while the bishop was administering the sacrament of confirmation and Holy Communion was being distributed at the altar, Vitas Karaliūnas and Vitas Savukynas assaulted a man in the church and dragged him outside by force. The victim began to call for help. Many men and women hurried up to try to save him. Although a third man had joined the two attackers, they were forced to release their victim, whom they had already dragged out into the churchyard. Waiting for them at the churchyard gate was policeman Giedraitis, to whom they complained that their mission had failed.

"During the services, at about 10 a.m., uniformed policemen Savonis and Giedraitis, cruelly twisting his arms behind his back, led out of the churchyard a blind old man who, they had noticed, had several rosaries and crosses on chains in his possession. At the same time Vitas Karaliūnas, together with another man, seized two shopping bags from a woman and made off with them.

"Just after the bishop's departure, policemen Savonis and Giedraitis, who had asked a teacher from the vocational school to help them, tried to take devotional objects away from some man in the churchyard, but the provoked crowd pounced upon the policemen and ejected them from the churchyard. The policemen called for help, but by the time it arrived, the people had managed to disperse.

"Such facts do not benefit, nor do they bring honor to anyone. Perhaps the Curia can take the necessary steps in the appropriate agencies to assure that such incidents would not be repeated elsewhere.

Veisiejai
August 3, 1973"

A Note from the Editor

At 5 p.m. on July 28, 1973, H.E. Bishop L. Povilonis was greeted ceremoniously as he arrived at the parish in Veisiejai. This was the bishop's first pastoral trip to the Vilkaviškis Diocese since his move from Telšiai to Kaunas.

Approximately 2,600 persons were confirmed at the church in Veisiejai on July 28-29. Some 10,000 people attended the ceremonies. About 3,500 persons received Holy Communion.

ŠAKIAI

On May 4, 1973, Father Gvidonas Dovydaitis, curate of this parish, sent the following written explanation to the vice-chairman of the Šakiai *Rayon* Executive Committee, to its chief of security, and to the committee's secretary:

"On April 24, 1973, I was summoned by the Šakiai *Rayon* Executive Committee to the office of Vice-chairwoman D. Noreikienė, who, together with the chief of security and the secretary of the Party organization, berated me.

"On the following day, Father J. Žemaitis, Dean of Šakiai, was summoned to appear before the *rayon* executive committee. He was told he was not to allow me to go to Plokščiai to perform religious rites. Aside from that, they threatened that they would forbid me to preach.

"Although, as ordered by the *rayon* officials, I had hurriedly submitted a written explanation, it was not detailed. I therefore wish to answer more fully all of the charges against me, which I consider unjust:

1. I was charged with preaching a sermon to the faithful during a retreat on the evening of April 16 of this year at Plokščiai.

    Because Father J. Adomaitis, pastor of the parish in Plokščiai, had been ill for some time, with his Memo No. 364 Bishop Labukas entrusted the Dean of Šakiai and me with the duty of providing religious services to the parish in Plokščiai. Inasmuch as it was more convenient for my pastor to remain in his own parish on Sundays and holy days, it was usually I who was sent to Plokščiai to provide religious services. I had to perform all of the liturgical rites, thus also to preach sermons.

2. I was charged with reading and explaining to the faithful during the services the Soviet laws regarding religious cults.

    a. What I read were Soviet laws and not those of some capitalistic country. Was that a crime?

b. What I read were not secret and prohibited matters but excerpts from A. Vesčikov's book *Tarybiniai įstatymai apie religinius kultus* [Soviet laws concerning religious cults], which was published by the State publishing house of political and scientific literature in Vilnius in 1963. Was that a crime?

c. The Republic-wide educational conference held to consider the education of citizens in legal matters took place in Vilnius on February 23-24 of this year. At this meeting LSSR Minister of Justice A. Randakevičius emphasized that 'the future development of the Soviet democracy will result in an ever-increasing role that laws will play in our political, economic, and cultural life. That is why the Party puts great significance on the improvement of Soviet laws, the strengthening of social justice and the legal system, and on the education of the residents on legal matters.' It was noted at this conference that 'as the citizens' legal awareness and their knowledge of the laws is strengthened, their criminal offenses decrease.' The participants of the conference stressed 'that the propagation of legal information and the education of working people in matters of law aid in augmenting the sense of responsibility each member of society feels for his own actions and those of others' (*Tiesa* [Truth], February 24, 1973).

Not all citizens are familiar with the Soviet laws regarding religious cults. We priests are often made aware of this fact. Many people complain to us that they are being persecuted for their religious beliefs. They tell us that their superiors at work forbid them to perform their religious duties, to attend church, or to receive the sacraments. In case of disobedience, they are threatened with a variety of punishments in an effort to forcibly turn them into atheists; attempts are made to intimidate them with the possibility of demotion or even the loss of their jobs. Students and their parents also very often complain that students are not allowed to attend church, to receive the sacraments, or pray. Which means that many of our citizens do not know that among us there are no laws which prohibit the practice of one's religion. Was it then a crime that in my sermon I explained all this to the faithful? After all, at the previously mentioned conference this very thing—that laws should be explained because then violations decrease—had been discussed.

3. I was also accused of mentioning during my sermon the complaint signed by parents of students of the secondary school in Lukšiai addressed to the Procurator of the LSSR about the discrimination against students because of their religion.

It is no secret that as they propagandize atheism many of our officials and teachers overstep the bounds of Soviet law. Many teachers and officials actually terrorize citizens and students who believe in God. Soviet laws provide for the punishment of such violators. Being aware of this, the more knowledgeable parents of students from the secondary school in Lukšiai wrote a collective complaint to the Procurator of the Republic. They acted correctly, of course. I cannot comprehend, therefore, why this should not be mentioned. Is that a crime? If I am censured and threatened with punishment, why then are the editors of newspapers and magazines and their correspondents not castigated for the many violations they publicize in their pages? My sermon was heard by only several dozens of believers, while thousands read the events described by newspapers and magazines. I do not understand why some violations can be talked and written about, but not others. After all, the very same constitution guards both public property and the freedom of conscience.

4. I was also accused of derogatory talk about the school at which I myself had studied and from which I grad-

uated. Bitter truth is always better than a sweet lie. It is shameful and demeaning, not to bring up mistakes, but to keep silent about them. Even F. Dzerzhinsky wrote: 'It is possible to go forward only when, step by step, you seek out wrong and vanquish it.'

"One could draw the conclusion that our constitution and our laws say one thing, but in practice it is otherwise. The laws exist only on paper. They are well formulated, but in reality they do not protect the convictions of believers. They are merely pleasant words of propaganda. Many atheists are guilty of violations against the freedom of conscience. Believers lament and complain, but not even once have the law enforcement agencies punished those who commit such offenses.

"One would wish that these fine laws regarding the freedom of conscience were not merely pretty phrases of propaganda, but that they would truly protect the sacred sentiments of believing citizens guaranteed by the freedom of conscience.

The Rev. G. Dovydaitis
Šakiai, May 4, 1974"

THE DIOCESE OF KAIŠIADORYS

KUKTIŠKĖS

On Easter Sunday, 1973, girls of this parish scattered flowers during services. Meškauskas, principal of the Kuktiškės eight-year school upbraided the girls for this "offense." Caricatures of some of the students appeared in the newsletter posted on the bulletin board. Kuktiškės Collective Farm Chairman J. Ryliškis censured [Mrs.] Veronika Katinienė for having organized the girls in the procession. He threatened that her plot of land would be taken away and that she would be refused pasture and fodder for her livestock.

***

A Request from the Editors of the Chronicle

Unsubstantiated information and inaccurate facts are not suitable for publication in the *Chronicle of the Catholic Church in Lithuania.* Such copy will not be printed in the pages of the *Chronicle.* Each news item, each fact or event relevant to the situation of the Catholic Church, to our nation's history, to the present, to the arbitrariness of the authorities, or to any repressions or other forms of discrimination must be scrupulously verified, clear, and precise. Numbers, dates, surnames, place names, and other data must be especially explicit, correctly written down, and verified.

no. 8

- *Visiting Italian journalist receives "objective" information about the situation of the Catholic Church in Lithuania*
- *Numerous raids by the security police are followed by interrogations*
- *Text of petition sent by 1,000 believers requesting an able-bodied priest for their parish; and its aftermath*
- *Priests are fined for catechization of children (Father Molis, Father Nykštus, Father Žvinys, Father Galvydis)*
- *Text of a declaration sent by Father B. Laurinavičius to various ecclesiastical and Soviet authorities*
- *Nuns are dismissed from their positions*
- *The authorities allow twelve candidates to enter the theological seminary*
- *The erection of a cross on the Hill of Crosses results in interrogations*
- *The authorities hamper believers on their way to a religious festival at Šiluva*
- *Pastor is upbraided for organizing volunteer workers to clean the church*
- *Confirmation rites are cancelled due to "harvesting"*
- *Tarasov of the Council for Religious Affairs declares that the believers of Klaipėda must be content with their overcrowded church*
- *Woman is fined for selling devotional articles*
- *Classmates are not allowed to attend a boy's funeral*
- *Schoolchildren are made to answer a questionnaire on religious topics*

THE CHRONICLE
OF THE CATHOLIC CHURCH
IN LITHUANIA

No. 8   1973

AN ITALIAN JOURNALIST
VISITS LITHUANIA

At the invitation of the press agency Novosti, the editor of an Italian Catholic weekly, Rugiero Orfeio, visited Soviet Lithuania. The guest from Rome toured the Vilnius home construction combination, viewed Lazdynai, Karoliniškė, the architectural landmarks of the old-town section, and spent some time in several churches during services. At the end of his visit, R. Orfeio stated, "Of great interest to me was the condition of Catholics under socialism. I was in [Saints] Peter and Paul's as well as [Saint] Ann's churches during services. After seeing the religious rites with my own eyes, I became convinced that Catholics are not being persecuted but are free to fulfill their duties. This impression of mine was confirmed by a lengthy and open discussion with Msgr. Česlovas Krivaitis, the ecclesiastical administrator of the Vilnius Archdiocese. This distinguished clergyman gave me an objective account of the field of action of the Roman Catholic Church in Lithuania and of the situation of the clergy and the believers. The concrete facts that he presented convinced me that the Catholic Church in Soviet Lithuania functions normally. Unfortunately, in Italy many individuals provide inaccurate information, with the goal of distorting and blackening the reality of this socialistic country. Upon my return to my homeland, I shall relate at great length my impressions of Lithuania, which has attained a number of worthy achievements" (*Gimtasis krãštas* [Native land], Nov. 8, 1973). To enable the formation of a more comprehensive picture of the situation of the Catholic Church in Lithuania, we shall present the following remarks:

1. For some reason the editors [of *Gimtasis krãštas*] failed to mention the title of the Catholic weekly, and therefore the thought comes to mind that the aforementioned editor is a member of the staff of *L'Unita* [Italian Communist newspaper]. Since when has the press agency Novosti become concerned about presenting "objective" information to the world through Catholic journalists?

2. Did the above-mentioned guest search for the truth on his own, or was he "assisted" in finding it by K. Tumėnas, the commissioner of the Council for Religious Affairs? There isn't a Catholic in Lithuania who believes in Tumėnas' good will as far as the Church is concerned.

3. Were not Orfeio's suspicions aroused because the same handful of priests has been trying for a number of years to sell to the world "objective" information about the situation of the Church in Lithuania?

4. We ask the guest from Italy (that is, if he has a conscience) to acquaint himself with all issues of the *Chronicle of the Catholic Church in Lithuania.*

5. After visiting only two churches in Vilnius, Orfeio managed to form an "objective" picture of the situation of the Catholic Church in Lithuania. How unfortunate that he failed to notice that the architectural masterpiece of Stuoka-Gucevičius, the Cathedral of Vilnius, has been converted into an art gallery, whereas other artistic churches, among them the churches of St. Catherine, the Trinitarians, and All Saints, have been turned into concert halls and warehouses, and St. Casimir's—into a museum of atheism.

6. It would be desirable that the small group of Lithuanian priests who have for many years been giving interviews to various foreign journalists would update their

"objective" information with the latest facts of Lithuanian Catholic life. To them is dedicated this issue of the *Chronicle of the Catholic Church in Lithuania.*

RELIGIOUS "FREEDOM" IN LITHUANIA

On November 14, 1973, the decision was made by the State Security Committee to organize a great number of searches in order to liquidate the secret publication *The Chronicle of the Catholic Church in Lithuania* and the underground centers at which prayer books and religious literature are printed and to destroy all literature of a religious nature.

RAGING RAIDS

Before dawn on November 20, 1973, a group of security police arrived to search the quarters of Father J. Lauriūnas, pastor of the parish in Kabeliai. In command was Capt. Kazanavičius of the State Security Committee Interrogation Department. The security police had brought with them from Druskininkai as witnesses Vytautas Žukauskas and Juozas Šlikas, who actually functioned as security agents during the search. Documents and literature slandering the Soviet form of government were sought in both the residence and the outbuildings. Taken during the search were two typewriters; nine typewriter ribbons; a goodly amount of writing paper; approximately ten typewritten religious books, among them, *Niekšybės paslaptis* [The mystery of iniquity], *Kristus ir krikščioniškoji asmenybė* [Christ and the Christian personality], *Viešpatie, ateik* [Come, O Lord]; some twenty metallic pictures, and a great number of various manuscripts. In one room even the floor was torn up. The secret police searched Father Lauriūnas as well. Since the search, the pastor has already been interrogated twice, and it is uncertain how long this vexation will be continued.

* * *

Early in the morning on November 20, the Interrogation Department's Senior Lieutenant V. Kontrimas appeared at the rectory in Valkininkai with his assistants and witnesses: [Miss] O. Važgytė, V. Novikov, and Valkininkai Locality Chairwoman M. Markevičienė. The purpose of this search was to obtain any articles and documents relevant to criminal case no. 345. Pastor A. Keina was away, so the security police presented their warrant to the rectory's housekeeper, and until 6 p.m. they carefully searched the dwelling and the outbuildings. Taken during the search was a typewriter, four issues of the *Chronicle of the Catholic Church in Lithuania,* fifty copies of the prayer book *Melskimės* [Let us pray], forty copies of *Sveika Marija* [Hail Mary] by K. Žitkus, six copies of Tihamér Tóth's *Jaunuolio religija* [A youth's religion], and some eighty religious books produced either by typewriter or photocopying machine, among them *Netikinčiųjų katekizmas* [Catechism for nonbelievers], *Marijos garbė* [The glory of Mary], *Milžinas, didvyris, žmogus* [Giant, hero, man], *Kunigas Dievo ir žmonių tarnyboje* [The Priest in the service of God and man], *Rekolekcijos apie Kristaus bičiulystę* [A retreat on the friendship of Christ], *Dievo Avinėlis* [Lamb of God], *Deimančiukai* [Little gems], *Žodžiai broliams* [Talks to the brethren], *Tėve mūsų* [Our Father], *Sekmadienių ir švenčių pamokslai* [Sermons for Sundays and holy days], *Katalikų katekizmas* [Catholic catechism], *O vis dėlto Šv. Raštas teisus* [In any case, the Bible is right]. Also taken were a few prewar books: *Tautinis auklėjimas* [Nurturing nationalism], *Jaunos sielos auklėjimas* [The nurturing of a young soul]. Three magnetic tapes, religious holy cards, religious albums, a stack of writing paper, various notes and manuscripts, a sheaf of newspaper clippings, various documents, *Beprotybės klausimas* [The question of insanity], and other items also ended up in the bags of the security police.

While the security police were resting after the search, Father A. Keina returned. He was not allowed to say mass for the people who had congregated; he was immediately taken to Varėna. His interrogation was continued also on the following day.

About twenty believers from the parish in Valkininkai

who came in search of their pastor filled the security police with dismay.

* * *

...On that memorable morning Father Boleslovas Babrauskas was hurrying to the bus station in Smilgiai (Biržai *Rayon*). Before he reached his destination, he was stopped by security officials. They said they wished to talk with him. Being unwilling to talk with the security police, the priest demurred. They then forcibly dragged him to the locality office and, presenting a warrant, searched his pockets and briefcase. The priest was taken to the church sacristy, where the pastor lived because the parochial buildings had been confiscated by the government. Some fifteen security agents, together with the two "witnesses" they had brought, scoured even the attic. The pastor was not allowed to invite any witnesses. All religious books in the sacristy were dumped on the floor. Then the "guests" ascended to the second floor of the sacristy—into the pastor's bedroom—and lugging out all his books threw them downstairs. The housekeeper's quarters were also thoroughly searched. They confiscated her Bible, a small prayer book, and other religious literature, even prewar editions. In the pastor's bedroom even the floor was torn up. The church was searched without the presence of a representative of the parochial committee. Even the tabernacles in the church were examined and some sheet music and all the hymnals were taken. The security agents hauled to the sacristy the religious literature that they discovered in the attic of the church. Nor were the outbuildings overlooked. The security police seized the audio tapes and the slides. The searchers' bags swallowed up even the holy cards. Over a thousand religious books were taken. The only items entered in the report of the search were issues of the *Chronicle of the Catholic Church in Lithuania*, several bags, and books. All the other books, haphazardly crammed into ten bags, ended up in the truck of the security police. After the search, Father B. Babrauskas was interrogated—where had he obtained the religious literature and the *Chronicle*?

* * *

On November 20, the Rev. Jonas Buliauskas, a retired priest from Krinčinas, was seized by the security police in Šiauliai, brought back, and searched. In the course of the search, the religious literature found in the priest's possession was confiscated. In the report of the search, the priest entered a protest, since the USSR Constitution guarantees the freedom of religion and the press, and declared that he would not respond during interrogation. To date, Father Buliauskas has not been summoned for interrogation.

* * *

Early in the morning on November 20, 1973, a group of security police arrived at the home of Augustinas Jaugelis, who lives at 16 Linkuva St., Kaunas, and at 7 a.m. searched the house and the outbuildings. The homeowner himself was also searched. The purpose of the search was to seize articles and documents "falsely" belittling the Soviet state and its social system. Maj. Vaclovas Raudys who was in charge of the searchers, included in his report of the search only nine religious books and six volumes of the prewar magazine *Ateities spinduliai* [Glimmers of the future]. Sets of the magazines *Šaltinis* [Source], *Saleziečių žinios* [Salesian news], *Žvaigždė* [Star], *Pranciškonų pasaulis* [Franciscan world], *Liurdas* [Lourdes], *Misijos* [Missions], *Šv. Pranciškaus varpelis* [Bell of St. Francis]; a typewriter; several religious books, among them, *Visi mes broliai* [We are all brothers], *Žmonės ir žvėrys* [Men and beasts], *Mokslininkų pasaulėžiūra* [World views of scholars]; sheaves of newspaper clippings; notebooks; and other items were all listed on separate sheets of paper and were not signed by Major Rudys nor by the witnesses. Jaugelis was given only the report of the search to sign.

While interrogating him, the security policeman angrily called the believers fanatics.

"If you were in power, you would twist our heads off," said the interrogator.

"If we gave you freedom of the press, you would demand that priests teach religion in the schools, and later,

that a Christian political party would be established.....
Through your libelous writings, you are ruining us economically. We need technology and computers, but the
American Congress is creating obstacles for us, on account
of the libelous propaganda about the so-called persecution
of believers."

***

On November 20, 1973, Captain Žilakauskas, an agent
of the state security organs, together with other security
policemen, began a search at 7:30 a.m. in the home of Virgilijus Jaugelis, who lives at 7 Kalnai St., apartment 4,
Kaunas, with the purpose of seizing articles and documents
of relevance in court.

In the course of the search they seized the following
books: *Dogminė teologija* [Dogmatic theology], *Evangeli-
ja gyvenime* [The Gospel in our lives], *Įvadas į filosofiją*
[Introduction to philosophy], *Stigmatizuotoji Teresė Neu-
manaitė* [The stigmatic Theresa Neumann], *Katalikas esu*
[I am a Catholic], *Jaunuolio būdas* [The character of a
youth], *Tikybos pirmamokslis* [Primer of the Faith], *Mo-
ralinė teologija* [Moral theology], and others. Unused stencils, notes, writing paper, and other items were also taken.

During his interrogation, Jaugelis explained that the
stencils and other articles found in a travel bag did not
belong to him, but to an unknown man who had asked
him to keep them for him.

Immediately after the search, Jaugelis wrote a protest
to the Procurator of the LSSR concerning the seized reli
gious books. In his statement Jaugelis argued that if the
Soviet government guarantees the freedom of conscience,
speech, the press, and other freedoms, then those who
seized his religious books are offenders whom the prosecutor should suppress.

***

On November 20, 1973, four agents of the security
police showed up early in the morning at the home of
Arimantas Reškevičius, a resident of Kaunas, and spent
seven hours searching for suspect literature. Seized during

the search was a typewriter, many manuscripts, one and one-half sacks of religious literature, and one issue of the *Chronicle of the Catholic Church in Lithuania.* After the search, Arimantas was questioned for a day and a half at security police headquarters as to where he had obtained the literature found during the search.

* * *

In the afternoon of November 19, 1973, six security policemen with two witnesses came to the home of [Miss] N. Cicėnaitė and [Mrs.] T. Mačiukienė. Two security men spent the night in their room, and in the morning, all six finished the search. Some poems, notes, *Maldynas* [Book of prayers], a new edition of the Bible, and a number of religious books were confiscated. Afterward, the interrogations began.

* * *

Early in the morning on November 20, 1973, five security policemen arrived at the living quarters of Juozas Turauskas in Kaunas and spent three hours searching his apartment. In the course of the search they seized the tricolor flag [of Independent Lithuania], some letters, a song book, five catechisms, three prayer books, and several religious books, among them, *Liturgika* [The Liturgy] and *Jaunuolio kovos* [Struggles of a Youth]. After the search Turauskas was interrogated.

* * *

On November 20, 1973, the security police failed to find [Miss] Monika Gavėnaitė at home; they therefore sealed her apartment (43 Kapsai St., Kaunas) and awaited her return. On November 26 Major Aleinikovas, together with other security policemen searched Gavėnaitė's apartment. A goodly amount of religious literature was taken during the search: *Šventųjų Mišių liturgija* [Liturgy of the Mass], *Mano malda* [My prayer], *Visa apimanti meilė* [All-embracing love], *Paprastas mąstymas* [Simple meditation], *Kristaus gyvenimas* [Life of Christ], *Jėzus Kristus* [Jesus Christ], *Kristus—mano gyvenimas* [Christ is my life], *Atlaidų rinkinys* [Collection of Indulgences], etc.

The security police also confiscated letters, brochures, writing paper, etc. The search took some two and one-half hours. After the search Monika Gavėnaitė was interrogated several times. The interrogator promised to question her many more times.

* * *

Early in the evening of November 19, 1973, Captain Marcinkevičius, the chief interrogator of the State Security Committee, together with other security policemen began looking for articles and documents that would be relevant in court at the home of Petras Pliuira, 50 Basanavičius Ave., apartment 208, Kaunas. Seized during the search was the *Chronicle of the Catholic Church in Lithuania* no. 1, and its Russian translation; the religious books *Krikščioniškoji šeima gyvenime* [How a Christian family lives], *Meilės ugnis* [Fire of love], *Šv. Mergelės Marijos gyvenimas* [Life of the Blessed Virgin Mary], *Atlaidų rinkinys* [Collection of Indulgences]; brochures reproduced by photocopying; notebooks; various notations, paper clippings with obvious markings made by a copying machine, etc. With the exception of the text *Kaip laikytis tardymo metu* [How to behave during interrogation], the confiscated literature was of a religious nature.

During the search [Miss] Ona Česnulevičiūtė came to Pluira's apartment. Found in her handbag and confiscated was the prayer book *Valandėlė su Jėzumi* [An hour with Jesus].

The search took about four hours. Afterward, Petras Pliuira was driven to security police headquarters and detained. He was accused of violating Article 68 of the Criminal Code—that he had disseminated libelous fabrications slandering the Soviet form of government.

* * *

On November 20, 1973, security police agent Senior Lieutenant Gudas searched the residence of Vladas Lapienis at 5 Dauguvietis St., apartment 11, Vilnius. Seized during the search were four bags of religious books reproduced either by photocopying or by typewriter, a typewriter, a large number of holy cards, ten copies of the *Chronicle of the Catholic Church in Lithuania*, and other items. During the search Father J. Zubrus happened to stop by to visit Lapienis and was also searched. (Seized were *Jaunuolio religija* [A youth's religion], several notebooks, and a few leaflets of religious nature.) The search lasted four hours. Afterward, Lapienis was interrogated many times and questioned as to where he obtained so much literature and the issues of the *Chronicle*. Many of the interrogators acted very rudely and threatened him with prison, with eviction from Vilnius, and made other, similar, threats.

* * *

On November 20, 1973, a search was made at the home of Vilnius resident Zenon Urbon, who lives on Baltarusiai St. The search lasted ten hours. Masters of the prayer book *Marija, gelbėk mus!* [Mary, save us!], a homemade printing press, several printed pages of the prayer book, and a number of holy cards were seized.

During his interrogation, Urbon said that he himself had obtained the printing facilities and had produced prayer books because he wanted to help the believers who lacked prayer books.

* * *

Early in the morning on November 20, 1973, security police began a search at the home of Jonas Stašaitis, a resident of Salininkai (Vilnius *Rayon*). For seven hours his home and outbuildings were thoroughly searched. The following were confiscated: several religious books, two prayer books, several notebooks, some holy cards, etc. After the search Stašaitis was interrogated at the headquarters of the State Security Committee (40 Lenin Prospect, Vilnius).

On December 4, Stašaitis failed to return from his interrogation. Two days later his wife received the following notice from the State Security Committee: "In accordance with the LSSR Code of Criminal Procedure, we hereby inform you that Jonas Stašaitis, son of Juozas, was arrested on December 4, 1973, by the State Security Committee, which is attached to the LSSR Council of Ministers, for committing the crimes specified in articles 18 and 162 of the Criminal Code of the LSSR and is being held at Vilnius a/d 17. [Signed] V. Pilelis, Chief Interrogator of the State Security Committee."

* * *

On December, 1973, a search was made of Father Prokofjevas' apartment in Vilnius. Seized during the search were old addresses, holy cards, etc. In the course of his interrogation he was threatened with prison because he had joined a delegation which had gone to Moscow on Church matters. Father Prokofjevas explained that it is not a crime to appeal to one's government.

* * *

Early in the morning on November 20, 1973, three security police officers began a search at the home of [Miss] Stefa Kriaučiūnaitė of Panevėžys. In her room and in the attic they found a great number of religious books. Seven security agents spent the whole day searching the place. In the apartment of Kriaučiūnaitė's tenant, [Miss] Ona Norkutė, the security police found, among other things, several prayer books, eighteen religious books, some pictures, etc. They accused Norkutė of black-marketeering.

The security police also seized seventeen religious books from [Miss] Liuda Razminaitė. The search ended at 9:30 p.m.

That same day the security police searched the apartment of [Miss] Nastutė, the janitress of the church in the old-town section. The search took three hours. A number of rosaries were confiscated and even the religious pictures cut out from *Žvaigždė* [Star].

* * *

On November 20, 1973, three security police agents from Panevėžys searched the apartment of [Miss] Julija Mickeliūnaitė, laundress of the church vestments in Ramygala. Among the items taken during the search were a few typewritten religious books, a notebook, and several small brochures.

* * *

On November 20, 1973, Senior Lieutenant Bankauskas searched the apartment of [Mrs.] Zita Razminienė in Šiauliai (35 Komunarai St., apartment 65). The purpose of the search was to seize articles and documents relevant to criminal case no. 345 for the "dissemination of fabrications belittling the Soviet state." The search lasted eight hours. Taken during the search was a typewriter; some books, among them, *Jaunoms širdims* [For young hearts], *Deimančiukai* [Little gems], *Moters gyvenimo ruduo* [Autumn of a woman's life], *Kęstutis* [Kestutis], *Katalikų tikybos kursas* [A course in the Catholic faith], *Mažasis tobulybės kelias* [The humble way to Perfection], *Jaunuolio religija* [A youth's religion], *Geroji kančia* [Worthy suffering], *Dora* [Virtue]; separate issues of the magazines *Židinys* [Center], *Pranciškonų pasaulis* [Franciscan world], *Saleziečių žinios* [Salesian news], *Misijos* [Missions], *Sargyba* [The guard], *Draugija* [The society], *Žvaigždutė* [Little star]; letters; postcards; notebooks; photographs, holy cards; etc. After the search, Razminienė was interrogated many times.

* * *

Early in the morning on November 20, 1973, security police agents began to search the home of Juozas Kopūstas, a resident of Semeliškės. The search lasted four hours. They were looking for an underground press. Taken during the search were two prayer books, the booklet *Tikiu* [I believe], and other religious books.

Kopūstas was interrogated—where had he obtained the religious literature?

* * *

On November 20, 1973, the apartment of Antanas Jasėnas in Vievis was searched. Bookbinding equipment and quite a number of partially bound copies of the prayer book *Aukštyn širdis* [Lift up your hearts] were found.

* * *

On November 20, 1973, early in the morning the security police started searching Dambrauskas and Kačergis, inhabitants of the town of Kapsukas (formerly Marijampolė) who lived on Krantas Street. They were looking for religious literature and a "firearm". The security police dug up the potatoes, rummaged through the wood pile, and even wanted to tear up the floor; however, when Dambrauskas protested, they relented. Items needed to support a case in court were not found.

* * *

On November 20, 1973, two security police agents searched the home of [Miss] Klementina Misiūnaitė in Kaunas. The search lasted seven hours. A typewriter and all the religious literature were confiscated.

* * *

For six hours, the security police searched the apartment of [Miss] Ona Tamulynaitė in Kaunas. Nothing incriminating was found.

* * *

At the home of Juozas Urbonas, a resident of Kaunas, a large quantity of religious literature was found. After the search, he had to undergo a lengthy interrogation.

* * *

In Šiauliai, at the home of Stasys Sipkus, the security police confiscated the entire library.

* * *

At the home of Antanas Ratkevičius of Pasvalys, the search took ten hours. All religious literature was seized.

* * *

In Viršužiglis Village, at the home of [Mrs.] Regina Strašinskienė, a typewriter and a large amount of paper were confiscated.

* * *

The *Chronicle of the Catholic Church in Lithuania* has been unable to register every search that occurred. Additional information will be presented in the next issue.

There is no news concerning the arrest and interrogation of Povilas Petronis.

The searches carried out by the state security organs indicate how much effort is being expended by the Soviet government in order to suppress religious thought and the truth about the present situation of the Catholic Church in Lithuania.

THE ARCHDIOCESE OF VILNIUS

MIELAGĖNAI

"To: K. Tumėnas, LSSR Commissioner of the Council for Religious Affairs
Rev. Č. Krivaitis, the ecclesiastical administrator of the Vilnius Archdiocese

A Petition from the faithful of the Parish in Mielagėnai in Ignalina Rayon

"Because the pastor of our parish, Father Vincentas Miškinis, is already eighty years old and afflicted with a great number of illnesses, he is no longer able to minister to our needs. Several years ago, during Lent, some neighboring priests came to minister to us (hear confessions and preach). At that time, Gudukienė, chairwoman of the Ignalina Executive Committee summoned Father Miškinis and upbraided him because other priests were helping out at Mielagėnai.

"Last summer, our pastor went away to undergo treatment. Practically every Sunday during his absence no services were held. We then appealed to the archdiocesan curia to appoint us a priest who was not incapacitated. We promised to maintain both priests, since the state grants no pensions to elderly priests or sacristans who are no longer able to work (even though ministers of the cult are required to pay sizeable income taxes to the state).

"Our pastor has been seriously ill and bedridden for the second month now. At the present time priests from neighboring parishes come here on Sundays to hold services, and then they hurry home. That is because there is a shortage of priests everywhere. The large parish of Adutiškis always had two priests, and now there is but one.

Ever since the closing of the church in 1961 during the tenure of Rugienis, the commissioner of the Council for Religious Affairs, Kačergiškė has had no priest. Some priests, for instance those in Ignalina, must even minister to two churches. It is obvious that they cannot also take care of the religious needs of our parish, of our sick, etc. "It appears as though the ecclesiastical administrator of the archdiocese, Rev. Č. Krivaitis, does not assign us a priest simply because there is a shortage of priests.

"We have heard, however, that there are priests who could minister to the faithful, but the government does not permit them to perform their priestly functions, for example, the Rev. Vytautas Merkys has been working in an arboretum in Vilnius for more than ten years.

"If such priests are allowed to work in governmental establishments, why are they not permitted to minister to us believers? Why are we being punished, for the Constitution guarantees the freedom of conscience?

"No one knows why our Bishop Steponavičius was removed from his position. No one knows why for thirty-five years no one has ever administered the sacrament of confirmation at our church in Mielagėnai. It grieves us that we have no regular services at our church, that our sick die without the last sacraments, that in our own church there is no one who could say mass for our intentions.

"It would not be so hard for us, the faithful, if we did not know that there are priests and bishops who are not permitted to carry out their duties.

"You have been appointed the new commissioner in charge of our—believers'—affairs. We therefore request you to find positions for all the bishops and priests who were displaced; to permit the ecclesiastical administrator of the archdiocese to appoint to our parish in Mielagėnai an able priest who would be capable of ministering to the needs of all the faithful, as demands humanity and the Constitution.

Mielagėnai
October 13, 1973"

This petition was signed by about 1,000 persons, not just Catholic Lithuanians, but also non-Catholic Russians; however, the petition was never submitted to K. Tumėnas, the commissioner of the Council for Religious Affairs, for the following reasons:

1. On October 19, 1973, M. Kolesničenko, head of the Ignalina *Rayon* State Security Committee, and A. Vaitonis, vice-chairman of the *Rayon* Executive Committee, started a hunt in the parish of Mielagėnai for the signed petitions. They went to Miečioniai Village, to the home of [Miss] Elena Jakštaitė, and tormented her for a whole hour, asking who had organized the petition and demanding that she hand over the petition together with all the signatures. She refused to comply with their demands. Her "guests" then threatened her with imprisonment and a search. The girl became frightened and surrendered the petitions.

Apparently the security agents were aware of who was gathering signatures since they went from Miečioniai directly to Kostas Bajorūnas in Buckūnai Village. Here again there were interrogations and threats. Kostas, deeply upset, told them that he had handed over the petitions to [Mrs.] Marijona Milikėnienė. Thereupon the security agents traveled to the residence of the Milikėnases in Malikai Village. Marijona was not at home. The whole brunt of the terrorization fell upon the shoulders of her husband, Stanislovas. He was not about to give in easily, but unfortunately the petitions had not been hidden, and so they were confiscated.

On that day petitions with several hundred signatures were seized in the villages of Miečioniai, Bernotai, Mašonai, Buckūnai, and Salomenka. They were unsuccessful in obtaining the petitions elsewhere.

Widespread panic arose. Some people began to talk publicly that at the present time in Lithuania the fate of the believer was worse than during the days of serfdom—the faithful are not even allowed to ask that a priest be assigned to their parish.

The people were not discouraged, however, and continued collecting signatures.

The security police did not forget to "pet" Juozas Bajorūnas, chairman of the Mielagėnai Parochial Committee. They berated him and told him that the writing of such and similar petitions and the stirring up of people was not allowed. On October 22 Bajorūnas was ordered to go to Ignalina to explain himself; however, on that day he did not go to the *rayon* headquarters himself, but rather his wife, Ona Bajorūnienė, went. Vice-Chairman Vaitonis, in an attempt to embarass her, upbraided her: "Why do you appeal to Vilnius? Write to us! You biddies know where to turn. Your children are in Vilnius; that's why you're so smart!"

2. After the security officials had confiscated the petitions with the signatures, on October 20 Dean Julius Baltušis brought to Father Antanas Mačiulis, pastor of the parish in Paringys, a communiqué from the Rev. Č. Krivaitis, the ecclesiastical administrator of the Vilnius Archdiocese, in which it was indicated that Father Mačiulis must minister to the faithful of Mielagėnai until a priest is appointed to that parish. The assignment was made completely disregarding the fact that between Paringys and Mielagėnai there is a distance of twelve kilometers, and there is only one passenger bus daily.

The security organs and the atheists have attained their goal. Now that the curia has appointed a priest, albeit a visiting one, it was unseemly for the believers to send another petition because both the curia and Commissioner Tumėnas would reply that they already have a priest.

While the signatures were being collected, Pastor V. Miškinis of Mielagėnai lay in the hospital at Švenčionys. His health was improving, but when he found out how the security agents were treating his parishioners, he became very agitated, and on October 27, 1973, he died.

RŪDIŠKĖS

Father Konstantinas Molis was preparing children for their first confession and First Communion. On May 27,

1973, a committee of six persons came to the church in Rūdiškės, where about fifty children had gathered. The members of the committee were very polite; they merely listened and waited in church for the end of the proceedings. When the priest, having finished with his explanation, dismissed the children, the members of the committee approached the parents. They asked why their children had assembled here. They wrote down the names of the parents and their addresses.

After several days, the Procurator of Trakai *Rayon* summoned many of the children and also Father Molis. During his interrogation, the priest admitted that he had been teaching the children. He said his conscience and his sense of priestly duties had compelled him to do so.

The people became frightened and addressed a petition to the Procurator of Trakai *Rayon*, which was signed by twenty persons. The petition pointed out that Father Molis was completely innocent because the parents had asked him to teach their children.

On June 28, 1973, the administrative commission of the Trakai *Rayon* Executive Committee ordered Father Molis to pay a fine of thirty rubles. All the committee members were polite and said little. The presiding officer asked Father Molis whether he felt that he had committed an offense. The priest did not reply. After a minute of silence, the presiding officer continued, "According to international law, you are not guilty, but according to our instructions— guilty. Since after our warning you no longer taught children, since you have not been punished previously for such incidents, and since you promise not to teach in the future, and also taking other factors into consideration, your fine will be only thirty rubles."

The administrative commission did not give the accused a copy of its verdict but merely ordered him to go to the bank and pay the sum of thirty rubles. The bank clerks would accept the money anyway.

ADUTIŠKIS

"To: Tarasov, the Commissioner of the Council for Religious Affairs Attached to the Council of Ministers of the USSR
H.E. Bishop J. Labukas, Apostolic Administrator of the Kaunas Archdiocese
The Curia of the Vilnius Archdiocese
K. Tumėnas, Commissioner of the Council for Religious Affairs
Purvaneckaitė, Chairwoman of the Švenčionys *Rayon* Executive Committee

A Declaration by the Rev. B. Laurinavičius, a resident of Adutiškis, Švenčionys Rayon, the LSSR

"On July 16, 1973, Adutiškis Locality Chairman A. Laurinavičius demanded the church keys. When asked for the reason, he replied, 'An important guest has come from Moscow—Tarasov. He wants to inspect the church.'

"In the churchyard I met you; K. Tumėnas, the LSSR commissioner of the Council for Religious Affairs; Purvaneckaitė, chairwoman of the Švenčionys *Rayon* Executive Committee; un unknown man; and A. Laurinavičius, chairman of Adutiškis Locality. You questioned me:

1. To the question 'How many come to church?' I replied that I did not know because we do not count. To enable me to answer your question, on July 22, 1973, we counted 722 persons. No conclusion can be drawn from this, however, since many are unable to come to church on account of distance, lack of transportation, and many other obstacles. For instance, one of my parishioners, Feliksas Kairys, bringing me home from sick call, on April 14, 1973, spoke to me with tears in his eyes: 'After working hard for some time, I bought myself a suit, but what's the use? It's been two years now that I've meant to put in on and go to church. Alas, I can't do it because I'm haunted by fear. In the spring, Director Galvydis of the Jakeliai State Farm

threatened me, "If you don't come to work on Sunday, you won't get a horse, neither for harrowing nor for bringing in wood, nor any hay for your cow, nor the use of the combine to thresh your barley." '

Povilas Burokas, who lives on the Jakeliai State Farm, got neither hay for his cow nor a prize solely because he would attend church on Sundays.

Burokas and the Steponėnas and the Trečiokas families were not allowed to buy wheat at reduced prices from the state farm also solely because they went to church on Sundays.

Those who attend church would find their names up on the [bulletin] board of shame.

2. To the question 'What is the number of believers in your parish?' I replied that I do not know. It has been over ten years since we were forbidden to visit parishioners during Christmas time, but an accurate list of the faithful can only be made by visiting the families. I can say only this, that before the war there were more than 9,000 parishioners.

3. You asked, 'What are the boards going to be used for?' The church floor needs to be replaced. You said that the flooring is still adequate. I proved that it has been ruined by fungi. The parish makes no unneccesary expenditures because there is no money.

You then emphasized that the church is a state building in which one may not even drive a nail without permission. When the church was nationalized, the living quarters next to it were also nationalized. That house had been built by the grandparents of the parishioners, and it is dear to all. The faithful are upset because it has been neglected and lacks a caretaker. The parochial committee therefore appealed to those presently in charge of the house—the Adutiškis Locality Executive Committee. I, too, as the tenant, made inquiries on May 31, 1968, February 24, 1969, January 28, 1970, and May 24, 1972, because whenever it rains, the roof leaks, and the chimney has begun to fall apart. In spite of the fact that a monthly rent of fifty-six rubles and forty-five kopecks is paid, the roof leaks to this day. Both the parochial committee and I have received the following reply by word of mouth: 'There is no organization which can make repairs.' Strange, that there is an organization to take the money, but none for making repairs!

The churchyard fence, particularly on the street side, has been deteriorating for several years. Passersby and motorists could have been seriously injured. The responsible *rayon* officials have taken no notice of it.

The parochial committee appealed to the *rayon* headquarters for permission to purchase some cement. The supplicants were told: 'We don't have enough cement for more important needs.' At times the *rayon* newspaper announces that building materials can be purchased, but when one wishes to buy some, one is told, 'We don't sell to the church.' That was the response in January of this year from the director of the Švenčionys *Rayon* building materials establishment.

Once the believers understood that the church was nationalized only in order that it might fall into disrepair and collapse (as has happened with many churches in Byelorussia), they began to buy building materials, to offer their services, and to repair it themselves.

In spite of the fact that the church has been socialized, the parishioners still consider themselves responsible, because their parents built the church themselves, without any assistance from elsewhere.

4. After having discovered that on July 15 of this year there was a religious festival at the church in Adutiškis, you warned me, 'You are not obeying the Soviet laws. You invited priests to the festival without the permission of *rayon* authorities.'

I did not request permission on the basis of the agreement which the parochial committee signed with the Švenčionys *Rayon* Executive Committee. The second article of the aforementioned agreement clearly states: 'Also granting the opportunity for its use by all other persons of that faith exclusively for the purposes of the religious cult, and preventing ministers of the cult, who are not registered by the LSSR commissioner of the Council for Religious Affairs from performing religious rites.' Thus, I invited the priests lawfully.

You then asked the LSSR Commissioner of the Council for Religious Affairs and the chairwoman of the *rayon* executive committee, 'Can such agreements be made?' They replied, as you did, that they cannot. It is most regrettable that neither you, nor your retinue, who have been charged with overseeing the affairs of the Church, know what is permissible to us. I advised you to get the secretary of the parochial committee. We could have cleared up the whole matter then and there, and become convinced of who was correct, but you quietly replied, 'If that's the case, we must take possession of the agreement.' It is regrettable that everything is done so one-sidedly. What was permissible according to the agreement is now forbidden.

Hoping to prove that neither you nor those who accompanied you were correct, but rather that I was, I am attaching to this petition a copy of the aforementioned agreement.

"In the Soviet Union the Church is separate from the State, and yet there is probably no other country in the world which interferes so much in Church matters.

"It is understandable that the state rules as it wishes, but the greatest misfortune is that it does not issue any written laws, granting instead unlimited power to vice-chairmen of *rayon* executive committees, and at times even to chairmen of village localities, who interpret all things as they see fit. They rule over the priests and instruct them even how they should perform religious rites.

"Everyone knows that in the Soviet Union patients are treated, medical students are taught, and in general specialists are prepared only by specialists; however, the Soviet government has entrusted the tutoring of priests to incompetent individuals, to fanatical atheists. Atheists are teaching priests how they are to perform religious rites.

"When I was working in Švenčionėliai, V. Bukielskis, chairman of the Švenčionėliai Executive Committee, instructed me, 'If you want to participate in a funeral procession, take off your vestments and walk behind the common folk. You may walk only in the rear.' When I asked on what he based this order, he pompously replied, 'It's a governmental regulation!'

"What would the faithful think and say if after the funeral procession to the cemetery I would recite only the ending of the prayer 'Eternal Rest' as I was instructed to do by the chairwoman of the Švenčionys *Rayon* Executive Committee on October 2, 1972?

"I cannot perform religious rites in any way other than that indicated by *Romos katalikų apeigynas Lietuvos vyskupijoms* [Roman Catholic book of rituals for Lithuanian dioceses], which was edited by the Liturgical Commission of the Bishops of Lithuania, censored by Soviet organs, and approved by the Congregation of Rites.

"In Soviet Lithuania an ecclesiastical hierarchy still exists—the bishops' curiae, even a ritualistic commission—but it is neither the curiae nor the ritualistic commission who issue instructions but rather utterly incompetent state organs; the curiae retain only the right of consultation.

"If a priest is out of favor with the government, he becomes a victim. I have had to suffer both morally and materially. Hereupon I present the facts. I was removed from the post of pastor of the parish in Švenčionėliai by blackmail: 'If you don't leave Švenčionėliai, you will be unable to do the work of a priest.' This was said by Rugienis, the commissioner of the Council for Religious Affairs.

"The house which I had built alongside the church at Švenčionėliai was confiscated illegally.

"On July 16 I explained that formerly we used to request permission for priests to come to the parish for religious festivals. With time, we stopped asking permission because the *rayon* official assigned to oversee Church affairs began to scoff at us. Vice-Chairman Telyčénas of the Švenčionys *Rayon* Executive Committee gave permission for retreats to be conducted on the very same day in all the parishes of the *rayon*. His purpose was obvious: to disrupt the retreats. No one condemned such derisive conduct on the part of an official of the executive committee. Wishing to justify his action you replied even more cleverly, 'You could have invited priests from some other *rayon*; from Vilnius, Palanga, or even from other Republics. You mocked no less. The priests of Vilnius have enough work in Vilnius. Palanga is too far away (463 kilometers), and besides, it has only two priests. Some *rayons*, e.g., Ignalina, do not admit priests from another *rayon*.

"So it is not even worth considering Palanga or any other *rayon*, to say nothing of other Republics. The priests of other Republics are not registered with the LSSR commissioner of the Council for Religious Affairs; therefore, according to the aforementioned agreement, they cannot minister in Lithuania.

"We priests wish nothing more than to be able to work according to Article 124 of the USSR Constitution and Article 96 of the Lithuanian Constitution, and also to perform religious rites in accordance with the above-mentioned book of rituals.

"On July 10 of this year (1973) the *rayon* authorities said that they would allow two to three priests to come to religious festivals. Only how could two or three priests have heard the confessions of some fifteen hundred believers on July 13?

"It has happened that priests in Lithuania have died from overexertion after a religious festival, e.g. Father Ražanskas in Šeduva; and Father Garuckas became seriously ill. I therefore invited as many priests as I am duty bound to do by the resolutions of the Synod of the Vilnius Archdiocese, in order that the faithful would find it convenient to get to confession and return home quickly, and most importantly, that they would not have to spend hours on end waiting at the confessional on a workday, since the majority would have come on a workday. I invited enough priests so that the people would be content and would not complain about the government or about me. For all this no debts or expenses were incurred by the *rayon*. I asked for no financial support for the priests' reception.

"During the czarist era, permission was required for priests to go to a religious festival—writes Bishop M. Valančius in his book *Maskoliams katalikus persekiojant* [Persecution of Catholics by Muscovites], Kaunas, 1929, p. 32, and A. Alekna in his *Bažnyčios istorija* [History of the Church], Tilžė, 1920, p. 213 ('In 1863, the following were forbidden: the construction of new churches, the repair of old ones, and travelling by priests to other parishes for religious festivals.')

"Only Lenin, by abolishing all decrees of the czar, undoubtedly abolished also the one which forbade the invitation of priests to religious festivals. No such or similar decree has been issued during the Soviet era.

Adutiškis, July 31, 1973
The Rev. B. Laurinavičius"

VILNIUS

1. [Miss] Bronė Pupkevičiūtė, candidate for a graduate degree in education, who had been working as a senior fellow at the Scientific Research Institute of Pedagogy. On May 7, 1973, V. Rajeckas, director of the institute, under pressure from the organs of state security, ordered her to submit a statement that she was resigning of her own free will. Pupkevičiūtė is accused of having been a nun.

2. [Miss] Domicėlė Gailiušytė, a French language instructor with a college degree, who had been working at the secondary school in N. Vilnia. She was discharged from work in May, 1973. Gailiušytė is accused of having been a nun.

3. [Miss] Elena Šulinauskaitė, chief laboratory assistant of the history department at the University of Vilnius (college graduate). In May, 1973, Assistant Rector B. Sudavičius informed her that it was impossible for her to engage in any educative work at the university because she was a nun.

4. Šidla Voldemaras, a graduate in economics, who worked as director of the School of Commerce. At the end of May, 1973, he was discharged because he would not expel two students who wanted to commemorate the sixteenth of February [Lithuanian Independence Day].

THE ARCHDIOCESE OF KAUNAS

KAUNAS

In 1973 the authorities allowed the seminary administration to accept twelve applicants to the interdiocesan theological seminary in Kaunas. Two candidates were struck off the list by the commissioner of the Council for Religious Affairs, K. Tumėnas. The most important role in accepting applicants to the seminary is played by the security police. If a candidate seems somehow unsuitable to them, he is not allowed to enroll.

As 1973 was ending, forty-eight seminarians were studying at the theological seminary in Kaunas. The Soviet government awaits the day when there will be no more applicants for the seminary; then they will abolish the limitation—anyone who wants to will be able to join.

It was suggested to the seminary authorities that they take over the care of the Church of the Holy Trinity. For many years the seminary had made use of this church, and it had been beautifully renovated; but the government confiscated it and turned it into a warehouse. Most probably the authorities would like the seminary to repair the church again, so that it could be confiscated once more. The bishop has refused to repair the church—let whoever did the wrecking repair it!

* * *

On October 3, 1973, workers at the woodwork plant in Aleksotas went out on strike. During the day shift 320 laborers refused to work, and on the night shift about 340. The cause of the strike was a reduction in wages.

On the day of the strike, police, security agents, and officials from the Kaunas City Executive Committee arrived at the plant. They tried to reason with the workers to persuade them to work. Even officials who came from the ministry were unsuccessful in convincing the workers. The next day, wages were increased.

An attempt was made to blame the youth for the strike, but almost all the strikers had been adults and even greyhaired people.

ŠIAULIAI

In Lithuania there is a famous fortress hill at Meškuičiai called the Hill of Crosses. At one time it was covered with a great number of crosses erected by many Lithuanians, but atheists have desecrated this sacred place many times, tearing down the crosses and burning them. People however have continued to cart, carry, and erect both large and little crosses on this hill so dear to the heart of every Lithuanian.

The Hill of Crosses had almost recovered from the damage it suffered during the devastation of 1961. Unfortunately, at the end of April, 1973, it was grievously ravaged once more; there was no sign left that once there had been crosses here. The desolate, denuded hill seemed to be waiting for believing hands and loving hearts to once more crown its desecrated head with the symbol of the Redemption—the Cross.

At midnight on May 19, 1973, an unusual procession appeared on the outskirts of the city of Šiauliai. A small group of serious and meditative young men and women were carrying a cross. They walked quietly, pensively, saying the rosary. From time to time the cross, measuring three meters (nine feet and nine inches) and weighing forty-five kilograms (ninety-nine pounds) was transferred from the shoulders of one youth to those of another. The cross was decorated with symbolic ornamentation: a heart pierced by two swords. On the handle of one sword was a swastika, and on the other, a five-pointed star. Lithuanian youths were carrying the cross, not in the quest of health, but in atonement for the desecration of the Cross and in reparation for the sins of our nation a-gainst the Redeemer. They carried the cross as a symbol of victory. On the night of May 19, many people knew about this procession with the cross, and they devoted an hour to prayer and the veneration of the cross. During that hour, many, with hands joined in prayer, carried the Cross of Christ in spirit. All the crossbearers had received Holy Communion the previous evening.

As preparations were being made for this procession with the cross, it was discovered that someone had informed the security police about the proposed journey. Security police agents traveled back and forth throughout the night along the proposed route from Šiauliai to the Hill of Crosses. To the crossbearers, the success of the procession seemed miraculous. At 2:30 a.m. on May 20, 1973, the Hill of Crosses was adorned with a beautiful new cross. Flowers were planted around it, and a candle was lit. Everyone knelt and prayed, "Christ our King, may your kingdom come to our country."

At 6:45 a.m. the sound of an automobile could be heard. The security police rubbed their eyes—all night they had been chasing the cross, and here it was! Evil hands uprooted the cross and hauled it off. By noontime, how-ever, another cross stood in its place. The atheists kept destroying them, but the crosses seemed to sprout from the earth.

Interrogations Concerning the Carrying of the Cross to the Hill of Crosses in May, 1973

In the evening of May 20, 1973, several security agents arrived at the home of Mečislovas Jurevičius, a resident of Šiauliai born in 1927, and took him to security headquarters.

There he was interrogated. Had he carried the cross? What route had they followed? How many persons had carried the cross? Who had organized the procession with the cross? Who had constructed the cross? Which priests had encouraged the carrying of the cross? Jurevičius replied that he had made the cross and carried it himself. Jurevičius was further asked on what charges had he been tried previously.

"For Stalin's errors."

"Stop slandering Stalin!" the interrogator shouted.

"Oh, how such as you need Stalin now!"

Jurevičius was further questioned as to which priests he knew, who served mass in the church, what people he had dealings with, etc. Jurevičius stated that he would answer no more questions. The interrogator called Jurevičius a fanatic and threatened that he would get a longer jail sentence than he had received the first time, that he would be hauled off to a lockup, be injected with drugs, etc. Finally, he was ordered to stand against the wall. Undaunted by the threats, Jurevičius was seated. This continued throughout the night.

In the morning the interrogation was resumed. Who taught the children to serve mass? With which priests did he speak most often? Who served mass? In the afternoon, the procurator came and asked him why he was remaining silent. "You're going to give me ten years anyhow," Jurevičius explained.

In the evening they allowed him to return home, with orders to present himself again on May 23. On that day, he was once more interrogated and threatened, but Mečislovas remained silent. He was again ordered to return to security headquarters on May 29. A security agent demanded that he write down everything; then he proceeded to explain about the freedom of religion—that supposedly priests were deceiving people, and so on. Jurevičius exclaimed, "If I'm guilty, put me on trial!"

"It's easy enough to convict someone," explained the interrogator, "but a man must be steered in the right direction." Letting him leave for home, the interrogator declared, "We know that you carried the cross in honor of Kalanta."

* * *

At noontime on May 20, 1973, several security policemen came to the residence of Zenonas Mištautas, fourth-year student at the Polytechnical Institute of Šiauliai, and took him away to their headquarters. They questioned him repeatedly as to what he had been up to the previous night, whether he ever served mass, which church he attended, who else served mass, who took part in adorations, and what priests said in their sermons.

At about 4 p.m. the security police brought Zenonas home, and without a warrant from the procurator, conducted a search. The security men ransacked all his books and notebooks. In the course of the search, they seized an exposed film and a notebook containing religious ideas. They returned the film after developing it but kept the notebook.

Upon the return to security headquarters, once again an interrogation. Zenonas was asked how many people had carried the cross, who made the cross, what route had they taken, at what time was the cross erected, etc. When they failed to get anything worthwhile out of him by using friendly tactics, the security police proceeded to try to intimidate him. Four interrogators surrounded Zenonas, threatened him with their fists, and showed him the kind of "sausages" would pop up on his back if he were to get a taste of the "banana" [club]. Three times they went out to get the "banana," saying, "Now we're going to bring in the 'banana.' When we pull down your pants and give you a thrashing, you'll tell us everything." The interrogators talked all sorts of nonsense about the Hill of Crosses, being unsparing even of obscenities. In concluding the interrogation, the security police tried to frighten Zenonas from ever carrying another cross to the fortress hill of Meškuičiai. He was ordered to present himself to security headquarters again on May 25. On that day once again he was questioned repeatedly about the carrying of the cross and about serving mass. When they failed to squeeze anything out of him, one riled security agent said that he would report everything to the school and that Zenonas would be expelled. Sending him home the interrogator gave him his telephone number and ordered him to call on May 28. Zenonas refused to call.

When the school year began, an attempt was made to "educate" Zenonas in the school, threatening him with expulsion if he insisted on sticking stubbornly to his principles.

On October 3, his homeroom teacher ordered Zenonas to present himself at security headquarters, but he demanded a written summons. Zenonas was reminded that he would be expelled if he refused to go to security headquarters. He did not go.

On October 10, the security police took Zenonas to their office. The interrogation lasted three hours. He remained silent for the most part.

Up to the present time, Zenonas Mištautas has not been expelled from the Šiauliai Polytechnical Institute.

* * *

At approximately noon on May 20, 1973, Virginijus Ivanovas was taken to security headquarters together with Zenonas Mištautas. At first the interrogator spoke calmly and read them the articles from the Criminal Code dealing with political offenses. Then he ordered Virginijus to describe in sequence everything he had done Saturday evening and night. When Virginijus stated that he would say nothing, the "politeness" of the security agent ended abruptly. Virginijus was called a fanatic and an ignoramus. "There's no place for you in a school of higher musical education, for if you become a choir director, you'll agitate among the choir members."

In the afternoon, Virginijus was brought back to his home, where a search was carried out (without a warrant from the procurator). During the search, the security police took several notebooks containing religious poetry. Afterward, the interrogation was continued. The security police would at first speak kindly, but after losing their patience, they would threaten to beat him and to stick him down in the cellar. The interrogation lasted until nighttime. During the night they did not permit him to sleep. Every two hours, a security agent would come and ask him questions about priests, church functionaries, and worshippers.

On Monday, at about noon, a security agent ordered him to sign a statement promising not to tell anyone about the interrogation. If anyone were to ask where he had been, he was to answer that he had been at police head-quarters and not at the security headquarters.

After that, Virginijus was summoned several times to meet with the security police. He did not go, and so he was expelled from the music school on the grounds that he had not taken his examinations. As a matter of fact, Virginijus had been excused from taking the examinations by a physicians' commission.

In July Virginijus' mother wrote the following complaint to the Procurator General in Moscow:

"Not far from Šiauliai is the Hill of Crosses. It has been dear to believers since ancient times. My sixteen-year-old son, together with several of his friends, carried a cross to that hill on the night of May 20. For this the security organs of Šiauliai took my son to their headquarters and kept him there a whole day and night without sleep or food. Aside from that, just recently my son was ill with in inflammation of the brain. He was excused from taking the spring examinations and was ordered to avoid emotional stress to prevent a relapse. Nevertheless, he was expelled from the freshman class of the school of higher musical education solely for carrying a cross to the Hill of Crosses.

"I request the Procurator General to investigate the above facts in detail and to reply whether the security organs were correct to have acted thus, since the Constitution guarantees the freedom of conscience and the freedom of worship to all believers. [Signed] Viktorija Ivanova"

Attached to the complaint was the note from the physicians' commission excusing the boy from the examinations.

In early September, 1973, the following reply was received from the Procurator's Office of the LSSR in Vilnius: "This is to inform you that upon investigation of your complaint of July 23, it has been determined that on May 20 representatives of the Soviet government spoke with your underage son Virginijus in the presence of his father, Ivanovas, concerning impermissible activities in which your son took part together with other persons in connection with an archeological monument—the fortress hill at Jurgaičiai.

"No impermissible actions on the part of the agents of the Soviet government who spoke with your son have been uncovered. [Signed] Bakučionis, Deputy Procurator of the LSSR"

This persecution by the security police not only failed to frighten people, but even inspired them with greater courage. One woman who had carried the cross has written: "Lithuanian, become aware of your strength! It is found in Christ and in our unity! Stand immovable, bravely guarding what is sacred and dear to your heart! Don't let them desecrate the Hill of Crosses. Don't leave it desolate and expectant. Bring to it your joys and sorrows, your hopes and victories; bring your love of God and your faithfulness to Him there: carry the Cross to the Hill of Crosses!"

The desecration of the Hill of Crosses gave rise to a new idea: if it is impossible to erect a cross on the Hill of Crosses, let us begin erecting them on our farmsteads, in our homes, in our own and others' hearts.

ŠIAULIAI

On October 30, 1973, Leonas Šileikis, a seventh-class student at Šiauliai Secondary School No. 5, was summoned to the teachers' room, where two security agents were waiting for him, and who took him to the students' room. Here they searched his book bag, examined his notebooks, and questioned him as to his friends. Then they took him to security headquarters and showed him some leaflets that Leonas had distributed in downtown Šiauliai. The leaflets contained the slogans "Down with the Soviet government!"; "Russians, scram from Lithuania!"; "Freedom for Lithuania!" Among other things, the interrogators wanted to know who had taught him to write such slogans, where he had gotten the idea, whether his parents criticized the Soviet regime at home, whether he went to church and to confession, whether he served mass or visited priests, whether his parents listened to the Voice of America, whether they had any religious literature, from what kind of prayer book they prayed—new or old. The interrogation lasted five hours. The following day Leonas had to undergo another interrogation.

A few weeks later, the principal attempted to "educate" Leonas and questioned him about the leaflets and particularly about church.

"I've been going to church, and I will continue to go," declared Leonas.

On hearing this, the principal announced her decision: to lower Šilekis' conduct grade.

On November 1, 1973, [Miss] Virga Šileikytė, an eleventh-class student at Šiauliai Secondary School No. 5, was summoned to security headquarters. An agent questioned her. Did Virga attend church? Who took part in adorations? How could one reconcile religion with science? Why hadn't she joined the Young Communist League? Which atheistic books had she read? Had she been at the Hill of Crosses? Did she know Ivanovas or Mištautas? Which priests did she know? He also asked many other questions.

The girl explained to the security agent that she did not know those who participated in processions, that she saw no good examples among League members, that the activities of the Pioneers had especially displeased her, that Ragauskas' books *Ite, missa est* [Go, the Mass has ended] and *Anuo metu* [At that time] had aroused feelings of disgust in her because of the nonsense they contained.

The security agent tried to explain to her that priests behave badly, that they had shot people.

"I believe in God, not in priests," declared Virga.

As he let her go back to her classroom, the security agent promised to summon her for another talk.

On October 31, 1973, Joana Šileikienė, the mother of Leonas Šileikis, was summoned to security headquarters and interrogated about her son's misdeed and other matters, such as whether there was anti-Soviet talk at their home, whether the children were given a religious upbringing, whether they met with priests, who else in their house attends church, and whether they had relatives abroad. The interrogation lasted two hours.

On November 1, 1973, Juozas Šileikis, the father of Leonas, was summoned to security headquarters. The interrogator asked whether the carpenters from the combine of the blind had not made the cross which had been borne to the Hill of Crosses, whether he went to church, whether he took part in processions, and who was in charge of processions?

Šileikis explained that he goes to church on Sundays and whenever he has time during the week, that he had never been in charge of a procession, that when he goes to church he prays and does not go around asking people's names. Šileikis was asked about Mečislovas Jurevičius and Stasys Čilinskas. He was upbraided for listening to the Voice of America, for Leonas' misdeed, for teaching religion to his children, and for not allowing them to join the Pioneers and the Young Communist League. The interrogator wanted to know whether Šileikis had any new religious literature.

On November 28, 1973, Juozas Šileikis and his son Leonas were summoned to a meeting of the Šiauliai city commission concerned with the employment of minors, at which some twenty-five persons from various agencies were present. The members of the commission asked about the leaflets which Leonas had distributed and about church attendance. Some members of the commission said that such a father ought to have his parental rights revoked, for he was ruining his child. The commission decided to expel Leonas from school but later contented itself with fining the father the sum of thirty rubles.

Šileikis blurted out to the commission, "If going to church is not allowed, then you should write on the church door that entry is strictly forbidden." One of the members of the commission replied that in that case the believers would go underground.

* * *

On October 11 Urbonavičius, chief of the Šiauliai security police, gave a lecture to students entitled "Contemporary Ideological Warfare and Youth." The security official spoke about the unrest in Šiauliai: how anti-Soviet leaflets had been posted in public places and even in schools; how on May 19, Jurevičius, Ivanovas, and Mištautas had carried a cross to the fortress hill at Meškuičiai. This had been done on the anniversary of Kalanta's self-immolation. The security chief said that in Jurevičius' case it wasn't surprising since he was a troublemaker; but there was concern for the youths. Priests, in the opinion of the security chief, were causing great harm. As he ended his lecture, Urbonavičius urged them all to renounce their "religious superstitions."

SURVILIŠKIS

In May, 1973, [Miss] Janina Ivanauskaitė, a tenth-class student at the secondary school in Surviliškis, was ssummoned to the teachers' room. There she was questioned repeatedly by Principal Stasys Bogušaitis, her class advisor [Mrs.] Nijolė Šilkaitienė, and some kind of *rayon* official. An attempt was made to shame the student, because it was supposedly not fitting for a member of the graduating class to go to church. If she continued to go to church, she would be expelled.

On the following day, the homeroom teacher reminded

Janina that if she wanted to go to church so badly, she should go where no one knows her.

On the last day of the school year, Ivanauskaitė was again "educated." Why didn't she join the Young Communist League? Did the priest visit her home? When did she become a sanctimonious granny? Did she go to church often? What did she do in church? What did she do on Easter morning? Did the priest ask her to scatter flowers in a procession?

ŠILUVA

In the early days of September, 1973, during the feast of the Nativity of Mary, huge crowds of people flocked to Šiluva. On Sunday, September 9, automobiles could no longer get into Šiluva and the fields around the town of Šiluva were full of cars. This year the auto inspectors were considerably more polite than they had been last year. Nevertheless, they still tried to nab the buses on which pilgrims were traveling to Šiluva. The pilgrims have recounted the following: "When we were about three kilometers from Šiluva, the auto inspectors and auxiliary policemen stopped our bus. For a long time our driver was grilled and accused of planning to let the passengers out at Šiluva and of not going to Pakruojis, for in the trip log, Pakruojis was listed as the final destination. After harassing the driver for half an hour, they confiscated his routing slip and passenger list, and issued him a permit to proceed only to Pakruojis. It was late at night when, after lengthy detours, the people reached Šiluva on foot."

On Sunday, September 9, the Raseiniai police confiscated the candles from vendors near the Šiluva chapel. They pushed one woman into their vehicle and took her away. On the evening of September 8, the police took away to Raseiniai an old woman who was shouting "People, help me!" as they drove off with her.

On weekdays many vendors of religious articles could be seen in the church itself. They had rosaries pinned on their chests beneath their outer garments.

BAISOGALA

Principal Šerkšnys of the secondary school in Baisogala and [Miss] Šidlauskaitė, homeroom teacher of the eleventh-class, berated and insulted eleventh-class students [Miss] Regina Jagėlaitė and [Miss] Vanda Aleksandravičiūtė simply because they had been flower girls in the Easter procession. The teacher tried to shame the girls before the entire class. When the girls explained that their mothers had told them to go to church, Šidlauskaitė retorted, "Perhaps your mothers will also tell you to go to bed with the pastor!"

Even though the girls were exemplary and good students, because of the flower-strewing incident their conduct marks were lowered and in the characterization in their school records the following entry was made: "Even though the girls were members of the Young Communist League, they have not yet developed an atheistic outlook because when they were in the eleventh-class they attended church." Such an official entry into the characterizations of students discriminates against believers and unmasks the Soviet claim that nothing concerning the religious beliefs of Soviet Union citizens is noted in any official documents.

Parents wonder how homeroom teacher Šidlauskaitė can nurture youth when she herself should be working on self-improvement.

Tenth-class student [Miss] Lionė Urbonavičiūtė was upbraided and an effort was made to compromise her for attending church. Her homeroom teacher threatened to note in the characterization in her school records that she goes to church.

The administrators of the school in Baisogala react somewhat more leniently towards other kinds of misbehavior by students. Several years ago, Vidas Varnas pilfered five coin boxes in the church and tore twelve votive offerings from the altar (damages totaled over 220 rubles). When Varnas finished the secondary school this year, his record was clean.

GIRDŽIAI

On September 1, 1973, an unknown official from Jurbarkas *Rayon* who came to the secondary school in Girdžiai, declared in a speech, "Don't you do as [Mrs.] Mockienė did."

People began to ask around to find out what this Mockienė had done. It turns out that on April 5, 1973, homeroom teacher Simanavičius had enrolled her daughter, Janina, an eleventh-class student, into the Young Communist League. The mother, deeply disturbed, burned the girl's membership card and sent the homeroom teacher the following note: "My daughter is not of age; therefore you had no right to enroll her without my permission. I consider her enrollment into the Young Communist League invalid, and as for her membership card, I sent it up the chimney in smoke."

Her husband expressed his fears that she would get a prison sentence for that.

"Big deal!" Mockienė retorted, "I'll sit it out and come home."

On April 19 Mockienė was summoned to *rayon* headquarters to explain her behavior.

"I burned the card," declared Mockienė, "because they enrolled my daughter in the Young Communist League without my knowledge. Nothing decent comes from those League members. The banks of the Mituva are covered with couples wearing their badges. They are an embarrassment to their parents. I don't want my daughter to grow up into a loose woman. Who robbed the store at Pavidaujys? Who threw up all over the bus passengers while drunk? It's always the students who are members of the Young Communist League. Why don't they put them in the newsletter posted on the bulletin board at school? But when some girl honor students took part in the Easter procession, their caricatures were posted in school. Finally, is enrollment voluntary or compulsory?" the woman asked.

"Voluntary, of course."

"Then why are they being forced? Children are being

intimidated at school. My daughter cried after coming home and couldn't fall asleep all night."

It was explained to Mockienė that her daughter would not be allowed to enroll into a school of higher education, and that she herself would be punished.

* * *

A few years ago, [Mrs.] Riklikienė burned her husband's Communist party membership card. [Mrs.] Stasė Banaitienė acted similarly. Summoned to explain her actions, she sent a note saying, "Two parties can't lie under one blanket."

PABAISKAS

At the secondary school in Pabaiskas, a conference on nurturing the spirit of internationalism was organized for the teachers in early March, 1973. Vladas Vembrė, head of the department of education for Ukmergė *Rayon* came to the conference. Principal [Mrs.] E. Stasiukaitienė made a mention of churchgoing pupils, complaining, "Previously it was easier to deal with students' church attendance. The new minister of the cult, however, is a most authoritative figure, and he knows how to attract everyone; but most importantly, in his sermons he "stresses the nationalistic question."

The head of the department of education said that it is important to pay great attention to the question of nationalism, since many pupils are causing incidents. Several occurred this year at the schools within Jurbarkas *Rayon* on February 16: one secretary of the Young Communist League distributed anti-Soviet proclamations, and other students raised the tricolor flag [that of independent Lithuania].

At the end of May, during the commencement exercises, school Principal E. Stasiukaitienė announced publicly that seventh-class student [Miss] Valė Amankavičiūtė had had her conduct mark lowered for attending church.

On June 29, 1973, the pastor of Pabaiskas, the Rev. V. Ramanauskas, was summoned before the Ukmergė *Ray-*

on Executive Committee for organizing on June 14 a group of volunteers to clean the church. The pastor had been denounced to the *rayon* authorities by [Mrs.] Boškevičienė, Party secretary of the Pabaiskas State Farm, and by the comptroller of Girdžiai. The chairman of the executive committee characterized the pastor as being the worst in the *rayon* because he was being reprimanded for the third time in two years. The pastor was told that the people earn his board for him, whereas he was interfering with their work. On account of the pastor's fault, three women had had their bonuses canceled (It later became apparent that these women had been assigned five days for weeding the gardens, which chore they could have finished in one day. Having finished the work at the farm, they therefore came to assist in the cleaning of the church.). The pastor told the committee that if the Ukmergė authorities were displeased with him they could request to have him transferred. The chairman replied that if they were to transfer him elsewhere, he would only cause trouble for others. At that point the pastor requested the chairman to hurry up and finish this discussion since it was the feast day of Saints Peter and Paul.

"What feast day?" shouted the official, actually jumping from his place, "I don't want to hear about it! It's haying time, and not a holiday! If the bishop ordered you to celebrate it, then we'll have to teach that bishop a lesson too!"

The pastor was then reminded of his other offenses: on Easter Day he had taken up a collection in church and ten children had taken part in the procession, etc.

About a month later, even the security officials upbraided the pastor of the parish in Pabaiskas for having organized the volunteer help. Moreover, they wanted to know where the people were getting their prayer books and catechisms, and who was typing their hymnals.

On October 5 the chairmen and treasurers of the parochial committees of the *rayon* were summoned before the Ukmergė *Rayon* Executive Committee. They were lectured on the laws dealing with cults and reminded of their duty to keep church money away from the pastor. The officials did not forget to remind them several times of the great "offense" committed by the pastor of the parish in Pabais-kas—the organization of a group of volunteers to scrub the floor, a job which had required all of four hours.

THE ARCHDIOCESE OF PANEVĖŽYS
SALOS
In July, 1972, the pastor of the parish in Salos, the Rev. Petras Nykštus, was accused of preparing children for their First Communion. On August 24, 1972, Father Nykš-tus was fined fifty rubles by the administrative commission of the Rokiškis *Rayon* Executive Committee. Below are presented several statements bearing witness to the self-will of teachers and various officials with regard to the faithful:

"To: The ecclesiastical administrator of the dioceses of Kaišaidorys and Panevėžys

A Petition from the Faithful of the Parish in Salos in Rokiškis Rayon

"We Catholics, Honorable Administrator, are well a-ware, and whenever we read the Soviet press we find it written that it is not permissible to assault or insult people. Those who do so are punished. Soviet laws give us believers complete freedom in matters of conscience and faith. Why, then, did [Mrs.] Didžgalvienė, a teacher from Salos; Principal Augulis; Steponavičius, principal of the agricultural school in Salos; and locality chairman Raugalienė without cause assault and accuse our pastor of teaching our children in church? Teacher Didžgalvienė and locality chairman Raugalienė went to the church to see for themselves which children were coming to church. Teacher Didžgalvienė, in fact, made Gradeckas' daughter go home. The teacher told her that children are not permitted to go to church. Frightened, the girl ran home, leaving her book in church. She had been afraid to pick it up in the teacher's presence.

"Augulis, principal of the school in Salos; Steponavičius, principal of the agricultural school; and locality chairman Raugalienė even visited the homes of the children who go to church. Taking some children without their parents' knowledge, with only the chairwoman and the principal of the agricultural school present, Principal Augulis ordered the children to write statements denouncing the pastor. The frightened children wrote exactly what Augulis dictated to them. When we parents discovered how wrongly the teachers had acted, we asked the children what they had written and why they had written what was not true? Then the children replied, 'We don't know. What the principal said—that's what we wrote. We were afraid that he might scold us.'

"Two of the children were actually given an already written statement denouncing the pastor. The children were simply told to sign it. Fearing their teachers, they signed. How can teachers act so unjustly? They dictate statements to the children and order them to write down their words. Later, taking these statements from the children, they filed a complaint with the Rokiškis *Rayon* authorities charging our pastor with the teaching of our children. The *rayon* authorities believe this unjust accusation by the teachers and are starting proceedings against the pastor.

"We ourselves taught our children their prayers and the entire contents of the catechism, and when the children had learned everything, then we went to the pastor and asked him to test, to question them in order to determine how knowledgeable they were and whether they could be allowed to go to confession and Holy Communion. We have already written to the *rayon* authorities and to the commissioner of the Council for Religious Affairs in Vilnius, stating that we parents have taught our children ourselves. But they do not believe us parents, who have taught our children ourselves, and are taking the pastor to court. Those parents whose children, at the insistence of their teachers, wrote denouncements against the pastor, have appealed a second time to the *rayon* authorities, informing them how matters stood and asking that the teachers be admonished; but everything remains the same.

"If teachers have the right to monitor what goes on in church, to count how many adults and children are present in church, then perhaps, Administrator, the priests will soon be setting foot into the schools? The teachers of Salos are already going to church and concerning themselves with the religious affairs of our children. If the priests are not allowed to enter a school, then we do not agree to the interference by the teachers of Salos in our matters of conscience.

"Honored Administrator, please help us Catholic parents so that, because of our children, our pastor would not be unjustly accused of teaching our children and punished. We parents know better than the teachers who it was that taught our children. The teachers are accusing us parents also, saying that we haven't the right to take our children to church.

"If you, Administrator, cannot help us in this matter, then please inform us where we should direct our appeal. We have once more written and will send another petition to the commissioner of the Council for Religious Affairs.

Salos, July 27, 1972"
The signatures of ten parents

On August 27, 1973, ten parishioners from the parish in Salos sent a similar petition to the commissioner of the Council for Religious Affairs, K. Tumėnas. The statement ends with the request: "We ask you, Commissioner, to keep teacher Didžgalvienė and Principal Augulis from harassing our children for attending church, not only in church, but also in school, for the children are afraid that the teachers will scold and punish them. Otherwise we shall be unable to send our children to the school in Salos."

Trying to defend their children from the terrorization, and also the pastor of their parish, the believers wrote a series of petitions to the officials of the *rayon* and the Council for Religious Affairs.

Albinas Jakūbonis wrote the following to the commissioner of the Council for Religious Affairs: "While I was at work and my wife was ill, the principal of the school in Salos came to my home and, bidding my daughter to go to another room, told her to write a denunciation against the pastor. The principal dictated and my daughter wrote down his words. I therefore request that you consider invalid what my daughter wrote against the pastor."

[Mrs.] Petrulienė wrote: "I taught my child all his prayers and the contents of the catechism myself ... We have rights over our children, and they go where we take them. We also have the freedom of conscience to go to church, but why don't the teachers permit this? Why do they monitor who goes to church? The priests don't go into a school and chase the children out."

Similar complaints were written by Stasys Gradeckas, [Mrs.] Elena Matiukienė, [Mrs.] Zose Didžgalvienė, and other believers. All of them complained that their children are being persecuted, that teachers are interfering in matters outside their field of competence, and that the pastor is being prosecuted unlawfully because they had taught their children themselves, and he had merely tested them.

The believers of Salos informed the ecclesiastical administrator of the dioceses of Kaišiadorys and Panevėžys, and the commissioner of the Council for Religious Affairs about how the faithful went to the trial of Father Nykštus, and how the Chairman of the Rokiškis *Rayon* Executive Committee had upbraided them.

[Miss] Elena Neniškaitė, a resident of Urliai Village, wrote the following to K. Tumėnas: "On August 24, 1972, I went to the People's Court of Rokiškis to see how the teachers of Salos were going to try our pastor. With me went [Miss] Julė Dambrauskaitė. In court, we were told that the pastor was being tried at the *rayon* office but that we would not be permitted inside because it would be a closed session. We therefore went to see the *rayon* chairman to ask why our pastor was on trial, and why they were calling no witnesses, why they were putting their trust in the teachers? The chairman did not answer our question, but angrily denounced the pastor and told us to leave. We then told him that we were believers and that we wished to know what our pastor was being tried for. The chairman did not answer our question but only shouted angrily at us, 'It's only from the believers that all the hooligans come from!' This comment by the *rayon* chairman offended me deeply. Never before in my life had I heard such a hurtful insult. I do not understand why it is so in Salos. I thought that teacher Didžgalvienė and Principal Augulis were being arbitrary in harassing the children and at the same time the believers, but here even the *rayon* chairman does likewise. Were teacher Didžgalvienė and Principal Augulis right to insult and to scandalize so many believers? They walk around with heads held high while they confer upon believers the 'honorable' title of 'hooligan.' Can we, the faithful thank them for such an epithet?"

In her declaration to K. Tumėnas Julija Dambrauskaitė wrote: "At the *rayon* office they told us that the pastor needs to be punished. But who will punish teacher Didžgalvienė and Principal Augulis?... Commissioner, I have been a believer all my life. I even worked for the bourgeoisie for seven years where I saw and heard all kinds of things, but the bourgeoise never said such words to me as the chairman did."

ALUNTA

On August 4-5, 1973, the Sacrament of Confirmation was to be administered at Alunta. Unfortunately, the rites were cancelled by telegram from the curia of Panevėžys "because of the harvesting." The telegrams were received on August 3-4, when it was already too late to even inform the people. A huge crowd of people gathered. There were also a goodly number of police. The people repeatedly cursed the government for interfering in the bishop's administration of the sacraments. People were saying that even during the days of serfdom it was possible to keep holy the Sabbath, but under the Soviet regime, people were expected to work like slaves all year long.

DABUŽIAI

During the summer of 1973, officials of Anykščiai *Rayon* checked on a total of three occasions to see whether the pastor of Dabužiai, Father Serafinas Žvinys, was teaching religious truths to children. They failed, however, to catch the priest in the act. The administrative commission of the Anykščiai *Rayon* Executive Committee fined the "perverter of youth" fifty rubles, explaining that a complaint had been made which had to be believed.

TRAUPIS

During the summer of 1973, as Pastor Stepas Galvydis was testing the children's knowledge of religious truths before their First Communion, the *rayon* chairman arrived, together with the school principal and the chairman of the collective farm. They wrote up a report stating that the priest was teaching religion to large groups of children. The administrative commission of the Anykščiai *Rayon* Executive Committee fined the pastor fifty rubles. Father Galvydis paid the fine and obtained a receipt from the bank marked "for teaching religion to children."

THE DIOCESE OF TELŠIAI

KLAIPĖDA

On July 14, 1973, the church in Klaipėda was visited by Tarasov, an official of the Council for Religious Affairs, accompanied by Commissioner K. Tumėnas, Ruginis, Vice-Chairman of the Klaipėda City Executive Committee, and a security official (see the *Chronicle of the Catholic Church in Lithuania*, no. 7). When the Catholics of Klaipėda learned that Tarasov had stated that the church in Klaipėda was no smaller than the Catholic church in Moscow, and that it was entirely adequate for the believers' needs, they were scandalized. The parish in Klaipėda has about 6000 parishioners. Every year, about 800-900 children prepare to receive their First Communion! The faithful must crowd into a church measuring 288 square meters, which doesn't even have a churchyard. On holy days and during religious festivals, even when it is raining or freezing the believers must stand in the streets since it is impossible for many of them to get inside the church. When the pastor of the parish in Klaipėda reminded Tarasov that the church could be enlarged if the sheds leaning against the back of the church were torn down, the latter replied, "We shall see later."

The Soviet press reports that the city of Klaipėda is growing, that new sections are being developed, and that living conditions are improving. Only believers wait in vain for the government to take note of their difficult lot and return the unlawfully seized shrine of Mary, Queen of Peace.

Can the believers of Lithuania respect a government which has desecrated a shrine dedicated to the Queen of Peace, while sending its builder, H.E. Bishop L. Povilonis, for propaganda purposes to a congress of peace advocates in Moscow?

* * *

In the month of October, 1973, [Mrs.] Augustinavičienė, a resident of Klaipėda, was apprehended and taken to police headquarters for selling religious articles at the church door. The People's Court fined Augustinavičienė twenty rubles and confiscated the religious goods.

In early 1973 government officials had instructed the pastor of Klaipėda to drive away from the vicinity of the church all vendors of religious objects. The police and the auxiliary police would rather not arrest those who sell religious objects right at the church door.

With such "freedom" of religion, where are the faithful to purchase rosaries, prayer books, or medals?

* * *

History teacher Mažeika of Klaipėda Secondary School No. 5 ridicules religion and students who go to church. As Easter, 1973, was approaching, teacher Mažeika threatened the students of Class 4 F "Don't try to go to church even on Easter Sunday because I'll be there to check on you. If I see anyone in church, remember, those will get a failing grade in history from me."

KAŠUČIAI

In September, 1973, a fourth-class student at the eight-year school in Kašučiai (Kretinga *Rayon*) named Andrijauskas died. His devout parents buried their son with religious rites. School Principal Povilaitis forbade the students to participate in their friend's funeral procession.

"Where the Church plays a role, that is no place for us," stated the principal.

Hearing the mournful funeral music, the students wept during the entire lesson, but they were not allowed to leave their classroom.

Whenever Principal Povilaitis sees any of his students in Darbėnai, where the church is located, he accuses them, "You've been to church, you degenerate!" The principal upbraids the suspects in class, and lowers their marks.

Povilaitis has been in charge of the Kašučiai eight-year school for eight years now. One former student recounts how the principal used to try to force them to join the Young Communist League. During class time the principal would pick out some student and demand, "Are you going to join the Young Communist League?" If the pupil refused, the principal would grab the student's hand and whack it against his desk. Some even had their knuckles bloodied. After one such execution, the students wrote a protest to the Ministry of Education. A commission arrived and supposedly checked out the facts, but the principal continues to terrorize the students who are believers.

ŠNAUKŠTAI

In 1970 [Mrs.] Domarkienė, head of the Pioneers at the Šnaukštai eight-year school, kept fourth-class students after school and pressured them to enroll in the Pioneers. The teacher "educated" those who did not want to join by striking their hands with a ruler. Two students—Lūžas and

[Miss] Veserytė—suffered the most. The teacher whacked at their hands until they bled. The parents of these pupils asked teacher Domarkienė who had given her the right to strike their children and to forcibly enroll them in the Pioneers? The blushing teacher tried to explain that all talented students are required to join the Pioneers. She had resorted to severe measures in an attempt to break down the stubborness of her pupils. The parents threatened not to send their children to school if such "educative" means were going to be used.

ŠILUTĖ

During 1970 [Mrs.] Arlauskienė, a teacher at the Ši-lutė eight-year school, spent much time trying to demonstrate to the sixth-class students that there is no God and that only the ignorant believe in him. "Let's all shout together now three times 'There is no God!'" the teacher urged. The only one who shouted out loud, however, was Arlauskienė, and only a few timid voices chimed in.

One seventh-class student says that at that time he knew nothing about God since his father was a zealous atheist.

"But now that I have gotten to know the truths of the faith, I would boldly cry out, 'Teacher, you're mistaken —God exists!'" the boy said.

KURŠĖNAI

On October 19, 1973, a questionnaire was distributed to the eighth-class students of the secondary school in Kur-šėnai, with the following questions:

1. Are your parents religious?

2. Do your parents force you to take part in religious rites?

3. Do you take part in religious rites (attend church, pray, observe holy days)?

4. Have you begun to doubt yet that our lives are ruled by supernatural forces?

5. Do you consider yourself a believer of religious dogma or a nonbeliever?

6. Are you convinced that religious superstitions are harmful, that explanatory education is necessary, and that an atheistic world view should be fostered?

7. Have you ever had to explain the antagonism between science and religion? How successful were you? Do you have the necessary information?

8. Have you read any scientific-atheistic literature, and what do you remember about it?

9. Do you think that religious superstition will disappear spontaneously, that no one will be interested anymore in such questions?

THE DIOCESE OF VILKAVIŠKIS

ŠAKIAI

On September 23, 1973, K. Tumėnas, the commissioner of the Council for Religious Affairs, gave permission to H. E. Bishop L. Povilonis to bless five new altars at the church in Šakiai.

When they learned of the bishop's forthcoming visit, government officials of Šakiai *Rayon* discussed how they might interfere with the ceremony. They were especially concerned with preventing the attendance of schoolchildren at the ceremonies. It was decided to keep the pupils occupied in some way when the bishop came to Šakiai. At one school they proclaimed a forester's day, at others field trips were organized, etc. Pupils were given strict instructions to come to school on Sunday and to take part in the planned activities.

The more knowledgeable students realized the true purpose of the planned activities and failed to show up. Only about half of the students came. Some "disobedient" ones were obliged to present written excuses from their parents, while others were threatened with work on collective farms after school. The teachers told the children to bring food, saying, "We're going to keep you until dark!"

People joked that the atheists of Šakiai had fled to the woods in fear of the bishop.

SKRIAUDŽIAI

In September, 1973, the principal of the Skriaudžiai eight-year school, [Mrs.] Albina Rinkauskienė, summoned from their classes to the teachers' room those pupils who had sung in the church choir.

"Children, write down who organized the children's choir, and where and when rehearsals are held. Write clearly since your writing is going to be read by someone. Write the truth, for if you lie, I'll call the police. Instead of cawing like crows in the choir loft, you would do better to spend your time watching television," the principal said.

The principal then addressed eighth-class student [Miss] Rasa Orintaitė, "You, Rasa, are a sanctimonious granny. Whenever there is a religious festival in the church, you scurry about like a ninny with flowers, avoiding me."

"Why did you go to sing in church, Nijolytė?" the principal angrily demanded of pupil [Miss] Nijolė Griciutė. "You've disgraced the school. For this you are going to get a bad characterization in your school records. Tell me, who asked you to sing?"

"My mother," replied Nijolė.

Some of the children wrote down on their papers that their mothers had told them to sing in the choir; others wrote that it was their fathers: still others wrote they had simply joined their friends. Being fearful of the police, two girls wrote that the organist had organized the children. Taking [Miss] Danutė Naujokaitė alone to a room and closing the door, the principal threatened her, saying that her parents would suffer if she did not tell who taught them and how many children there were. Now the girl no longer goes to school because other children tease her maliciously.

The principal's husband, Viktoras Rinkauskas, is the chairman of the Skriaudžiai Collective Farm. On Sundays he goes to the post office and observes who is coming to church. Later, he makes use of every opportunity to ridicule them, especially the youngsters. He harasses people and makes mean retorts. Collective farm workers complain that Rinkauskas is more concerned with ridiculing believers than he is with running the farm. The chairman of the collective farm is partial to unethical persons, tolerating their unconscientious work, and yet he ought to remember that the majority of people on his farm are believers.

* * *

On September 28, 1973, [Mrs.] Kazė Kairiūkštienė visited the principal of the school.

"Why do you threaten my children with the police?" asked the woman. "One of my girls wakes up in the night crying, 'The police, the police!' I'm going to take her to a physician. What have the children done that you should harass and frighten them so?"

"You turncoat! You bamboozler!" shouted the furious principal, calling Kairiūkštienė the worst possible names.

Then the woman asked the children, "Children, did the principal threaten you with the police?"

The bolder ones confirmed it, while others said they hadn't heard clearly. Using intimidation, the principal learned the surnames of the children who had made their First Communion during the summer, not only those from the Skriaudžiai Collective Farm but also from Leskava. On September 28, taking with her all those children's "writings," the principal went to Prienai. There, at a meeting of atheists, she reported on the "offense" committed at Skriaudžiai. The participants discussed how to punish those who were trying to "ruin" children.

Soon afterward the interrogation of the children's parents began, increasing the feelings of disgust among the people against the "Red sanctimonious grannies." That is how people call fanatical atheists.

KYBARTAI

At the secondary school in Kybartai, with the approach of the commemoration of the October Revolution, there was a plan to increase the number of the Little Octobrists. Some of the pupils and parents objected. The mother of [Miss] Zita Menčinskaitė gave her daughter a note to take to school, directing the teacher not to enroll Zita in the Little Octobrists. Disregarding all excuses the homeroom teacher of the first-class students enrolled her entire class in the organization. For those who demurred, she even purchased the badges. Some of the pupils came home from school crying. The more timid parents kept quiet. The mother of the Jurienis girl went to [Mrs.] Česnienė, demanding that her daughter be dropped from the membership of the Little Octobrists.

"If you don't want your daughter to be a Little Octobrist," retorted homeroom teacher Česnienė, "take her to a capitalist country. Here, everyone must be a Little Octobrist!"

no. 9

THE CHRONICLE
OF THE CATHOLIC CHURCH
IN LITHUANIA

No. 9   Lithuania, 1974

Read and pass on!
Published since 1972!

IN THIS ISSUE:

The Freedom to Die
The Komsomol Convention
Gromyko Visits the Pope
Raging Raids
Interrogations
The Trial of A. Terleckas
News from the Dioceses

THE FREEDOM TO DIE

During December and January [1973-74], an article entitled "Tarybinis įstatymas ir religija" [Soviet law and religion] by Pranas Mišutis, advisor to the Council of Ministers of the LSSR, was reprinted in the *rayon* newspapers. The weekly newspaper *Kalba Vilnius* [Vilnius speaks], 1974, no. 5, published a long article by Mišutis entitled "Bažnyčia ir religingumas mūsų dienomis" [The Church and religiosity in our day]. Appearing on the radio program "Akiratis" [Store of knowledge], the advisor to the Council of Ministers attempted to convince the populace that the Soviet laws governing religious cults are very humane.

Why has atheistic propaganda been intensified? "It is our obligation to unmask the attempts by propagandists from abroad and local reactionaries to slander Soviet reality and distort the actual situation," wrote Mišutis (P. Mišutis, "Tarybinis įstatymas ir religija" [Soviet law and religion]). The atheistic propagandists hope to convince the people at any cost that "our laws governing religious cults are democratic" (ibid.).

Let us analyze just what Mišutis stated concerning the extent of the "freedom" of the Church and what he failed to mention.

"Priests are prohibited from catechizing children, from allowing minors to take an active part in religious ceremonies, from interfering in the nonreligious affairs of the believers, from making traditional yearly visitations to the homes of their parishioners during the Christmas season, and from organizing various groups, meetings, discussions, trips, and the like. The priest has no right to handle financial affairs, to hold services in the open air (including funeral processions with religious overtones and the consecration of wayside crosses without the appropriate permit except in a churchyard or cemetery), to incorporate nonreligious propaganda into his sermons (such as urging parents to raise their children in the faith—ed.), or to interfere in the managerial matters of cemeteries" (ibid.).

We would respect Mr. Mišutis and those he represents if he had come to the following conclusion: "The clergy and the believers have been granted the best possible conditions and are utterly free *to die*."

What do priests do under the present conditions of "freedom"?

"At the present time," according to Mišutis, "the majority of the priests are more or less loyal to the Soviet government. . . Some of the clergy today are somewhat passive and take only a formalistic view of their duties."

In truth, there are "loyal" priests. The Lithuanian believers consider some of them traitors to both Church and nation. There are only a few of these. In his article

"Kovoje prieš klastingą melą" [In the struggle against deceitful lies] J. Aničas mentioned several Lithuanian clergymen who have openly stated that the Church in Lithuania is free (*Gimtasis kraštas* [Native land], March 5 and 13, 1973). While reading this article one Catholic was overheard deeply sighing and exclaiming, "Lord, have mercy!" To those clergymen who try to justify themselves with the excuse that the Soviet press was distorting their statements, the faithful reply: "If statements never uttered are attributed to you by the atheistic press, at least renounce them in your private conversations and refuse to give further interviews."

"There still are quite a few clergymen," wrote Mišutis, "who actively participate in the struggle to maintain the influence of the Church among the people... Some ministers of the cult do not limit themselves to the religious activities prescribed by law but interfere in public life, implant bourgeois-nationalistic ideas within the minds of the people, proclaim the concocted thesis that atheism aids in the denationalization of Lithuanians, incite distrust of the the Soviet system, and spread various rumors and fabrications..." (P. Mišutis, "Bažnyčia ir religingumas mūsų dienomis" [The Church and religiosity in our day]. "Minors are still being used as servers during religious rites. There have been instances of organized catechization.... In some areas, disloyal priests have intensified their activities. They have a negative influence on the loyal priests; they incite the clerical elements and the illegal convents; they encourage the writing of complaints and petitions; they strive for changes in the laws governing religious cults; and they struggle for so-called total freedom. Reactionary priests try to stir up discontent about the so-called servile position of the church and interfere with the normal relations between Church and State" (P. Mišutis, "Tarybinis įstatymas ir religija" [Soviet law and religion]).

The Soviet press heaps scorn and threats upon the so-called reactionaries. *Raudonoji vėliava* [Red flag], the newspaper of Varėna *Rayon*, reports the following about the Rev. Algimantas Keina (ordained in 1962), pastor of the parish in Valkininkai: "Over a period of several years, and without the knowledge of his parishioners, the pastor purchased various construction materials, spending more than 20,000 rubles for the repair of his church.... He induces children to participate in religious ceremonies, threatens the believers who are beginning to fall away from the Church, violates the set procedures of religious ceremonies, and so forth. These are not just occasional errors, but the purposefully chosen course of a proponent of ignorance. This, we repeat, cannot be tolerated" (Jan. 10, 1974).

Mišutis mentioned illegal convents. It is strange that during the entire postwar period the atheists never mentioned convents, as if there were none in Lithuania. But they existed and they still exist. Fortunately for them, they are underground institutions, and therefore the Soviet government has little control over their operations and postulants do not have to undergo the trials which must be endured by those desiring to enter the seminary. The number of vocations is not decreasing but is in fact increasing. Of particular merit among the activities of these institutions is the catechization of children and their work among the youth. Regretfully, too little attention is devoted to the preparation of religious literature for the laity. The interest shown by the government in these institutions is a good sign indicating that their existence is not pointless.

Who are those so-called clerical elements mentioned by P. Mišutis?

They are the believers who are actively concerned about the life of the Church and its future. It is no secret that almost all prayer books, catechisms, and religious literature are produced by these "clerical elements" under extremely unfavorable and dangerous conditions. For this, they deserve our respect.

Mišutis threatens: "At the present time there are some clergymen and certain particularly active believers who are violating the laws. With them it is a different story.

There can be no concessions, and there will be no concessions in their regard" (P. Mišutis, "Tarybinis įstatymas ir religija" [Soviet law and religion]).

"A ritual, a prayer book, *Vatikano susirinkimo nutarimai* [Documents of the Second Vatican Council], the Bible, as well as other essential literature have been published to meet the requirements of the believers," further asserts the propagandist.

If we can believe what Mišutis states, twenty thousand children received their First Communion in Lithuania in 1972. How many children then, have received their First Communion since 1945? And how many prayer books have been published for them? Only a few limited editions. What textbooks were provided for the hundreds of thousands of children who were preparing for their First Communion, if "the most democratic government in the world" has up to the present refused to grant permission for the publication of even one edition of a Catholic catechism? Those who wanted to help the faithful, however, were and still continue to be tortured in prison! It remains for us only to cite the usual Soviet platitude: "One of the most wonderful manifestations of the triumph of Soviet democracy in our country is the firm right to the freedom of conscience" (*Agitator*, 1973, no. 21).

"The decrease in the number of believers," expounds Mišutis, "has led to the merger of a number of religious communities, especially in the cities. . . . No one is desecrating the churches that have been closed" (P. Mišutis, "Bažnyčia ir religingumas mūsų dienomis" [The Church and religiosity in our day]).

Had the number of believers decreased when the Soviet authorities were closing the Cathedral of Vilnius, the Sobor [former garrison church—tr.] of Kaunas, the Shrine of the Queen of Peace in Klaipėda, and a large number of other churches? Is it possible to desecrate churches worse than has been done by the Soviet government? which converted a large number of them into warehouses, gymnasiums, movie theaters, and atheistic museums.

"In 1972, about 20,000 children received First Communion, though there were more than a quarter of a million in the first through fourth classes" (ibid.). In this instance, Mišutis stated an untruth. During the 1972-73 school year, about 57,000 children were registered in the first four classes (see *Lietuvos TSR gyventojai* [Residents of the LSSR], vol. 5, 1973, p. 175); that is, less than a quarter of a million. Aside from that, only children of a single age bracket are prepared for First Communion each year. Twelve percent of the children living in Lithuania are non-Catholics: Russians, Jews, Latvians, etc. Thus about 50,000 children should be prepared for First Communion each year. In fact, no less than 44,000 are thus prepared. The number of 20,000 cited by P. Mišutis is absolutely incorrect since it was only in 1973 that the authorities began to insist that the priests present them with the statistics on children preparing for their First Communion; however, even in the future governmental statistics will also be incorrect because some priests do not turn in any information about the catechization of children, and others, "hoping to ease the atheists' heartaches" present the sort of statistics that the atheistic government desires.

"Observations show," relates Mišutis, "that of 350,000 students in the upper classes, only several percent are believers."

This is also untrue. For example, in January, 1974, a questionnaire distributed to the students of class 10A at the secondary school in Lazdijai contained questions such as: Do you believe in God? Do you go to Church? Sixteen of the twenty members of the Young Communist League in the class admitted that they believe in God. [Mrs.] Malinauskienė, a teacher and the League's secretary at the school, was particularly enraged.

An open meeting of the school's Young Communist League was called. Malinauskienė characterized the frank admissions of the students as being an embarassment to the entire school. A representative from the department of education also noted that it did not matter what the students thought, but that they should have put down "the required answer."

On that occasion, one tenth-class student said: "You force us to join the Young Communist League. You tell us that we don't have to tell our parents that we joined, and that we can even attend church. Even now you have advised us that it is possible to think in one way but to write differently. How are we to understand all this?"

In November, 1973, when the tenth-class teacher of the secondary school in Raudondvaris began to talk about an approaching League holiday, the entire class burst out laughing. As a result, the conduct mark of two students were lowered. When the students in this class were asked, "Who attends church?" a whole forest of hands shot up.

How reliable are the statistics presented by Mišutis?

"No one persecutes the church," he asserts. "Only those clergymen have been punished who, in their efforts to re-establish the bourgeois system, have exchanged their ideological weapon for a firearm" (P. Mišutis, "Bažnyčia ir religingumas mūsų dienomis" [The Church and religiosity in our day]).

An interesting question is whether Mišutis himself believes what he writes. Between 1944 and 1962, solely from the smallest diocese in Lithuania, Kaišiadorys, forty-one priests were given prison sentences. A majority of them, who had never had a firearm in their hands, were given ten-year sentences, and some were even sentenced to twenty-five years in prison. For example, Prelate J. Labukas-Matulaitis (present apostolic administrator of the Archdiocese of Kaunas and of the Diocese of Vilkaviškis) was sentenced to ten years in prison in 1945 for delivering sermons, even though, as vicargeneral, he had never preached any sermons. The majority of the priests were rehabilitated after Stalin's death. Is it possible that Mišutis does not know this either?

"Whoever want to believe in God and to worship Him in his own way or to participate in religious rites has every opportunity to do so," asserts Mišutis.

In their desire to divert believers from the active practice of their religion, atheists frequently make use of whatever means are necessary to achieve this goal. Several examples from both the present and the recent past follow. On Palm Sunday in 1972, a huge crowd of people packed into the Kaunas cathedral and its churchyard. When the services began, the employees of the Žilvinas Youth Club across the street opened their doors and windows and began to broadcast loud popular dance music while those attending the dance created quite an uproar on the club's balcony. As a result, the people gathered in the churchyard were unable to follow the services.

Each year the believers attending the Palm Sunday services at the Kaunas cathedral had been able to purchase symbolic palms in the churchyard. Children would bring juniper branches, pussy willows, and other greenery from the forest. The faithful were grateful for these services. In 1973, the atheists decided to disrupt the solemnities. When the services began, the police arrived and began to apprehend those who were selling the palms. Some of them were arrested and taken to police headquarters. On the Sunday after Easter, the police again showed up at the cathedral and began apprehending those who were selling religious articles. The police did not even show mercy to a crippled old woman. She too was placed in the paddy wagon and taken to headquarters.

During the Khrushchev era, the authorities had set up a loudspeaker near the church in Žiežmariai which carried local radio broadcasts. For several years the believers participating in church services had to put up with the disturbance from the loudspeaker; prayer was difficult. No one paid any attention to the requests of the pastor or his parishioners that the loudspeakers be moved farther away from the church.

On the first Sunday of July, 1969, the author of these lines had occasion to participate in the religious festival at Žemaičių Kalvarija. Pilgrims who had thronged here from all parts of Lithuania prayed in the church and the churchyard. When the church bell signalled the start of the high mass, a whistle in the stadium next to the churchyard signalled the start of an athletic event. A group of seminude youths participating in the games hollered and made so much noice that it was difficult to pray in the churchyard. The people were scandalized by this disturbance organized by the atheists. Usually the participants at such athletic or other events sponsored by the atheists are herded in by force and through the use of intimidation. Few people participate voluntarily on such occasions.

A few years ago the atheists of Vilkija conferred on how to divert large numbers of people from the religious festival of St. Ann. They decided to sponsor a very interesting program at the cultural center at the same time as the high mass. At noon only one spectator could be found in the hall—the center's caretaker. The atheists were forced to postpone their program.

On July 22, 1973, we were traveling through Dzūkija. Nowhere did we see anyone working in the fields. Only when we arrived at the parish in Leipalingis, did we notice large numbers of people at work. It turned out that the Feast of St. Ann was being celebrated in Leipalingis that day, and the collective farmers were being forced to work.

Those who work on Sundays get double pay from the government.

Next Sunday, July 29, the bishop administered the sacrament of Confirmation in Veisiejai. Again the people were being made to work that day.

During the summer of 1960, I happened to visit the birthplace of Vaižgantas [noted Lithuanian priest and author—tr.] in Anykščiai Rayon. The collective farmers in the area complained bitterly that they were being subjected to an unprecedented oppressive serfdom, with no opportunity to rest even on Sundays. Anyone failing to show up for work during religious festivals is docked several days' pay by the collective farm chairman.

It is a common practice to block the roads leading to churches at which a religious festival is scheduled. Those traveling in trucks or horse-drawn wagons are turned back. Sometimes the atheists become very "inventive." In 1963, in Rumšiškės, the travelers to the Festival of the Nativity of Our Blessed Lady came up against roadblocks. The officials on guard explained that admittance was being forbidden because of an outbreak of foot-and-mouth disease. Those who were traveling in horse-drawn wagons were turned back. Everyone was surprised, for prior to the festival no one had heard about any such outbreak. They were even more surprised to see the barricades come down after the services. That is to say, the outbreak of foot-and-mouth disease was over. In addition, the priests in Rumšiškės were ordered not to celebrate high mass or to have a procession on that day. The people joked: "Perhaps even the singing of hymns spreads foot-and-mouth disease?"

During the religious festival of the Nativity of Our Lady in 1963, the confessionals in Šiluva were practically besieged by crowds of penitents. Yet the government allowed the pastor to ask only several priests to come to assist him.

In what is probably his most interesting assertion, Mišutis discusses pilgrimages to shrines, alleging that each year the shrines are visited by fewer number of believers. As an example he cites the case of Šiluva as having had only 1,300 visitors in 1972. As a mater of fact, the church in Šiluva alone can hold three times that number. Everyone who attended the religious festival in Šiluva in 1973 was a witness to the fact that the church in Šiluva was packed with people during every mass. On Sunday, the cars inundated not only the town of Šiluva, but the surrounding countryside as well. During a single day, the auto-inspectors counted about 1,000 cars.

"Only about 1,000 persons visited Vepriai Kalvarijos [The Stations of the Cross in Vepriai—tr.] in 1972. No one visits Vilnius Kalvarijos [The Stations of the Cross in Vilnius]," exults Mišutis, "though about a dozen years ago ten thousand would come" (P. Mišutis, "Bažnyčia ir religingumas mūsų dienomis" [The Church and religiosity in our day]).

Particularly fanatical were the atheists in trying to disrupt the pilgrimages of believers to the Stations of the Cross in Vilnius. In 1961 this author witnessed such an effort. On Pentecost morning, notices appeared on the bulletin boards of the town's taxi garage announcing that travel on the road to the shrine was prohibited. One taxi driver categorically refused our request to take us there on the grounds that the police were stopping cars on the road and were confiscating the licenses of drivers heading in that direction. The taxi driver suggested that we go by way of Antakalnis and cross the Neris River by rowboat at Valakumpiai. When we arrived at Valakumpiai, however, we were unable to cross the Neris because the police were on guard to prevent such attempts. Local residents tried to assist the pilgrims. They advised us to go through the shrubbery beside the river bank toward Nemenčinė, where there were no policemen. Here too, however, after rowing us across the Neris, the boatman was assailed by several auxiliary policemen, who warned him not to bring anyone else across.

These methods proved ineffective. Believers streamed on foot in large groups toward the Vilnius Kalvarijos. The forests along the banks of the Neris rang with the sound of hymns and litanies. In 1962 the atheists, with military reinforcements, dynamited the Stations of the Cross in Vilnius and trucked away the rubble that very night. Dirt was brought in, and the sites where each station had stood were leveled.

Since then, attendance really did decrease at this holy place but did not cease altogether. Pilgrims from all over Lithuania gather here on Pentecost and walk the seven kilometers of pathways where the stations once stood. The sites of the former stations are marked by crosses fashioned of loose stones placed there by unknown devout hands, which also decorate the sites with flowers.

The Stations of the Cross in Vepriai (Ukmergė *Rayon*) were also destroyed by the atheists; however, on Pentecost huge crowds of pilgrims still throng to the site of the demolished stations. The destruction of the Stations of the Cross at Žemaičių Kalvarija was also attempted. The pictures had already been removed; however, the Samogitian people crowded to the site and stood guard for more than ten days, determined to defend to the end this place that was holy to them. As a result, the Stations of the Cross at Žemaičių Kalvarija were saved.

In concluding these brief comments on Mišutis' articles and speeches, it is necessary to add that these articles and speeches are not really his own but are the voice of the Party misleading uncritical minds.

THE KOMSOMOL CONVENTION

In mid-February, 1974, the Eighteenth Convention of the Komsomol Leninist Young Communist League of Lithuania, held in Vilnius, devoted particular attention to the Communistic education of the young. First Secretary of the Central Committee of the League, V. Baltrūnas, boasted of the results that have been achieved in educating the youth in the spirit of patriotism and internationalism. According to Baltrūnas, the all-Union campaign to mark and preserve places of note relating to the revolutionary battles and deeds of the Soviet workers had produced favorable results. During the three-year campaign, the participants dedicated about 150 obelisks and memorial tablets, and furnished a total of 678 museums, memorial rooms, and smaller sites honoring those who had participated in the struggle. In the future the special task of the Komsomol and Pioneer organizations would be to instill in the youth a respect for and loyalty to their *multinational* homeland.

In his address Lithuanian Communist party Central Committee Secretary A. Barkauskas stated: "Each collective must plan for the internationalistic and patriotic education of its youth, making more intelligent and inventive use of the examples of the revolutionary movement and of the Great War of the Fatherland, of museum exhibits, exhibitions, meetings with Red Army soldiers, veterans, former members of the underground, and of organized trips to historical sites of past struggles and triumphs."

Both speakers condemned so-called nationalism. Experience shows, however, that it is useless to attempt to vilify or eradicate the history of a nation while attempting to legitimize its occupation as a "heroic achievement of the populace." For example, the youth and students of Lithuania never neglect to mark in some way February 16 [Lithuanian Independence Day—tr.]. As many as three of the yellow-green-red flags of independent Lithuania were flown in Alytus; in Jonava proclamations were distributed, etc.

A. Barkauskas said that "the enemy is stubbornly trying to maintain a torrent of lies about alleged violations of human rights in the Soviet Union and attempting to arouse national discontent and encourage religious fanaticism."

For two years the *Chronicle of the Catholic Church in Lithuania* has been documenting the violations of human rights in Lithuania. If these are lies, then why have the Soviet propagandists not denied any of the facts which have been cited in this publication?

The Lithuanians respect people of other nationalities, but they cannot remain detached when the past of their nation is derided under the guise of the evils of "nationalism," or while denationalization is carried out under the guise of "internationalism."

The Secretary of the Central Committee of the Lithuanian Communist party did not overlook the opportunity to denounce once again Nobel Prizewinner Alexander Solzhenitsyn, whom he called a traitor, a renegade, and a degenerate.

As for the Catholics of Lithuania, they salute and pray for this fine author. Solzhenitsyn's work *The Gulag Archipelago* reminded many Catholics of Lithuania of the sufferings they themselves or their parents had endured in prison camps, prisons, or during exile. Solzhenitsyn serves as an example to the Catholics of Lithuania of how one should love one's country and truth, and refuse to surrender to violence.

The participants of the Komsomol convention were urged to devote more attention to antireligious activities.

"It is essential," exhorted Baltrūnas, "to use all the means at the Komsomol's disposal to deal with the clergy's attempts to influence youth, and essential to struggle as a matter of principle against every example of religiosity on the part of youth."

"It is most annoying that some young people about to be married still avail themselves of the services of a clergyman," complained Barkauskas. "Of course, what is even more disturbing is that Party and Young Communist League members also avail themselves of these services."

The Catholics of Lithuania would salute the members of the Young Communist League if they directed their efforts to the struggle against what is truly evil. For example, at the present time about 10 liters (10.56 quarts) of whiskey, 14 liters of wine and 30 liters of beer, as well as entire rivers of moonshine are consumed by the average resident of Lithuania.

"We have something to show," Barkauskas boasted. "We have strong arguments for each and every discussion. Truth is on our side."

For some reason this "truth" must be upheld by force and violence. Since November, 1973, the broadcasts of Radio Vatican have been severely jammed in an effort to prevent Lithuanian Catholics from hearing any other kind of truth. During searches, the security agents confiscate even prewar magazines in an effort to keep them from impairing the Soviet "truth." Believers have been arrested, interrogated, and charged with the propagation of non-Soviet truth, i.e., Pliuira, P. Petronis, and J. Stašaitis in late November, 1973.

GROMYKO VISITS THE POPE

In our times it is very fashionable to talk about dialogue. Both Communists and Catholics strive for it. Some time ago the papal nuncio visited Moscow, and on March 24 of this year USSR Foreign Affairs Minister Gromyko called on Pope Paul VI.

What do the Catholics of Lithuania expect from any future dialogue with the Communist government?

The Catholics are convinced that dialogue is necessary, but they are not yielding to any illusions. Dialogue can be useful only when both sides demonstrate good will. The "good will" of the Communist government is evident from the trials of priests charged with the catechization of children, from the incarceration of the believers P. Pliuira, P. Petronis, and J. Stašaitis for producing prayer books and religious literature, from the interrogations of those found with religious literature in their possession, from the prohibition against the filing of complaints with the government in cases where administrative measures have been used to persecute believers, and from the lies to the rest of the world about the situation of Lithuanian Catholics. To date, in dealing with believers the Communist government has made use solely of lies and force. It seems to need this dialogue with the Church only as a means of convincing the Vatican to remain silent about the religious persecution that exists in the Soviet Union in the hope that conditions might eventually be eased for the believers. The purpose of this dialogue is to mislead the world's public opinion into the belief that there truly is religious freedom in the Soviet Union.

RAGING RAIDS

(Continued. For the beginning of this listing see the *Chronicle of the Catholic Church in Lithuania*, no. 8.)

On November 19, 1973, Vytautas Vaičiūnas, an employee of the Kaunas Executive Committee, returned home for lunch at noontime after visiting a number of construction sites in the city. At his home (46 Hippodrome St.) he found an old acquaintance, Povilas Petronis, a former teacher. After about fifteen minutes, an unknown man rang the doorbell. As soon as the host opened his door, six men ran up from the staircase and forced their way into the room. The intruders, who did not identify themselves or produce any documents, took Povilas Petronis away with them. They left, but not all of them—three remained until 6 p.m., when a search of the apartment was begun. In charge of the search was the security agent Major Limauskas, the interrogator for particularly important cases. Vladimiras Gluščevskis and Vladimiras Engelhartas were "witnesses." The security police usually call in their own people to act as witnesses. Since the search could not be completed on November 19, Major Limauskas dismissed the witnesses at 10 p.m. and departed, leaving three security men on guard in Vaičiūnas' apartment. One of them, Vilimas, later interrogated the landlord.

On the following morning, Major Limauskas showed up with another security man and the witnesses. The search was resumed. A few hours later, three security men took Vaičiūnas' wife, Leonora, to a garden house, where she was searched. After searching her, the security police took [Mrs.] Vaičiūnienė to the Kaunas security police headquarters for an interrogation which lasted nine hours. She was interrogated for another seven hours the following day.

Before starting the search, Major Limauskas announced that the decision to search Vaičiūnas' apartment and to seize significant articles and documents had been made on November 14. The search was concluded at 4:20 p.m. The following items were taken:

1. A large number of folders containing religious and anti-alcoholic-beverage articles, among them: "Katalikų tikėjimo pagrindai" [Principles of the Catholic Faith], "Kad kūrentųsi ugnis" [So that the flame may keep burning], "Stebuklai ir tikėjimas" [Miracles and faith], "Kelias į laimę" [The way to happiness], "Degtinė ne atlyginimas" [Whiskey is no reward], "Šventumo keliai" [Pathways of

holiness], "Tėvų pavyzdys" [The example set by parents], "Tikėjimo pagrindas" [The foundation of the Faith], "Tikėjimas išgelbėjo" [Saved by faith]—in all, about seventy articles.

2. Numerous sheets of paper containing various notes.

3. The prayer books: *Aukštyn širdis* [Lift up your hearts], three copies; *Jėzus ir aš* [Jesus and I], four copies; *Prie altoriaus* [At the altar], four copies.

4. Notebooks containing various notes.

5. Newspaper clippings.

6. A large number of notebooks containing various religious and anti-alcoholic-beverage articles.

7. Religious magazines published before the war: *Draugija* [The society], one copy; *Saleziečių žinios* [Salesian news], three copies; and *Žvaigždutė* [Little star], five copies.

8. A number of religious books, among them: *Tikiu* [I believe], *Raupsuotųjų kunigas* [Priest of the lepers], *Tėve mūsų* [Our Father], *Auklėjimo menas* [The art of Nurturing], *Ką apie Dievą sako šiuolaikiniai mokslininkai* [What the scholars of our day say about God], *O vis tik Šv. Raštas teisus* [In any case, the Bible is right]—about sixty books in all.

9. *Naujasis Testamentas* [New Testament], two copies.

10. Many photographs and religious pictures-photographs.

11. An envelope addressed to "The Honorable Povilas Petronis."

12. Magnetic tape (two reels).

13. Several maps of Lithuania on which certain locations were marked off.

14. A rubber stamp marked "Med. f. P. Petronis."

Vaičiūnas explained to the security policemen that the items turned up during the search were the property of P. Petronis.

The security police also found various parts of a paper cutter, several sheets of paper containing diagrams of various details, a technical description of the model Era-M-015, copying machine, etc. V. Vaičiūnas was interrogated for four days. Each interrogation lasted from five to eleven hours.

* * *

On November 19, 1973, the security police searched the home and outbuildings of Kazimieras Gudas, a resident of Šlienava Village in the locality of Samylai, Kaunas *Rayon*. Among the items confiscated during the raid were 2,500 unbound prayer books, as well as an unassembled homemade ERA photocopying machine. During his interrogation, Gudas was repeatedly beaten.

* * *

On November 20, 1973, two carloads of security policemen stopped at the home of Parturbavičius in Ežerėlis. Some of the security men went to the home of a neighbor, Žareckas, where they also conducted a search. The security men even searched through a pile of gravel in the backyard.

A typewriter and an ERA copying machine were found at Parturbavičius' home. The security men alleged that the *Chronicle of the Catholic Church in Lithuania* was being duplicated here.

Before leaving with their plunder, the security men arrested the resident. Members of the family are being interrogated.

* * *

On November 19, 1973, the home of [Mrs.] Janina Lumbienė at 13 Marksas St., Apt. 4, Kaunas, was searched. During the raid, a typewriter, a number of poems about Romas Kalanta [a young man who immolated himself in protest against the Soviet oppression of Lithuania—tr.], and a copy of the 17,000 signatures to the petition sent to the Secretary-General of the United Nations were confiscated. During the search, Lumbienė fainted, and an ambulance was summoned. The search was followed by an interrogation.

* * *

On the evening of November 19, 1973, the security police began a search of the apartment of Y, a resident of Kaunas (9 Baršauskas St.). The search turned up 250 kilograms of type for a book entitled *Jaunuolio pasaulėžiūra* [A youth's world view] and for the prayer book *Aukštyn širdis* [Lift up your hearts] which were being readied for publication; two suitcases filled with various literature; a homemade printing press; P. Petronis' surgeon assistant's diploma and his license to operate a motorbike. The security men ordered the resident to operate the printing press while they photographed him. The search was followed by an interrogation.

* * *

On November 20, 1973, Major Eismantas of the security police conducted a search at the home of Juozas Tarnauskas (See the *Chronicle of the Catholic Church in Lithuania*, no. 8, at 12 TSRS 50-čio Street, Apt. 28, Kaunas. His apartment, a storage area, and his place of employment —the Ragutis Plant—were all searched. Among the items confiscated during the search were: the religious books *Liturgika* [The Liturgy], *Jaunuolio kovos* [Struggles of a Youth], *Jaunos sielos religinis auklėjimas* [The religious nurturing of a young soul]; several poems; a notebook, a sheet of paper on which was the color combination yellow-green-red [The colors of independent Lithuania—tr.]; several copies of the prayer book entitled *Jėzus ir aš* [Jesus and I].

* * *

On November 20, 1973, a search was conducted at the home of N., at 67 Biliūnas Ave., Apt. 8, Kaunas. Seized during the search were: 1,000 unbound copies of the prayer book *Aukštyn širdis* [Lift up your hearts], two rolls of mimeograph paper, and a papercutter. On November 20 and 21 the inhabitant of the apartment was interrogated by Major Glušovas. In December, he was summoned to the headquarters of the security police in Vilnius, where he was interrogated by Markevičius.

* * *

On November 21, 1973, the security police searched the apartment of [Miss] Marija Vilkutė, at 23—XIV Krantas St., Kaunas. The search was witnessed by P. Vilkas and Grajauskas. During the search, a suitcase full of books and various papers was confiscated.

* * *

In the early morning hours of November 20, 1973, security policemen began their search of the apartment of J. Gudelis at 5 Vyšnios St., Kaunas. The searchers took five hours to go through the apartment, the attic, and various storage areas. They were looking for a "weapon"! Religious literature, notes, and the *Chronicle of the Catholic Church in Lithuania* [in Lithuanian] were confiscated during the search. The tenant was interrogated at security headquarters in Kaunas and Vilnius.

INTERROGATIONS

On January 18, 1974, Virgilijus Jaugelis was ordered to present himself before the Vilnius State Security Committee. Lazarevičius, the interrogator, attempted to find out the name of the person who had given Jaugelis a satchel containing mimeograph stencils. Jaugelis explained that, in his opinion, the search that had been conducted in his home was illegal since freedom of the press is guaranteed by the constitution. Those who had conducted the search were, in fact, lawbreakers, and that for this reason he was refusing to say anything. One of the interrogators expressed the opinion that V. Jaugelis should be taken to a mental hospital to have his health checked.

Jaugelis was interrogated again on the following day. He was asked whether he knew Petronis, Father Zdebskis, and others. Jaugelis was fingerprinted and had to provide samples of his handwriting.

* * *

On February 25, 1974, the Rev. Jonas Buliauskas was ordered to appear before the Vilnius State Security Committee for questioning. The priest, however, refused to answer the interrogator's questions on the grounds that the latter had no right to interrogate him concerning religious matters.

* * *

In January, 1974, Arimantas Raškinis (a graduate student of technology) was ordered to report to security police headquarters in Vilnius for questioning. His wife, Danutė Raškinienė (a graduate student of physics and mathematics), is employed by the V. Kapsukas University in Vilnius as an instructor in the department of physics and mathematics of the evening school in Kaunas. Both were warned that in the future they might lose their jobs because of their religious convictions.

* * *

On Ash Wednesday, 1974, the Rev. J. Zdebskis was ordered to appear for questioning before the Vilnius State Security Committee. In the opinion of the security police, he is the "General," that is, the leader of the anti-Soviet activities. His interrogation lasted until the evening of the following day.

* * *

Many other persons were also interrogated by the Vilnius State Security Committee. Among these were K. Tarutis [Mrs.] A. Pliuirienė, and [Miss] N. Stašaitytė. The security police were interested mostly in their acquaintance with those who have been arrested, and with others.

There is no information about the interrogations of some of those arrested, namely, P. Pliuira, J. Stašaitis, and others. One security policeman was heard to remark that the interrogations would take about a year since "that's the style nowadays." One prisoner made the following statement about the present methods of interrogation: "If one compares interrogations conducted in 1958 with those being conducted now, they are as different as heaven from hell."

Being unable to physically ease the suffering of those who have been arrested, the believers of Lithuania remember them daily in their prayers.

It is widely said that during the interrogations attempts are made to recruit certain persons into working for the security organs.

THE TRIAL OF A. TERLECKAS

On December 19 and 20, 1973, the People's Court of Lenin District in Vilnius heard a case against the "embezzlers of state property." Presiding was Judge Stankevičius. In the bill of indictment, which took Procurator Dėdinas about three hours to read, A. Terleckas was charged with violating Articles 160, 157, and section 2 of Article 94 of the LSSR Criminal Code. The second part of the last-mentioned article deals with crimes committed jointly by a group of individuals, however, A. Terleckas was alone in the dock.

From the indictment it became clear that A. Terleckas is a college graduate with a degree in economics. He also studied history. In 1958, he had been on trial for a political crime in violation of Article 58 of the Criminal Code. There has been talk that Terleckas was a "major irritant" in the eyes of the Soviet government, which therefore was seeking revenge. This opinion was fully confirmed by the proceedings of the trial.

Since 1972, A. Terleckas worked in the Confectionary Department of the Bureau of Cafeterias and Restaurants. From the fall of 1972 to mid-April, 1973, he headed the department, and subsequently, until May 24 he was in charge of the department's supplies' warehouse. On May 24, 1973, he was arrested. After his arrest, his apartment was searched for the purpose of investigating the alleged misappropriation of state property. It is strange that the magazines *Naujoji Romuva* [The new Romuva], *Mūsų Vilnius* [Our Vilnius], and others were confiscated. What is the connection between them and buns?

During the preliminary investigation, instead of ascertaining the actual embezzlers, the investigators made use of unseemly methods, seeking to obtain from the witnesses the desired though untrue testimony implicating Terleckas.

When an attempt was made to force Terleckas into signing a falsified transcript of the proceedings, he demanded that the procurator be summoned. In an effort to break Terleckas, the investigators grasped at extreme measures—he was locked up in the psychiatric section of Lukiškiai Prison.

The trial of the "embezzlers of state property" began on December 19, 1973. Judge Stankevičius frequently demonstrated his lack of objectivity by asking witnesses leading questions and pressuring them to give the desired answers. He browbeat witnesses and made sarcastic comments when their testimony displeased him, but he overlooked contradictions when witnesses became confused while giving false testimony detrimental to the defendant.

The indictment comprised six volumes.

The procurator's charges were serious; the alleged crimes were grave. Terleckas was charged with stealing raw materials such as butter, sugar, salt, eggs, etc., from the warehouse. He supposedly instructed the bakers to produce low-quality goods, and the truck drivers and shipping clerks to make unauthorized deliveries of the finished goods and to turn over the cash obtained in these transactions to Terleckas.

The litigation revealed that the facts were otherwise. On May 23 to 25, 1973, officials of the OBCHS (Ministry of the Interior department in charge of combating the embezzling of state property), had halted the trucks operated by the drivers Geic and Svirskis while they were making deliveries of the finished goods. Upon checking their records, the officials found that some of the goods in the trucks were not listed. It turned out that these two men would make money on the side by selling these products for cash. By some "lucky" chance, however, neither Geic nor Svirskis was charged. (Their offense was considered by a lenient court.) By putting the blame on Terleckas, they became the key witnesses against him.

The questioning of the witnesses showed that the shortages of raw materials in the warehouse were the direct result of improper bookkeeping to which no one had paid any attention from the very inception of the department some ten years previously. Not one department head was charged in the case except Terleckas, who had headed the department for only a few months. The bakers and their manager were fully responsible for what was being produced and its quality, and not Terleckas, who was merely in charge of the warehouse. For this reason, those charges were later dropped. The charges of the violation of section 2 of Article 94 of the Criminal Code (crimes committed jointly by several individuals) were based only on the oral testimony of Geic and Svirskis, which really should not have carried much weight in the proceedings. It was these two, in fact, who should have been in the dock. Their testimony was very confused. They stuttered, blushed, and contradicted their barely uttered statements. Finally, Svirskis became completely silent, not knowing how to answer the questions of the attorney for the defense. When Svirskis' truck had been halted, other unaccounted-for products were found, such as sausages, which are not produced by the bakery-confectionary department. These same drivers also delivered identical goods from other bakeries-confectionaries; therefore it was impossible to determine whether the goods found in the truck had been taken from the department in which Terleckas was employed. This was confirmed by the testimony of the director of the laboratory which had conducted a chemical analysis of the products.

Notwithstanding the fact that after all the testimony it was obvious that Terleckas was innocent—a fact admitted by the procurator himself when he asked that many of the charges be dropped—on the basis of the (completely unconvincing) oral testimony of Geic and Svirskis the procurator demanded four years in a strict-regime prison.

After the procurator had completed his summation, in his reply Defense Attorney Kovarskis asked whether the words of Geic and Svirskis were as infallible as those of gods that their statements were being believed so readily when they themselves should have been on trial. By admitting to the court that they had taken part in Terleckas' crimes they had risked nothing, for they had been acquited and were no longer in jeopardy. Why was the testimony of other witnesses being ignored?

Judge Stankevičius announced the verdict of the court on December 26, 1973, that is, following a four-day recess after the examination of the witnesses. The defendant was sentenced to one year in a strict-regime prison, including the time that had elapsed since his arrest. The judge added that the sentence should have been harsher since this was the defendant's second offense, but that it had been reduced for "humane" reasons (while trying an innocent man), because of the defendant's poor health and tragic family circumstances—the critical illness of his wife and the presence of three small children.

This is how the Soviet courts are used to deal with those who have displeased the security police.

THE ARCHDIOCESE OF VILNIUS

VILNIUS

"To: The Procurator of the LSSR

"From: Lapienis, Vladas, the son of Antanas, residing at 5 Dauguvietis St., Apt. 11, Vilnius

A Petition

"In accordance with Article 242 of the LSSR Code of Criminal Procedure, I wish to inform you that on Nov. 20, 1973, security police under the leadership of Lieutenant Gudas, while conducting a search of my apartment, violated Article 192 of the LSSR Code of Criminal Procedure by taking away to their headquarters the following religious books which were not listed in the report of the search nor in the addendum."

(V. Lapienis enumerates the exact titles of fifty-nine religious books, and notes many other books, pamphlets, and loose sheets of paper confiscated and taken to security headquarters that were not mentioned in the report of the search or in the addendum—ed.)

"Article 192 of the LSSR Code of Criminal Procedure clearly states: 'All confiscated documents and objects must be shown to the witnesses and all others present, and must be enumerated in the report of the confiscation or search or in an addendum attached thereto, indicating their quantity... and an official seal must be placed on the items at the scene of the search or confiscation.' In reality, completely ignoring Article 192 of the code, the security policemen willfully took the above-mentioned and many other books without listing them either in the report or in the addendum, placed them in bags, and without sealing them loaded them into an automobile and took them away. Before leaving, Lt. Gudas stated, 'These books might be returned.'

"The security police violated not only Article 192 of the LSSR Code of Criminal Procedure but also Article 10 of the LSSR Constitution (The books are my own personal property, since they were purchased with my earnings.); Article 96 (which guarantees freedom of conscience); and Article 97 (which by law guarantees citizens the freedom of speech and the freedom of the press). Furthermore, these actions violated several international agreements, namely, the Universal Declaration of Human Rights and the Convention Against Discrimination in the Field of Education.

"On November 30, 1973, I wrote to the Chairman of the State Security Committee requesting the return of my books. On Dec. 21, I received the following reply signed by Capt. J. Morkevičius: 'The questions raised in your letter of November 30, 1973, will be answered during the course of the preliminary investigation.'

"Therefore, in accordance with Article 24 of the LSSR Code of Criminal Procedure, I request that you take steps to redress the above-mentioned violations of the law and to return all my religious books, brochures, papers, notebooks, J. Mockevičius' manuscripts, and all other items taken to security headquarters...."

(V. Lapienis then notes that there is a deep chasm between the tolerance for believers evident in the writings of Lenin and the security officials who confiscate religious literature. This fact could turn believers against the present system—ed.)

"The demand that believers should not possess or read religious literature is like demanding Communists not to own or read Marxist-Leninist works, or atheists—atheistic literature.

"How is the believing public to understand Article 97 of the Soviet Constitution,which guarantees the freedoms of speech and of the press, when the publication of almost all religious literature is prohibited, except for extremely small editions of prayer books and an even smaller edition of the Bible, and when even religious books that are typed out or privately duplicated by the faithful themselves are confiscated and those possessing them are threatened with punishment? These and other related facts lead the believing public to suspect that the freedoms of conscience, speech, the press, and assembly, including the holding of mass meetings, guaranteed in the LSSR Constitution, as well as by the signing of the Universal Declaration of Human Rights are but empty words because some (all—ed.) of the security policemen disregard the basic rights and freedoms of citizens.

"In his report to the Twenty-fourth Party Congress, Leonid Brezhnev declared: 'Respect for law should become the personal conviction of every human being. This should be especially true of the actions of public officials. No attempt to deviate from or to bypass the laws for any reason whatsoever, can be tolerated. Neither can violations of personal rights be tolerated, nor anything that lowers the dignity of citizens. For us Communists, who adhere to the most humane of ideals, this must be a matter of principle' (*Tiesa* [Truth], Dec. 5, 1973).

"If I do not receive a reply within one month, I will take my appeal to the Procurator General of the USSR.

V. Lapienis
January 4, 1974"

(This is an abridged version of the petition—ed.)

In his letter dated January 14, 1974, Bakučionis, the Chief Deputy Procurator of the LSSR, informed Lapienis that "the search conducted in your apartment was sanctioned by the procurator in connection with the investigations being carried out in a criminal case. The question of the confiscated literature will be decided during the course of the investigation. You may obtain further information on this matter in person from the Procurator's Office of the LSSR."

Lapienis had complained that the security police had violated the law by failing to make a record of all confiscated items, whereas Bakučionis replied that the search had been sanctioned.

IGNALINA RAYON

The funeral of the late pastor of the parish in Mielagėnai, the Rev. Vincentas Miškinis, was held on October 30, 1973. A great number of people participated in the rites. Among them was [Miss] Albina Meškėnaitė, the director of the pharmacy in Ignalina, and Dr. [Miss] Vitalija Juzėnaitė, the director of the local medical laboratory.

Meškėnaitė had come to the pharmacy in Mielagėnai, which was under her supervision, on business. She found the store closed since the local pharmacist, even though she was a Russian, had gone to the funeral—everyone is interested in the burial rites of a priest.

Present on this occasion for reasons of surveillance were [Mrs.] Pivoriūnienė, an official from the Ignalina Bureau of Vital Statistics and [Mrs.] Karoliūnienė, the representative of the *rayon* executive committee. They later reported the presence of Meškėnaitė and Juzėnaitė at the funeral.

On the following day, [Mrs.] Gaigalienė, the chief physician at Ignalina Hospital, and Meškėnaitė, the director of the pharmacy, were ordered to appear before the Ignalina *Rayon* Executive Committee. Meškėnaitė was ordered to submit a written explanation. She wrote that her job had necessitated a visit to the pharmacy at Mielagėnai, but she made no mention of the funeral. Her explanation was considered unsatisfactory, and the government officials ordered her to rewrite it. They threatened to report her to the Pharmacy Board if she would refuse to do so, which in fact was done.

[Mrs.] Gudukienė, chairwoman of the *rayon* executive committee shouted at her that persons in leadership positions who attend funerals of priests bring shame on all. The chairwoman inquired what Meškėnaitė would be doing in the future: whether in matters of ideology she would work with them or against them? Meškėnaitė was reproached for neglecting to nurture the spirit of Communism in her subordinates and for neglecting the political aspects of her position. As for leaders whose ideological views are opposed to those of the executive committee— they are unfit for their posts.

That same day, that is, November 1, Dr. Gaigalienė also called Dr. V. Juzėnaitė into her office and instructed her to write an explanation. In reply to the question whether she would give up her religious superstitions in the future, Dr. Juzėnaitė answered in the negative. Dr. Gaigalienė then suggested that she look for work in another *rayon*, threatening to create intolerable working conditions for her. She also threatened Dr. Juzėnaitė with the loss of her secondary position. (Dr. Juzėnaitė has a part-time position in the epidemiologic sanatorium of Ignalina.)

On November 2, summoning Dr. Juzėnaitė into his office, Dr. Andriuška, the chief physician of the epidemiologic sanatorium once again ordered her to present a written explanation.

A Party meeting of the leaders of the *rayon* executive committee was called at Ignalina Hospital on November 1, in order to discuss how to punish pharmacy Director Meškėnaitė and laboratory Director Dr. Juzėnaitė.

On November 13, Pharmacy Board Deputy Chairman Sakalauskas arrived at the Ignalina pharmacy and announced that the services of pharmacy Director A. Meškėnaitė were being terminated and that she was being denied the right to work in Ignalina *Rayon* even as an ordinary pharmacist. Sakalauskas did not even bother to listen to Meškėnaitė's side of the story.

Having no one to replace Dr. Juzėnaitė, who was in fact a most conscientious worker, the committeemen contented themselves with posting an official reprimand upon the bulletin board.

VILNIUS

Toward the end of 1973 Vladimiras Prokopivas, a Ukrainian Catholic priest residing in Vilnius was arrested in Lvov. After his arrest, he was reportedly transported to the Kiev Psychiatric Hospital.

It turns out that Ukrainian Catholics in the area of Lvov had gathered 1,200 signatures on a petition requesting that, on the basis of laws in effect in the USSR, they be allowed to reopen the Catholic church. Father Prokopivas had accompanied the persons presenting the petition to Moscow. Upon his return to Vilnius, he found that his apartment, located at 13 Milda St., Apt. 3, had been searched. The Ukrainians who had taken the petition to Moscow suffered a similar fate.

The security police also arrested another Ukrainian priest, Father Mickevičius, who had worked in the city of Stry. Both priests had protested more than once that the security police have been confiscating the Blessed Sacrament, which was being secretly kept in the homes of the faithful.

The Rev. V. Prokopivas was born in the Carpathians in 1914. He received a degree in theology in Rome. He later carried out priestly duties in the Ukraine, was banished to Kazakhstan, and served as a missionary in Akhmolinsk. With the start of the systematic arrests of the clergy, he went to Lithuania, where, working as a laborer, he was able to serve the faithful of Vilnius and of the Ukraine only in secret.

Father Prokopivas is a holy and self-sacrificing man.

* * *

[Miss] Aldona Matusevičiūtė was a teacher at Vilnius Nursery-Kindergarten No. 81. On September 27, 1973, she was charged before the Vilnius Department of Education with being a nun, and forced to sign a statement that she was "voluntarily" resigning her position. On October 13, Matusevičiūtė was dismissed from her position.

* * *

Toward the end of May, 1973, Stankaitis, an instructor of atheism at the State Pedagogical Institute of Vilnius, stated while delivering a lecture to fourth-year students of preschool education and psychology in the evening session: "Kindergarten teachers who overhear a child mentioning God must consult with his parents. If this fails to produce the desired results, it is permissible to contact the parents' places of employment and to take action through their labor unions and Party organizations."

* * *

On February 18, 1974, the Supreme Court in Vilnius began to hear the case of V. Povilonis, A. Sakalauskas, S. Žukauskas, Rudaitis, and Mackevičius. All five were arrested in March, 1973, and charged with anti-Soviet activities. The trial is expected to last about two weeks. Further information will be presented in issue no. 10 of the *Chronicle of the Catholic Church in Lithuania.*

THE ARCHDIOCESE OF KAUNAS

KAUNAS

Having learned that one of his employees, Monika Gavėnaitė, was a nun, the director of the Šviesa Publishing House declared, "It's best to have nothing to do with sanctimonious grannies," and ordered her to sign a statement that she was leaving her position "voluntarily." On February 11, Gavėnaitė was discharged. The firing of M. Gavėnaitė was undoubtedly sanctioned by the security organs. (See the *Chronicle of the Catholic Church in Lithuania,* no. 8).

* * *

On January 7, 1974, while [Miss] Valerija Grincevičiūtė, a resident of Kaunas, was at work, a security official
went through her books, notebooks, and photographs. The
only other person present in the room at the time was an
underage boy.

ŠIAULIAI

On December 18, 1973, S. Kulevičius was sent to Juozas Šileikis, of Šiauliai, for the purpose of convincing him
to renounce his faith, if only for appearance' sake. Šileikis
replied that he would never be a hypocrite.

In early December, 1973, the homeroom teacher of
class 11B at Šiauliai Secondary School No. 5 demanded
that students who were not members of the Young Communist League were to bring notes of explanation from
their parents. J. Šileikis wrote the following: "My daughter, Virginija Šileikytė, is a believer, and since she does
not want to be a hypocrite, she will not join the Young
Communist League."

On December 26, 1973, Šileikis was again summoned
to a parents' meeting. Once again the conduct of Leonas
Šileikis was being deliberated upon. He had been accused
of distributing anti-Soviet leaflets in Šiauliai (See *Chronicle of the Catholic Church in Lithuania*, no. 8). [Mrs.]
Kaunienė, a teacher, reproached Juozas Šileikis for speaking "a lot of nonsense" at previous meetings. The homeroom teacher complained to the parents that there still
were many believers among the students. Subseqently, the
homeroom teacher spoke about the offense of seventh-class
student [Miss] Nijolė Martinaitytė. Nijolė had beaten up
an innocent girl and had stabbed her several times with a
knife. The homeroom teacher spoke very briefly about this
misdeed, mostly how to help Nijolė avoid punishment.
The girl herself stated that she wanted to go to prison,
where she could really learn how to fight!

On the evening of December 26 Juozas Šileikis was
visited by Kaunienė, Attorney [Mrs.] Petrauskienė, and

Judge [Mrs.] Norvilienė, the purpose of whose visit was an attempt at re-educating the family.

"When did you last attend Church?" they asked Leonas. "Do you read the Gospels?"

"I was in Church on Sunday. That was where I last heard the Gospel."

"Have you read the books written by Ragauskas?" [An ex-priest and atheistic propagandist—tr.]

"Yes."

Juozas Šileikis explained that his children read both religious and atheistic books and can distinguish what is the truth by themselves. For this reason, the atheists are unable to uproot their faith.

"Why do you believe in God so blindly?" they asked their host.

"Actually it is the atheists who are blind in their non-belief. Many of them have never read a catechism, yet they insist that there is no God."

"Why do you oppose the line taken by the Party and refuse to allow your children to join the Young Communist League?"

"I don't see the necessary good examples. Gather all the hooligans in the school, enroll them into the Young Communist League, and re-educate them into being decent people; then I will be able to entrust you with the training of my children."

"How come you have such strong convictions?" the educators asked Šileikis.

"Because of my religion. Secondly, Lithuania has been crisscrossed by many invaders, and if Lithuanians would have been influenced as easily as down blown by the wind, it is doubtful whether nowadays any of them would even know how to speak Lithuanian. Consequently, let us hold fast to the heritage of our forefathers."

JONAVA

During the 1972-73 school year at Jonava Secondary School No. 1, the homeroom teacher of class 4A, [Mrs.]

Šlapkauskienė, frequently scolded and derided her pupil Leonas Rosinas for attending church. Following the teacher's example, the class acted no better than she.

During the 1973-74 school year, the education of Leonas was undertaken by another teacher, [Mrs.] Valeravičienė, another atheist. She ridiculed him in front of the class for going to church with his mother. Upon returning home from school, the boy would frequently complain that he had been pushed around and beaten by the schoolboys.

Once Valeravičienė and her husband assailed Leonas' mother for being a backward, uneducated person who believed in some kind of imaginary God. [Mrs.] Rosinienė explained to her in a kindly manner that she was thoroughly convinced of the existence of God. The homeroom teacher then attempted to convince her to at least stop taking Leonas to church.

"I am responsible for the upbringing of my child," she replied, "and if I didn't take him to church, I would be sinning against my own conscience. As long as he is in my care, I will continue to bring him up in the Faith."

"If you do so, the boy will remain an ignoramus to be scorned and pushed around."

The mother began to weep and returned home with a heavy heart.

On October 5, Leonas returned home from school all beaten up. He was pale and complained of a headache. His mother called an ambulance, which took him to the hospital. The doctor called the police and informed them of what was going on at the school. Though the underage brawlers were taken to the children's section of police headquarters, they went unpunished.

Leonas had to stay home from school until October 15 and was unable to participate in physical education classes until December.

JAKUTIŠKIAI

The directress of the cultural center in Jakutiškiai received the Sacrament of Matrimony at the church in Deltuva during the summer of 1973. Immediately after committing this "crime" she was dismissed from her post.

Gimtoji žemė [Native land], the local newspaper of Ukmergė *Rayon* published the following on January 10, 1974: "[Miss] Laima Atkočiūnaitė (now [Mrs.] Starkienė) betrayed the Young Communist League, upon joining which she had promised, among other things, to strive against religious superstition.... Two years ago, [Miss] Vida Pakėnaitė, Commissioner of the USSR Reconstruction Bank in Ukmergė *Rayon*, betrayed the League in the same shameful fashion...."

By being forced to join the Young Communist League, believers are taught how to become hypocrites. Later there is resentment when they continue to practice their religion.

THE DIOCESE OF PANEVĖŽYS

UTENA

On the night of January 30, 1974, evildoers broke into the church in Utena and stole two chalices, two ciboria, and two reliquaries. The host was pierced and desecrated. The criminals have not been apprehended as yet.

People say that the Museum of Atheism in Leningrad is buying up religious articles. Otherwise, thieves would have nowhere to dispose of those stolen goods.

The Museum of Atheism in Vilnius has also announced that it purchases religious items. Some professors at institutions of higher learning in Lithuania will sign a receipt for a prayer book or religious book which has been turned in.

SMILGIAI

"To: The Procurator of the LSSR
"From: Citizen Balys Babrauskas, the son of Anupras, residing in Smilgiai Village, Biržai *Rayon*

A Petition

"On November 20, 1973, security officials of Biržai *Rayon* under the command of Capt. Jasinskis, searched the church, the sacristy, the outlying buildings, and my living quarters in the sacristy. I have been forced to live there because both the old and the new rectories built by the parishioners for their ministers have been confiscated by the Biržai *Rayon* Executive Committee.

"Much of my religious literature, hymnals, and writing paper was confiscated during the search, together with my typewriter and all of my magnetic tapes, both blank and those containing mainly recordings of hymns. Also taken were all the copies of the hymns used by the religious community of Smilgiai.

"I consider the search to have been completely illegal for the following reasons:

1. The search was conducted without any witnesses, because those listed as such themselves took part in the search, and I was not permitted to ask anyone to serve as a witness.

2. My confiscated property—the religious literature, etc.—was taken unlawfully because both the Natural Law and the constitution permit the profession of any religion whatsoever and the free use of religious literature, no matter how it was produced, whether by pencil, ink, or on my typewriter.

3. The warrant that was displayed did not authorize the confiscation of these items, but the officials conducting the search claimed them under the cover of that warrant.

"Two months have passed since the search, and during this time none of the confiscated materials have been returned. For this reason, I am turning to you with the request that you remind them of the elementary principles of law, and that they should return my property, since as far as the law is concerned, I cannot understand their actions.

"Just how blameworthy are the most ordinary religious literature and hymns whose posession and use are guaranteed by both the constitution and Natural Law? On this basis, I consider the confiscation of my religious literature and hymns to have been plain robbery.

"What is the legal basis for the confiscation of my magnetic tape, which can be purchased in stores? I do not understand. The confiscation of my late mother's recorded words (the container carried the notation 'Mother's Words'), which was one of our family's most cherished treasures—the only recording in the posession of the five children she raised—was an action I consider an unprecedented act of barbarism by the officials involved, an act for whose condemnation I cannot find the words.

"What blame can be laid on the plain white writing paper or the carbon paper, both of which were purchased in stores? Unless perhaps we can quote the words of the officials conducting the search: 'It's hard to get (carbon paper). This will be enough for a number of offices.' It is easier for officials to steal from a citizen than to look for paper in the stores.

"I was surprised at the rumors started by the perpetrators of the search regarding what they saw and found. I consider all that to be due to the immaturity and lack of culture—hooliganism—on the part of some of the officials conducting the search.

"On January 22, 1974, I was summoned by A. Tumėnas, chairman of the Biržai *Rayon* Executive Committee, who threatened that my income taxes would have to be increased because I was capable of paying a larger sum. He then began to enumerate what the searchers had noticed and turned over to him, starting with my bankbook and ending with the several pairs of gym shorts found in my room. This only proved the prevalent unwritten rule that anything goes as far as believers—and especially priests—are concerned: the most barbaric assailment, discrimination, and as on this occasion, even robbery. Such actions force even me to believe that in the case of a priest everything is permissible.

"The confiscation of the copies of hymns belonging to the religious community of Smilgiai is an example of extreme arbitrariness because the hymns are the property of the church in Smilgiai. The search of the church was carried out in the absence of a representative of the religious community of Smilgiai, who could have been found, not several kilometers, but only a few steps away, in the self-same Smilgiai Village.

"On the Sunday after the search, failing to find their copies of the hymns, the representatives of the religious community came to me and demanded an explanation of their disappearance. They were very surprised and scandalized by these arbitrary actions of the government officials and they began to collect signatures on a petition concerning this robbery that had occurred at their church. I asked them to wait in the expectation of your support, Procurator, which would demonstrate that the country is being run on the basis of law and not the arbitrariness of its representatives.

"On this same basis and, in addition, with the belief that the state is governed according to the laws, I have written this petition, appealing to you to correct the injustice done me, and to order the persons involved to return all the confiscated religious literature, hymns, magnetic tapes, paper, and typewriters.

"At the same time, in order to alleviate the people's anxiety and to relieve them of the strain of collecting signatures and of sending delegations to officials, I request that you return the copies of their hymns.

Smilgiai, January 24, 1974
The Rev. B. Babrauskas"

To this petition, LSSR Deputy Procurator J. Bakučionis replied in his usual manner: "In reply to your petition of January 24, 1974, I must report that the search of your premises on November 30, 1973, was sanctioned by the Procurator of the Republic in connection with a case that is under investigation."

Since the petition sent by Father Babrauskas already mentions the sanction of the LSSR Procurator, Bakučionis' reply can be considered nothing more than the mockery of a citizen, proving the assertion stated in the petition: that in the case of a priest, anything is permissible.

SALOS

The *Chronicle of the Catholic Church in Lithuania,* no. 8 reported the persecution of the Rev. P. Nykštus, pastor of the parish in Salos, for preparing children for their First Communion. Although the Rokiškis *Rayon* Executive Committee had decided to penalize Father Nykštus with a fine of fifty rubles in an effort to avoid further vexation of the believers, on the eve of the meeting of the administrative commission the meeting was called off. Thus, the pastor remained unpunished.

THE DIOCESE OF TELŠIAI

ŠILALĖ

On January 8, 1974, the curate of the parish in Šilalė, the Rev. A. Šeškevičius, sent a letter to the Commissioner of the Council for Religious Affairs inquiring why the vice-chairman of the Šilalė *Rayon* Executive Committee had forbidden him to assist the chairman of the parochial committee in taking up the collection.

"Does not the chairman of the parochial committee have the right to select any citizen to assist him in taking up the collection?" asked Father Šeškevičius. "And is not the priest a citizen?"

"I have been told that a priest may participate in taking up the collection, but that in no case can he carry the plate. It is useless for a priest to 'assist' in taking up the collection, if he has no useful function, for then he will appear to be an overseer, which only irritates the faithful."

"How can these prohibitions be coordinated with Article 96 of the LSSR Constitution, which provides for the separation of Church and State? For here the state is telling the Church how to conduct its collections. Do not such actions make a thinking-20th-century-man's head spin?" (The letter has been condensed—ed.).

UPYNA

With the approach of Soviet Constitution Day in 1973, [Mrs.] Jurgaitienė, a teacher at the secondary school in

Upyna, posed the following question to the students of one class:

"Which holiday is approaching?"

"Christmas," they replied.

The teacher blushed and stated, "Nowhere will you find such ignorant parents and students as in Upyna."

FROM THE ARCHIVES OF THE CHRONICLE OF THE CATHOLIC CHURCH IN LITHUANIA

On August 7, 1968, the Rev. V. Šlevas, pastor of the parish in Adakavas, sent the following petition to Comrade Kosygin, chairman of the Council of Ministers of the USSR:

"The Lithuanian SSR is a country of believers. At present it has about three million inhabitants. About two million believe in God and make use of religious services. As a rule, neither the clergy nor the believers oppose the present form of government. (Diplomatic phraseology— ed.). The Lithuanians are industrious, conscientious, earnest, and friendly, as well as amenable; however, we are aware of certain restrictions and deficiencies on the part of some of the governmental representatives of our Republic. Therefore, I am appealing to you, Honorable Prime Minister, requesting your assistance and support in the name of all the priests and the believers:

1. There are about 800 churches served by the priests in the LSSR. Yet there remains but one seminary for six dioceses, whereas previously there were three. Only a limited number of seminarians—about thirty—are permitted to study at this sole seminary. Each year barely five or six priests are ordained. Of what significance is such a number for six dioceses? Between twenty-five and thirty priests die or leave their posts yearly because of ill health. Parishes suffer greatly when they lose their spiritual leaders. Such groundless limitation severely restricts the freedom of religion of the Catholics, thus violating the laws of the Soviet Union.

Moreover, the pertinent government officials interfere with the ordination of seminarians who have completed their studies. Our spiritual leaders are not allowed to perform the ceremony without official permission. (That is, ordain priests—ed.). This is intolerable; it is arbitrariness.

2. The churches of the LSSR have been electrified, the same as other buildings. It is still unclear to us why the church has to pay such a high fee for its electric power. *Collective farmers pay four kopeks per kilowatt for their power; collective farms pay one kopek per kilowatt for the common use of electric power; the church, which is supported by these very same collective farmers, as well as other people, has to pay as much as twenty-five kopeks per kilowatt.* We do not know the reasons behind this.

3. Lithuanian believers lack prayer books. Some are outdated; others have become worn out. A good prayer book (*Liturginis maldynas* [A liturgical prayer book] —ed.) has been readied for publication, and the permit for publication has been obtained, but its appearance has been repeatedly delayed for several years on the pretext that there is a paper shortage.

"I believe in your sincerity, your friendliness toward our nation and its believers. For this reason, we await your sincere assistance. We are convinced that the quota system limiting the number of candidates to the seminary will be abolished and that the payments for electricity will be equalized with those of the collective farmers, at four kopeks per kilowatt; we also sincerely believe that the prayer book will soon be published and will be allowed to circulate freely among the believers in Lithuania.

"Respectfully, gratefully, and hopefully,
                                        The Rev. V. Šlevas"

A similar petition was sent to the USSR government by the Rev. Alfonsas Pridotkas, the pastor of the parish in Batakiai.

On October 5, 1968, the chairman of the Skaudvilė
locality informed Father Šlevas that on October 7 he was
to call on Rugienis, the Commissioner of the Council for
Religious Affairs.

On October 7, both "culprits," the Rev. V. Šlevas and
the Rev. Alfonsas Pridotkas went to see Rugienis, who
greeted them angrily and berated and threatened them.

Soon after the "visit" with Rugienis, both priests were
transferred to other parishes.

At the time when the clergy of Lithuania were first
starting to send petitions to the Soviet government concerning the restrictions in Lithuania, both the priests and
the believers in all of the dioceses supported the idea that
it was necessary to fight for their faith. Many regretted
that they had waited too long without taking any action.

THE DIOCESE OF KAIŠIADORYS

JIEZNAS

On October 26, 1973, Mykolas Jaudegis, organist of
the parish in Jieznas was summoned before the Prienai
Rayon Executive Committee. Its administrative commission
(Chairman Stakenis, Vice-Chairman Arbačiauskas, Secretary Ramanauskas, and members [Mrs.] Mickienė and Sve-
žauskas) fined him thirty rubles for "violating the laws
governing religious cults." It turns out that children sing
in the choir at the church in Jieznas and that is already a
"serious crime."

***

On August 20, 1973, the curate of the parish in Jieznas, Father K. Žilys (ordained in 1973), was ordered to
present himself before the Jieznas Executive Committee.
The government officials demanded that he banish the
children from the altar.

"A priest's duty is to draw children to the altar and
not to drive them away," explained Father Žilys.

A short while later, Father Žilys was being "educated"
again. The principal of the secondary school in Jieznas

accused him of organizing a children's church choir and insisted that he would not permit the religious education of children. The curate even had to present a written explanation. Father Žilys explained that it was his duty as a priest to help people. He had agreed to teach hymns to the children because the believers had asked him to do so. On October 31, 1973, both priests from the parish in Jieznas, Fathers V. Sidaras and K. Žilys, were ordered to appear before the Prienai *Rayon* Executive Committee. The curate was warned to stop violating Soviet laws: to cease the holding of choir practice and the teaching of groups of children. Father Žilys declared that he was unable to obey such laws that were aimed against the Church. He refused to sign a written warning. The *rayon* officials warned him that they would not tolerate such a priest in their *rayon*, and that such actions of his would have serious consequences.

On October 29, 1973, the vice-chairman of the Prienai *Rayon* Executive Committee, K. Morkvėnas, had sent Father Žilys the following written warning: "It has been ascertained that children and youths act as servers during religious services at the church in Jieznas, thus violating the Soviet laws. You are hereby warned that these illegal actions with regard to the education of children must not recur and that further violations of the laws governing the cults must be prevented."

The principal of the secondary school in Jieznas took harsh disciplinary measures against those students who served mass or sang in the church choir. The children were ordered to present written explanations of who was teaching them the hymns. Calling one of the students, [Miss] L. Kvederavičiūtė, into his office, the principal warned her that her father would be jailed and fined fifty rubles. In addition, the priest would also be punished. The principal also called in the parents of the students involved, warning them that their children's conduct mark would be lowered, that they would be expelled from school, etc. This zealous apostle of atheism even began to visit the homes of some of the students, but gave up the practice after one of the parents treated him with disdain.

On January 2, 1974, both priests were again summoned before the Jieznas Executive Committee. Since the order was given orally, Father Žilys did not show up. The pastor was then scolded for not keeping his curate in line.

On January 20, 1974, the faithful of Jieznas organized a farewell party in the curate's apartment for Father Sidaras, who was being transferred to Vievis. The parishioners even brought their children, who sang a few songs and hymns.

Meanwhile, traipsing about and keeping watch under the curate's window were the director of the boarding school, the principal of the secondary school, and [Mrs.] Kačergienė, a member of the boarding-school staff.

The watchers noted the names of some of those present. On the following day, the secondary school principal assailed the children for having visited the curate. Several girls were ordered not to come to school without their parents. The children were upbraided for singing in the church choir. The more timid ones signed explanations stating that the curate had taught them the hymns. Some of the parents were particularly brave, stating, "Our children will continue to sing in the choir and to serve mass!"

On January 23, the director of the boarding school, the principal of the secondary school, and executive committee Chairman Aganauskas gathered at the headquarters of the Jieznas Executive Committee and once again attempted to re-educate the curate.

"Even though you were guilty and had organized everything, we punished the organist. But you continue to interfere with our efforts of educating the children as atheists," stated the principal.

Father Žilys commented that no favorable results of their atheistic education were readily apparent. In 1973 alone, some students from Jieznas had burglarized the church a total of four times. A group of eleven students—thieves was found to have been responsible.

The curate was reproached for purposely disregarding the authorities, most probably in the hope that he would be declared a saint.

The curate refused to sign a copy of the proceedings.

On February 1, 1974, the administrative commission of the Prienai *Rayon* Executive Committee fined Father Žilys fifty rubles for violating the laws governing religious cults. Father Žilys explained that, being a priest, he had no right to chase children away from the choir loft or from the altar. Besides, the decree of the Presidium of the Supreme Soviet of the LSSR handed down on May 12, 1966, prescribes the punishment for organizing children in matters unrelated to the practice of religion, but the singing of hymns is a part of such religious practices.

"Why should we bother to explain?" asked a member of the commission. "Complain to the courts. They'll explain it to you. We came here not to explain but to punish."

FROM THE PUBLISHERS OF THE *CHRONICLE*

Despite governmental repression, the *Chronicle of the Catholic Church in Lithuania* will continue to be published in the future. Publication will cease only when the authorities grant to the Church and the believers at least as much freedom as is guaranteed in the Constitution of the USSR.

Readers are requested to continue to assist in collecting information for the *Chronicle of the Catholic Church in Lithuania*. Without your help, many of the facts in the life of the persecuted Church would be forgotten.

The *Chronicle of the Catholic Church in Lithuania* cannot make use of any vague or incorrect information. Such items will not be published. Every news item, fact, or incident having to do with the situation of the Catholic Church, with the present state of the nation, with the arbitrariness of government agencies, with repressions or other forms of discrimination must be carefully ascertained, clear, and exact. Numbers, dates, names, locations, and other data must be especially clear, correctly written down and doublechecked. We await your information.

INDEX

INDEX

abortion, 54
Adakavas, pastor of parish in. *See*
   Šlevas, Father V.
administrators, church. *See*
   ecclesiastical administrators
Adomaitis, Father J., 305
Adutiškis, 151, 153, 162-63, 165,
   325, 330, 336:
   church in, 162-63, 330, 331-32
   parochial building repairs, 331-32
   pastor of parish in; *see*
      Laurinavičius, Father B.
   petitions from believers in,
      166-68, 204
   religious festival in, 332-33
Adutiškis Parochial Committee,
   168-69, 331-33, 335
Aganauskas (Jieznas Executive
   Committee chairman), 411
Akmenė, 48, 85
Akmenė *Rayon*: executive commit-
   tee fines Father Lygnugaris, 48
   People's Court, Bičiušaitė and,
      46-47, 85
Akstinas, Father D., 46
alcoholism, 117
Aleinikovas, Major (KGB agent),
   319
Aleksandravičiūtė, Vanda, 349
Aleksotas, 88, 144, 338
Alksninė, pastor of parish in. *See*
   Antanaitis, Father Br.

All Saints Church, 313
altar, blessed in Šakiai, 362
altar boys. *See* mass servers
Alunta, 276, 357-58
Alyta (student in Lukšiai), 71
Alytaitė, Janina, 70, 71, 73, 75
Alytienė, Ona, 72, 76
Alytus, 285, 380: dean of, 88, 129
   prison camp, 8, 184
Alytus *Rayon*, executive committee,
   Father Tamkevičius and, 129-30
Amankavičiūtė, Valė, 351
Andrašiūnaitė, Birutė, 240
Andrijauskas (student in Kašučiai),
   360
Andriuška (physician in Ignalina),
   396
Andriuškevičienė, S., 64
Andriuškevičius, Father A., 46, 279,
   280
Andriuškevičiūtė (student in Urkio-
   nys), 64
Aničas, J., publications by, 67-68,
   107-108, 148, 151, 192-93, 370
Antakalnis, 378
Antanaitis, Canon B., 85
Antanaitis, Father Br., 142
Antanavičius, Father, 160
antireligious campaign, 381:
   clergy ensnared in, 145-49
   methodology, 138
   reason for, 233
   review of, in Soviet press, 92-93

416 INDEX

Anykščiai, 191
apostolic administrator. *See* Labukas-Matulaitis, Bishop Juozapas
appeals: by Astrauskienė, 216-17;
by believers in Ceikiniai, 205-
207, 211; by believers in Ignalina, 79; by believers in Prienai, 5; by Bishop Steponavičius, 189; by Brilienė, 105, 106,
108-11; by the clergy, 145; by
Father Bubnys, 31; by Father
Gudanavičius, 86, 126-28; by
Father Keina, 34-37; by Father
Laurinavičius, 161-62; by Father Liesis, 286-92; by Father
Šauklys, 86, 123-26; by Father
Šeškevičius, 37-38, 136; by Father Zdebskis, 27; by the Kučiūnai Parochial Committee, 114,
116; by Povilonis' mother, 247
regarding cemetery monument's
destruction, 216-217; church in
Ignalina, 79; church in Kučiūnai, 116; church storehouse repairs in Ceikiniai, 205-207, 210,
211; concessions not to be
made, 145; dismissal from job,
105-10; Father Zdebskis, 5;
fines, 34-37, 86, 122-28, 286-92;
the forwarding of the memorandum to Brezhnev, 54-55; the
harassment of Father Šeškevičius, 136; "pastoral letter", 57;
Povilonis, 247; priestly duties,
189; refusal of registration certificate, 38; teachers and
schoolchildren's beliefs, 264-67
signed by 109 priests, 145
to bishops and ecclesiastical administrators, 145; to Brezhnev,
116; to Canon Bakšys, 37; to
the clergy, 57; to the Council
for Religious Affairs, 5, 38,
136, 206, 207; to the Human
Rights Committee, 38; to the
Ignalina *Rayon* Executive Committee, 79, 205, 207, 211; to
the Lithuanian Communist
party, 247; to the LSSR Council of Ministers, 38, 207; to
the Procurator's Office, 5, 38;
to the Palanga Executive Committee, 216; to the Palanga police, 216; to People's Courts,
34, 36-37, 86, 105, 109, 122-23,
126, 162, 286-89; to the Procurator of the LSSR, 5; to the
Supreme Court, 10, 27, 31, 34-
35, 85, 106, 110-11, 123-28, 161-
62; to teachers, 264-67; to
U.N. Secretary-General Waldheim, 51, 54-55; to the USSR
Council of Ministers, 217; to
the USSR Procurator General,
38; to the USSR Procurator's
Office, 5, 35
see also complaints; petitions;
Supreme Court; trials
Apytalaukis, 144
Arbačiauskas (Prienai *Rayon* Executive Committee Administrative
Commission Vice-chairman), 409
Archdiocese of Kaunas. *See* Kaunas
Archdiocese
Archdiocese of Vilnius. *See* Vilnius
Archdiocese
Ariogala, 213
Arlauskienė (teacher in Šilutė), 361
arrests, 381: because of petitions,
50, 51, 55
during Kalanta's self-immolation
anniversary, 284
for anti-Soviet proclamations, 247;
for the *Chronicle of the Catholic Church in Lithuania*, 385;
for protesting the destruction
of a cemetery monument, 217
in Kaunas, 9, 140, 247, 284; in
Klaipėda, 61; in Prienai, 3; in
Veisiejai, 303
of Astrauskienė, 217; Bičiučaitė,
47; bystanders at the trial of
Father Zdebskis, 9; Mackevičius, 398, Parturbavičius, 385;
Povilonis, 247; priests, *see*
priests, arrested; Rudaitis, 247;
Rugys, 247; Sakalauskas, 247;
sellers of religious articles, 303,

456 INDEX